Praise for Casey Parks's

Diary of a Misfit

"Parks's engrossing book is an excavation—emotional, familial, spiritual, and perhaps above all else, regional."
—Ariel Levy, author of *The Rules Do Not Apply*

"The beauty of *Diary of a Misfit* is that it [allows] Parks to unfold her family's history, her understanding of herself, and her obsession with Roy slowly and methodically. . . . Parks's book is a wonderful addition to the genre."
—NPR

"Parks's moving, empowering, searching tale is one of the modern American South, of mother-daughter breaking and bonding, of the pernicious effects of homophobia and bullying and hate. . . . Parks has written a memoir that will serve as a beacon for many others still yearning to no longer feel like misfits."
—Oprah Daily

"Like Harper Lee, Parks evokes the simmering suspicions of a small Southern town. Like Eudora Welty, she tells a poignant story of people trying to fit into a way of life that once suited them but no longer wears well. And like Truman Capote, she packs her memoir with eccentric characters. . . . Parks's dazzling narrative gift imbues *Diary of a Misfit* with all the makings of a great Southern story that readers won't be able to get out of their minds."
—*BookPage* (starred review)

"Parks's work of self-investigation is a fascinating, engrossing tale about identity and belonging."
—*Booklist* (starred review)

"A tantalizing blend of personal history and reportage. . . . Parks's writing is a marvel to witness."
—*Publishers Weekly* (starred review)

Casey Parks

Diary of a Misfit

Casey Parks is a *Washington Post* reporter who covers gender and family issues. She was previously a staff reporter at the *Jackson* (Mississippi) *Free Press* and spent a decade at *The Oregonian*, where she wrote about race and LGBTQ issues and was a finalist for the Livingston Award. Her articles have appeared in *The New York Times Magazine*, *The New Yorker*, the *Oxford American*, ESPN's *The Undefeated*, *USA Today*, and *The Nation*. A former Spencer Fellow at Columbia University, Parks was most recently awarded the J. Anthony Lukas Work-in-Progress Award for her work on *Diary of a Misfit*. She lives in Portland, Oregon.

caseyparks.com

Diary of a Misfit

Diary
of a Misfit

A Memoir and a Mystery

Casey Parks

Vintage Books
A Division of Penguin Random House LLC
New York

FIRST VINTAGE BOOKS EDITION 2023

The Library of Congress has cataloged the Knopf edition as follows:
Names: Parks, Casey, [date] author.
Title: Diary of a misfit : a memoir and a mystery / Casey Parks.
Description: New York : Alfred A. Knopf, 2022.
Identifiers: LCCN 2021049946
Subjects: LCSH: Parks, Casey. | Lesbians—Biography. | Gender
identity. | Sex (Psychology). | Self-actualization (Psychology). |
Investigative reporting.
Classification: LCC HQ75.4.P36 A3 2022 |
DDC 306.76/63092 [B]—dc23/eng/20211206
LC record available at https://lccn.loc.gov/2021049946

Vintage Books Trade Paperback ISBN: 978-0-593-08110-5
eBook ISBN: 978-0-525-65854-2

Book design by Maria Carella

vintagebooks.com

Printed in the United States of America
10 9 8 7 6 5 4 3 2 1

For Wanda Louise, who taught me to stay out of the meanness.
And for Rhonda Jean, who always jumped right in.

So much

For despair.
Thomas, go home.

—RITA DOVE, "AURORA BOREALIS"

Diary of a Misfit

Prologue

(2002)

A FEW MONTHS AFTER my pastor asked God to kill me, my mom ran to the bathroom, and I ran after her. She shut the door before I reached it. I knocked, but she didn't answer. The rest of our family was in the dining room, eating spareribs at my grandma's good table, or maybe, by then, they were listening to hear what I'd say to my mother. I pushed the bathroom door open. My mom was sitting on the toilet, bent over, crying into her hands. It was a small bathroom, only as wide as my wingspan, and my mom was heavy enough that she often told people with some mix of pride and horror that doctors considered her morbidly obese. I stepped around her, squeezed myself into a space between the toilet and the tub, then I touched her back. She spoke without looking at me.

"I could lose my job," she said, half whispering, half crying. My mom answered phones at a church for nine dollars an hour, and my dad sprayed bugs for less than that. They had no savings account, no reserve to cover whatever my love life cost them. I knew my mom was right: One disapproving preacher could bankrupt our family.

"Mom," I said. "I'm not going to be gay anymore."

I had kissed only one girl one time. Her name was Ellen. We'd been listening to Pink Floyd and drinking Jones soda in the dark when Ellen leaned toward me. My twin-sized dorm bed felt like a gulf I'd never cross, but then the song crackled, my heart beat triple speed, and the space between us disappeared. Her lips had been so much softer than a boy's. We'd kissed for just a moment, not even the length of the chorus, but those few seconds felt like a revelation I wasn't sure I could forget. I told my mom I was gay a few weeks later, in church, on Easter Sunday. I did not tell her about the kiss.

In the bathroom, my mom cried so hard her body shook, and I racked my mind for ways to fix myself. It was 2002, the summer after my freshman year of college, and I was stuck in West Monroe, Louisiana, until at least August. I wouldn't see Ellen all summer. She lived in Jackson, Mississippi, a few miles away from the private liberal arts college I was attending on scholarship. Maybe that break was long enough, I told myself. Maybe if I didn't see Ellen, maybe if I kissed the right guy, I would feel straight again. I thought, suddenly, of the tall teenage boy who worked alongside me Friday nights at Blockbuster Video.

"Mom," I said. "I'm going to date Richard from Blockbuster. He's six foot five, like Aidan in *Sex and the City*."

My mom's nose started to run, so I pulled a few squares of toilet paper off the roll and handed them to her. I wished I could tell her about that transformative kiss. I had told my mom about every kiss since I was fourteen, when an exchange student from Mexico smashed his lips against my teeth during the homecoming dance. I'd come home late and beaming, and my mother had driven me straight to Waffle House, even though it was after midnight and my hair spray had stopped working. I'd described everything—his cologne, the way his spit had overwhelmed me, the moment he'd whispered, "I love you." My mom ordered a second plate of cheese-covered hash browns and asked me what song had been playing. I told her it was "Love of a Lifetime," then she slow-danced with her fork toward the jukebox to see if the Waffle House had it. I'd told my mom about every other boy I'd kissed—six in the four years since—but watching her sob in my grandma's bathroom that Fourth of July, I knew I would never tell her about the Jones soda or the Pink Floyd song. I would never tell her about the girl whose lips I imagined every night while I fell asleep.

My mom cried without words or sounds, and I told her about Richard's car. It was a beat-up sedan, and his head touched the top of the sagging roof. His hands were big, and his Blockbuster uniform was so short it showed his torso. My mom listened, but she didn't say anything. I sat on the side of the bathtub. I knew she thought Satan had claimed me. She'd told the president of my college and any professor whose phone number she could find on the school's website that I would spend eternity in Hell. She'd even persuaded a campus security guard to barge into my room periodically to make sure I wasn't doing anything gay. Aside from that one kiss, I was never doing anything gay, but it didn't matter. Just a few nights earlier, she'd told me that thinking of me made her want to throw up.

"Mom?"

I wanted to tell my mother that I didn't want to lose her, not forever, not for the summer, but when she looked up, I saw that her mascara had run black rivers down her face, and I lost my will. She'd forced me to wear mascara in middle school, but I'd never learned to put it on myself, so I didn't wear it anymore. I knew she would reapply hers before we left the bathroom—she believed in makeup the way she believed in God—and I considered asking her to put some on me, too. Maybe then, I thought, she'd love me again.

The bathroom door banged open before I could ask. My grandma stood in the entryway, wearing black slacks and a lime-green V-neck T-shirt. She threw her hands up, exasperated, then she jigsawed her way into a spot near the sink.

"Rhonda Jean," she said, jabbing a finger at my mother. "Life is a buffet. Some people eat hot dogs, and some people eat fish. She likes women, and you need to get the fuck over it.

"Now come eat," she said, then let herself back out.

I waited a minute, stunned. Some people eat fish? I swallowed hard. I asked my mom if I could do anything, but she didn't answer. Instead, she pulled a stream of toilet paper from the roll and used it to wipe away the ruined mascara. Neither of us mentioned my grandma's speech. My mom threw the paper into the little trash can under the sink, then she looked at me from the toilet.

"Can you get my makeup bag?"

THE REST OF THE day passed in a blur. I ate banana pudding alone in the carport. I read *Beowulf* in the backyard. I had started to imagine myself as someone outside of my family, and I believed then that if I read all the classics, the rest of my years would somehow be better than the eighteen I'd already lived. I barely understood Old English, but I pressed on until the voices in the house quieted, until my mom and everyone else went to the carport to smoke. I opened the back door. I found my grandmother in the kitchen, washing the serving spoons we'd left behind. She turned off the water, then wiped her hands on the dish towel she kept tucked into her pants pocket.

"Sit down," she said.

Though she'd defended me in the bathroom, I was nervous to spend any time alone with my grandmother. She was tough, foul-mouthed, and prone to yelling. She wanted the TV off, the screen door closed, and everyone's shoes wiped free of dirt. I couldn't remember a time she'd ever told me she loved me. She'd already cleaned the cherry dining table, so we sat down at the smaller, rustic pine frame she kept in the kitchen. She'd found it in a dumpster years ago, painted it white, then declared it "good as new," but it wobbled as I leaned into it. We sat there awhile without talking. My grandmother fumbled with a pack of Virginia Slims, and I ran my hands over the buzz cut I'd given myself in Jackson. My grandma cleared her throat.

"I grew up across the street from a woman who lived as a man," she said.

I leaned closer. This was 2002, years before people began signing their emails with their pronouns. There was no Caitlyn Jenner, no transgender tipping point. There was only my grandma, making the most unlikely of declarations at a wobbly pine table while our family members smoked nearby.

My grandmother had spent her childhood forty miles away, in a rural town called Delhi. Though Delhi was spelled like the capital of India, people in Louisiana pronounced it Dell-HIGH.

The man's name was Roy, my grandma said. He was five foot flat with a sandy blond crew cut and skin so fair it blistered in the sun. Roy made his living out in the elements, picking cotton or mowing lawns, and his face stayed freckled because of it. In the evenings, my grandma said, he sat on his porch and strummed Hank Williams songs for a dozen neighborhood kids. Roy sang, too, but his voice never dropped low enough to hit Hank's deeper notes.

"It was the most beautiful music I ever heard," my grandma told me.

I'd only met one trans person—a trans guy who hadn't changed his name or pronouns yet, just the hoped-for trajectory of his life—and I asked my grandmother questions that day I wouldn't ask now. I asked about Roy's body. I asked if anyone knew he was really a woman. My grandma shook her head no. Roy's real identity, she said, was a secret. He was raised by a lady named Jewel Ellis, but Jewel was not his real mother.

"On her deathbed," my grandma said, "Jewel pulled my mother close to her, and she said, 'Roy is as much a woman as you or I.'"

Jewel said she'd met Roy when he was a little girl named Delois. My grandmother couldn't remember where they'd lived—maybe Arkansas, maybe Missouri—but Jewel said that Roy's real parents abused him.

"So Jewel stole Roy," my grandma said. "And thank God she did."

My brain short-circuited with questions. When had Delois become Roy? Had Jewel told anyone else? Did Roy *want* to be a man? I bit my fingernails and looked at my grandma, a sixty-two-year-old with short gray spokes for hair. She wasn't wearing makeup, I realized. She never wore makeup.

"What did you think of Roy?" I asked. "Were you shocked?"

My grandma reached for my hand. "Honey, it didn't matter. Everyone loved Roy, because he was a good, Christian person."

I wanted to believe my grandma. I wanted to believe that people would accept me just because I was good. I wanted to believe that my mother would forgive me, that she'd love me again the way Jewel seemed to love Roy. But could I call myself a Christian? When Ellen kissed me, I'd felt a light inside. So *that* was what kissing was supposed to feel like. There'd been no extra spit, no time to worry whether our tongues would meet up right. It was the kind of magic I'd only experienced in church.

"Grandma? Was Roy happy?"

My grandmother said she didn't know. Once, long ago, Roy had been the most important person in her life, but she'd lost touch with him in the 1950s, and she wasn't sure if he was still alive. His whole existence, she said, was a mystery.

"It's eaten at me all these years," she said. "Am I going to die without finding out?"

My grandma picked up her cigarettes, then she headed to the carport to smoke. I sat at the table, alone for half an hour, imagining Roy. My grandmother said he wore Wrangler jeans and a big belt buckle. Still, he was fuzzy in my mind. I pushed my brain to fill in the outlines, and eventually, I scooted away from the table. Over time, my reasons for wondering about Roy have changed, and I can't remember anymore what compelled me that day. I stood. I traced my grandma's path toward the carport. I stepped down into the fog of her cigarette smoke. I know the rest of my family must have been there, but when I think about that day, all I see is myself, standing in the smoke, head angled up as if I were brave.

"I'll go to Delhi," I announced. "I'll find out about Roy."

Chapter One

(2009)

MOM EASED OFF THE gas, and her Buick sank down the hills I knew by heart. We had to make two stops, she said, before I asked any questions. First we'd go to my grandma's house in West Monroe, then we'd drive to the Delhi police station. "Just go meet Rufus," she said, pulling off the interstate. "Tell him you're a young journalist back in town to document the real South."

I rolled down the window. Christmas was only three days away, but thick North Louisiana heat rushed in. I stuck my hand out to feel it. *This,* I thought, *is what weather is supposed to feel like.* My mom's SUV lurched forward, and the town I'd tried to forget suddenly surrounded me. We passed Walmart and a Chick-Fil-A, two Waffle Houses, and the Captain D's where we used to eat free kids meals every Thursday night. The car slowed, and everything I'd once loved seemed small—my school, a park, the empty lot where I'd spent hours talking about boys with my best friend Ashley. Mom reached across the console and held my hand.

"You haven't been home in so long. Does it look different?"

She turned left in front of the drive-through daiquiri shop, past the Blockbuster Video where I'd last tried to be straight. Our old church, I knew, was only a mile away.

"No," I said. "It hasn't changed at all."

———

IT WAS 2009, and I was twenty-six. I hadn't been home in six or seven years, not since college, not since I'd promised my grandmother I'd find out about Roy. I had wanted to learn about him, but something unnameable had stopped me. At the end of the summer of 2002, I'd gone back to college in Mississippi, then I'd gotten a newspaper job in Portland, Oregon, a scrappy, liberal city twenty-three hundred miles away from home. *The Oregonian* was a good paper with a big circulation and seven Pulitzers, and I was a staff reporter, a position I knew my mother bragged about to her sisters. No one else in the family had the kind of job one might call a career. My mom thought I was on my way to becoming some kind of writing superstar, but the reality was less exciting than I'd let her believe. A few months earlier, the managing editor had demoted me to a night shift where all I did was listen to police scanners and write the occasional brief. I'd done so poorly at that beat, the editor had moved me again—to a low-level reporting job in the suburbs. I didn't tell my mom I mostly wrote about the suburban planning commission, a wonky board that approved developments and debated the urban growth boundary. I didn't tell her that my latest article was about something called an intermodal transit facility, the most boring topic I could imagine.

I'd only returned to Louisiana because I believed that a good Southern tale might turn my work life around. I'd decided, after my second demotion, that I wanted to work for *This American Life.* I had no audio reporting skills, but I thought if I produced one great podcast, *This American Life*'s editors would recognize my talent. I'd bought a seven-hundred-dollar recorder, watched a spate of YouTube how-to videos, then started brainstorming ideas. I'd considered other family stories—one about the years my mother spent trying to get on *Oprah* to meet the Bee Gees, another about the aunt whose husband bought a thirty-year supply of salt just because it was on sale—but then I'd remembered Roy, and I knew his was the story that would get me a new job.

My mother drove, and I looked out the window and understood, for the first time, that my hometown was ugly. All the stores were chain stores, and every tree looked scrawny and bare. I told my mother that the West Coast had spoiled me.

"In Oregon, some trees stay green all year."

I told her she should come see the evergreens, but she nodded without saying anything. I'd lived in Portland three years already, and my mom had never once offered to visit. I squirmed in my seat, and she turned up the radio, a country station, then we careened along the curves toward my grandma's house. When we arrived, my mom parked crooked, half on the street, half on the grass, and I stared out for a moment before unbuckling my seatbelt. My grandma's two-bedroom brick house looked as pristine as it had when I was in college. Her lawn was edged and mowed, the shrubs trimmed straight. She'd left the garage door half-open, and with my window down, I could hear her yelling from the carport.

"Rhonda Jean? Casey? Is that y'all?"

The garage door rose. My grandma surged into the yard with a half-smoked, unlit Virginia Slims in her right hand. She'd turned seventy that year, but she looked exactly as she always had. Her gray hair shot out as if she'd stuck her finger in an electrical socket, and her mouth seemed to be resisting a smile. "Look at you," she said, surveying my outfit with a grimace as I stepped out of the car. I wore a red plaid shirt and a G-Star Raw jacket I'd spent half my paycheck buying in New York. My mother dug a pack of Capri menthols out of her purse, and my grandma shooed us toward the carport. The yard was too perfect, and her house too pressure-washed clean to stand in front of it smoking. My grandma grabbed my hand and held it as we walked up the driveway past her ancient Crown Victoria.

"Are you going to tell Rufus you're here, Casey?"

I rolled my eyes, hoping I seemed like a badass brave journalist, but the truth was I'd looked in the hotel mirror that morning and realized I was scared to interview anyone in Louisiana. My haircut was boyish, I still didn't wear makeup, and the four flannel shirts I'd brought all looked hopelessly gay. On the way into town, my mother and I had stopped at a gas station to use the bathroom, and an attendant had directed me toward the men's facilities. I'd whispered a correction— "I'm a girl"—then, on my way to the women's bathroom, I'd realized just how foolish this reporting trip might turn out to be. Who was going to talk to a woman who looked like me about a person who lived like Roy? I wasn't even sure yet what I wanted to know. All I had to go on was my grandma's fifty-year-old story and a bleak obituary I'd found on *The Monroe News-Star* website a few weeks earlier:

> DELHI—*Roy Delois Hudgins, a yard maintenance worker, died Wednesday. Graveside services are 2 p.m. Sunday at Delhi Masonic Cemetery.*

The obituary was dated March 9, 2006. Roy had been alive when my grandmother first told me about him, but I'd waited too long to keep my promise. Now he was dead, and I'd have to find strangers willing to talk about him. But how could I find those strangers? Obituaries are supposed to list the names of the people a person leaves behind. They're supposed to be long and loving chronicles, with paragraphs that describe everything memorable about a person's life. Roy had no survivors, the obit suggested. He hadn't even had a real funeral in a church. The only thing worth remembering about him, the obit seemed to say, was his job, a blue-collar gig someone had gussied up with a fancy title.

My grandma ignored my forced bravado, then motioned toward the house. "Are you hungry?" she asked. She disappeared into the kitchen before I could answer. I looked at my mom and followed her into the carport, a cement square filled with canned Cokes, rusted tools, and the kind of fold-up plastic chairs we used to sit on at church potlucks. My mom's older sister Cindy stood in the middle of it all, menthol held up like a conductor's baton waiting to start the show. I hated that my family smoked. I hated the smell, and I hated that my mom spent money on cigarettes when she and my dad owed thousands of dollars in medical bills. My mom and aunt flicked their lighters in unison, then they plopped down in front of two space heaters, their skinny cigarettes mirroring the heaters' electric red glow. My aunt picked up a remote, and the garage door eased down. She pointed her cigarette at my face.

"You favor me."

I shook my head in protest. I loved the colloquialism, the funny Southern phrase that meant I resembled her, but I felt sure I didn't look like anyone in our family. Both my aunt and mother were big women with big hair they molded stiff into styles more Paula Deen than Dolly Parton. They kept their locks cut short but used curling irons and three kinds of spray to spike and arch their hair into poofy, wavy helmets. Their eyes were so dark and deep that they looked like circles of coal nestled under smoky lids. My hair fell and curled without purpose. My eyes were a shallower brown. I was five foot four and so skinny everyone in my family called me "runt."

Cindy had been the prettiest of my grandma's four daughters, and perhaps because of that, she'd been married three or four times. I watched her smoke, and I tried to remember the uncles I'd had and lost, but I could only conjure Stanley and Monty. They'd both been old, gregarious men who drank a lot and made the kinds of jokes that always seemed sexual, even if the words were clean. Cindy and Stanley had two kids, Jennifer and Joey, both of whom were just a few years older than I was, but I hadn't talked to my cousins in years. Jennifer had gotten pregnant when she was fifteen. Joey had gone to prison soon after.

"So," I said. "What did Roy look like?"

"I can tell you exactly," Aunt Cindy said. "Roy was short. Very fair-complected. Blond. Had a butch haircut."

"It was a crew cut," my mom said. Her voice seemed both louder and more Southern than her usual twang, and I couldn't tell if she was correcting my aunt or just adding detail. She loved to interrupt people.

"Butch haircut," Cindy said again. She puffed her menthol, then cleared her throat. "Don't take this the wrong way. Roy looked like if he were, if she was, a lesbian, she was the male counterpart of that relationship. The dyke. Is that the right word for it?"

My mom looked at me with either pity or apology, I wasn't sure which. It had been years since she'd last told me I disgusted her, and she scolded strangers if they used the word "faggot," but she never asked me about my girlfriends. I'd been dating a woman for a year, and no one in my family had ever met her.

"As I got older," my aunt continued, "I became more aware of different things and different types of sexuality, and my assumption of Roy was he was transgendered. Whether she was forced transgendered, or if it was something that just happened, I don't know."

My mom and aunt changed Roy's pronouns as they talked, sometimes mid-sentence. She looked like a boy who hadn't gone through puberty, they said. He didn't have an Adam's apple. She wore Aqua

Velva, a men's aftershave that came in a blue bottle. Eventually, they dropped pronouns altogether. "The voice was very mild," my mom said. "Very soft."

My mom pushed the end of her cigarette into a ceramic seashell ashtray on the table between them. She moved it back and forth, longer, I thought, than she really needed to. She dropped the stub, then she leaned forward. In the 1970s, she said, people in Delhi had called Roy "he-she-it."

"People were not kind to outsiders back then," she said. "We were outsiders, too."

Aunt Cindy shook her head in agreement. "Family issues."

I knew they had another sister who ran wild, then ran away, but my mom and aunt seemed to be alluding to other, unspoken issues. They smoked and seemed lost for a moment, collectively remembering secrets I didn't know.

"I worked at the drugstore," my mom said. "People would come in, and they would let me take their order, but they wouldn't put their money in my hand. The preacher of the First Baptist Church wouldn't put his money in my hand because I was a Carter."

I didn't say anything, but I wondered what my mom meant. I knew she'd grown up poor, but what was so bad about being a Carter?

Roy, my mom explained, didn't look down on the Carters. He came into the drugstore every afternoon, and he used a quarter to buy a fifteen-cent lemon-lime soda. He put the money right in my mom's palm, then he took the change back. Some days, he'd ask for two nickels instead of a dime, and he'd leave her one as a tip.

"He was just good to me. I didn't have a lot of that."

I stared at my mom for a few seconds. I wanted to study her the way I did people I wrote about. I wanted to dig into her past and ask her all the probing questions I didn't mind asking strangers, but I was too nervous to look at her for long. We'd been close when I was young. We'd studied the Bible together, we'd giggled at the checkout stand in Walmart, and she'd helped me get ready for all my middle school dances, but it had been years since we'd done anything like that. I'd walled myself off that first summer after college, and once I moved to Portland, I stopped telling my mother things. I didn't tell her when a girl broke my heart.

I didn't tell her about the work demotion. I didn't even tell her which TV shows I liked. I kept up with my dad and brother, but my mom and I went months without talking. I told myself I didn't call because my mom was often fogged on pills she said doctors prescribed for the dozen or so maladies she cycled through. I couldn't stand the slow way she talked when she used pills. But that wasn't the only reason I stayed distant, I knew. I didn't call even when my dad promised me that my mom was healthy and talking clear.

I stood. I stepped through the door that connected the carport to the kitchen, then I watched my grandmother lift a cast-iron skillet out of the oven. My stomach growled. No one in Oregon made biscuits the way my grandma did. Hers were tangy and soft with a satisfying outer crunch.

The door opened and closed behind me, and a waft of cigarette smoke briefly overpowered the biscuits.

"I think I'll get on the road soon," I told my grandma.

"*We* will," my mom said. "After you call Rufus."

THE THERMOMETER OUTSIDE MY grandma's house had edged above sixty degrees by the time we left, but my mother cranked the heat in her Buick. We listened to the Dixie Chicks for a while, and I stared out the window. The dull expanse of yellow grass and gray-brown trees dragged by. As soon as we were outside the Monroe city limits, my mother turned to me.

"Growing up as a little girl, my uncle Herman was the chief of police. Rufus was his deputy." She turned the stereo off. "Last night, I called an old friend's dad. I told him we were going to Delhi, and he asked, 'Have you called Rufus yet? You need somebody who is somebody to go up there, someone who is good folks to vouch for you so they don't throw y'all in jail.'"

Her voice fell to a near whisper. "I would think I would count as good folks since my uncle was the one who hired Rufus, but apparently because I'm a Carter, I'm still not a good folk yet."

I turned the radio back on. I didn't know what my mom meant by "good folk," and I didn't care if she was nervous to visit Delhi. She owed me. A few years earlier, I'd discovered that my mom had accrued twenty thousand dollars of debt in my name. She'd started charging the summer before I left for college. The people who made the *Who's Who Among American High School Students* book mailed a black MasterCard to my house, and my mom kept it, then swiped it until it stopped working. Afterward, she applied for another card in my name, then another, until she had seven or eight maxed out with plus-size blouses and fancy mops and other purchases she forgot as soon as she made. I didn't find out about the debt until the year I moved to Portland and tried, unsuccessfully, to open my first bank account. My mom had confessed—or rather, she'd left the house and had my father confess on her behalf—but she'd never tried to pay back what she'd stolen, and I had never pushed her to. Instead, I'd sent half of my newspaper checks to credit card companies, slowly working down her arrears. My mom was only driving me to Delhi as some sort of penance. A few weeks earlier, I'd finally blown up at her about the money. I'd wrecked my car and had no way to finance a new one, so I'd called her late and sobbing. I told her she'd ruined my credit and my life, and she'd stayed silent on the other end as I cried. Later that night, she emailed me a letter she said she planned to get notarized. It was an affidavit of sorts, a note addressed to the police, admitting that my debts were hers. "I am more sorry than you know for this," she'd written. "I want you to know that even if I go to jail I will work tirelessly to get your name cleared." I'd called her the next day. I'd told her to delete the letter. I didn't want her to go to jail, but I did want her to pay me back somehow, so I'd offered a compromise. "I'll keep paying off the credit cards if you help me do this project about Roy."

I told myself that I asked my mother to go to Delhi because she could help me find sources. I was scared that strangers there might see me as an outsider or something worse, but it was my mom's hometown, and I thought her country way of talking might put people at ease. It was unorthodox, I knew, taking one's mother to an interview. My best friend, an older reporter at the paper, suggested that maybe I'd invited my mom because I wanted to spend time with her, but I protested. I thought of myself as tough then. I didn't need or want anyone. Of course now, when I watch the grainy videos I taped that weekend, the truth creeps in around the edges. I can see how my twenty-six-year-old self looked at my mom, nervous, goofy-eyed, and hoping for something neither of us knew how to give. I wanted to love my mother. I wanted her to love me, but I didn't know how to ask for that, so instead, I asked her to drive.

We bumped east on the interstate in near silence. I couldn't bring myself to tell my mom anything personal, so instead, we rode the forty-five minutes like strangers, only talking to note bad drivers or the three dead armadillos we spotted belly-up one after the other on the gravel-strewn shoulder.

"There it is," I said finally. "The Delhi exit."

I held my breath. I'd visited Delhi a few times a year as a kid, and I'd driven past it on the way to and from college, but I couldn't remember the last time I'd actually stopped in the little town. I hadn't known how to emotionally prepare myself for this trip, so back in Portland, I'd done what editors always told me to do when starting a new article: I looked up statistics. Only 8 percent of Delhi's three thousand residents had a college degree, I learned. A third of the town lived in poverty, and the per capita income was $11,000—less than a fourth of the national average.

We veered left toward town. The strip of gas stations could have been any junction, I thought, except horses grazed the fields beside them. We passed a grocery store and a funeral home, then the little community appeared. I counted churches as my mom drove. First Baptist was big, white, and ominous. Its steeple stretched three stories, the only brick in Delhi's sky. Down the road, stone and glass mosaic narrowed to a point at the Presbyterian sanctuary. The Church of Christ was a dour off-white, stubby and triangular with the town's thinnest cross nailed to the front. I tallied nearly a dozen others as we meandered through town, the churches only slightly outnumbering the hair salons that dotted the rutted roads. I made a list in the slim reporter's notebook I'd taken from work. The British *u* in Glamour Cuts suggested something classier than the shearing one might endure at N'Tangles. I admired the promise of New Attitude Hair Design and the no-frills efficiency of the single-wide trailer with a HAIRCUTS $7 sign taped to the front. Delhi seemed to have only three restaurants, a Pizza Hut, a Sho-Nuff Good Chicken, and a converted gas station called Hot Wings Heaven. My mom pulled her Buick close to the wing shop's front door. A construction-paper sign promised fifteen flavors—Heavenly Mild, Heavenly Atomic Hot, Heavenly Honey Gold, plus a dozen other heavenly flavors—but a sign noting the store's hours had been left blank after the colon.

"I'd eat Heavenly Lemon Pepper right now," my mom said with a sigh.

"I'm a vegetarian," I told her, though she already knew.

The Main Street tour took two minutes, then my mother told me it was time to talk to Rufus. She wheeled us toward the police station, an unimposing wood-frame house nestled between pecan trees just across the street from the towering First Baptist. My mom pulled a flip phone out of her red corduroy jacket and dialed as she parked.

"We're here," she said into the phone. A few minutes later, Rufus strode toward us. He was tall, beefy, and Black—the first African American police chief the town had ever had, my mom told me, though Delhi had long been home to more Black people than white.

"Hello, sir," I said.

Rufus grabbed my hand to shake it, and his class ring bit into my skin. I couldn't tell how old he was, maybe in his fifties, maybe sixty-something. He wore slacks, a black tie, and a white button-down shirt with two police department patches sewn on each shoulder. Over that, he had buttoned either a thin bulletproof vest or repurposed fishing attire; I couldn't tell which. My mom caught my eye, then nodded toward his hat. Rufus had on a blue baseball cap with "Chief Carter" stitched in white on the front. I turned back to her, eyes wide. Rufus was a Carter? Though he was Black, I could see now that Rufus looked remarkably like my grandfather, who was white. They had the same tiny eyes, wide face, and thin lips. I'd read somewhere that most people in Louisiana probably had mixed blood, and I wondered if Rufus and my mom's father were related. No one in my family had ever mentioned Black relatives, but maybe, I thought, that's what my mother meant when she said people disliked her because she was a Carter. Maybe they were just racist.

"Chief of police," he said, dropping my hand. "Rufus. What can I do for you ladies?"

My mom told the chief that I was a journalist working on a story about Roy Hudgins. Chief Carter didn't say anything, so I told him my grandmother wanted to know if Roy had a family. The chief shook his head no. "She rode a bicycle, but I don't remember any family."

As we talked, "O Little Town of Bethlehem" started playing loud and clear. My mother and I searched the street for its source.

"First Baptist," Rufus said. "They do that every year for Christmas."

We listened to a few lines, the ones about the hopes and fears of all the years, then I told the chief I hoped to shoot some video around town. My mom knew one woman, a friend of Roy's who'd said she would talk to me, but otherwise, I needed to knock on doors to find people.

"My mom thought y'all might get reports. She's worried I'll get arrested."

Chief Carter laughed. "Probably would."

My mom smirked, and I pretended to listen to the music. "Well," I said finally. "I don't want to be arrested. I'm just doing this for my grandma."

At that point, I wasn't doing anything for my grandmother. I'd been excited back in college when she stood up for me, but that Fourth of July had turned out to be an anomaly. We still weren't close. I'd worked up a story, though, that I told myself was true, a story I thought might make people in Delhi more willing to talk with me. If people saw me as a kid working to give her grandma answers, maybe they'd soften. Maybe they'd talk. I smiled at Chief Carter in a way I hoped looked innocent.

"I'll tell the deputies," he said. "If they stop you, just tell them you talked to me."

A radio crackled from inside one of his vest pockets. "Silent Night" replaced "O Little Town of Bethlehem," and I could tell our meeting was over. We shook hands, then Rufus pulled me into a hug. Most people I knew in the South had no problem embracing strangers, but I'd never gotten used to that kind of physical intimacy. Back in Portland, I had years-long friends I'd never once hugged. Rufus held on for a few seconds, then he let me go. He watched as we walked toward my mom's car.

"He has cancer," my mom told me once we'd climbed into the Buick. "It was very nice of him to take time to talk to you when he's sick."

She cranked the heat again, and we cruised down cracked asphalt. She turned right at Uncle Pete's Discount Tobacco. She looked at me, then looked away. I asked her what she was thinking.

"Do you mind if I drop you off?" she asked. "I need to go see someone."

I clenched my jaw. Of course, I thought. My mom had promised to do something for me, and now she was going to leave me with strangers who'd probably condemn me to hell the second they saw me.

"You're not going to stay with me?" I asked. "I don't even know who we're meeting."

"Her name's Ann McVay."

I slumped into the passenger seat, took a deep breath, and tried to reply with more calm than I possessed. "Are you going to go in? What if they tell me to leave?"

I wasn't sure why I suddenly felt nervous. I'd interviewed armed bandits in the Central African Republic, and a few months before, I'd grilled a suburban school superintendent after he'd used district funds to buy Viagra for himself. Neither of those interviews had scared me. But I started sweating, imagining knocking on Ann McVay's door.

"Casey," my mom said. "I need to go see Mrs. Milton."

My legs went numb. We rode a block in silence, and I longed for First Baptist to interrupt us with a carol. I'd grown up hearing stories about Cam Milton, my mom's high school boyfriend, a straight-A student and four-sport athlete who killed himself two weeks before their senior prom. My mom met my dad just ten days after Cam died. She got pregnant with me a few months later and married my dad that fall. My dad was nothing like Cam. He didn't play sports, and he'd barely graduated from high school. I don't remember if my mom ever told me directly, but I knew that Cam was the love of her life. My dad and I were just accidents she'd stumbled into while grieving.

My mom pulled the Buick up to a beige brick house. "I'll be back in an hour."

"Are you sure Ann knows I'm coming? She doesn't mind talking about Roy?"

My mother shook her head yes, then no. She seemed in a hurry to leave. I grabbed my new audio recorder, a video camera, and a cheap tripod, then I stumbled out into a shallow ditch. I watched from the dry grass as my mother disappeared down the street. I turned to face Ann's house. The driveway was empty but long enough for two vehicles, and I could hear a soap opera playing on the TV inside. I knocked on the screen door.

"Ay-lo?" a woman called.

"Hi," I said through the screen. "My name is Casey, Rhonda's daughter? She said you were willing to talk about Roy."

Ann took a few minutes getting to the door, long enough for *The Young and the Restless* to go to a commercial break. "Yep," she said, when she appeared. She was plump and straight-faced with short blond hair that she'd topped with a pair of reading glasses. I held up the video camera and asked if I could film her. She looked back into the house, a 1970s-era model with wood veneer paneling and thick, unvacuumed carpet.

"I need to put my teeth in first," she said, waving me in.

I followed her, and she gestured toward a man standing along the back wall. "This is Tommy. Me and him got married in 1966. He grew up with Roy."

"Sure did," Tommy said. Tommy was as lanky as Ann was round. He nodded at me, folded himself onto a floral-printed couch, then clasped his hands together. He surveyed the room as if seeing it for the first time. His couch looked toward the back of another floral-printed sofa, and someone had left a purple recliner with the footrests still jutting out. A large gold lamp cast a triangle of light over Tommy's graying brown hair. He looked at the lamp, then scooted away from its gleam. I told him I lived in Oregon, and he widened his eyes. "Far away," he said.

Ann reappeared with teeth. She sat down on the couch next to Tommy, smoothed her gray T-shirt, and said she was ready to talk. I set the camera on the tripod, six feet away from the couch. I stood for a moment behind the camera, but they looked so startled, I reconsidered.

"Have y'all ever been on video before?"

"Nope," they said in unison.

"Do you think I'm crazy for doing this?"

"Nope," they said again.

I pressed record and sat down on the other side of Tommy, hoping they'd eventually forget I was taping.

"Hello," Tommy said. He laughed a sweet, gravelly laugh. I fumbled with the microphone I'd brought along, and I pressed every button on my audio recorder, but none seemed to make the machine work. Ann and Tommy just watched me, generous in their silence. I removed the batteries, then put them back in. I shook the recorder. It still seemed dead. Finally, I gave up, hoping the audio from the video camera would be good enough for *This American Life*. The microphone wasn't connected to anything, but I held it up, just for show.

"Okay, hello," I said. Tommy laughed again. He had deep dimples and no teeth.

"So, um, you knew Roy?" I asked.

"We played softball," Tommy said in a deep voice that came out crackling and flat. "Me and my four brothers played with her. She was real good. I used to go to the dump on Sundays. Roy'd always go with me, and we'd dig through it. I was about seven."

I asked how old Roy had been when they'd pawed through the trash. Tommy shrugged.

"Well," Ann said. "We really don't know. She couldn't get a birth certificate or anything because she never found out where she was born. What she told me was that her parents gave her away because she was a real tiny baby. She fit in a shoebox, she was that small. That's what her mom and dad, as she called the Ellises, told her, so that was all she had to go by. She wrote to all the surrounding states trying to find out who her birth parents were. Once the Ellises died, she had no one."

Ann talked for a while without prompting. She told me she'd met Roy through Tommy. She said she and Roy spent most of the 1970s together, drinking coffee and playing dominoes. They sat in the kitchen and talked about the weather or the Bible. Roy read from Genesis to Revelation every year.

"When you first met her," I said. I stopped mid-sentence. When I listen to this tape now, I feel a sinking guilt every time I hear myself say "her." I didn't think of Roy as a "her." My grandma had always described Roy as "he," and though I didn't know for sure how Roy described himself, I suspected he would have preferred to be called that. Maybe I'm projecting a modern sensibility on Roy. Maybe he didn't even think about pronouns. All I know is that when I thought about Roy—his name, his hair, his clothes—"he" felt right. But I wasn't confident enough at twenty-six to assert myself. Ann used "she," and I worried one word might derail our conversation, so I used "she," too.

"When you first met her," I said again, "did you care if Roy was a woman or a man?"

"It didn't make me no difference," Ann said. "Later, when we became good friends, she opened up to me, and I found out she was completely female, but had been raised up like that. She was comfortable being as a man, wearing her jeans with her hair cut short. She wanted to be buried in blue jeans and a flannel shirt. She wasn't comfortable with the idea of being a woman. She was very uncomfortable because she was a female and had monthly periods."

Ann told me she'd taught Roy how to use Kotex pads when he was, she assumed, about forty-five. He'd used rags before he met her, she said, because he was too embarrassed to be seen buying sanitary products at the grocery store. Tommy nodded in silent agreement. Ann raised her eyebrows in a way that suggested I should ask another question. I looked down at my outfit and remembered Ann had said Roy preferred flannel shirts.

"You mentioned Roy wanted to be buried in jeans. Did that happen?"

"I don't know," Ann said.

She was quiet for a moment, the first time she'd been since we started talking. My arm was hurting from holding the microphone, so I set the mic down for a second, then picked it back up.

"She kept animals," Ann said. "Between cats and dogs, she had more than a dozen. She said that was her family. It got so bad that you couldn't even go over there. You couldn't stand the stink. You had to stand outside of her house to talk to her. Eventually, you stopped going."

Ann had switched to the second person, I noticed. She wasn't saying *she* couldn't stand the stink. She was saying no one could. I tried to imagine a smell worth abandoning someone over, but even the worst odors fell short. I didn't understand. Ann didn't care if Roy was transgender. She didn't call him a "he-she-it." She'd loved Roy in men's clothes and women's Kotex. That love seemed like such a daring and subversive act to me, but then Ann had just given up on Roy—not because he was different, but because his house smelled bad.

"About ten years ago," Ann continued, "Roy stopped going to church. We had a dinner every Sunday after the service, and one time she just showed up for the meal. She didn't go to church, but she came in and fixed herself a plate. After that, she had to go to the nursing home."

Ann went quiet again, and I asked if she'd visited Roy at the nursing home. Ann shrugged her shoulders and shook her head no. She didn't look sad or remorseful, just resigned.

"I saw a picture," she said. "And Roy had the most beautiful long white hair you've ever seen. My sister-in-law had the picture, and she said, 'You know who this is?' And I said no. She said, 'It's Roy.' Roy had on a pink sweatsuit because in there they treated her as a female. It was no more binding the breasts."

I swallowed hard. A pink sweatsuit. Roy must have felt so betrayed.

"How did y'all feel about them doing that to Roy?" I asked.

"Fine," Ann said. "Roy wasn't working or anything anymore. I thought it was nice."

I'd learned long ago to conceal my feelings when interviewing someone. I could keep my face calm, even if something roiled inside me. But I wanted Ann to reckon with Roy's fate, so I asked if she wondered how Roy felt about the pink sweatsuit.

"She wouldn't have liked it," Ann said. "At all."

She answered me in a matter-of-fact tone that verged on defiant. I wasn't sure what to ask after that, and maybe Ann wasn't sure what to say. She stood, went to a back room, then returned with five photographs. She handed them to me, turned upside down. They were sticky on the back, and I wondered if they'd been taped into an album. I knew without looking that they must be of Roy. I held on to the stack, torn between rushing through them and delaying what I suspected would be a big moment. I'd spent seven years thinking about Roy, but I'd never once seen a picture. I'd invented a Roy in my mind, a Hank Williams with softer features, a stone butch in a plain white tee. I'd researched Billy Tipton and Alan Hart, transgender men who'd lived around the same time Roy had, and I'd imagined a person who looked like them. I knew when I turned over the photographs that Ann's images would replace the Roy I'd envisioned, that he'd seem real in a way he hadn't before. I ran my finger over the sticky residue, then I flipped the first photo over. Roy was old in the image. His hair had gone white, but it was still cut short—the way he'd kept it before going into the nursing home. Ann pointed to the second photo, a close-up portrait of Roy grinning in front of a plate of food. He wore a brown workman's shirt, unbuttoned to reveal a white ribbed tank top. A reel-to-reel recorder sat behind him.

"This is a picture I made of Roy when she was sitting at her desk in her living room. She sat there for everything. She had her phone there. She ate there. She read her Bible there."

I studied each picture for clues. In one, Roy wore black plastic glasses and a denim shirt. His freckled hands reached for a bag of coffee filters, partly cut off by the image's frame. He stood outside in another photograph, a short man beside a white house, and I wondered if that was the home my grandmother remembered. Ann handed me another snapshot of Roy at his desk, his hands thrown up in mock exasperation. I tried to look behind him to see the stuff that must have made up his life. There was a framed collage of photos on the wall. Nearly everyone in the pictures looked like a child. They were so small I couldn't make out any distinctive face, but I believed—mostly because I wanted to—that one looked like my grandmother. Every other object felt like a hint. Roy had been drinking a Coke from a glass bottle. He'd lined the desk's shelves with books and wedged additional volumes on top of those. I tried to decipher the titles but couldn't. What did it mean that he kept Lysol on his desk?

Ann smiled as I scrutinized the tiny, square artifact. "She had notebooks where she wrote down every day what happened. It might not have been anything but what the weather was like, but she did that every day."

Roy kept a diary? I'd spent all these years wondering what Roy thought about his life, and somewhere out there, he'd left a notebook with answers. Maybe he wrote about the kidnapping, I thought. Maybe he explained what his life was like. I wondered if he'd ever written about my grandma, if he'd recorded any of the lyrics to his songs.

"Do you know what happened to those notebooks?"

"Yes," Ann said. "Her neighbor has them. Mr. King."

A car pulled into the driveway, and I figured it was my mom. Ann must have sensed our time was over, because she stood.

"Roy was a really good friend to me. In fact, she was probably the best friend I had in my adult life."

My stomach hurt. I liked Ann. I wanted to believe that she had been good to Roy, that she had loved him enough, but I didn't understand how someone could abandon a best friend.

My mother knocked on the door. Ann told me I could take the photographs to make copies, so I thanked her and slipped them into my jacket pocket. Ann opened the door, and my mom hugged her hello. Tommy stood, and my mom embraced him, too. I worried that any one of them might try to hug me, so I slid out the door as my mom asked about Tommy and Ann's Christmas plans. A few minutes later, my mom danced down the driveway, vogueing in a way that suggested she wanted me to ask how her visit with Mrs. Milton went, but I was too hurt to ask. Why did she always abandon me when I needed her?

We climbed back into the Buick, and I told my mother what Ann had said about Roy writing in notebooks. My mom stuck the key into the ignition but waited to start the car. She told me she had seen Roy once, sitting in the softball field bleachers, scribbling into a thick composition book.

"At the time," she said, "I kept a journal. And Cam Milton kept a journal. I thought we were the only two people in the whole world who kept them, so Roy took on a different meaning for me at that point. I spent my life wondering what he was writing about."

"Ann said Roy's neighbor has the notebooks. Do you know a Mr. King?"

My mom's dark eyes lit up. She fished her phone out of the Coach knockoff purse she carried everywhere. "His wife, Cheryl, was my PE teacher." My mom started dialing, and I thought maybe she knew the Kings' number by heart. Every number in Delhi started with the same three digits, a fact so taken for granted that one of my cousins once told me that boys didn't ask for a girl's full number there. Instead, they'd say, "Hook me up with those last four digits." But my mom pressed only three buttons.

"I'm calling information," she said.

An operator gave her the number, and my mom sprung for the extra charge and told the woman to patch her through. A few seconds later, a twangy male voice said hello.

"Is this Mark?" my mom asked.

My mom kept her Nokia turned up so loud I could make out most of the words the man on the other end said. He wasn't Mark, he told her. He was Mark's brother, Keith. Mark had left town for Christmas. My mom told Keith we were hoping to talk to his brother about the neighbor he no longer had, and Keith laughed. "I remember Roy. I went into her house. It was horrible. Like thirty or forty dogs. We finally had to trap the animals and take them out to the country and turn them loose. Honestly, that lady's house was about two feet deep in trash in every room. I shouldn't even be telling this, but they had to put that lady in the psych ward."

I wasn't sure whether to be skeptical or horrified. It seemed like Ann would have told me if someone had put Roy in the psych ward.

"Well," my mom said. "Everyone has told us that the best way to get to know the personal side of Roy is to talk to Cheryl and Mark."

My mom had always been a great bullshitter. She would have made a good journalist, cajoling her way into interviews, but she'd had me so young that she never made it to college, let alone a real career. She'd cleaned houses and cooked dinners for an old lady when I was younger, and she'd worked the front desk for a construction company while I was in high school. She hadn't worked in a few years, but she was smart enough, I thought, to do anything.

"I don't know you," Keith said. "But if you want to come get me, I can take you by where Roy's house was."

He told my mom to turn around, go straight past where the high school used to be, then turn right at the closed-down convenience store. My mother told Keith to look for a white Buick Rendezvous. She steered back onto the asphalt, then followed Keith's directions—past the high school that burned down her junior year, right in front of a shuttered A-Mart. We rolled down Edgar Street and found Keith standing outside. He was blond and thin enough that his long-sleeved hunting-themed T-shirt hung loose around his arms. His stonewashed jeans billowed and bunched the same way his shirt did.

"Before we go any further," Keith said, twisting a pencil between his hands, "y'all should know I'm gay. I don't care what you think about it, but I just thought you'd want to know."

My mom looked over the front of the Buick, nodded at me as if to say I should tell him I understood.

"We're fine with that," I said. My mom shot me a disapproving look. I assumed she wanted me to tell Keith that I was gay, too, but I didn't say anything else.

"Are you a hairdresser?" my mom asked Keith. I cut my eyes at her, then pursed my lips in a way I hoped made clear that not all gay men cut hair.

"No, that was Donnie," Keith said, seeming to take no offense. "Donnie was my best friend. He passed away two years ago. He was in a car wreck and got addicted to opiates. He died of an overdose."

I looked at my mom. She seemed okay on this trip, but in the past, she'd often floated in and out of a pain pill haze. She always had a few prescriptions for Percocet filled, and the year before, my brother had stopped talking to her because he believed she'd stolen his OxyContin after he had shoulder surgery. But my mom wasn't addicted like Keith's friend Donnie, I thought. The fogs were just lows she sometimes staggered through.

As Keith talked, I noticed a figure appear behind the screen door one house over. A woman, I realized, seemed to be rambling to herself or to me, loud enough that I could hear but too quiet for me to understand.

"Are you talking to me?" I called out—sweetly, I hoped. The door flew open, and the woman rushed out. Her hair was a frizzy gray mane that seemed to blow everywhere as she ran toward me. "Y'all never cared about Roy when he was living. Tim McGraw already stole Roy's songs. You're just here to make more money off him."

Tim McGraw had grown up in Delhi around the same time my mom had, but it seemed impossible to me that a country music superstar would have had any reason to steal from Roy. My grandmother had said Roy played bluegrass Christian tunes. Tim McGraw sang catchy pop with a twang.

"Which songs?" I asked, but the woman turned away. She stomped inside, and the screen whacked the frame behind her. A few seconds later, a different woman—an older woman—slinked through the doorway, careful to guide the screen back against the jamb. She sauntered toward me, holding a folded piece of paper that had gone brown with time. She unfolded it and tugged a ribbed purple sweater down over her wrists.

"I'm Mary Rundell. Don't mind my ugly hands."

She held the paper out. Her palms were weathered and wrinkled, but lovely, the kind I'd seen in artistic black-and-white photographs.

"Roy wrote this," she said. "It's a poem, or maybe a song, I don't know."

Roy had typed his name at the top, then, underneath, he'd hammered out four stanzas, each with four lines. Every word was capitalized, and his *A* key must have been messed up because every *A* dipped below the other letters. He'd typed commas in a few places that didn't need them, but his rhyme scheme looked perfect.

MY LIFE IS NEARLY OVER, AND I LOST MY WAY
I HAVEN'T GOT A CHANCE, IS WHAT PEOPLE SAY
I WAS ON MY WAY TO HEAVEN, BUT I SLIPPED AND FELL
AND I CAN'T GET TO HEAVEN, BY GOING THROUGH HELL

I'VE LIVED IN HELL FOR THE MOST OF MY LIFE
NOTHING BUT HEARTACHES, SORROW AND STRIFE
YOU CAN'T GET WATER, FROM A DRY WELL
YOU CAN'T GET TO HEAVEN, BY GOING TO HELL

I'D LIKE TO PICK MYSELF UP, AND TRY AGAIN
BUT IT SEEMS SO HOPELESS, I JUST CAN'T WIN
MY LIFE IS EMPTY, JUST LIKE THAT DRY WELL
AND I CAN'T GET TO HEAVEN, BY GOING THROUGH HELL

THIS PAIN IN MY HEART, CUTS LIKE A KNIFE
I GOT TO GET IT TOGETHER, AND STRAIGHTEN UP MY LIFE
IF I COULD FIND THAT PEACE, IT WOULD SURE BE SWELL
I CAN'T GET TO HEAVEN, BY GOING THROUGH HELL

I looked at Mary and searched her face for some recognition of how sad the poem was, but she just smiled. My throat tightened. As much as I hoped my grandmother was right, as much as I wanted to believe that everyone loved Roy, I'd started to doubt my grandma's rosy view of his life. Had he really ended up in a psych ward? How long had he had to live in a pink sweatsuit? I turned back to Keith.

"Do you know where Roy is buried?"

"Masonic Cemetery," Keith said. "Same as everyone else. You want to go?"

My mom unlocked the Buick before I could say yes. She told Keith to sit in the front, so I waved goodbye to Mary and found a space in the back seat next to my suitcase. The graveyard was less than a mile away. As we edged closer, Keith pointed to a chain-link fence and a gate that hung tilted on the hinge. He said he didn't know exactly where Roy's tombstone was, but he knew it was under a tree somewhere. I looked out. The graveyard was mostly dead grass and tombstones spaced far apart. I spotted only two trees—a skinny pine and a sprawling live oak close to the road. We walked toward the bigger one.

"There's Cam Milton's grave," my mom said, pointing toward a huddle of plots.

"He was, what, seventeen when he went?" Keith asked. "That's always been a mystery why that boy did that. I think a lot of people do that sort of thing when they think they're gay."

I stopped walking. Cam was a ghost whose presence I took for granted, but I'd never heard another person mention him. I definitely hadn't ever imagined him as gay. My mom looked at Keith and smirked.

"Oh, Cam wasn't gay." Usually my mom talked fast and brassy, but she slowed these words down. She winked, and I tried to catch her eye, but she and Keith walked ahead of me. She was eighteen when she got pregnant with me, and I'd always assumed she hadn't had sex before my dad. But maybe she had. Almost everyone I knew in the South lost their virginity by sixteen; why would my mother have been any different?

"Then why'd he do it?" Keith asked. "He wasn't on drugs."

"You know," my mom said, lowering her voice. "I got a suicide note, so I don't feel like I can tell his secrets."

"All right, then," Keith said, content not to ask any more questions. He gestured toward the live oak and suggested Roy's grave was probably somewhere close. We walked in circles with our heads down until Keith squealed. "There it is, right there."

My mom bent down to brush three felled branches off Roy's headstone. It was flat, two feet long, and a marbled gray. Both of his names—Roy and Delois—had been carved into the rock, along with two flowers and a set of praying hands. It was nicer than I'd expected it would be, given that his obituary hadn't listed any survivors. Ann had said Roy didn't know his birth date, but the tombstone listed one.

"April 19, 1926, to March 9, 2006," my mother read out. "She was eighty years old. Just a month shy."

I pulled out my camera to snap a few photographs, and Keith and my mother kept on chatting about people they knew who used or sold drugs. Eventually, my mom brought up the woman behind the screen door. "She feels like we're wanting to make money off this, but that has nothing to do with it. I'm not going to bust out and tell every single person, 'My daughter is gay, and this is a journey of self-acceptance.'"

In 2009, I thought my mother had my mission pegged wrong. This wasn't a personal journey. I had already accepted myself. But if that were true, I think now, why did I do what I did next? On the video, which my mother was running at that point, I can see that I moved the camera away from my glasses. I lowered my voice into a tone I hoped was stern. "Don't tell people I'm gay," I told my mother. "That's not why I'm doing this."

My mom looked at me, confused or crestfallen, then she walked off with Keith. I watched from Roy's grave as they shrank toward the horizon. The tombstone didn't tell me much, and I wasn't sure I could trust what it did. Roy's last name was spelled differently than it had been on the poem—Hudgens instead of Hudgins—and the date of death was a day later than the obituary had pegged it. How could I trust that the birth date was correct? I kneeled in front of the marble, and I thought about Cam, about Donnie the hairdresser, and Roy in a pink sweatsuit. The cemetery seemed too big for a town so small.

WHEN I FLEW HOME to Portland a few days later, I wrote Cheryl and Mark King a letter. I said we'd met Keith, that he'd told us great things about them. I reminded Cheryl that she'd been my mother's PE teacher. I mentioned Roy's journals but didn't ask to see them. "It would help me greatly to sit and talk with you to learn more about who Roy was," I wrote. "Would you be willing to do that?" I sent them my phone number, but they never called. A week later, their reply came in the mail. I opened the envelope slowly, careful not to tear the yellow paper inside. I unfolded it, hoping the legal-size sheet would be filled with the Kings' memories of their old neighbor. But Cheryl had written only one line—a warning in blue cursive.

"For due respect to Roy's life, leave this story alone."

Chapter Two

(1920s–1950s)

THE DELHI MY MOTHER and I explored in the winter of 2009 was cracked and desolate. Whole blocks sat empty, and vines crawled through the broken windows of the city's shuttered municipal buildings. It looked nothing like the city my grandma described when she talked about Roy. Though I'd waited seven years to go to Delhi, my grandma and I often talked about him while I was in college. Every time I went home, she'd tell me a version of the tale she first told me in the summer of 2002. She'd bring up the kidnapping, then she'd end by saying she was sure Roy was "an earthly angel." At first, the story took just a few minutes to unspool. I told myself back then that my grandma wanted to tell the story, but I can see now that I was the one who pushed her to recount what she'd already told me. College had turned me into something of an alien in my family. It felt as if every book I read or girl I kissed yanked me farther away from them, but when I talked about Roy, I fit. My aunts chimed in with memories they'd recovered, and even my uncle—a former baseball standout who'd told me, repeatedly, that God would "destroy" me—asked how my project was going. Roy gave me a reason to call my grandmother. He gave me a reason to go home.

After my mom and I went on that first trip, my grandma's stories went on for longer. When I asked how she met Roy, she told me she had to start at least a decade or two earlier. In order to understand why Roy mattered to her, my grandma told me, I had to understand the life she'd lived before she met him. Most of the time, on the phone or in her carport, I'd settle in with the cheap recorder I used to tape interviews at work and let my grandma talk until she exhausted herself.

My grandma, Louise, was born in late August 1939, the third of four children raised by a couple pulled together by cotton.

Her father, Golden Huffman, started working as a day laborer in south Missouri when he was five. He spent a dozen seasons there, snaking white lint from sharp bolls until his fingers—six on one hand—bled and calloused. Golden had planned to stay in Missouri forever, my grandma told me, but in the late 1920s, when Golden was eighteen, he got the plantation owner's daughter pregnant. Maybe Golden was scared, or maybe he was just irresponsible. When the plantation owner came after him one afternoon, Golden fled, abandoning a sack of cotton and a child he'd never meet. He ran toward the railroad. He rode south through the Ozarks, and when the train stopped at a depot in north Louisiana, a man told Golden the cotton grew tall and thick that close to the Mississippi River. Golden stepped off and went looking for work.

My grandma's mother, Rita Mae Hoover, spent her childhood sharecropping in Mississippi. Rita Mae's family never stayed on any one farm for too long. They worked a season or two, just long enough to break even, then they pushed east toward the alluvial plain in search of more fertile dirt. Eventually—my grandmother never knew when—Rita Mae's family rented a wagon to carry them over the Mississippi River. By 1930, Rita Mae was living and picking cotton just outside of Delhi.

No one ever explained to my grandma how Golden found Rita Mae, but sometime in the early 1930s, they met, then married a week later. My grandmother filled in the blanks for herself. Her father, she imagined, liked the way her mother stood straight-backed, a miracle for a woman who'd spent her life stooped over rows. Rita Mae was a day laborer, the same as Golden, but she had an air of mystery that other field girls lacked: Her father was a Frenchman who'd allegedly traded two fur pelts and a box of farming supplies to marry her mother, a six-foot-tall "Blackfoot" Indian. Maybe, my grandma told me, Golden loved Rita Mae more than he'd loved the plantation owner's daughter, or maybe he'd just lost the will to run.

Usually, I stopped my grandmother there. What did Golden and Rita Mae have to do with Roy? And how could Rita Mae's mother have been a member of the Blackfeet Nation? As far as I knew, that tribe mostly lived in Canada and Montana, not Mississippi. My grandma always hushed me, then kept on with her story, even after I interrupted, again, to tell her that Hoover was a German—not French—surname.

"Just listen, Casey," she'd say. "I'm trying to tell you a story."

Soon after Golden and Rita Mae met, my grandma told me, they went looking for work on a knot of small plantations fourteen miles south of what they called the city. They found an owner who agreed to go halves on the season—he'd buy the seed and the tools; Golden and Rita Mae would work his land—then they made their home on a slough in a shack made of unpainted wood. City people called them "swampers," dwellers of a nameless place. But soon after my grandma was born, in the earliest days of World War II, her brothers taught her that the soggy, rich fields they lived on did have a name, even if the census workers were too obstinate to record it.

"This," my grandma's oldest brother told her, "is Frog Island."

It wasn't an island, my grandma told me, just a lowland community with a pond full of frogs and dirt farmed by sharecroppers who couldn't afford to buy their own parcels. My grandma's slice was a twenty-acre plot hemmed in by pines, a woodsy cut where quicksand pooled and Spanish moss hung in curtains. My grandma wasted as many hours as she could, racing through the woods, catching fireflies and searching for blue robins' eggs, but her family needed money, and the world's appetite for Louisiana cotton seemed endless then, so my grandma joined her parents and brothers in the fields before she was old enough to go to school. Rita Mae slipped a canvas sack over my grandma's shoulder, showed her how to tug the tufts clear out of the bolls, then left her to work a row alone.

My grandma usually narrowed her eyes when she reached this point in her story. I felt like she was trying to shame me. Though I'd grown up poor, my family's situation had been lavish compared to hers, and I'd never had to work a job as hard as picking cotton. I'd only worked at newspapers and video stores. My fingers had never calloused. I never argued with her—I knew how lucky I was—but I did want my grandma to see my career as worthwhile, so in those early days of reporting this story, I tried to use my journalism skills to connect with her. I downloaded almanacs and agricultural reports, and I told her I'd learned that the value of cotton jumped up and down the first ten years of her life. I'd read off statistics as if I'd been there, as if I knew anything at all. In 1940, I'd tell her, the price for a hundred seeded pounds dropped to only fifty-five cents, roughly half of what it had been a decade earlier. She'd told me that on Golden's fastest days, he managed to get two hundred pounds, a haul my tallies told me was worth just over a dollar, half of which, my grandma reminded me, the family owed to the man who owned the farm. I could see in old farm reports that the price of cotton eventually ticked back up, topping out at nearly three dollars per hundred pounds in 1948, but I knew that the extra cents had done little to lift my grandma's family out of poverty.

She never complained exactly. She just narrowed her eyes and said what people of her generation often did: She hadn't known she was poor. Even though she seemed to want me to know how good I had it, she romanticized the life she'd had back then. She complained that grocery store produce tasted empty and flat compared to the rutabagas her family wrested from Frog Island's soil. Life was simple there, she'd tell me, by which she seemed to mean better. Golden killed a hog once a year, and the family ate off its salt-preserved meat until every part of the pig was gone. Rita Mae fashioned what my grandma believed then were beautiful dresses made from twenty-five-pound flour sacks, each of which came with a different print just after the Great Depression. At night, after the family had picked themselves exhausted, they'd crowd around a kerosene lamp and tell stories about a pair of pump-hole-dwelling ghosts they called Rawhead and Bloody Bones. The family's only extravagance was a wood console radio that Golden bought from a man at the cotton gin. They set it up in the living room, and every Saturday night, my grandma, her brothers, and a new baby sister named Shirley bunched together to listen to the *Grand Ole Opry* pipe in sounds from places my grandma believed she'd never see. The world was worlds away then. Even Nashville felt as distant as the moon.

My grandma's face looked different to me when she talked about her childhood. Her toughness fell away, and the stern line of her mouth curved into the kind of smile I knew she'd worked hard to erase. She looked almost dizzy with nostalgia. The first time she told me this story, I kept scrunching my face up in disbelief. The girl of Frog Island seemed so simple and sweet, but the grandma I knew was sassy and hard-charging. How could they be the same person? My grandma softened as she told the story, though, and over time, I began to understand how she became herself.

Back then, in the early 1940s, my grandma told me, she assumed she'd pick cotton forever. Then, in the fall of 1944, the radio announced that a man had built a machine that would one day put sharecroppers out of business. That October, three thousand people traveled to a plantation near Clarksdale, Mississippi, to watch as eight red machines picked cotton sixty times as fast as any man could. On Frog Island, listening from the floor as the radio announcer spoke in awe of what the machines had done, my grandma's brothers told her they were doomed. What farmer would want a bunch of sharecroppers skimming half his profits, if a tractor and claw could do the work for free?

"That's enough," Golden interrupted, twisting the radio's knobs until the signal faded and the threat disappeared. He told his family that the machines were too expensive, that harvesters wouldn't make their way to Franklin Parish. The family picked another six seasons, eventually forgetting about the inventions that had robbed sharecroppers in Mississippi of their jobs, but one afternoon in 1951, Golden came home from the gin and admitted he'd been wrong. Four corporations were manufacturing mechanized cotton pickers by then, and the competition had reduced the price enough that even semi-broke farmers had started to pool together the money to buy one. The machines were just a part of it. Other companies were making herbicides that would reduce the amount of weeding sharecroppers had always done by hand. Boll weevils chewed down so many flowers that year, parish officials declared it a disaster. And federal lawmakers, in an effort to curb overproduction, were threatening to limit the amount of cotton each person could grow.

"We have to leave the farm," Golden told the family. It didn't make much sense to sink all their prospects into one place, so Golden told the family he would head to the Pacific Northwest. He'd spend the winter picking apples in Washington, he explained, and the boys would look for public work in Ohio and New Mexico.

"You girls are going to live with my mom in Delhi."

My grandma ran deep into the woods to cry. Though picking was miserable work, she loved Frog Island. She was happy roaming its swamps and teaching her brothers everything she learned at the country school she attended most mornings while they chopped and hoed. That night, she wandered through the pines, trying to memorize every branch. She was only eleven, but she'd lived a life on Frog Island, and she didn't want to lose it. She spent an hour breathing in the moss. She stuffed leaves she wanted to remember into her underwear and she stared at the quicksand until her eyes throbbed, but she knew no amount of looking could preserve the life she loved. She was going to lose Frog Island. Eventually, my grandma fumbled her way home, guided by moonlight and a sense of duty. She stepped into the shack and told her father she'd go.

Golden told my grandma that Delhi was close, but ten miles seemed as far as ten thousand to my grandma, and just before her father left for the train station, she asked him if Delhi was close to the Grand Ole Opry. Golden laughed and said he'd take her to Tennessee to see country music someday, but for now, Delhi was the farthest she could go.

Soon after my mom and I took that first trip, I signed up for a subscription service that allowed me to read all of Delhi's old articles. I thought I'd impress my grandmother by adding detail to her story. The next time I went down, I plopped onto one of those plastic chairs in the carport, and I told her that prospectors had found oil near Delhi in the mid-1940s. By 1951, the surrounding Richland Parish was outproducing every other region in the petrostate. The city opened its first public swimming pool a few months before my grandmother moved there, and that fall, they began installing the city's first dial telephone system.

"I saw in one story that barons brought so much money into Delhi that the bank had to hire three extra tellers to process the cash!" I told her.

She nodded, lit one of her skinny cigarettes, then told me that her father read the newspaper, too. Before he left for Washington, he told her that Delhi had movie theaters and paved streets.

"Now," she'd say. "Do you want to hear the rest of my story?"

Golden told my grandma he'd found them a house, a clapboard bungalow with a real working toilet—the family's first—and a porch swing where they could relax in the evenings.

"Don't know if you'll want to sit outside, though," Golden said.

"People say the neighbors are unruly. They even changed the name of the road."

Officially, Golden said, the house was on Chatham. "But everyone calls it Hell Street."

The family didn't have enough money to stage an elaborate good-bye. My grandma and her siblings ate what was left of the garden, then Golden and the boys took the family wagon to sell at the depot, leaving the girls without a way into town. The next morning, a man from the other side of Frog Island knocked on their cabin door and said he was a few hundred pounds short of a full five-hundred-pound bale of cotton. If Rita Mae and Louise helped him pick what he lacked, he said, he'd drive them to Delhi on his way home from the gin.

They worked all morning, until Rita Mae's bag held 111 pounds and my grandma's had an even hundred. They gathered their belongings—a collection my grandma described to me as "meager"—and carried them to the man's horse-drawn wagon. He dumped their canvas sacks on top of the pounds he'd already picked. Rita Mae and Shirley took the front seats, so the man ushered my grandma to the back. She smoothed her flour-sack dress, then climbed on top of the bale.

The man hit the horses, and they were off, coughing dust on their way toward town. My grandma had never left Frog Island, so she watched wide-eyed as they rode down barren streets. The trees were stark sentinels with leafless branches that my grandma feared were an omen. Plenty of families had made similar trips. In Louisiana, the number of sharecroppers dwindled from ninety thousand to fifty thousand between 1930 and 1950, a drop that would soon inspire the Census Bureau to stop counting sharecroppers altogether. But that afternoon, my grandma thought she was the only girl in the world who'd ever moved from the swamp to the city. She'd always made the honor roll at Frog Island's country school, but now she worried city students would think she was uninformed. The clothes she'd loved suddenly looked just like flour sacks cut and sewn into poor facsimiles of the dresses they'd never be. Even the new house worried her. How could anyone make a home on a street people called Hell?

The horses slowed to a stop at Baker's Ginnery. After the machines removed the seeds and pressed the cotton into a tight bale, the man gave my grandma a few coins from his profits. She held on to them all the way to Delhi, until the money grew sweaty in her palms. The wagon bounced up a gravel highway. Then, all at once, the ride turned smooth. The man stuck his head out the side and told my grandma that the paved roads meant they'd almost made it. The wagon climbed north, and my grandma glimpsed the world her father said would be hers. Delhi was two and a half miles wide and bisected by highways—Louisiana 17 running north to south, and U.S. 80 cutting east to west. They passed the swimming pool and two movie theaters, the bank and a pharmacy full of lunchtime customers. The main drag had streetlights and store lights that shone brighter than Frog Island's stars ever had. Cars dashed ahead of the wagon. My grandma's new home was north of the railroad tracks, a distinction that residents paradoxically used to mark the beginning of the neighborhoods they called "the Belows." The wagon crossed over, and within a few blocks, my grandma was home.

They unloaded and cleaned all night. The next morning, after Shirley went to school and Rita Mae went looking for work to cover the twenty-five-dollar-a-month rent, my grandma eyed the coins the man had given her. She knew she should head to school, too, but she couldn't stop thinking about the shops they'd passed the day before. She grabbed the change, then strolled toward town, buoyant with possibility. She stopped at the grocery store first and felt overwhelmed by its colors. Heaven, she thought, must look a lot like the stack of Chiquita bananas the grocer had piled high near the checkout stand. My grandma bought a bundle and bit into the fruit before she left the store. She'd never tasted anything so yellow. She walked next to W&W's five-and-ten-cent store, where she spent the rest of her money on half a pound of cashews and a dark blue bottle of Evening in Paris perfume. She spritzed her wrist. The perfume smelled floral and fruity, sophisticated in ways my grandma worried she'd never be. She breathed the city in, then made her way back toward the bungalow.

She walked north on Hell Street, ambling and gawking at every block. The road before her looked like someone had designed one home, then copied it lot by lot. Every yard had an oak tree whose branches sprawled high above the beams. Each house was painted the same flat white. The homes were shotguns with wraparound porches, a swing, and a set of steps. Only Miss Mattie Smith's house, a wood-frame mansion on a corner lot, dared to break the blueprint. Golden had said Miss

Mattie owned much of Delhi and all of Hell. She was eighty-seven and sick enough that the newspaper charted her visits to the sanatorium. She'd never married and had no children, distinguishing facts the newspaper took care to note, but her house was big and stately, unlike any my grandma had ever seen. On Frog Island, even the plantation owner had lived in a modest cabin, so my grandma stopped to admire the white hulk that shadowed her new street. A breeze blew. The trees rustled, and my grandma continued on to her bungalow. She sat on the steps and smelled her wrist again, but the scent of Paris was little solace for the emptiness she suddenly felt. She missed her father and the unpainted shack she'd always called home. She wanted the quicksand and the robins whose eggs had been the bluest part of her world. What if her father did what he'd done in Missouri? What if he found a new family and abandoned the one he'd made first? The sun sank behind the oak trees, and my grandma buried her face in her arms.

Later, she could never remember how long she'd sobbed into her scented self. Those few days seemed to last years in her memory. All she remembered is that someone walked up to her porch, cleared his throat, and began to speak.

"I'm playing music on my porch tonight," Roy said. "Would you like to come?"

When my grandma looked up, blurry-eyed with loss, she didn't notice that Roy was short and round in a way her father and brothers weren't. All my grandma saw was the banjo in Roy's hand.

Every time my grandma told me this story, she paused there and looked up to make sure I understood how big that moment had been for her. She raised her eyebrows, and she scooted to the edge of her seat. Once, she paused with such dramatic effect, I thought she was about to tell me she was gay.

"That was the beginning of *me* coming out . . ." she said, waiting just long enough for my heart to clench in excitement before she added "of my shell" to the end of her sentence. Maybe I looked disappointed. I wanted to feel like I wasn't the only freak in the family. But she wasn't talking about her sexuality, at least not in any overt way. She slid back into her chair, cleared her throat, then finished her thought. "*That* was the beginning of my life as I know it."

MY GRANDMA HAD NEVER seen a musical instrument before, and Roy's banjo made her so nervous, she stuttered her reply. Eventually, she managed a "yes," then she hurried inside to finish her chores before the concert. She swept the floors and scrubbed the bathroom. She wiped down the counters and fixed Shirley a sandwich. An hour later, my grandma watched from the window as young people raced toward Roy's front porch. She counted more than a dozen children, most of whom looked to be around her age. The boys had crew cuts and button-up shirts; the girls wore red and green jeans. They laughed as they climbed Roy's steps and huddled around him, but then Roy tapped his foot on the porch, and the children went quiet as he began to pick a song my grandma recognized from the *Grand Ole Opry*:

Some bright morning when this life is o'er
I'll fly away

Roy launched into the chorus, and my grandma couldn't bear to listen from a distance anymore. She grabbed her younger sister's hand, yanked her out the front door, and sped across the street. They tiptoed up the stairs, careful not to interrupt a verse. They claimed a spot on the porch's edge, and my grandma opened her eyes as big as she could, too spellbound to blink. Roy's hair was brushed back in a pompadour. His jeans were rolled into cuffs. He left his plaid shirt unbuttoned at the top, and my grandma thought that must be how country stars wore their clothes in Nashville. Years later, my grandma would tell me that she should have known then. Roy's version of "I'll Fly Away" was weary and beautiful, but it didn't sound like a man's. When he sang, the verses came out in a light, lilting warble.

The children clapped, and Roy said he'd play a new song next. This one, he explained, was by a man named Hank Williams. Hank had gotten his start on the *Louisiana Hayride*, another Saturday-night show, before joining the *Grand Ole Opry* in 1949. He was from Alabama, but he'd lived in Shreveport, just a few hours west of Delhi, and his success gave Roy hope. As Roy talked, my grandma tried to guess his age. He looked just a few years older than her, eighteen at most, young enough, she thought, to make it to Nashville.

Roy plucked the banjo, and his voice dropped an octave as he sang the opening notes:

Hear that lonesome whippoorwill
He sounds too blue to fly

My grandma gasped. She felt Frog Island in those lines. The way Roy dragged syllables gave voice to feelings my grandma couldn't articulate. He sang about robins weeping and leaves dying, and my grandma could smell the pines whose needles used to fall on her farm. She closed her eyes and thought of her father, picking apples thousands of miles away. Roy paused. My grandma opened her eyes just long enough to recognize in Roy the pain she'd started to feel. He wailed the final line:

I'm so lonesome I could cry

The second night was as thrilling as the first. My grandma vowed never to miss a concert. When she got a job working at Harris's grocery store, she asked for a shift that ended before Roy's nightly performances began. Over time, my grandma came to realize that Roy wasn't the only musician in town. Other people strummed guitars in their living rooms, and the churches had a few good bands. As oil transformed Delhi, the city's population doubled, and money-minded men built concert halls to lure entertainers from out of state, but no city excitement compared to what my grandma felt sitting on Roy's porch. No singer had his conviction. No one else longed the way she and Roy did for a world beyond.

My grandma talked to Roy only in snatches, so a year went by before she knew much of anything about the boy whose songs lit up her nights. Roy's parents were as poor as hers. His father, John, drove an ice truck, delivering frozen blocks to households up and down Highway 80. Roy's mother, Jewel, caught the cotton truck to work one of the few fields that hadn't yet replaced its workers with machines.

"I used to pick with her," Roy told my grandma, holding out his hands to show where dried bolls and sharp seeds had scraped shallow grooves into his palms. "Now I just mow."

Almost everyone on Hell Street was a former sharecropper who'd moved to Delhi when the work ran out. Some still caught the cotton truck; others came home at night black with oil. No one was any richer than they'd been back on the rented farms, so they made their entertainment out of what they had. People fought in the street, and one lady ran a brothel on the corner. The residents couldn't agree whether it was the punches or the prostitution that had earned the street the nickname Hell, but they were shunned as a street together. People from other neighborhoods wouldn't have them, so most Hell Street residents loved and mingled on their own block.

My grandma wasn't beautiful. Her hair was a short wave unfashionably pinned back, and she had the straight flat build of a prepubescent boy. She watched from her porch as the other teenagers paired off. By 1954, everyone on Hell Street seemed to have someone. Everyone except my grandmother. Everyone except Roy.

Roy was good-looking, my grandma thought, but she never saw him go on a date. He worked. He played music. And he talked to his mother, a tall, ruddy-complected woman named Jewel Ellis. Jewel kept her hair tied in a long, dark braid, and her face was square and stern. Other day laborers said Jewel never talked in the cotton fields. She just picked and boarded the truck. But Jewel must have decided eventually that she needed at least one friend, because after a year or so, she knocked on my grandma's door and asked to have coffee with Rita Mae. My grandma longed to eavesdrop, but her mother sent her down the road for flour and a jug of milk. Jewel came back the next week, and eventually she and Rita Mae settled into a Saturday-morning ritual, a quiet conference they shared over coffee. They talked about the weather, Rita Mae told my grandma, and sometimes they talked about men.

Life kept on the same way until one night—my grandma never remembered the day, month, or year—Roy banged on the door in the middle of a rainstorm and begged Rita Mae to come see Jewel. They rushed across the street. The screen door slapped behind Rita Mae as she stepped into Roy's shotgun house. John was off on a long ice route, Roy explained, and Jewel hadn't known who else to call. Roy pointed toward the bathroom, then he sat down at the kitchen table. Rita Mae pushed the door open and saw Jewel, naked in the bath.

"I've glimpsed Heaven," Jewel said.

Rita Mae picked up a sponge and a bottle of rubbing alcohol to pour over Jewel's body. The nearest hospital was forty-five minutes away, so the women had long depended on home remedies. Alcohol cooled the skin down, sometimes fast enough to break a fever. Rita Mae worked the sponge in circles, but Jewel's skin, wrinkled and worn from a life spent working in the sun, never cooled.

"You need to get to a hospital," Rita Mae said, but Jewel grabbed the sponge out of Rita Mae's hands and interrupted her with a whisper.

"No one can know what I'm about to tell you."

Thirty years earlier, Jewel explained, she and John had lived on a farm next to a family. Their neighbors had a child, a little girl named Delois, and Jewel had loved the girl as soon as they met. Jewel was in her thirties then, but she'd worked so much that she'd never had time to give birth to any of her own children. Over time, she came to think of the girl next door as something like a stepdaughter. Jewel picked flowers for Delois and saved the best bits of supper to sneak over after dark.

"The parents were abusive," Jewel told Rita Mae. "They beat Delois. They didn't feed her neither."

Eventually, the fields Jewel and John worked gave out. Farmers could only grow cotton in one place for a few years before the dirt stopped producing. Jewel wanted to find another farm nearby, but John said they'd have better luck in Louisiana. The night before they left, Jewel sneaked down the road and told Delois to meet her at the fence post the next morning. Delois was only four, but she seemed to understand. At sunrise, the little girl was out there, waiting for whatever Jewel had in mind.

"I took her," Jewel told Rita Mae. "I changed her clothing. I changed her name."

Rita Mae looked at Jewel, confused and searching.

"Where's the girl?" Rita Mae asked.

Jewel pulled herself out of the bath, then leaned as close as she could to Rita Mae.

"Roy is as much a woman as you or I."

WHEN MY GRANDMA TOLD me the story fifty years or so after Jewel told Rita Mae, she said it slow, careful to let the drama of every line hit. The alcohol hadn't worked that night. Jewel died soon after her confession. My grandma believed that Jewel had told Rita Mae the story because she didn't want to leave Roy alone with such a secret.

"What about John?" I asked my grandma. "Didn't he know?"

"He was a drunk, Casey. He couldn't take care of Roy."

She first told me the story at her rickety table that summer after my freshman year of college, and she told it again when I returned in 2009. When I went back the next year to try to find Mark King, I asked my grandma to tell the story one more time. She told it the same way she had when I was in college. She described the houses, the banjo, the confession, then she stopped somewhere in the 1950s. She was still a teenager in the retelling, still alone on Hell Street and watching Roy play.

"What happened after that?" I asked.

"I married your grandfather, and I left Hell Street. I went to El Paso and Germany, places Roy never went."

I knew she had eventually returned to Delhi because my mother grew up there. We'd celebrated Thanksgiving and Christmas in the squatty brick house my grandparents owned on a lot they shared with neighbors. I thought back to the visits, but I couldn't remember seeing anyone who looked like Roy.

"Did you keep in touch with Roy?"

My grandma closed her eyes and said she didn't want to talk about Delhi anymore. I asked a few more questions, but she told me to stop. She grabbed my tape recorder. She turned it off.

"Why did you tell me the story, then?" I asked her. "Why did you tell me about cotton and Hell Street and Jewel's big confession if you didn't want me to ask any questions?"

Outside, the racoons she fed every night scratched at the door. She stood up to gather food scraps for them, then she turned back to me.

"Do you want the truth?"

She sounded exasperated and angry. I rolled my eyes. Yes, I told her, I wanted to know the truth.

"Because I knew," she said. "About you."

Chapter Three

(2010)

EVERYTHING FELT LOST TO me in the spring of 2010. A month before I returned to Delhi, my girlfriend broke up with me, and the editor of *The Oregonian* laid off thirty of my coworkers. I somehow managed to keep my suburban bureau job, but everyone at work suspected the editor would lay off another hundred people before the end of the year, and I figured I wouldn't survive another cut. One of my three best friends left Portland to teach in Africa, and the other two moved back to their hometowns in Nebraska and Mississippi. "Which is great," I wrote in my journal. "It'll finally just be me, alone with my apartment." I spent March staring at the crown moldings. Outside, the trees bloomed bright blossoms, and I lay on the floor and reminded myself that *this* was the life I'd dreamed of. It didn't matter if everyone left or I lost my job. I'd made it out of Louisiana. That was good enough.

Early that April, I called my mom with nothing to say. My brother, Dustin, and his girlfriend had just had a baby, and my mom told me she'd been trying out nicknames for herself. She didn't want to be called mammaw or meemaw or any of the other cutesy words people in the South use for grandma. She was only forty-five, too young to take on a title like that.

"What do you think of the name GG?" she asked. "It stands for 'Gorgeous Granny.'"

I told her that name sounded weird and even older than mammaw, but she ignored me and asked when I planned to meet my new nephew.

I stuttered and shuffled papers. I hoped she thought the sound meant I was looking at a calendar.

Dustin had always wanted a family. When we were young and our parents were fighting, we'd often retreat to the woods a block away from our house. One year, we spent so much time in the trees, my brother decided to turn a small clearing into a second home. He carried blankets and lampshades through the pines, and he set up a coffee table where we could play Spades underneath their skinny branches. I never wanted a second home, though. While he hung curtains and swept the dirt into an even floor, I lit dead grass on fire. The rest of our lives had gone pretty much the same way. He tried to build things; I burned them down. He joined the army and married his first girlfriend a few months after he turned eighteen. She left him while he was serving in Iraq, and soon after their divorce was final, he found a new girlfriend, a sweet Starbucks barista who rode her skateboard to work. Now they were raising a child together. I knew I would never have a life like my brother's. I wouldn't have kids or a girlfriend to marry. Gay marriage wasn't legal, but that only barely mattered to me then: I'd cheated on my last girlfriend, and I'd cheated on the one before her. Seeing my brother just reminded me of the ways I'd always failed to be normal.

"I was thinking I'd come to Louisiana first," I told my mom. "Maybe we could work on the Roy project."

This American Life had never responded to my application, but after the last trip, my mom had urged me to think bigger. We should abandon the podcast idea, she said, and turn Roy's story into a film documentary. I told my mom I could fly down in two weeks, just in time for her forty-sixth birthday. We could spend a few days in Delhi together, then, after that, I'd drive to Texas to meet my new nephew.

"You should make flyers," she said. "Make it like one of those missing-children posters. Put a picture of Roy on there, and we can tape them around Delhi so you can find people who knew him."

I spent the next few hours designing a flyer out of one of the photographs Ann McVay had given me. I chose the nicest picture, a portrait Ann said Roy had had made for the church directory, and typed a message across the margins: "DID YOU KNOW ROY HUDGINS? We need people to interview who remember Roy." Underneath, I listed my phone number and email address in a font I hoped was eye-catching. I didn't finish until after midnight Pacific time, 2 a.m. in Louisiana, but I emailed my mom a copy, and she called a few seconds later.

"Don't put your phone number on there. No one's going to dial long-distance."

I told her Delhi didn't seem like a place especially wired to the web. The old people who remembered Roy probably didn't have email addresses. My grandmother had never even gone online. My mom allowed that that might be true, but still, she said, my Portland phone number wouldn't work.

"Your number is going to scare people off. They'll think you're from out of town."

"I *am* from out of town. I don't live there."

My mom sighed and told me to hold on. She put the phone down and seemed to bang around the kitchen for a minute before coming back to the line. She lit a cigarette, and her first exhale whooshed into the receiver.

"Okay," she said. "Use mine."

TWO WEEKS LATER, in late April, I drove to the airport with the flyers and two filmmaker friends in tow. I acted nonchalant when I told my mom I'd found people to work on the documentary, but I felt stunned with disbelief. The filmmakers were cooler and much more accomplished than I was, and yet, they'd both offered to help me after I'd blogged about the first trip with my mother. They'd even offered to pay for their own tickets. Aaron was my college roommate's older brother, an introvert with long hair and a degree from Savannah College of Art and Design. My roommate and I used to wear out the mixtapes he'd send from Georgia, and when I first met him in Portland, I felt as if I were meeting a celebrity I'd admired from afar. *This* was the guy who introduced me to Joni Mitchell and the Velvet Underground. The other filmmaker, Aubree, hosted Portland's coolest gay dance night and once starred in a Sleater-Kinney music video. (At the time, I thought of Aubree as a gay woman, but years later, after we'd been working on this story for a decade, Aubree came out as nonbinary and started using "they/them" pronouns.)

At twenty-six, I didn't spend much time wondering *why* Aaron and Aubree wanted to help me. They were Southern—Aaron was from Memphis, and Aubree from Louisville—and that seemed reason enough to me. Maybe, I thought, they had their own ghosts, or maybe they just liked making things. Now, in my late thirties, I see those early investments as incalculable gifts. Up until then, the only person who really believed in my project was my mother. But Aubree and Aaron were artists. They'd made films that had screened in actual theaters, and they believed my little idea was worth pursuing.

On that first trip, the three of us flew into Shreveport, a mid-sized city a hundred miles from Monroe, because that's where my mom lived in 2010. My phone rang almost as soon as the plane landed. I answered expecting my mom to tell me she was waiting on the other side of security. She always got to the airport an hour early to pick me up. But her voice sounded thin when she said hello.

"Baby. I'm not there. They're putting me in the ER."

My mom went to the emergency room at least a few times a month. Over the years, she'd suffered from shingles, cellulitis, kidney stones, stomach issues, and severe headaches she said she'd started having in 1982 when, at Cam Milton's funeral, a branch fell off an oak tree and knocked her unconscious. In 2006, a brown recluse spider bit her in Oklahoma, and she spent the next three years logging regular hospital stays, trying to recover from the bite. Maybe she *was* sick, but I suspected that she usually went to the hospital to treat something that had nothing to do with the spider bite or the headaches she said she'd have for the rest of her life. When I was young, the drawer of our TV stand stayed stocked with Vicodin and Percocet, pills my mom bought from neighbors or persuaded doctors to prescribe. She kept a narcotic called Stadol, a nose spray that worked immediately, hidden between pairs of underwear in her top dresser drawer. Most of my earliest memories of her are manic ones, nights where she didn't sleep or drove stoned to a Walmart in another town. She'd call at three in the morning, not knowing how she'd drifted beyond city limits. My dad seemed to believe her every time she said she was sick, but I could sense a subtle difference in her voice. It was creaky and weak when she was ill, slurred and low when she was high. There were other signs—her right shoulder shrugged, her left eye drooped, and her mouth fell into a perfect frown—but her voice was the giveaway. I didn't need to see her to know why she wasn't at the airport. Her words sank and dragged, and I knew she'd made herself sick with pills.

The flight attendant said it was safe to grab our suitcases, so I told my mother I had to go. She asked me to bring two bags of Dove chocolate candies to the hospital, and I whispered that I didn't want my friends to see her that way. She started to cry.

"Just come alone," she said.

A trip to the hospital would cost us a whole reporting day, but I relented. I dropped Aubree and Aaron off at my parents' house, then rode with my dad to a Walgreens close to the hospital.

I can't remember what my dad and I talked about on the drive, but I'm sure we didn't talk about my mother. We never talked about her. When I was young, I thought of my dad as my favorite parent. He was as easy and unremarkable as a seventy-degree day. He never yelled or lost his temper, and he didn't even cuss until I was fourteen or fifteen. He stuttered the first time he said "bullshit," as if the word weren't just unnatural but painful rolling through his mouth. He laughed a lot and delighted in coming up with the least grammatically correct sentences possible. Double negatives were his specialty. He read the newspaper every morning, but he didn't talk about anything serious. On drives like the one we took to the hospital that night, he mostly recounted weird things he'd seen at work or on TV. My favorite story is the one he told about a woman named Gretchen who knocked on my parents' front door one summer afternoon after my brother and I were grown. Gretchen was wearing a towel and a bathing suit, and as she talked, a dead frog fell out of the bottom of the towel. Neither she nor my dad acknowledged the frog. They locked eyes with each other, and eventually, Gretchen squatted, picked up the frog, then stuffed it into the top of her one-piece without ever looking down.

"But why did she knock on your door?" I'd ask him.

"She said she wanted to see my glow-in-the-dark turtle."

"Do you have a glow-in-the-dark turtle?"

"No," he'd say, collapsing into a high-pitched giggle before telling the story again in her voice. "My name is Gretchen. I wanted to ask about your turtle."

Usually, I felt grateful that my dad didn't force me to talk about my mother. I thought if we pretended that her incidents weren't happening, we could somehow keep her issues from leaking into our own lives. I thought of her hospital visits as the kind of white noise that drives you crazy when you first move into a new apartment—a loud refrigerator or the beep of a neighbor's dying smoke alarm—the kind of noise your ears eventually tune out. But on that trip, I remember I was angry as we pulled into a Walgreens parking lot near the emergency room. I thought my dad was enabling my mother by taking her to the hospital when surely nothing was wrong. But I didn't tell him that. I held my jaw a little tighter. I didn't laugh at whatever story he told. I thought then that I just didn't want any extra conflicts messing up my reporting trip, but I see now that I never asked my dad why he didn't intervene with my mother because I was worried he'd ask me the same question. I spent my life largely ignoring my mother's dips, but my dad never got a break. He lived in her throes.

At the Walgreens, I bought two bags of milk chocolates. I held tight to the candy as I lugged myself down the hospital's fluorescent hallways and into my mother's room. She was watching a trashy talk show at a volume so low I could hear her IV dripping small drops down the tube. I set the candy on top of her chest. She told me she loved me, and I didn't say it back.

"What am I supposed to do about the flyers?" I asked her. "They have your number on them."

I don't remember how long we lingered or how I said goodbye. I stayed up late that night, thinking Roy was lucky. Jewel had wanted him so badly she'd stolen him. My mom had stayed clean for my brother when his son was born, but when I needed her, she disappeared. I dreamed all night about cotton, and the next morning we drove to Delhi. I barely spoke to Aubree and Aaron as we headed east. *They probably think I'm a jerk*, I thought. I'd planned this whole trip around my mom's birthday, and now I was abandoning her. What kind of daughter leaves town while her mother is in the hospital? I didn't want to tell them about the pills or the nose spray, and I didn't want to talk about the hours I'd spent in emergency room lobbies, watching late-night TV from yellow vinyl chairs as I waited for my mom to emerge woozy and wobbling. I could still picture the snack bar at the hospital where we'd spent most nights my fourth-grade year, and as I drove my friends to Delhi, I remembered that I'd once stolen a Snickers bar while my mom begged for a shot.

"Okay," Aubree said, picking up a camera and turning it toward me. "Should we start filming?"

Aubree asked questions, but most of my answers were mumbled fragments. I said "um" and "I don't know." I told Aubree I was too nervous to be interviewed. At work, I asked the questions.

"Just explain what we're doing. We can edit it later."

I looked back and forth between the road and the wide-angle lens a few times before answering.

"We're going to Delhi," I said finally. "My mom's hometown."

WHEN I TURNED ONTO Main Street a few hours later, the abandoned buildings felt like landmarks, souvenirs of the time I'd spent with my mom four months earlier. Hot Wings Heaven was still closed, and the old A-Mart, where we'd turned to meet Keith King, remained dark. A WELCOME TO DELHI, HOME OF sign hung incomplete and rusted from a pole. The only new business I spotted was a shack whose unfinished front doors advertised pecans and locusts for sale. We had an hour of daylight left, so I drove along Delhi's two highways, pointing out the cemetery, the nursing home, and the drugstore where my mom had worked as a teenager. I wasn't ready to track down Mark King, so I steered away from his neighborhood, pressing past the barber shops and churches, until the highway ran through nothing but fields.

The sun sat low in the west. We planned to spend the week in a cabin on Poverty Point Reservoir, a man-made lake two miles north of town. Poverty Point is Delhi's lone tourist attraction. It's a national monument, home to what the cabin reservation website described as a prehistoric archaeological site with five mounds and six C-shaped ridges. Native Americans built the earthen structures between 1700 and 1100 BC, but I don't know what those original inhabitants called the land. Most websites say the area's former name is unknown, and all of the official documents I dug up started with the history of one very rich man.

Just before the Civil War, a farmer from Kentucky bought the land and started calling it Poverty Point Plantation. I don't think he named it after his own circumstances. All the records I found showed that he had $120,000 cash by 1860—a purchasing power equal to nearly $3 million when we visited in 2010. I unearthed one newspaper article that said he named it after a place his wife loved in Kentucky, and another that said he'd chosen it because the people in North Louisiana were fairly destitute. I don't know which is true, but by the time I pulled my rental car close to the site, the name felt disturbingly accurate. In 2010, forty percent of Delhi's families earned less than $25,000 a year—half of what I made at the newspaper.

The name wasn't new to me. When I was in middle school, my class took a trip to Poverty Point to look for arrowheads, and I remember we made fun of the name on the way home. Someone pointed to a boy who was wearing cheap-looking sweatpants, then asked if he'd bought them at Poverty Point. Everyone laughed, and I did, too, even though my own clothes were layaway specials paired with Adidas knockoffs my mom had bought half-off at Payless. I knew what poverty was. I even wrote a whole journal entry in seventh grade about how unfair it was that my family "lived in poverty." But I don't think the name fully hit me until I returned to work on the documentary. How long had this place been poor? Maybe that farmer had been wealthy, but I suspected most people who lived here never had.

I turned right at the reservoir, then followed the rim of the lake back toward our cabin. The lake hadn't existed back when I came on the school trip. Lawmakers had voted in 2001 to dig it out and fill it up. They'd done so hoping a basin full of bass would bring fishermen to town, but when I looked out at the water, I saw only one canoe. Birds cut across the road, and a possum darted through the grass. Yellow signs warned of alligators and black bears. A dead snake baked on the shoulder. Ours was cabin 7, the second to last on the map, but the last one standing. I'd read online that cabin 8 had burned down in the middle of the night a few weeks before. Three of the four people staying there had managed to rush down the long boardwalk that connected the cabin to the parking lot, but one person had had to jump. All that remained was a few charred pegs. Aubree eyed the burnt remnants with trepidation, then turned to me.

"Do you think it was lightning?"

The newspaper promised a storm later that week, and I was sure Aubree was wondering whether we'd survive a stay in a place so full of beasts and bad weather. Our whole cabin looked like kindling. I said I didn't know, but suggested we leave our suitcases packed by the front door. We lined up the camera equipment, then we stepped out onto the porch to survey the lake. Catfish circled what was left of cabin 8. Mosquitoes bit my legs.

I knew I had to find people for us to interview, but I was nervous to work the phones. One reason I worried I'd lose my job in the next round of layoffs was I never felt comfortable calling strangers. It felt so invasive, dialing someone's private line and demanding to talk. But I knew Aubree and Aaron had flown down expecting to film people, so I whispered a pep talk to myself. "No one here knows you. If they hang up, don't let it bother you. You'll never see them again."

I couldn't bring myself to try anyone from the phone book, so I called relatives until I had a short list of names, people who knew Roy and might be willing to talk to three strangers with video cameras. One of my aunts told me she'd introduce me to people, but only if I promised never to tell anyone I thought Roy was a lesbian. I told her that I didn't think Roy *was* a lesbian, that wearing men's clothes didn't mean he was attracted to women, and anyway, I couldn't imagine myself saying the word "lesbian" out loud in Delhi. My aunt ignored me. "Promise me," she said.

"Okay. I won't tell people that I think Roy or anyone else is or was ever a lesbian."

Satisfied, she gave me the number of a man named Teddy Rockett. He answered when I called, but apologized and said he couldn't talk because he was working on an oil rig in the middle of the Gulf of Mexico. I hung up without asking him what it was like to be out there. Two days before we flew down, the Deepwater Horizon rig had exploded off the coast of southeast Louisiana, and as I talked to Teddy, I could see Aubree and Aaron watching news reports on the cabin's TV. Deepwater was still on fire, spewing thousands of gallons of oil and natural gas into the gulf, and somewhere out there, Teddy Rockett was answering my call.

I dialed disconnected numbers and reached other people who said they didn't know enough to speak with me. I left messages in a voice twangier than my usual accent, hoping I sounded like I belonged in Louisiana. Finally, I found Ricky Ellis, a fifty-something who lived near Roy when Roy was older. Ricky said he'd never heard of Jewel Ellis, but he did know that Roy was "a morphodite."

"What, what's that, what's a morphodite?" I asked. Ricky laughed uncomfortably, and neither of us said anything for a few seconds. Ricky laughed again to break the silence.

"Half man, half woman," he said. "Roy had the top part of a woman. I mean, you know, breasts."

Ricky didn't describe Roy's bottom half, and I didn't dare ask. I changed the subject to Roy's music, and we talked about the guitar and the Bible for a while. Ricky told me that his parents didn't go to church, so Roy taught him how to decipher the Old Testament. I asked Ricky if he'd ever heard that Roy had been kidnapped. He said no. No one talked about Roy's past. The only explanation Ricky had ever heard is that Roy's was a body made up of mismatched parts.

"I thought he was a guy. Just a regular guy until my mother told me. He lived in a regular wood-frame house, nothing fancy. He always lived by hisself. Never had kids, and that's the way he liked it."

Ricky told me I'd learn more from older folks, people who'd lived in Delhi when Roy was young and Jewel Ellis was alive, but most of those people were dead or down with dementia in the town's only nursing home. Ricky suggested we call Delhi's state senator, a man who now lived on the good side of town but who grew up near Hell Street on a road named Race. When I called my grandma later that night to ask if she remembered the senator, I could almost hear her smirking over the phone. She and Francis Thompson were about the same age and had lived one street apart, she told me, so of course she knew him.

"We sat in the same classroom together," she said. "In fact, he sat in front of me. And can I tell you something?"

She sounded hyped and angry, wily in the way she got when she wanted to make a point. She didn't wait for me to ask "what" before she answered her own question.

"He is state representative, okay? I was nothing but a housewife."

I could hear her sister, Shirley, talking in the background, bad-mouthing the senator and other people they thought had judged them for never accomplishing enough.

"He was no more intelligent than I was," my grandma said. "He didn't make any better grades than I did."

"Okay," I said. "So, do you want me not to call him?"

I didn't need to see her to know she was probably smiling smug, the way she always did when she wanted to see some drama play out. She told me to go right ahead.

"Now, Casey, did y'all see the news? Y'all need to be careful, baby. These are end times. The world is going up in flames."

FRANCIS THOMPSON WAS IN Baton Rouge when I called him, but he said he'd be back Sunday afternoon. We hadn't found anyone else to interview yet, so we drove around Saturday pasting flyers to abandoned store windows. I sent messages to everyone who'd subscribed to a Facebook group celebrating Delhi's olden days, then we waited for Sunday to come. Wind whipped at the cabin Saturday night, and the news briefly interrupted the oil rig coverage to announce that one tornado had killed ten people in Mississippi and another had flattened homes and ripped metal from the ground in Tallulah, a Louisiana town less than twenty miles east of Delhi. Aubree and I looked at each other nervously.

"Should we put our suitcases in the car?" I asked.

The lake sloshed against our windows all night, but the sun was shining when we woke Sunday morning. Dead bugs covered the windshield of our rental car, so I drove toward the senator's house with the wipers waving back and forth. Francis Thompson lived as far away from Hell Street as a person could within Delhi city limits. His house was on the south side, two miles from the railroad tracks, set back behind a maze of other roads. We wound around them, and I felt like I was in a different city altogether. The streets on the north side are straight sticks, thoroughfares with intersections but no curves. The south side seemed to be all cul-de-sacs and sharp joints tucked away from the main drag. A few roads in, we circled a pond and watched ducks waddle along the bank. Every block looked beautiful. Brick houses rose several stories into the sky, and the roads were named Little John and Robinhood—all paved new and smooth.

The senator's street was particularly lovely. Every yard had at least three oaks, each thick with leaves and the kind of branches a kid could climb. The senator's house wasn't the biggest on the south side, but it wasn't a home I'd call modest. It was built from good bricks, the light kind with bleached-white mortar. Two columns stood between a row of doors that led out to a perfect lawn. His driveway could have held half a dozen cars.

The man who opened the door looked years younger than my grandmother, even though they were both born around the start of World War II. Francis Thompson was handsome in a boyish way. His blond hair had barely grayed, and his blue eyes were clear bright circles. He moved easy through the living room as he ushered us inside. He wore a sport coat with a red tie and a pocket square that didn't exactly match. I handed him two release forms, papers that gave us permission to film the interview, and the senator bragged that we were his second news crew of the day. He eyed the papers and said he'd better ask his wife before signing off the film rights to their house.

"Marilyn," he called. "Do you agree they can film your house?"

We hadn't met Marilyn on our way in, but I could hear her rustling around the kitchen. Her voice curled out in a soft twang I'd only heard among the gentry. She joked that we could film as long as our lenses weren't good enough to show the dust, and when she said it, she made three syllables out of one-syllable words.

"You know," the senator said, "Roy dressed like a boy, but it came out from later accounts that Roy was actually female but took on the lifestyle of a male."

He widened his eyes in a way that suggested he was revealing something to me for the first time. I'd decided on the drive over that I wouldn't tell anyone what my grandmother had told me. I wanted to see what people would offer up before I pushed them, so I widened my eyes, and Francis continued talking.

"I'm sure that he or she or, um . . ." he said, trailing off. The senator explained that he didn't know which pronoun to use, but he could say with authority that no one in Delhi had ever thrown rocks at Roy. In fact, the senator said, he'd never even noticed anything unusual about Roy. Roy was just a hard worker who mowed lawns, and that made him a valuable community member. Marilyn was still in the kitchen, but she hollered an addendum: "I never saw him or her with anybody."

Francis ignored his wife and waited for me to ask a question. Suddenly, I felt hesitant to probe deeper, even though I'd flown all the way down to learn about Roy. Something about the way the Thompsons called Roy "he or she" made me uneasy, so I stalled by asking the senator questions about the town he'd represented for nearly forty years. He said Delhi had been different when he was growing up.

"People raised gardens in their backyards. They talked over the fence to their neighbors. When one suffered, all suffered."

I looked around the living room and thought of the poem Roy had written, comparing his life to a dry well. I doubted the senator had suffered alongside Roy. The Thompsons had a fireplace, a piano, and, most important, each other. Roy had described his life in that poem as one of "nothing but heartaches, sorrow, and strife."

Marilyn tiptoed in and took a seat. She wore the same short and sprayed hairstyle most of the women I knew in the South did, but she looked slightly stately in a boat-neck sweater and gold hoop earrings. I smiled, then turned back to her husband and asked what had happened to Delhi. The pool that opened the year my grandma arrived had closed decades before, and so, it seemed, had everything else.

"Delhi doesn't have a large tax base," the senator said. That was largely a function of geography, he thought. The parishes that line the Mississippi River in North Louisiana are among the poorest in the whole nation, and those parishes border Delhi. I waited, but the senator didn't offer any other explanation for Delhi's decline. He reminisced about the days when the train used to stop downtown, funneling visitors and traveling salesmen into the city's core, then he lost track of what he was saying. He looked to his wife for help. Marilyn didn't speculate about the town as a whole, but she said the north side had always been bad. "I didn't live over there," she said. "I mean, to me, that was—in my view—the worst area in town."

Francis allowed that Marilyn was right. When he was growing up, the only community poorer than the one my grandmother had lived in was the Black neighborhood, a cluster of homes just a few blocks away from Hell Street on the lots that bordered Race. The senator kept both his legs and his hands crossed in a stance that seemed diplomatic. I knew he'd grown up on Race Street, but he didn't describe his childhood the way my grandma did. In his memories, nothing was hard or painful, nothing was wholly lost or found. When I asked if he missed the oil-rich Delhi that used to be, the senator shook his head no.

"I'm very happy with my station in life right now. I've never had it so good."

He told me Conagra planned to open a sweet potato factory later that summer, and Delhi would probably come up after people found jobs there. I was skeptical, but I could tell by the way the senator pawed at his wireless mic that the interview was over. I looked down at my notebook. I'd planned to ask if he knew what happened to Roy's music career after my grandmother left, but I hadn't asked that. I hadn't really asked much of anything about Roy. The senator stood, so I closed my notebook. He said I should call Dorothy Bradley, a ninety-six-year-old woman who worked, unofficially and without pay, as the town's historian. Marilyn said Dorothy lived within walking distance on a street that backed into undeveloped land.

"Of course she has a gorgeous yard," Marilyn said. "She has a staff and somebody who lives with her."

The senator motioned for Aaron to unclip his microphone, so I stood to say goodbye. Marilyn continued sitting.

"I have to say this," she said. "Everybody knew Roy was different. He was definitely a novelty."

"He was what?" the senator asked.

"A novelty," Marilyn told her husband. "You said you didn't notice. I mean, there wasn't anyone who didn't know that."

She squinted in disbelief. I was sure Francis was just being senatorial, careful with his words. He mumbled and said he'd been a child when Roy was around, but Marilyn shook her head. She was three years younger than her husband, but she'd always known Roy was different.

"I grew up knowing he was a novelty," she said. "People didn't know if he was a boy or a girl or what."

Marilyn said Roy was just one of the town oddities, a cast that included a woman who walked the street with a big goiter hanging from her neck, and another person they called Big Boy. Big Boy's name was lost to time, but Marilyn remembered that he was so fat he couldn't get into his own car. The senator walked off to take a phone call from the governor, who was in town to survey the tornado damage.

"And also," Marilyn said, "Hell or whatever was a street unto itself. I went to school with two girls who lived on that street, nice girls, but I remember finding out they lived on that street and thinking, 'Are they like me?'"

Her scowl told me all I needed to know. Whatever it was that made my mom and grandma feel like outcasts must have started fifty years ago on Hell Street. The senator reappeared and told his wife they had to go. The governor was waiting. The senator scribbled down Dorothy Bradley's phone number on the back of an AARP magazine. He told me he hoped my reporting went well. When we climbed back into the rental car, I told Aubree and Aaron that I had to see the street that shaped me in ways I didn't yet understand. I had to see Hell.

I edged north out of the Thompsons' driveway, back toward the main drag, and I imagined my grandma riding the bale of cotton. The wagon must have traveled the same route, up and over toward Chatham. I knew my grandma's old clapboard bungalow was gone, but maybe, I thought, we'd see Miss Mattie Smith's mansion or one of the lesser, look-alike shotguns my grandma had described. I turned left, then right. I rolled slow down the block. The street was a single lane without sidewalks, but people stood talking up and down the span. Men sat in lawn chairs, and women waved from stoops. Kids clustered around a basketball that seemed at least half-flat. Most of the homes weren't houses; they were trailers, and each was painted a different color, though they all seemed to be built with aluminum that had weathered decades ago. The two wood houses that remained both looked abandoned. One was blue and boarded up, the other white and rotted out.

I waved but felt voyeuristic. Every single person on the street was Black, and I, a white person, worried I appeared slow and lurking. The rental-car plates said Indiana, and I suspected everyone could tell this street wasn't mine. I tried to look like I knew where I was going, but my grandmother had never told me which intersection she'd lived closest to.

I grabbed my notebook and searched for Mark King's address. Roy had lived next to Mark, Ann McVay had told me. And my grandmother had lived across from Roy. If I found Mark's, I could find my grandma's.

We eased up until we saw Mark's home, a red single-wide flanked by vacant lots. I parked a few trailers down, then took stock of the street as Aubree and Aaron unloaded their camera equipment. I'd lived in trailers twice growing up. One was a double-wide with a Jacuzzi tub, the nicest place we ever lived. The other looked just like Chatham's single-wides, old and dented with rickety steps we'd pushed against the base. Ours was an off-white tube stuck between pines on a plot way out in the country west of Monroe. The walls were made of warped, wood veneer paneling, and the carpet was green shag. I hadn't lived in that trailer since 1997, my freshman year of high school, but standing on Chatham that afternoon, the years crumpled away. The trailer had had only two small bedrooms, I remembered. My parents took the larger one, a 9 x 6 space that fit their queen-sized bed and nothing else. I refused to share the other. I was a teenager, I'd argued, a high schooler who needed privacy to talk on the phone at night. I couldn't sleep so close to my twelve-year-old brother. I don't know why my parents didn't force us to bunk together, but my brother carved himself a bedroom out of the kitchen using empty boxes as a wall. The first night we moved in, a stray Catahoula cur gave birth to a litter of puppies under the trailer, and we stayed up late listening through the floor as the puppies cried. By the end of the school year, my parents had separated. My mom was heavy on the nose spray then, so I didn't want to live with her when our family split. Instead, my dad and I moved to an apartment, a two-bedroom behind a Sonic Drive-In close to West Monroe High School, and my mom and brother went to Delhi to stay with my grandma. We lived apart for two years, until my junior year, when my parents reunited in a town ninety miles south. By then, whatever had held us close listening to the puppies had been too damaged to recapture.

I lingered on Chatham, and I prayed nobody invited me inside. I didn't want to think about the trailer's vinyl flooring or the pathetic "room" I'd forced my brother to accept. I recalled, suddenly, that my best friend and I had taken baths together in the single-wide, even though we were in high school, and arguably too old. I stared at her body with what I told myself was innocent curiosity, but maybe my gay feelings started there. When we first moved in, I'd covered the fake wood walls with posters of Joey Lawrence and Jonathan Taylor Thomas, but when we left, I threw them all away.

Aubree and Aaron were waiting in one of the vacant yards, so I shut the rental car door and moved toward Mark's. This was the walk my grandmother must have made, I thought, the night she first heard Roy play music. These must be the oak trees that shaded her house. This must be the way the air smelled. I was lost in her world, stepping one foot at a time, so I didn't notice the police car speeding north until it cut me off from Mark's driveway. A cop rolled down the passenger-side window and leaned over to ask what we were doing with the cameras. My heart beat loud and quick. The officer was young and Black, and I felt, again, like I was trespassing in a neighborhood that didn't belong to me. I wished my mother were there.

"Dispatch got calls," the officer said.

"Um," I answered. "My grandma lived here. I'm making a documentary for her. Rufus, I mean Chief Carter, said it was okay."

I tried to come up with a story, something to tell the officer if he asked what the documentary was about. I didn't want to say it was about Roy. *If I tell him*, I thought, *he'll know about me.*

"Really?" the officer asked. "Which house was your grandma's?"

I scanned Chatham, still unsure of where my grandma must have lived. I didn't want to point to anyone's trailer, so I motioned toward one of the vacant patches. "She lived there in the fifties. She hasn't been back in a long time, so I'm filming to show her the old neighborhood."

"Well," the cop said. "Don't look nothing like it did back when she was here, but all right."

He told me not to film anyone's front door, then he rushed off with his lights on. I told Aubree and Aaron we should leave. They insisted on getting at least a bit of footage, but I hung back while they filmed the empty lots. It had only been four months since Mark's wife had told me no, and I thought I should give the Kings more time before I asked again. Next trip, I promised myself, I would ask Mark and Cheryl to let me see Roy's journals. I nodded as people walked past me, and eventually I got back in the car. I wrote a list of questions on a yellow legal-sized notebook. *Did Roy ever lose his temper? Is Delhi a welcoming place?* I wondered what Roy thought of Hell Street. Did he ever mow the perfect lawns on the other side of town?

THE NEXT MORNING WAS my mom's birthday, and I called her before we started reporting. She sounded the same as she had a few days earlier, hollowed out and weak with medicine. It had been years since I'd seen her on her birthday, so I had forgotten how much she hated it. As she talked, I remembered that she'd spent her birthday on pain pills every April since 1996, the year she turned thirty-two.

It was the spring before we moved to the single-wide trailer. I was a month shy of thirteen. We lived in a white house that sat crooked on a lot close to the levee, a house where rats and cockroaches skulked through the cupboards. My mom was using the nose spray then, and when I begged her to take me to a Christian pop concert at the civic center, she'd been too drugged to say yes. Her eyes were vacant, and her hair stuck up, wild and unbrushed. She was wearing a nightgown, even though it was daylight, even though it was her birthday. It was a Saturday, and I cried that afternoon until my dad agreed to take me and my brother to the concert. My dad's best friend was staying with us, I remember. When we left, the man was reading a book in my room, and my mother was watching *Oprah* in hers. We stayed out late because I wanted to meet the band, a quartet of beautiful women called Point of Grace. By the time we made it home, my dad's best friend was gone. I was still buzzing from the concert, so I called out to my mom in a voice I'm sure she found too loud and happy. A few minutes later, she teetered into the kitchen, empty-eyed. All my joy sank into anger when I saw her, and I told her one day she'd regret not spending time with me. She punched me in the stomach.

My parents were the kind of Southerners who believed the Bible condones spanking, and they whipped us a few times a week. My dad used a belt on my bare butt, and my mom slapped my face every time I said "yeah" instead of "yes ma'am." But that night was different. I collapsed against the refrigerator, but she kept punching. My mom was unrestrained, flailing and full of hatred. I know I fell down, and I know she kept punching. She hit my legs, my back, my jaw. I could hear my brother screaming from somewhere. My dad pulled my mom off, and I stayed on the ground while he dragged her somewhere else. My brother bent down and asked if I was okay. I don't remember the rest of the night. I don't remember when or how my mom broke the news that my dad's friend had raped her while we were gone, but I remember she told me he'd shoved a knife inside her, that he'd said if she didn't take it, he'd find me instead. I'd just gotten my period a few months earlier, and I remember I didn't sleep that night because I was worried he'd come after me. I was old enough to get pregnant, my mother had taught me, and I knew, because she'd told me, that nothing ruined your life like getting pregnant too young.

The reception was bad at the cabin, so my mom and I talked in staticky clips, then she made an excuse to get off the phone. I felt embarrassed that I hadn't remembered what her birthday meant when I'd first suggested the trip, but I couldn't bring myself to tell her I was sorry. I worried if I did, I'd just remind her that I'd abandoned her that night in 1996. Her lows had lasted longer since that night. Every birthday, she became that person I'd seen in the kitchen, teetering and gone.

I walked out to the lake and wished I knew how to be close to her. The only time we'd spent together since I went away to college was that first trip to Delhi, and that was just a day trip, abbreviated time that hadn't brought us together in the way I'd imagined it might. I told myself I would return to Louisiana in a few months, maybe in the summer when my mom was feeling buoyant and clean. I wandered back into the cabin, grateful lightning hadn't burned it down, and I asked Aubree and Aaron if they were ready to do one last interview.

THE SOUTH SIDE'S curvy streets didn't surprise me the way they had earlier in the week, but I grimaced, again, seeing how segregated Delhi was. How could neighborhoods so close look so different? The south side didn't have a single trailer, only homes with yards and covered porches. Dorothy Bradley's house was nestled in a bend, and as we rounded the curve, I saw that her lawn was as beautiful as the senator's wife had promised. The grass was edged in straight lines, the bushes pruned into perfect circles. I stopped counting trees when I reached a dozen. We parked in the shade under a towering oak, but when Aubree and Aaron reached for their cameras, I suddenly felt scared. I told them to wait. I'd called Dorothy the day before, and she'd said that we could come by her house, but I thought she sounded suspicious of me. She'd asked if I planned to "tape" her, and I'd mumbled something like "We'll see." Aubree and Aaron didn't film that conversation, so the only record I have is my own memory, and the conversation has grown dim with time. All I remember is that I told Aubree and Aaron that we should take in only one camera, the smallest one they'd brought, instead of our usual fleet.

We walked up to the house, a one-story ranch with a brick facade and brick-paved walkways. Dorothy's assistant led us through a parlor. I was almost twenty-seven then, and Aubree and Aaron were a few years older, but when we stepped down into the living room, Dorothy's assistant announced that we were teenagers interested in learning about Delhi's past. I half wanted to go along with the ruse. If Dorothy assumed we were young, I thought, maybe she'd be open to letting us film her, but I knew I couldn't lie my way into bravery.

"Actually," I said, "I'm twenty-six."

Dorothy seemed to survey me for half a minute, then she nodded her head.

"By golly, you're not a teenager, are you?"

She told me she was ninety-six and a half, and as I eased around the couch, I looked at her and thought she looked at least a decade or two younger. She'd dried and curled her white hair, painted on red lips and brown eyebrows. Her eyes and shawl-collared sweater were the same shade of turquoise. She was healthy, she told me, though her body had been crimped by polio when she was two.

I don't know if I asked her if we could film her or if Aubree just turned on the camera, but in the footage of that day, I can see that I asked Dorothy to introduce herself. She spoke to me at an angle, her head turned and trained on the air just left of me. "I'm Dorothy Phillips Bradley, and the Phillips name has just about disappeared because we were girls who married men. Now we have other names."

She talked another ten minutes without interruption. She told us she still owned forty of the six hundred acres her ancestors acquired through a land grant during the Louisiana Purchase. They'd handed it down, generation to generation, she said. Dorothy assumed she, too, would leave the land to her children, but both her son and her daughter had left Delhi years ago, and as far as she could tell, they had no plans of coming back. Dorothy talked about the Siege of Vicksburg, and she explained to us how the railroad had turned the dirt around the Bayou Macon into a town. When she was young, Delhi was just a boat ramp, but then trains brought people, and the people built Delhi up. In the early days, Dorothy said, Chatham was a good street. The town's only school was there, as were two churches, but then, in 1927, the Mississippi River flooded and ruined most of the low-lying communities outside of Delhi. People moved inland, out of the Delta and onto Chatham, and when they arrived they brought a brand of rowdy that hadn't existed in town before.

"I don't mean they killed anybody," Dorothy said. "But maybe they did."

I asked if she remembered the days when Chatham was called Hell Street, and Dorothy laughed so hard she coughed. "It still is. I used that term just last week."

She told me she didn't mean anything derogatory. "Hell" is just what people called it. I couldn't tell if she was snobby or a straight shooter. She said she didn't know why Chatham had become Hell during the Great Depression, but the town had been very prejudiced back then, and Chatham very poor. The name change probably grew out of that.

"Did you, uh," I said, stalling. "Did you know Roy Hudgins who lived on that street?"

Dorothy adjusted the shawl on her sweater, and I noticed, for the first time, that polio had reshaped her hands. Her fingers were bent in half, and her left palm seemed to be clutching an invisible tennis ball. She stared into space for a few seconds, then began talking without looking at me. "I did. I knew her for years and years. She was tied to Chatham, but she rode her bicycle all over town. She mowed yards and took care of herself. I don't know where her family was."

I could see Aubree zooming in closer on Dorothy's face. I asked if it was unusual back then for someone to live without a family, and

Dorothy said yes. That's why people remembered Roy. Adults aren't meant to live alone forever. Dorothy had been widowed in 1958, but she had kids and her assistant. I thought of my Portland apartment, of the girlfriend who'd dumped me and the friends who'd moved away. My brother would have his family, and I would live in that apartment, alone, like Roy.

"She kept her hair cut short, I know that," Dorothy said.

I shifted in my seat, stupidly hoping that Dorothy hadn't noticed that my hair was short, too. I wanted to leave, but I knew I couldn't end another interview the cowardly way I had the senator's. I'd spent the whole trip scared. I hadn't asked Francis Thompson any real questions. I hadn't gone to the Kings' house. Now the trip was ending, and the only things I'd learned were the things I already knew: Roy rode a bicycle and mowed lawns. He lived alone. No one had confirmed my grandma's kidnapping story or Ann's report of the pink sweatsuit. No one had told me how Roy *felt*.

"Roy is a man's name," I said. My voice snagged and quivered. I hadn't actually asked a question, I realized, just noted the disconnect between a name and Dorothy's "she."

"Yes," Dorothy said, dragging out the *s*. "I didn't know whether you wanted to talk about that or not. That's fine. In my opinion, she was just a homosexual."

The next few seconds felt like they lasted a million minutes. My ears rang with a noise that felt heavy. *She knows*, I thought. *She knows about me.*

"She wore men's clothes," Dorothy said. "Doesn't mean a thing. You see, I have friends."

Dorothy trailed off, then relaxed, just a bit, into her chair. She said she'd been a counselor before she was a volunteer historian, and she'd met lots of gay men working in the field. She'd gone out to eat pizza and drink beer with two gay cops, and she found them elegant and fun. They never bothered anyone, Dorothy said, and neither had Roy, but homosexuals kept to themselves for a reason.

"Nobody gets close to these people," she said.

Dorothy wiggled her right hand when she said "these people." I had no idea what that motion meant. I could feel sweat collecting underneath my arms. My heart beat so fast I worried Aaron's professional microphone might pick up the sound. Dorothy turned her body so she was looking right at me for the first time. Roy, she said, stayed on the outskirts.

"And I never really knew where she belonged," Dorothy said. "Did you ever know where she belonged?"

I thought of my apartment, so unlike that trailer or crooked white house. And I thought of my mom, wasting another birthday in a haze. I wished I could go back to 1996 and skip that Point of Grace concert. I wished I could give my mom everything I knew my brother would.

"No," I told Dorothy. "I don't know where Roy belonged."

Chapter Four

(1982–1992)

ONCE, WHEN I WAS young and trying to prolong the moments before bedtime, I asked my mother to describe Heaven. We were devoted Christians then, and we talked about the afterlife as if it were as real as Walmart, a warp world just a level above or below us. My mom tugged my twin-sized sheets up to my neck. She kissed my nose, then described the path to what she called the pearly gates.

"When we die," she said, "we leave our bodies behind. Only our spirit goes to heaven."

She told me my soul would slip through my chest, float up through the clouds, then land in front of Saint Peter and his giant tome of judgment. "When you get there, he'll flip through the Book of Life until he finds your name. He'll look at everything good and bad you've ever done, and he will decide if you should take your place among the angels."

I wiggled under my Holly Hobbie sheets, imagining the ascent and Peter's big book. I wondered if its holy pages would show the times I screamed at my little brother, if Peter would know I called the 1-900 wrestling hotline, racked up a five-hundred-dollar phone bill, then lied to my mom and said a kid down the road had broken in and used our phone. I'd prayed and asked God to forgive me for those sins, but did that mean they'd disappeared? I still hadn't told my mom I'd lied. Maybe Peter would use that as evidence to keep me out of heaven.

"And then what happens?" I asked.

"If you get in, you'll walk the streets of gold."

I wanted my mom to sit on my bed a little while longer, so I asked all the questions my seven-year-old brain could conjure. Did God build the streets out of gold bars or gold nuggets? Did he arrange the pieces like cobblestones? Did they stick up in rocky crags that scratched the angels' feet?

"No, baby," my mom told me. "The gold is smooth. Everyone glides along barefoot and singing hallelujah."

She turned off my light, and I imagined Heaven's glow. I asked if we would still live next to the same people in the afterlife. I didn't want to spend forever with that neighbor boy. I didn't want him to bring up the wrestling hotline in front of Saint Peter.

"I don't know," my mom told me. "But I do know everyone gets a mansion."

I closed my eyes and imagined a gigantic house on an open plot of land. I told my mom I would fill my mansion with Barbie dolls and the American Gladiators figurines my little brother and I collected. I'd have a pool in the backyard and a porch swing in the front.

"You and me can drink coffee there," I said. "With lots of milk. Every morning, we'll swing and watch the hummingbirds."

She didn't say anything, and I kicked the covers off, worried that my vision of paradise didn't sound appealing. "Or we can just read," I said. "We don't have to look at the birds. They have books in Heaven, right?"

My mom exhaled, then smoothed the sheets back down. She called me "baby." Her voice turned serious.

"When we get to Heaven, I won't be your mother anymore."

All the heat in my body rushed to my head. I asked my mom to repeat herself, but I covered my ears so I wouldn't hear her say it again. Still, I could make out every muffled word.

"I won't be your mother."

My bedroom didn't have curtains, and I worried my mom would see my face in the moonlight, so I pulled the sheets back over my head and hid as the first few tears slipped down my cheeks. I tried to take a deep breath, but my lungs seized up. I could feel the fear in my throat.

"No," I said, from under the covers. "That doesn't make sense. You have to be my mom."

I cried long wails, and my mom cried, too. I begged her to tell me she was lying. She pulled me into her arms, and I cried until my sheets were sweaty and her neck was soaked with snot and tears.

"Please, Mama, I don't want to go to Heaven. I don't want to spend forever without you."

I don't remember how long she held me, but it felt like we both cried till daylight. I promised to be good if she'd take it all back. She told me it wasn't punishment, just God's will. He wanted everyone to love each other equally in Heaven, she said, so there couldn't be any special relationships. She wouldn't be my dad's wife. She wouldn't be my grandma's daughter. She wouldn't be my little brother's mom, and she wouldn't be mine.

I woke up the next morning puffy-eyed and afraid. I didn't ask my mother if it was different in Hell, if the trade-off for burning was recognizing everyone on fire next to you. But I feared the afterlives equally after that night. When our preacher talked about Heaven, I didn't imagine mansions or gold or Saint Peter. Without my mother, I knew, Heaven would be as miserable as Hell.

I DON'T REMEMBER A time in my life before church, but my mother did not grow up devout. Her parents were part-time Christians, weak believers who spoke about God in the dry, generic way many people in the South do—constantly, but without real conviction. My grandparents knew the Lord's Prayer, and they believed in Heaven, but my mom grew up thinking God was little more than an old man with a big red pen. He lived on the outskirts of her imagination. Then Cam Milton died, and my mom turned to God in a desperation she later described as hope.

My mom told me over and over again when I was young that Cam was the only person who understood her. I hated hearing about the boy she loved more than my dad, but my mother talked about Cam anyway. They met on the first day of sixth grade, when a football Cam threw long hit my mom on the head. She was Rhonda Carter then, and new to Delhi. Though my grandma always described Delhi as the most important place in her life, she left a few years after she moved there from Frog Island. She met my grandfather at the edge of Hell Street in 1955. Then, when he joined the army, they moved to El Paso, Texas, and Lawton, Oklahoma, before settling down for a few years in Germany. My mom was born in 1964 in Oklahoma, the fourth of my grandma's five children, and she did most of her elementary schooling in Germany on an army base called Bad Tölz. When my grandpa retired in 1975, he told my grandma they could move anywhere. She said she wanted to go back to the first city she'd loved. She wanted to return to Delhi.

My mom enrolled at Delhi Middle School that January. She was nosy, so she was looking around as she approached the building, but she didn't see Cam until his football skidded across her face. She fell into the dirt. Cam rushed over to help, and when my mom looked up, she was too spellbound to care about the welt forming below her eye. Cam was handsome and skinny, with a long face and deep brown eyes. My mom told me she loved him immediately.

Cam played golf and basketball, but he was also an intellectual, the only Delhi student who made straight A's every report card. My mom was one of a handful of kids who regularly earned a spot on the honor roll, and her idea of a perfect day was hiding in the closet and reading three or four books. Cam liked to read, too. He kept a journal and wrote my mom long notes. They joined the Beta Club and the yearbook staff together, and for a while, they were next-door neighbors one street east of Chatham. My mom told me she spent most afternoons staring out the kitchen window of her family's single-wide trailer, waiting for Cam to appear. He was one of the few people in Delhi who never called her white trash. Other people gossiped about my mom's drunk father and her runaway sister, but Cam never treated my mom as an extension of what other people considered a wayward family. He saw a bookworm with unlimited potential.

Sometimes my mom and Cam dated, but mostly they were best friends. Before Cam died, my mom considered the biggest heartbreak of her life to be the day he asked Cindy Homan out. By the end of their senior year, my mom and Cam were "together" enough that he agreed to take her to prom. She saved all spring to pay for a dress. She worked doubles at the Jitney Jungle grocery store, and she babysat for extra money. By early May, she had enough. She skipped school one Friday and drove to Monroe to buy a gown worthy of the boy she loved. She picked out something modest but lacy, a purple floor-length, and as she carried it in clear plastic through the Pecanland Mall, she saw someone she knew from Delhi. The friend waved her down, and my mom walked over, smiling until she got close enough to see the pain on her friend's face.

"Cam died," the girl said. "He shot himself."

My mom often talked about Cam's funeral when I was growing up. He died May 7, 1982, a few weeks before the end of her senior year. Three pastors preached at his service, she told me, and just before the graveyard workers lowered Cam's casket into the ground, a heavy branch fell off an oak tree and knocked my mom unconscious. She left the funeral in an ambulance. An emergency room doctor prescribed her first Percocet, and the pill filled her with a woozy relief.

My mom spent a few days in the hospital. One evening, she was watching TV, flipping through the channels, when she stopped on Pat Robertson's show, *The 700 Club*. Robertson was a folksy preacher and a keen media mogul, and *The 700 Club* was his daily talk show. (He later ran an unsuccessful bid for president.) Each episode of *The 700 Club* was like a news program mixed with a revival. Robertson interviewed guests, and he preached a rousing sermon. He would claim miracles in the name of Jesus, then announce that God had told him that someone in the television audience had just been healed of hemorrhoids or cancer. My mom watched the evangelist from her hospital bed, and she decided to give praying a shot. She asked God for solace, and she begged him to let Cam into Heaven. She worried then, and for many years after, that suicide was the kind of unforgivable sin God refused to ignore. But she prayed, hoping God worked miracles retroactively. She told herself that maybe Cam had repented right after he pulled the trigger, that he'd made it past Saint Peter, and she'd see him in Heaven someday.

When my mom got out of the hospital, she prayed and searched for the same kind of relief the Percocet had provided, but whispering into the void did not transport her the way she hoped it would. She tossed around in bed, blaming herself for not filling whatever holes Cam felt in his life.

A week after Cam died, my mom decided she couldn't stand to live in Delhi without him, so she moved forty-five minutes west to live with her older sister Ann in Monroe. She met my dad in a park that weekend.

He was drunk, and she was heartbroken. My dad wobbled back to his car holding an emptied case of beer, and he found my mom sitting on the hood, looking out at nothing.

"Hey," he said. "Do you cook?"

My mom turned around and tried to make sense of my dad, a lanky white teenager with a curly Afro and hazel eyes she thought looked lonely.

"Yes," she said.

"Do you smoke?" My mom shook her head no, and my dad smiled. That was the right answer. He stepped closer, and she could smell the beer he'd been drinking all day.

"Do you want to go out Friday night?" he asked.

My parents spent their first date in Delhi, in Cam's kitchen, talking to Cam's mother while the rest of my mom's classmates got ready for prom. My mom watched as her friends spilled out from a back bedroom, dressed in taffeta, happy despite the circumstances. She and my dad lingered in the kitchen long after everyone was gone. Eventually, Cam's mom said she was ready for bed. My dad didn't have rhythm or a tuxedo, but when they left Cam's house, he asked my mom if he could take her to the dance. He drove her home so she could put on the dress she'd bought for Cam, then they sped down Main Street, a boy and his grieving date. They didn't take pictures that night, so I've never seen the dress or the khakis and polo shirt my dad wore, but when I was a kid, my parents told me their clothes didn't matter. What they remembered was the music. As soon as they stepped into the gymnasium, my mom grabbed my dad, then she held him close through "Endless Love."

As a kid, I always thought theirs sounded like the weirdest first date ever. Who takes a girl to her dead boyfriend's house? But my dad was an only child whose parents rarely spent time with him. He was hungry for any kind of love.

After the dance, my dad dropped my mom off at her parents' house. He walked her to the door, and she lingered on the steps while her father flicked the porch light off and on. My dad cleared his throat.

"This is the part I've been dreading my whole life," he told my mom. "I've never kissed anyone."

My mom leaned in, stole a quick peck, then hurried inside before she could see my dad's reaction. I don't know if they were in love or just lonely enough to tell themselves they were, but they hung out every day after that, and by August, my mom was pregnant with me. They were both eighteen.

Neither of their families offered to help buy the things a baby would need. My mom's parents were perennially broke, and my dad's were stingy. His parents had good jobs and a steady stream of side income they earned off the mineral rights their parents secured when prospectors first found oil in Louisiana, but they didn't give my parents any money when my mom got pregnant.

In a way, my dad was happy. He was free to start a new family on his own. He didn't earn much driving a delivery truck for Coca-Cola, but he promised my mom he'd work extra shifts so she could focus on college. He'd never excelled in school, but he knew my mom longed to keep studying. She loved math and dreamed of becoming a nurse or an accountant, a career woman with a bachelor's degree. That fall, she registered for classes at the local university, but when she arrived the first week, a guidance counselor told her she couldn't attend. It didn't matter that she'd already been accepted, or that she'd made the honor roll every semester in high school. The college didn't want pregnant students, the guidance counselor said. My mom left the campus and started working at the fast-food restaurant Hardee's instead. "A dream job," she told me when I was young. "I was the chocolate chip cookie and salad girl."

I asked her all the time when I was little if she regretted choosing me over college. I knew by the way she talked about school that she was smart enough to have become anything she wanted. She'd scored two points shy of perfect on the ACT, and she used big words like "mellifluous" and "transmogrify." I knew, because I'd read in her high school journal, that she loved physics and trigonometry and planned to take both in college. But every time I asked, she'd make a face and shake her head as if she hadn't thought twice about keeping me. "Being a mom is the best thing I've ever done," she'd tell me, conveniently wording her response so as not to address the things she didn't do. I always dropped it, knowing in my heart that she was disappointed in ways she couldn't tell me. Not only had she missed out on college, but she had to spend her life with my dad, a guy who'd misspelled "parents" as "parnets" in the first letter he wrote to her.

My mom was three months pregnant when she married my dad in November 1982. Cam had been dead six months. My mom woke up that day ill with morning sickness, and when she tried to recite her vows at a country church on the highway between Delhi and Monroe, she threw up on the preacher. My parents had to sit to say "I do."

They didn't go on a honeymoon because they only had thirteen dollars between them after the ceremony. Instead, they used a buy-one-get-one-free Burger King coupon to celebrate with two Whoppers and a single Coke. They survived the rest of the month on a bag of rice and a pound of potatoes. They spent most of their time in a decrepit one-bedroom apartment with a view of the grassy levee that protects West Monroe from the Ouachita River. They pretended their complex was a country club, and they told each other that apartment "I" stood for "in love," but they grew restless after a few weeks inside. Looking for free entertainment that winter, they started going to church.

They flipped through the phone book, picking out the congregations with the biggest ads. They spent a few Sundays with the Methodists sitting upright on hard pews. They tried the Baptist church that my mom's algebra teacher attended, and they yawned between the droning hymns. Then, one weekend in January 1983, they visited a Pentecostal-style evangelical church, and my mom believed she'd found the thing that would distract her from her grief.

My mom could tell, as soon as she and my dad took seats in the back, that the church was different. The choir performed as if they were a rock band with guitars. The pastor shimmied around the pulpit, punctuating scriptures with leg kicks and tiny dances. His was the kind of sermon Pat Robertson preached on TV. In the audience, people closed their eyes and raised their hands, and they prayed in an incomprehensible language that made my mother believe they'd surrendered everything, even their capacity for speech, to God. She watched in envy. At the end of the service, she staggered toward the altar and asked God to take her pain away.

That May, a year and twelve days after Cam died, my mom gave birth to me. She told me later that she prayed when she first held me. She asked God to turn her into a tower of strength, and she promised she would raise me to believe in Him. A few years later, when my brother, Dustin, was a newborn, my mom sat me down and explained that as long as I was a Christian, I would never feel alone.

"God is a wonderful friend," she told me. "He loves you even when you feel unlovable."

We never missed a church service when I was young, and we always tossed a handful of dollar bills into the offering plate as it passed our row. The preacher said God would reward anyone who tithed—not just in Heaven with a mansion, but here, on earth. God would reach through the clouds, the pastor said, and pour out so much money that the tithers wouldn't even have space to store it all.

My family needed that blessing. When I was born, oil profits accounted for nearly half of Louisiana's state budget, and when the price per barrel plummeted in the mid-1980s, the state's economy collapsed. By 1986, one in eight Louisiana workers was unemployed, the highest rate in the nation. My mom lost her job at Hardee's. She tried to open her own daycare, but no one else had money to spend, either. My dad kept his job, but he earned only $110 a week driving a truck for Coke, so we lived off rice and gravy in a wood-frame house my dad's grandmother owned. It was drafty and old, painted in a peeling gray whose flecks worked their way into everything. When I was young, my mother talked about our poverty as if it were some failing of my father's. *He* wrote hot checks to keep the lights on, she told me. *He* pawned their wedding rings to cover the checks. I remember waiting in the car with her while he slinked into a pay-day loan agency, trading what last bit of shame he had for money to buy the rings back, but I didn't understand then that there were forces greater than one man's bad decisions. He was the head of our house, my mother taught me, and that meant he was supposed to provide.

The only way to forget disappointment, my mother told me, was to lose yourself in God and stories. She prayed for hours every morning, and she checked out library books a dozen at a time. She imagined herself as someone else. She listened to the Bee Gees and danced alone in the living room, her eyes closed and her hand held up, as if an invisible person were guiding her along the carpet. Her make-believe worlds never lasted, though. Whatever pain she buried found its way to the surface. She'd call a neighbor, or she'd go to the doctor, then she'd return with bottles of Percocet, and she'd sleep the rest of the week.

AS A KID, I didn't understand what drove my mom toward the pills. She seemed to me then to be such an ancient, wise figure. She was my mother, and she'd read every book in the fiction stacks. She taught me how to read and write whole paragraphs long before I started school, and she could recite Bible stories from memory. But when she took pills, she seemed like a child herself. She cried a lot. She begged for attention. She needed things the way a kid does—desperately, irrationally. I realize now she was twenty-two.

By 1988, my mom had five doctors and eleven different prescriptions for Percocet. My dad couldn't afford to cover all her medical bills with the little he earned driving a truck, so that summer, broke and worried about the hot checks he couldn't repay, my dad enlisted in the army. The military promised him a $3,000 signing bonus, plus roughly $750 a month to work on a base near Savannah, Georgia. He used the signing bonus to buy a used Ford Tempo, then we headed east. I was five, and my brother was three.

We spent a year in a brown, two-bedroom apartment. After that, when my dad got approved for free military housing, we moved into a neighborhood with streets named Hero, Courage, and Liberty. Our new home was a two-story brick town house that had carpeted stairs and a tiny backyard full of azalea bushes. We didn't own it—we would never own anywhere we lived—but my mom scrubbed the surfaces every afternoon with Pine-Sol and Comet as if the town house were an investment she couldn't let degrade.

When she wasn't scouring our place, my mom cleaned for a rich old lady whose house looked haunted. It was big and gray and full of old dolls. The woman's daughter had died by suicide a year earlier, and the old woman mostly sat in a rocking chair and cried. In the refrigerator, she kept a tube of lipstick she said the mortician had used on her daughter at the funeral. My mom took us with her to the house most afternoons, and she forced us to sit in a corner far away from the old lady and all the dolls. My mom would pray that nothing demonic there took hold of us, then she'd begin working her way around with a broom. Occasionally, she'd stop and tell the old lady that she'd lost someone to suicide, too, and the old lady would stand, and they'd hug and cry, and I'd watch from the corner, hating Cam for hurting my mother.

My mom didn't have special sponges or even plastic gloves like other cleaning ladies had. To mop, she dunked an old towel into boiling water spiked with Pine-Sol, then she spread the towel on the floor, bent down on top of it, and scooted across the ground in circles, using all her weight to scrub the dirt away. The job left peeling sores all over my mom's hands, but she seemed energized by the move to Georgia. She made a best friend at the commissary, and they talked on the phone every night. My mom sat with me while I finished my first- and second-grade home-work, and some evenings I found her at the table, working ahead in my textbooks, filling in vocabulary words or writing out the times tables I hadn't yet learned. She did my science fair project for me two years in a row, and I won both times. She tested paper towels one year to determine which brand held up best while cleaning spills. The next year, she asked our neighbors to put clothespins over their noses while they ate bites of onion, apple, and potato, so she could see whether they could taste the difference without smelling the bites. She let me keep the first-place rib-bons. For her, learning was prize enough.

She was good at every school subject, but she thrived most at church. In Georgia, we attended Live Oak, a mixed-race megachurch with vel-vet pews and a spotlight that followed the pastor across the stage as he broke down the New Testament in punchy, half-hour sermons. My mom taught Sunday school and joined the board of a Christian women's group, and she helped organize the after-church potlucks we held in the smaller sanctuary everyone called the children's church. My mom cooked gumbos and butter-rich casseroles that disappeared before any other dishes did. Some weeks, as soon as the pastor said amen, people rushed over to the children's church to spoon out heaps of my mother's manicotti before the pan was scraped clean. They'd call later that eve-ning to ask for her recipe, but she always left out one ingredient.

"I don't want anyone to know my secrets," she'd tell me.

———

WE JOINED LIVE OAK instead of another church on base because the congregation there spoke in tongues. To us, "tongues" was a holy gibberish, heavy on Hebrew-sounding syllables that our pastor said were proof that God was speaking through us. At most Live Oak services, one person stood, said an incomprehensible string of sentences, then waited until someone else rose and interpreted the message. Other people fell to the ground, writhing and praying in a way that we called "slain in the spirit." I can't remember what I thought the first time I saw this spectacle, but I imagine I must have been scared as I watched adults lose all control. Time seemed to stop in a creepy way when an interpreter stood to decipher a message. My mom taught me that speaking in tongues was the highest manifestation of God, though, and by the time I was seven, I was begging the Lord to fill me with the spirit, too. Our pastor told us we were just like the apostles who'd spoken in tongues after Jesus ascended to Heaven. He pointed us toward the book of Acts, where, in chapter two, during the time known as the Pentecost, the apostles saw tongues of fire, then began speaking in other languages. My mom loved Acts. She highlighted, underlined, and starred its verses, and some nights, at home cooking dinner with her Bible propped against the coffeepot, she'd lean into the stove and start speaking a babble she said was sacred.

Back then, I assumed that our way of worshiping was the only way of worshiping. Everything else was a cult, my mom told me. Especially Catholicism. Years later, long after I'd left the church, I discovered that the version of Christianity I grew up with wasn't the same brand people had been practicing for millennia. In the United States, there's no modern record of anyone speaking in tongues before 1900, when a preacher named Charles Fox Parham founded a church in Topeka, Kansas. Like other evangelical Christians, Parham wanted to preach the gospel across the world, but he couldn't speak any foreign languages. Hoping to remedy that, Parham started a Bible school in a stone mansion, and he taught his students that if they could get the Holy Spirit the way the apostles had, they'd be able to preach in every country, no matter which language the locals spoke. The class met for an all-night prayer party on New Year's Eve, and just after midnight, one of the students began muttering random syllables. Parham believed that the Holy Ghost had empowered the woman to speak Chinese.

"In a few moments, we realized what it was, and we fell on our knees and gave thanks to God," Parham told a reporter at the Chicago *Inter Ocean* newspaper.

By the end of the week, Parham's students believed that they could speak Japanese, Arabic, and a dozen other languages. Parham called reporters across the Midwest, and his students spoke their foreign languages into the phone, but the journalists remained unconvinced. They mocked Parham's miracle, and they described the supposed holy tongues as gibberish. After Parham sent in a sample of the "Chinese" characters a student had written, *The Topeka Daily Capital* ran a picture of the scribblings with the caption, "specimen of Miss Auswin's handwriting which the Apostolic brethren claim is inspired by God himself." The script looks nothing like Chinese. It's swoopy and disordered, the kind of messy graffiti a child might pen. Parham's message spread anyway. He traveled across the Midwest and the South, preaching and opening Bible schools. In 1905, William Joseph Seymour, a Black man whose parents had been enslaved in South Louisiana, met Parham in Texas. Parham was a KKK sympathizer, but he needed converts, so when Seymour showed up to Parham's Bible school in Houston, Parham told Seymour to sit in the hallway and listen through an open door. Even at a distance, Seymour was persuaded. The next year, he moved to Los Angeles and opened a church in a former stable. Soon, Seymour's congregants were spinning, shaking, and speaking in tongues the way they believed the apostles had.

A few years later, Parham was arrested in Texas for a sex act many speculated was a homosexual dalliance. He lost his Bible schools, but Seymour's congregants started their own churches, and within a decade, people were speaking in tongues across the world. Still, Pentecostals were considered a fringe group in the early twentieth century. The *Los Angeles Times* covered Seymour's church under the headline WEIRD BABBLE OF TONGUES, and a reporter wrote that "night is made hideous in the neighborhood by the howlings of the worshipers." Other newspaper dispatches from the early 1900s made Pentecostalism sound like an incoherent cult. In Alabama, reporters described the worshipers as religious brawlers under a spell. And in Vermont they were roaring dervishes, crazed people who ran around a movie theater, searching the seats for

Satan. Pentecostals rolled around on straw floors in Pittsburgh, and in Chico, California, a pastor beat a man with a chair because he mistook his red hair for the Devil.

The denomination became more normalized after World War II, as churchgoing increased across the United States. Pentecostalism eventually split into a web of sub-denominations, and as it did, it reached even more worshipers. Among those was the Assemblies of God, the majority-white Pentecostal offshoot that my parents first joined in Monroe. Between the 1960s and the 1980s, the number of people who attended Assemblies of God churches quadrupled to two million. Live Oak was Church of God, another Pentecostal-style denomination, but we rarely used that term. We just called ourselves evangelicals.

Today, people use "evangelical" as a catch-all term to describe the conservative Christians who help Republicans win elections. But back then, when nearly a third of Americans identified as evangelical, we used it to describe our mission. Evangelical meant that we tried hard to tell other people about Jesus. At school, I passed notes to other students, inviting them to attend any Sunday or Wednesday. I told my teachers about the sermons, and I bribed neighborhood kids with promises of potluck lunches that always included at least six kinds of cake. It was easy to persuade people to visit because Live Oak was genuinely fun. We hosted Christian rap concerts and carnivals, Saturday-night slumber parties full of pizza and s'mores. Every summer, my brother and I went to church camp and vacation Bible school, retreats where we pretended to be Moses wandering the desert or Joshua blasting our trumpets toward Jericho. We were Shadrach, Meshach, and Abednego, wading through fire, untouched by the flames.

Live Oak's congregation believed in biblical infallibility, which meant that I grew up thinking every word was literally true. I believed that God created the earth in six days and Mary was still a virgin when she gave birth to Jesus. Some Sundays, our pastor spent the whole service digging into one story, but mostly he jumped around, reading out verses as if each were a commandment.

Years later, I tried to look for the line that made my mom believe we'd be strangers in Heaven, but I never could find one, so I asked her which it was. She remembered that she'd been heartbroken to discover it—not because she wouldn't be my mother, but because she thought it meant she wouldn't recognize Cam. But she didn't remember where she'd learned the verse. Maybe someone had said it on *The 700 Club*, or maybe she'd read it in one of the Christian books she checked out from the church library. Most of those books promised a kind of doom far scarier than any horror movie. She kept them in the freezer, tucked behind packages of hamburger meat, as if that might lessen their blows. The books had names like *This Present Darkness* and *He Came to Set the Captives Free*, and they all chronicled a spiritual warfare marked by demon possession and eternal damnation. In the early 1990s, my mom read a book called *Turmoil in the Toy Box*, and afterward, she told us that the devil lurked in mundane places. We could catch a demon watching the Care Bears or the Smurfs. Video games were evil. Impure thoughts were evil. If we let them consume us, the pastor said, God would forsake us, and we'd burn in Hell forever. Most of the sins confused me. I knew I shouldn't lie or scream at my parents, and I definitely had no plans to murder anyone, but what was a false idol? Why was Super Mario sinful? How could I stop myself from coveting the Barbie Corvette richer girls owned?

We talked about Satan as if he might show up unannounced any minute. Twice, our pastor cast a demon out of a woman he said had been possessed. The woman's name was Trana, and it took three men to drag her down the aisle toward the pulpit. I remember she wore a purple blouse and blue eye shadow, and she sobbed as the men pulled her to the front. Trana kicked the pastor, and my mom told me to close my eyes. She pressed her hands over my ears so I wouldn't hear the demon hiss into the microphone.

"You can't cast me out," the demon said. "I dwell here."

It was scary and thrilling, and for weeks after, I stayed up late, listening to my own brain replay the demon's hiss. I worried something evil would possess me. I knew what demons looked like because I'd seen them in Christian music videos. A singer named Carman was big then, and in each of his songs, Satan and a band of demons set out to destroy humanity. Carman's videos were heavy on special effects, as slickly produced as the Terminator movies, and they rendered Satan's ghouls with a frightening specificity. The demons were green and pointy-eared mon-

sters in "Revival in the Land." They were short and burnt-looking in
"Satan, Bite the Dust." Their skin was always wrinkled and covered in
warts, and their voices were a high-pitched wicked. As an elementary
school kid, I believed if I sinned for even a second, one of those creatures
would creep after me, and take hold of my life. I shuddered in my bed.
The demons alone were horrifying, but what I feared most was not the
monster. Instead, I stayed up late, terrified that our pastor might someday drag me to the front of church to cast the devil out.

I know we read the Bible every night, but now, as an adult, I can't
remember much beyond a few stray verses and the most famous stories.
I had my own Bible, a Precious Moments edition that my mom gave
me in April 1990, the first time I got saved, but the stodgy language
eluded me at six. I'm not sure I ever understood the context behind
the verses my mom adopted as edicts. Some people at church switched
Bibles every year, but my mom always used the same one, a creased and
coffee-stained New International Version. It was a women's devotional
Bible, so it was pink and included easy-to-read summaries after each
chapter. My dad gave it to her a few months before his unit left to fight
in Saudi Arabia, and she used it as a surrogate journal in his six-month
absence. She wrote people's phone numbers on the inside flap. She highlighted and dated verses she found comforting, and she added her own
commentaries in blue cursive throughout. Next to a Leviticus scripture
about "mediums" and "spiritists," she wrote "psychos." And in 1991, she
highlighted Psalm 34, verse 18, "the Lord is close to the brokenhearted."
Next to it, she wrote, "I am not alone."

The movie *Ghost* came out the year before my dad went to war, and
while he was gone, my mom moped around the house, carrying her Bible
and listening to "Unchained Melody" on repeat. I could never tell if she
was missing Cam or my dad, but I watched from the carpeted stairwell
as she led herself around the living room in a solo slow dance. Most days,
she called the *700 Club* Prayer Center or the Richard Simmons Deal-a-
Meal hotline, sometimes seeking advice, sometimes just wanting to talk.
At night, she sat in the bathtub and read *Anna Karenina*. She told me it
was her favorite love story, even if Anna killed herself in the end.

We couldn't call my dad in Saudi Arabia, and the internet didn't
exist yet, so my mom talked for hours into a recorder, then mailed the

tapes to his base. Every Sunday night, we read the week's newspapers, and we cut out articles about the war. I imagined my dad in the desert, dodging bombs and defeating Saddam Hussein as part of the 24th Infantry's Victory Division. I felt closer to him when we read the articles, but my mom seemed to grow more depressed. She used pills in stretches, though I didn't know back then what caused her eye to droop and her words to slur. Usually, it started with her not sleeping. She'd wake me up in the middle of the night to tell me she'd spent two hours bleaching the bathtub, a chore that was supposed to be mine. Or she'd turn on my light to present a plate of pork chops she expected me to eat before dawn. The next day, she'd drag around the house begging for attention. She'd complain that her head hurt, and she'd blame the oak tree from Cam's funeral. Eventually, she'd keel over somewhere, and she'd sleep five days before she returned to normal. Maybe my mom could feel a spell coming on because she always stocked the freezer with our favorite TV dinners before she passed out. My brother liked Salisbury steak and a brand called Kid Cuisine, but I preferred Hungry-Man's "Mexican style fiesta," a supposed pound of enchiladas, refried beans, and a wiggly dessert the brand called "cocada pudding." On the nights my mom was zonked, I'd pry two dinners out of the cardboard, slit their plastic coverings with a butter knife, then slide them into the oven. Some mornings, she'd drift around the kitchen, somehow able to cook a cheese omelet with her eyes closed, and other days, we ate Pop-Tarts or cereal, then took ourselves to school. Just as I was starting to tire of the cocada pudding, my mother would wake up, clear-eyed and cooking for the church potluck as if nothing had ever happened.

I thought she just suffered from insomnia, so I didn't understand why she went to the altar after her spells. I didn't know what she meant when she begged God to deliver her from the chains that bound her. I'd whisper to my little brother, ask him if he'd seen any chains. He'd shrug his shoulders, and we'd watch her, wondering what spiritual shackles held her down.

A YEAR OR TWO into the cleaning job, the rich old lady asked my mom to start cooking for her. The old lady was a retired librarian. I have no idea how she came into her money, but she had enough that she could afford to pay my mom to stick around the big gray house a few hours longer each day. Every week, she gave my mom a blank check, then sent her to the good grocery store across town, and my mom returned with supplies far nicer than the ones we usually bought at the military commissary.

After a month, the old lady told my mom she'd passed a secret audition. I don't remember the exact dialogue, but the old lady said she'd found a few recipes that her late daughter had written, and she wanted to build a Southern cookbook around them, but she needed my mom to write and test the recipes. The old lady didn't have a publisher, but that didn't matter. She had money. She told my mom she planned to start her own publishing company. She'd bankroll all the grocery shopping, and she'd pay my mom overtime to stay late, baking cakes and casseroles until they settled on the right measurements.

My mom was thrilled. Her name wouldn't be on the front of the cookbook, but she'd still be a published author. All the famous people used ghostwriters, she told me, and this was basically the same thing. She gave the old lady her gumbo recipe—the real one, not the shy-of-an-ingredient instructions she shared with people from church—and she offered up the salmon croquettes her grandma Rita Mae had somehow learned to make on Frog Island. The recipes were all heavy on butter and either salt or sugar, but my mom treated each one as if it were up for some kind of award. She'd spoon over bites to me and my brother, then she'd watch with big eyes as we rolled the fudge or shrimp Matilda around in our mouths.

"Tastes good!" I'd say, and my mom would furrow her brow, then tell me I was supposed to offer a more in-depth critique than that.

"It tastes very good?" I'd try.

My mom mostly stayed clean of pills during the year she and the old lady worked on the cookbook. She spent hours each night trying her hand at pecan divinity and other temperature-sensitive candies. She made what felt like a thousand adaptations of bread-and-butter pickles and expected me to try every limp version. None tasted as good as the big dills we plucked from a barrel at the corner store, but I tried to fake enthusiasm. My mom was alert when she was cooking. She didn't cry or pray about shackles, and she didn't talk about Cam Milton. At church, when new people joined and asked her what she did for work, she said she was writing a cookbook. If I chimed in and told people she also cleaned an old lady's house, she pinched my leg and said she was just doing that while my dad was at war.

"As soon as he returns," she said, "I'll be on the cookbook full-time."

MY DAD CAME HOME from Saudi Arabia in April 1991, a few weeks after my mom first told me we'd be strangers in the afterlife. I can't remember now if my father seemed different after the war. He was our silly parent, the one whose emotions never wavered. He only spanked us when our mom forced him to, and every night, he tickled us or told funny stories until we laughed ourselves to sleep. He was not open with his feelings. He didn't tell us what made him happy or what made him sad, and when he returned from Saudi Arabia, dark-tanned from six months in the desert, he didn't talk about what he'd done there. At the library, I searched newspaper articles for clues, and I wondered, when my dad flinched during Fourth of July fireworks, what the quick pops reminded him of, but I never asked, and he never volunteered answers.

In my memories, he came home as cheery and solid as he'd always been, but my mom seemed to topple off some unspoken edge after he returned. She stopped sleeping again, and soon her left eye was drooping the way it did when she took pills. That fall, the old lady put the cookbook on hold, so my mom came home smelling like Pine-Sol instead of chocolate cake. We ate bologna slices wrapped in American cheese while she lay in bed, watching soap operas she'd taped during the day. She'd spend hours underneath the covers, sometimes watching an episode of *The Bold and the Beautiful* two or three times until she fell asleep.

One afternoon in early 1992, my brother and I rode our bikes home from school, and we found my mom sitting at the wood veneer table with a kind of rabid look in her eye. I worried a demon had possessed her.

"Mom?" I said.

She turned to me with a smile I thought was creepy.

"Oh good," she said. "You've come home from college to visit me."

I looked at my brother, confused, and we held hands as we tiptoed closer to her. He was in the first grade, and I was in the third.

"We're not in college," my brother said.

"Not you, Dustin," my mom said. "I know you're in the army. You always come to visit me, but Casey never wants to come home from college. She only cares about getting a *job*."

I remember snow falling in specks, which was weird because it never snowed in Georgia. My mom handed my brother her car keys, then she pushed us into the backyard and made us sit in a plastic kiddie pool. She opened a window and screamed that someone named Owen had stolen her class ring. He'd pawned it, she said, and she wanted it back. I think a few days went by before I understood that she thought that my dad, whose name is Alan, was the Owen who'd taken her ring. My dad told us that she'd fallen down the stairs at the old lady's house, that she'd hit her head, and a doctor had concluded that the injury had aggravated whatever damage the oak tree had done at Cam's funeral. I told my teachers about it, and they asked me every morning before school if my mother was my mother again. For weeks, the answer was no. I was embarrassed and scared, but mostly I was sad. Why did she think my brother would visit her but I wouldn't? Why did my mom think I'd go to college and forget her?

I wriggled around in my Holly Hobbie sheets every night, crying and asking God to fix my mom before it was too late. I worried she'd die the way Cam and Anna Karenina and the rich old lady's daughter had. I was eight years old, but I understood already that some people went crazy, then disappeared forever. I was going to lose my mom, I realized. On earth, if not in Heaven.

Chapter Five

(2011)

I WENT TO DELHI a third time in the spring of 2011, and this time, my mom didn't stand me up. My filmmaking friends and I landed in Monroe sometime Thursday afternoon, and my mom was waiting for us, upright and glowing, as clear of pain pills as I'd ever seen her. I stepped through security, and she ran at me. We hugged, and I could tell by the way her body shook as she held me that she was crying.

"You're really coming with me!" I said, relieved.

"I'm really coming with you."

I'd rented a car for the week, so we caravanned, cutting through sunshine on our way to a crawfish restaurant across the river in West Monroe. I let out a happy yelp. My mom was lucid, and I was home.

The crawfish place was in a strip mall with a furniture rental store and the Blockbuster where I'd worked the summer after my freshman year of college, but the restaurant seemed to be trying to evoke a Mississippi Delta jook joint the night we ate there. The inside was neon-lit and full of plastic tables covered by plastic tablecloths. The plates were big circles advertising Budweiser, and everyone around us was downing buckets full of beer. We picked a table and ordered our own bucket of Coronas. My dad, Aubree, Aaron, and I plowed through a dozen pounds of crawfish, but my mom took her time. Every ten minutes or so, she'd peel one, then gingerly eat the small tail she'd freed from the shell. The rest of us pressed on, sucking the crawfish heads, eating as fast as our fingers could work. My mouth burned a little from the spice, so I guzzled Coronas to ease the sting. Soon I was light-headed and laughing at everything.

"I'm so happy," I said, to myself or to everyone, I'm not sure which. I worried I'd forget how happy I felt, so I pulled my camera out of my book bag and started shooting video. My mom closed her eyes.

"No pictures of me while I'm eating," she said.

I frowned. She'd turned forty-seven a few days before, but she looked younger than she had the last time I'd seen her. She'd lost a bunch of weight, and her skin looked brighter, but I knew she still felt self-conscious about her appearance. She'd often told me that kids in Delhi had called her "Fat, Fat, the Water Rat" when she was a teenager. As an adult, she never wore white because she worried she'd look like a giant jug of milk, and she hated all-you-can-eat buffets because she thought someone would accuse her of sneaking seconds or thirds.

I lowered my camera but kept it in my lap, hoping my mom would change her mind. I didn't plan to use the clips in my documentary. I didn't plan to do anything with them. I've just always felt compelled to document everything. I've kept a journal since I was five, and I used to carry a tape recorder around middle school so I could interview my classmates about our teachers. I made zines in college, and in Portland, I usually put together a video every season showing what my friends and I had done the previous few months. I took notes when I rode the bus. I posted pictures and mini essays on my blog a few times a week. And every time I saw my parents, I forced them to do something I could tape. By 2011, I had a hard drive full of recordings marked "family stories." I told my parents and myself that I was practicing for the great journalism job I eventually hoped to get, but I see now that I didn't know how to talk to them without pretending I was at work. The camera and the audio recorders emboldened me. When I was in reporter mode, I could ask my family anything.

We finished eating, and I was tipsy, so I swayed out of the restaurant holding my mom's hand. The sun had set, but it was still seventy-something outside, thirty degrees warmer than it was in Portland, so I spun around in the mellow heat. Nothing too momentous was happening. We were dawdling in the parking lot, talking about things I was sure I'd soon forget, but I felt high on the pedestrian joy of being with my family, so I pulled out my camera again and started filming. My mom was standing in front of a shuttered Goodwill store, digging into her purse for a pack of cigarettes. My dad danced without rhythm behind her. My arms weren't steady, so the picture jerked around, losing focus as I wobbled. The parking lot lights were bright, blurry orbs. I zoomed in on my dad, and he contorted his face into silly expressions. He stuck his tongue out, crossed his eyes, then moved so close to my lens that his face went fuzzy. I swung the camera toward my mom, and she held her hand over her face.

"I don't want my picture made."

She turned to hide her face, but I kept filming—closer, closer, as if proximity alone would reveal everything I wanted to know.

MY MOM AND I woke up early the next morning to watch the royal wedding. My dad was out buying a newspaper, and everyone else was asleep, so there was plenty of space in the living room, but still, we sat close to each other on the couch.

"I thought you'd grow up and marry Prince William," she said, leaning into me. "Now he's taken, and you're gay."

She sighed, and I cackled and told her the world wasn't ready for a princess like me. I was hungover and clumsy, completely lacking in grace. Plus, I thought, you had to come from a good family to marry into royalty, and I was sure ours didn't count. Prince William appeared on-screen, balding and regal in a red tunic with a blue sash. I crinkled my nose in mock disgust.

"I'm sorry, Mom. I do not find him attractive."

"You used to," she said. "You had his picture on your wall."

She frowned, and I wanted to tell her that I'd been twelve when I did that. Back then, Prince William had looked more like Ellen DeGeneres than a man, and I'd come to realize that boys like that had been gateways to girls for me. I'd longed for this prince because my mother wanted me to long for a prince. For her, nothing was as important as storybook love. I nodded. I didn't want to ruin this trip or whatever unrealistic fantasy my mom was holding on to, so I told her she was right. I *had* had Prince William's picture on my wall. When his younger brother appeared on

DIARY OF A MISFIT

the screen, I pretended to faint with lust. "Now, Prince Harry is a different story. I might be willing to go straight for him."

My mom grabbed my hand and held it as the royal brothers made their way down a red carpet. The cameras zoomed in on Harry, resplendent in a blue uniform draped with gold cords, and my mom fanned herself.

"Oh, yeah," she said. "He is hot."

We catcalled Harry every time the cameras showed him, and I longed to tell my mom that I'd signed up for OkCupid and had spent the last few weeks emailing a girl in San Francisco something like love notes. But I couldn't bring myself to tell my mother anything so personal, and anyway, I already knew I didn't feel whatever my mom had felt for Cam. On TV, bells chimed, William walked the aisle, and ladies in fancy hats waited for the woman who would be princess. Maybe, I thought when Kate Middleton appeared, I could become someone different, the kind of girl who wears a dress and drifts along to the wedding march.

When the wedding was over, my mom pulled a Dell laptop from underneath the couch. She typed fast, then turned her computer around for me to see. She'd logged on to Facebook. "Calling anyone from Delhi who might have known Roy Hudgins," she'd typed. "My daughter is filming a documentary and wants to finish up by interviewing anyone who might have known Roy. If you can help, please drop me a message."

We watched the post-wedding commentary until everyone else woke up. My grandma started mixing flour and buttermilk to make biscuits, and Aubree and Aaron packed our film equipment into the rental car. I kept refreshing my mom's Facebook page, hoping someone had responded to her post. We planned to interview my mom outside the drugstore where she'd worked as a teenager, but I didn't have any other appointments lined up. I'd messaged a bunch of people on Facebook, but no one wanted to commit ahead of time. And I'd decided not to call Mark King yet because I was worried he'd balk if I told him I was coming. We'd just show up, I thought. The Kings would see my mom, and they'd soften.

It was almost eighty degrees by the time we were ready to leave the house, but I put on my tightest skinny jeans anyway. My mom wore camouflage-patterned shorts with little drawstrings around the knees.

She had on a pale green shirt that matched the lighter tones in the cam-ouflage, and her sandals were the exact same shade. Even her earrings, dangling teardrops that looked like miniature avocados, matched.

"You're wearing shorts?" I asked when I found her in the carport smoking with my grandma.

"Why?" my mom asked. "They don't look good?"

"No, I just didn't think you wore shorts."

She winked at me in a way that suggested she was feeling good. She told me she liked to wear "whatever's in style," then she stubbed out her cigarette and followed me out to the car. I can't remember now what we talked about or what music we listened to on the hour-long trip to Delhi, but I know we got to town a little after noon. The sun hit straight down. My stomach rumbled with hunger, but I wanted to film my mom while she was happy, so I suggested we start the interview right away. I drove to Thompson's drug store, the pharmacy and soda fountain where my mom had sold Cokes to Roy. We got out of the car, and as Aubree and Aaron set up their tripods in the parking lot, I asked my mom to tell me more about Roy. She talked about herself instead.

"I started here when I was fifteen. I used to come in in the morning and make thirty-five cans of tuna fish salad. I'd go to school still smell-ing like it," she said. "Girls would turn their noses up at me."

Now that I'm in my late thirties, I look back at video footage of that interview with my mother, and I understand that she was trying to tell me how hard it was for her to return to Delhi. But in April of 2011, when I was twenty-seven and standing in front of her, I only wanted to hear about Roy. I didn't acknowledge the tuna fish or the girls who made fun of my mom. Why was I suddenly so disinterested when, the night before, I'd been desperate to tape her? I didn't write in my journal that trip, so I don't know what I was thinking. I can only hear myself on the tape, ignoring my mother's painful story, then asking her, again, to tell me about Roy.

"Um," my mom said, obviously hurt by my lack of interest. "Every time Roy would come in, I'd stare. I was trying to find an Adam's apple."

I started to tell her that kind of snooping is offensive, but before I could, she looked away from me and stared at a group of girls leaving the shop next door.

"Look at their dresses," she said. "It must be prom day."

Her eyes glazed over, and I wondered if she was thinking about Cam or my dad, the prom she'd dreamed of or the prom she'd had. I thought about asking her, but a loud whistle shrieked, and a freight train rattled along the rails behind us. It was too loud for us to talk to each other, so we watched as it heaved forward, kicking up rocks and dust. The train created a wind that blew my hair crazy, but my mom's was so shellacked with hairspray, it didn't budge. After a few minutes, the caboose crossed into the distance, and I turned back to my mother.

"Do you remember when grandma first told me about Roy?"

"I remember you were fascinated by it," my mom said. "After that, it was every phone call from you. 'Tell me a little bit more about Roy.' I didn't want Grandma to tell you, because I was afraid we'd be doing what we are now."

She motioned toward the video cameras, then she swung her arm around as if to implicate the entire town. "I was afraid because your hair was really short. There was no makeup."

A motorcycle zipped through the parking lot, then three or four pickup trucks rambled by. Every engine was loud, and eventually Aubree suggested we cut and find somewhere quieter to film. I exhaled in relief. I wanted to learn about Roy, but I did not want to talk about my short hair or lack of makeup. That wasn't the point of the story, I thought. We got back into the car, and I drove around, looking for a spot to film. I turned right on Highway 17, and my mom pointed to a boarded-up storefront. "Grandpa's shop was right here."

She sighed and leaned her head against the window. I'd forgotten that her father ran a store in Delhi after they moved back from Germany. She was quiet for a moment or two, then she began to talk in a voice more wistful than the one she usually used when telling stories.

"In this town, things were a certain way. If you weren't, like, born-and-bred Delhi, with deep roots in the community, they could close ranks on you very quickly. Unfortunately, when we came back here from Germany, we all dressed differently. We didn't have a lot of money, and he couldn't find a job, so he opened a little antique store right there on the corner."

Initially, my mom said, her father only sold on weekdays. Then, one day in 1977, a man came from out of town and asked my grandpa to host an antique auction that Sunday. My mom's dad wasn't religious, but he did understand that most people in town were, so he told the man they'd have to wait until church let out if they wanted any customers.

When Sunday arrived, my grandpa stood in the street, waiting until people in sundresses and three-piece suits spilled out of the sanctuaries. At 12:05, he started the auction.

"The next Sunday," my mom said, "the pastor of First Baptist got in the pulpit and said my dad was an infidel."

She closed her eyes. She didn't say, but I assumed the pastor had been angry that my grandfather had worked on the sabbath. We had never been particularly strict about that rule when I was growing up, but I knew some denominations were. I stopped at a red light, and my mom started talking again. After the auction, she said, customers stopped visiting, and my grandpa had to close the shop. He left Delhi to try to sell life insurance on the road, and girls who'd invited my mom to their birthday parties told her they needed the invitations back.

"They weren't allowed to have anything to do with me because of my family."

My mom went quiet, and I drove around in circles. I knew the kind of horrible power some pastors can wield. When I was young, I thought preachers were as good as angels, holy emissaries sent to do God's work, but I'd changed my mind since then. I'd experienced too many bad pastors, too many holy men willing to destroy a person's time on earth under the guise of delivering them to Heaven.

Eventually, I pulled over to search my notes for ideas about who else we could interview. I flipped through the legal-sized yellow notebook where I'd kept all my reporting from previous trips. I read off names people had suggested, and my mom shook her head no after every one.

"Ki Allen?"

"Not with me in the car," my mom said.

"Why not? Do you have a problem with her?"

"I'd rather not talk about it," she said.

I rolled my eyes, then kept flipping through my notebook. I stopped on a page that mentioned the old woman who'd given me Roy's song lyrics the first time my mom and I visited Delhi.

"What if we go see Mary Rundell again?" I asked.

My mom didn't protest, so I dialed the number I'd written down in my notebook. An old lady with a high-pitched voice and an almost incomprehensible accent answered.

"Miss Mary?" I asked. "My name is Casey. I met you probably a year and a half ago. I've been working on a memorial for Roy Hudgins. You had some old poems, or songs, that Roy had written. Would you be okay if—"

Mary must have cut me off, because in video footage of that day, I go quiet and listen to the phone for a while. My mom leans in and whispers to me, "Tell Miss Mary I worked with her at Jitney Jungle." In the video, I hold my right hand up to shush my mom. She keeps talking anyway about people she knows who might know Mary. After three or four minutes, Miss Mary must have told me to come on, because I got off the phone smiling, then told my mom and the crew that we were heading to an interview.

"What's the address?" my mom asked.

I looked down at my notes. "I forgot to ask."

I was too embarrassed to call back, so I told my mom I was sure we could find Mary's house without an address. I remembered that it was somewhere west of the high school, and I figured if I drove in that general direction, I'd recognize it as we passed. My mom shook her head as if that was the dumbest idea she'd ever heard. I started the engine anyway. I drove for a while, but none of the houses looked familiar. My mom eventually grew annoyed, took my phone, and pressed redial. Mary's sister answered.

"This is Rhonda Parks," my mom said in her sweetest, most syrupy tone. "She's expecting us to come over. My daughter just talked with her, and we're on Edgar Street, but I can't for the life of me remember what house number she lives at."

My mom listened for a few seconds longer, then she held her phone out, puzzled.

"She hung up on me," she said.

I pulled the car forward a few blocks, rolled down my window, and asked a group of kids playing basketball if they knew where Mary lived. They stared at me, slack-jawed and silent, as if I were an alien there to steal their brains. I rolled the window up, and my mom said she was done.

"I'm not going to somebody's house after they just hung up on me," she said.

I was nervous, too, but I didn't want my mom to know that, so I told her that was stupid, then I got out of the car and knocked on a random door. No one answered, but eventually I spotted Mary down the road, standing in a dry ditch, waving and waiting for us to arrive. I got back in the car, shot my mom a look, then eased down the block. Mary was standing in front of a white house with faded plastic flamingos in the yard. She looked hunched in half by age and a lifetime of service jobs, and her hair was so white it was pink. She directed us toward a fenced-in area, a kind of makeshift porch created out of the driveway. She'd arranged six green plastic chairs into a circle around a wooden spool she was using as an outdoor coffee table. We sat, and Mary's face lit up as she recognized my mom.

"We go back a ways," Mary said in surprised delight.

"We do," my mom said. "We used to work at Jitney Jungle in the deli."

Mary said she was "proud" we'd come to visit her. She recounted every dish she and my mom had made in the deli—doughnuts and roast chickens, spaghetti and fried potatoes. Mary said she'd been out of a job for a few years, and she'd give anything to be back working again. I could tell by the way she talked that she didn't remember that we'd come to see her before. She tried to calculate the last time she'd seen my mother, and she figured it had been at least thirty years. My mom shook her head in affirmation. "I left Delhi in 1982. Cam Milton and I were really good friends, and after he committed suicide, I couldn't stand it."

Mary nodded, as if she understood. She said her husband had passed away years ago. "I just get dull thinking," she said. "I get in the house, and I just sit there. I used to keep the road hot. I like to have my feet in the road, but I don't have nobody to put the feet in the road with me now."

She looked at me, and I didn't have any loss to talk about, so I asked about Roy.

"Oh, Roy was real nice," Mary said. "She was real nice. Her mama said the only reason she put her in pants was she couldn't afford dresses. I went with her to the Church of Christ once. What amazed me is, there they have no instruments. Roy loved music, but there, they don't allow it."

She clasped her hands together, then raised both eyebrows in a way that suggested Roy's churchgoing seemed suspicious. I nodded. It did seem odd that Roy would spend Sundays in a sanctuary without music. Mary's twin sister and a daughter came out onto the porch, and they listened as we talked. Eventually, Mary's daughter interrupted and asked if we'd talked to Mark King. I told her I'd tried, but he'd turned me down.

"Mark took care of Roy the last few years she was living," Mary's daughter said. "He has all that music she wrote and everything."

Mary nodded, as if to confirm that what her daughter said was true.

"The Lord let me write two songs once," Mary said. "I try to play the piano, but people have to suffer when I play because I don't know music. It might hurt your feelings to hear it."

Aubree and I told Mary we didn't believe her. We begged her to sing for us. After a few minutes, Mary cracked her fingers, then stood.

"If you can take it," she said, "I might try to play a little for you."

Mary opened the screen door, and we followed her into the living room. Every light in the house was turned off, and thick patterned curtains shaded the windows. It was so dark inside, I couldn't make out anything but the white piano keys. Mary sat down and tried the first verse of "How Great Thou Art," then she transitioned into one of the songs she'd written herself. It was a song about Jesus. The first verse started slow, then picked up momentum, and as Mary leaned into the chorus, my mother gasped. Mary played with all of her fingers moving. Her thumbs pounded hard notes, and the other fingers skipped and slipped across the keys. The chords seemed to shimmer. I've never studied music, so I don't know if Mary was right, if the way she played was wrong, but the song sounded both rich and airy, like a whole choir singing in an open country church. A light breeze swished through the screen door, and my mom reached for my hand. I felt like I was young again. It was dark enough that I didn't need to close my eyes, but I did, and I pictured myself back in Georgia at Live Oak, sitting next to my mom on a velvet pew, full of love and the Holy Spirit. I squeezed my mom's hand.

Mary sang in a low alto that stretched for high notes in the chorus.

Her voice cut through the twinkling melody, and I couldn't remember a time when I'd ever been happier. Later that night, over Gchat, I told the girl in San Francisco that I'd felt like I was in the exact right place at the exact right time, like God or someone had just handed me all of my best memories to relive through one song. It had been years since I'd been to church, and I'd convinced myself that the music no longer belonged to me, but listening to Mary, I started to believe that it could again.

Mary finished with a high-C flourish, and we all clapped as she stood and asked for a hug. She held her hands out and looked at them in wonder. "I'm shaking."

She turned on a light and told us she'd look for more of Roy's songs that weekend. As we edged toward the door, Mary blew us two kisses and told us, again, that she hated spending all her life alone in the house. "I wish I could be in the road. Out of here."

I stepped outside, and the sun hurt my eyes, so I tried to blink them into working as we climbed into the car. My mom pulled out her phone, then she did a little celebratory whoop. A woman named Lynda Best had responded to the Facebook post my mom had written that morning.

> Roy attended some Bible studies with me for a few weeks. She said she was a man born with a woman's body, that she had not worn a dress since she was a little girl and really didn't remember wearing one at all. The only reason she confided these things to me was because I was a member of the United Pentecostal Church in Delhi, and our doctrine forbade women to wear pants. She knew the pastor in Delhi would never accept her as a true member as long as she refused to wear a dress. She said she just could not put one on; it was too hard mentally. However, she did testify that she had received the baptism of the Holy Ghost with the outward evidence of speaking in other tongues as the Spirit gave the utterance; and she did permit our pastor to baptize her in Jesus' Name as the apostles did in the New Testament. She was definitely a Christian woman.

"Shall we go?" I asked.

My mom shook her head no, then pointed out the window. My dad had arrived, and he was waiting in the Buick.

"My knight in shining armor is here to take me away," my mom said.

"What?" I asked. "You're supposed to do the interview with us."

"I did an interview with you. Now I want to go home."

The rental car idled, and my dad's car idled, and neither my mom nor I said a thing. Why did I keep getting my hopes up? Why had I let myself believe that this trip would be different? I watched the kids down the road play basketball, and I willed myself into needing less.

"Okay," I said. "I guess I'll see you at Grandma's."

My mom stepped out of the car and into my dad's SUV. I waited until they drove off, then I checked her Facebook page again. She'd already updated it with a new status.

> *What an emotional day it was for me to be in a town where life was so hard, and yet it was such a good day . . . i was able to show off my daughter and show them that I didn't turn out so bad after all.*

Lynda lived north of the manmade lake, way out in the country on a narrow highway marked by signs that advertised an exotic zoo. Yellow-green grass rose high out of the marshy land around her house, and the blades must have concealed a bunch of bugs, because the birds were diving and chirping loud. I pulled up the gravel driveway and parked under an oak tree late afternoon. Lynda's house was long and white with wood columns, but it was not fancy. It was a single-story with three brick steps leading up to it. The screen door looked old, and the rocking chairs out front were chipped. I knocked, and Lynda answered immediately.

"Well, y'all come in," she said.

Lynda had a voice like Blanche Devereaux's on *The Golden Girls*. She spoke low and slow, with a dragging hint of drama, and I could tell after a few sentences that she liked to talk. She led us through a dark living room decorated with a few dozen replicas of porcelain cowboy boots, then she settled into a plush brown recliner.

I asked how she knew Roy, and Lynda said they'd met through the Pentecostal church. It took a while for the Pentecost to make its way from Topeka to Delhi, Lynda told us. After William Joseph Seymour opened the Azusa Street Mission in Los Angeles, Pentecostal churches sprouted across the United States. A few opened in Louisiana in the 1920s, and Lynda visited one in a country town near Monroe in the 1950s, but Delhi didn't get its own Pentecostal church until August 1967, when two men from nearby Epps opened one next to a butane plant off Highway 80. The first congregants drove in from all the surrounding towns to worship with Lavelle Hales, a big jowly preacher with a high forehead and a plain way of talking.

Lynda was in her thirties then. She was married and had two small kids, a boy and a girl, and she joined the United Pentecostal Church of Delhi almost as soon as Pastor Hales opened it. In his first sermon, the preacher told the group that this new denomination had stricter rules, and they'd be following every one. Women, he said, should wear long dresses and abstain from cutting their hair. They should defer to their husbands and stay silent in church. Lynda told me that she hadn't minded back then that she couldn't wear pants or jewelry or makeup in the new church. She'd loved the way the music filled the building, and she wanted to speak in tongues.

The church stayed packed until December, Lynda said. Then, late in the middle of the night a few days before Christmas, the butane plant caught fire. Crews from four cities tried to extinguish the flames, but by the next morning, the plant and the church had burned down.

"We got a tent and put it out there," Lynda said. "Then a hurricane came and blew the tent down. We went through the fire, then we went through the water, as they said. Finally, we decided to build somewhere else."

After the disasters, the congregation bought a building on Fifth Street, just a block from Roy's house. The offering plate alone couldn't refinance what the church had lost, so they started hosting revivals in the spring of 1970, hoping week-long services might attract new members and enough donations to finance a new organ. Pastor Hales brought in evangelists from Texas and gospel choirs from Mississippi. He took out ads in the paper, promising "special singing" and "a special move of God." Lynda volunteered to knock on doors to drum up interest.

Lynda told us that she and a woman named Cookie set out one Saturday morning and made their way up and down the north side of Delhi. When they reached the wood-frame house just north of Cuthbert

Street, they heard music playing inside. Lynda knocked on the screen door. After a minute, the music stopped, and Roy opened the door wide enough that Lynda could see inside his cluttered home. It was full of books. A guitar hung on the wall. Lynda's heart skipped a half beat. She'd seen Roy riding a bike through town, but she'd never spoken to him before.

"Roy was a strange woman to us," Lynda told me. "She was different, kind of an outcast. People in Delhi didn't know who she was. They didn't know what she was. They say she's a man. They say she's a she. They say she's a morphodite."

Roy stood in the doorway, waiting for the women to say something, and finally Lynda handed over a religious tract about speaking in tongues. She told Roy that a couple was coming up from Franklinton to preach and sing some "jam-up good music." Roy was quiet, Lynda said, cordial but shy. He said he'd be there.

That Sunday night, Roy showed up wearing a cap and a pair of pants. Lynda told me she didn't remember who took Roy aside and explained that he'd have to wear a dress next time, but she said everyone at church agreed with the sentiment. Someone went to the front and recited Deuteronomy 22:5: "A woman shall not wear anything that pertains to a man, nor shall a man put on a woman's garment, for all who do so are an abomination to the Lord your God."

Roy returned the next night and the night after that, and both times he wore pants. He joined an outside Bible study with Lynda, and he wore pants to those, too. Sometimes, after the studies, he'd linger and talk. Lynda said Roy told her he'd known since he was young that he ought to be a boy. At one Bible study, he said he was a man who'd been sent to earth in a woman's frame. "Roy told me, 'It would be just like your husband trying to go down the street in a dress. I feel the same way.'"

Lynda told me she'd never thought Roy was lying—he really seemed to believe he was a man—but in the 1970s, Lynda didn't understand how his brain and body could feel so disconnected. She pressed him for a clearer explanation. Finally, at another Bible study, Roy told Lynda he'd been in an accident when he was twelve. A piece of farm equipment hit him on the head, he told her, and he hadn't matured into a woman after that.

"She never had a menstruation, never had a period, never had children," Lynda told me. "I doubt she ever had sex to be honest with you. She never had a boyfriend or a girlfriend that I know of."

Maybe Roy hoped the farm accident story would give him a reprieve, but no one at the church relented. Every week, the pastor or someone else told Roy he had to wear a dress if he wanted to be Pentecostal, and every week Roy returned wearing pants. In a way, Lynda told us, she admired Roy. He must have really believed in the Pentecostal church. Otherwise, why would he have put himself through that?

"It was terribly embarrassing for her to come to our church. It really was, because she felt out of place. And to be honest, we felt out of place to have her. If she was going to be a woman, people thought she ought to look like one."

Lynda didn't look like any other Pentecostal I knew. All the Pentecostal girls I grew up with wore ankle-length skirts. Most had never cut their hair, so they kept their locks tied back in long braids that stretched almost as long as their skirts did. Lynda's hair was only shoulder length. She was wearing black dress pants—women's pants, but pants nonetheless.

"Back then," I said, "when Roy was going to church with you, did you wear long skirts and long hair?"

Lynda shook her head yes. "Always. But Roy didn't. Roy's hair was cut like a man's. Hers was cut like yours."

She pointed at me, as if I somehow might have missed that I was the girl with man hair. I didn't want to draw more attention to myself, so I asked Lynda if she'd stopped being Pentecostal. She said she hadn't.

"But you cut your hair now?" I asked.

Lynda told me she'd had it cut three weeks earlier. Her hair had been falling out in hunks all year. Every time she washed her face or combed her hair, "fistfuls" fell out. After a few months, she had big bald patches across her head.

"I thought, 'Why?'" she said. "If that is part of the salvation, why is God taking that away from me? Think about it. If hair is part of the salvation, if you've got to have long hair, why would he take it away from you? He died for your salvation, now he's going to take some of that back? He's going to take that hair away from me? That didn't make sense to me."

Lynda's voice turned rascally and agitated. She creased her forehead in confusion, and she put a finger on her chin to show she was really thinking this dilemma through. She reminded me of myself, of the way I'd wrestled with my identity in college. I'd spent months my freshman year wondering how God could let me be attracted to women, and I'd wondered why he would condemn me to Hell for something I couldn't stop from happening. The way I understood the Bible then, it didn't matter if I ever kissed a girl. The thoughts alone were punishable. But why? Why did God care about hair or pants or something as innocuous as attraction?

"I went to the beauty shop," Lynda told me. "And I said, 'Something is wrong.' The beautician said my hair was too long. It was getting stringy. She did cut it then, and it's quit coming out like that."

Lynda said that after she got her own hair cut, she started looking at other Pentecostal women differently. She noticed how many had just a few strands of hair twisted into a braid. Their hair looked scraggly, she thought, not at all godly.

"So is your pastor okay with you cutting your hair?" I asked.

Lynda shook her head no, then smiled what I thought was a forced grin. "I don't get to teach Sunday school or sing in the choir anymore. But that's okay. I have a personal relationship with God. I think the older I get, the more lenient I become. I'm not saying about sin, because I still believe sin is sin. Swearing. Adultery. Stealing. That's sin. Mistreating people. Gossip. But I just don't think God can be put in a little box and say, 'Okay, this little group right here is going to do what you say, and everybody else is going straight to Hell.'"

I told Lynda I liked the way she thought. I hoped that the God I'd grown up loving wouldn't care if we cut our hair. Lynda laughed.

"But I don't think I could wear hair like yours," she said. "I really don't."

I ran my right hand through my wavy bangs and said I didn't have much of a choice. Even when my hair was long, it had always turned unruly in the humidity. My cowlicks were easier to tamp down when they were short.

"It's really cute," Lynda said. "But I personally couldn't wear it. That comes from First Corinthians. It says if a woman has long hair, it's a glory to her."

She laughed. I couldn't tell what Lynda thought of me, or what she'd thought of Roy long ago. I told myself it didn't matter; I'd probably never see Lynda again. But listening to her reminded me of all the other people in my life who'd told me that the Bible says that the way I am is wrong. My chest burned. I had gone so long in Portland without feeling ashamed of myself, but sitting in a recliner in Lynda's living room, all the strength I'd built elsewhere faded away. I felt eighteen again, judged, vulnerable, embarrassed for being myself. I tried to joke about my cowlicks, but the words caught in my throat.

"Mine, uh, didn't feel like a glory when I had it long," I said.

Lynda laughed again, and we talked for a while about other things.

After twenty minutes or so, Lynda stood, leaned on a cane she hadn't used earlier, then walked us toward the front door. I asked her if the Pentecostal church was still near Roy's old house, and Lynda said the congregation outgrew it long ago. Now they were in a big building on Highway 17, but new people kept joining, she said, and soon, they'd have to find a place even larger. She told us we were welcome to drive by and see it, but she didn't invite us to attend. I ran my hand back through my short hair, and I thought Lynda must not want to relive what had happened with Roy. I knew without Lynda telling me that no Pentecostal preacher would want me in the pews. I'd learned that long ago, and I didn't want to relive it, either.

Aubree, Aaron, and I got into the rental car, and I drove a few miles, remembering things I'd spent years trying to forget. I hung a right on Highway 17, and I drove as slow as I legally could toward town. I'd never told Aubree or Aaron why I stopped going to church. I'd never told anyone. I turned to face my friends, then I looked back at the road. The Pentecostal sanctuary appeared on the far horizon. Maybe, I thought, it was time.

Chapter Six

(1994–2001)

MY DAD LEFT the army in late 1993 with a broken ankle and lungs clogged by chemicals he inhaled during the Gulf War. We lost our free housing on the base in Georgia, so we moved across town to a moldy brown ranch house tucked against a forest slated for development. My dad became an exterminator, and my mom took a second job to help pay the rent. She still cleaned the old lady's house on nights and weekends, but during the day, she started working at my elementary school as a teacher's aide. Other kids teased me for having my mom at school, but I liked tiptoeing down the hallway, looking into her classroom, and waving. After school, I'd wait in the parking lot, and I'd ride with her to the old lady's house. We did that every day until I was ten or eleven, until one afternoon, while my mom was mopping on her hands and knees, I sneaked into the old lady's closet and pulled out one of her porcelain-head dolls. The old lady jumped out of her rocking chair and charged toward me to snatch the doll back. She sneered, then told my mom not to bring me or my brother to work with her anymore.

After the incident, my mom hired a girl from church to babysit my brother and me. Toni was twelve and tall with tawny skin and tight black curls she kept pulled back in a ponytail. She had a deep voice and breasts so big that when she first came over, my mom exclaimed, inappropriately, "Wow, Toni, you're built like a brick house." Toni covered her chest with her arms, and she slunk into our house. I shot my mom a look, but she rolled her eyes as if it were perfectly acceptable to tell a teenage girl how womanly she looked. Toni hated Barbie dolls but loved football, and most afternoons she chased my brother and me around the yard until the sun set. I don't remember how many times she babysat us, but I remember the last day clearly because it was the first time anyone ever suspected I was gay.

We were playing football in the yard. My brother threw the ball, and I caught it. I ran toward the tree we'd designated as the end zone, and Toni sprinted after me, then grabbed me by the hips. She tackled me, and I collapsed against the ground, giggling as her legs pinned mine to the grass. She held my arms down. Her ponytail holder had fallen off, and her curly hair tickled my face. I brushed her hair aside and looked up at her. She stared back a few seconds too long.

"I like you," she said.

I knew without knowing what she meant, knew that "like" meant something awful, so I squirmed out from under her and ran toward our neighbor's yard. They had a trampoline, and I climbed up its metal side, then started jumping. Toni walked over, pulled herself up, and bounced alongside me. She seemed so much older to me then, though now I can see she was just a kid. We jumped the way children do, high and wild, but I felt tethered by an unnameable electricity. Every spring felt heavy.

"Do you like me?" Toni asked.

I told her I didn't know. I asked her what she meant. I tried to leap higher.

"I mean, I like you," she said. "Like, like-like." She hopped off the trampoline and peered at me from the ground. "I know you are, too," she said.

I plugged my ears with my fingers. I closed my eyes and jumped until it was dark, and my mother called me inside.

I couldn't sleep that night. Every time I closed my eyes, I could hear Toni, asking if I liked her. Her voice made my insides spark and jump. I felt drawn to Toni in ways I didn't understand, ways I suspected were sinful even though they were devoid of sexual feelings. When I thought about Toni, I didn't think about kissing or anything else physical. I was ten. I didn't think about anything, really, except seeing her again.

A week later, my mom came home smelling like Clorox. She told me she needed to talk to me. My dad and brother were gone, and all I could hear was the refrigerator buzzing in the kitchen.

"I need to tell you something," my mom said. "One of your friends is gay."

My stomach stung with guilt or fear, and I blurted out a response as if I were gasping for air. "Toni is not my friend. I hate her."

My mom must have asked me follow-up questions, and I must have told her what happened, but I don't remember the details. My mom swirled around the house the rest of the evening, calling people from church and screaming every cuss word she knew. She drove to Toni's house and chewed out her mother, then she came home and cussed some more.

By Sunday, everyone at church had heard because my mom had called and told everyone. The pastor strode up to the pulpit that morning and announced that he planned to deliver a special sermon in the evening. Afterward, he said, we'd take a vote. Neither the pastor nor my parents had ever talked much about homosexuality before Toni, but I knew somehow that what had happened between us in my front yard was a sin. I felt sick all Sunday. That night, our pastor preached out of the Old Testament. He quoted Leviticus, and he told the story of Sodom and Gomorrah, two cities he said the Lord had destroyed as punishment for their homosexual activity. Afterward, the pastor said it was up to the congregation to decide whether we would allow Toni and her family to keep worshiping with us.

"Raise your hand if you want to rebuke Satan. Raise your hand if you want this family to leave."

I didn't need to look at my mother to know how she was voting. I could feel her arm brush past mine as it shot into the air. My dad must have been there, and he must have voted, but he and my brother are both missing in my memories. All I can remember is the pastor's voice, my mother's arm, and my own hand, timidly reaching toward Heaven to vote Toni out.

I TRIED FOR TWENTY years to forget Toni. I tried to forget the way her legs pressed against mine, and I tried to forget her voice, soft and pleading. I never let myself wonder how she felt when I raised my hand that Sunday night. But after I started going to Delhi to learn about Roy, I couldn't stop thinking about Toni. I drove away from Lynda's that afternoon in 2011 thinking I was no better than the people who'd told Roy he had to leave the Pentecostal church. Later, in the cabin, I googled Toni's name over and over. I tried three or four spellings, but I never got a hit. I paid for a Classmates.com account, and I searched for the middle school I remembered her attending, but the school didn't have any yearbooks online. I even messaged an old friend of my mother's to ask if she'd kept up with Toni's family. She hadn't. I think I wanted to tell Toni I was sorry. I'd been so sure at ten that I had no choice, but I know now that demons wouldn't have come to claim me if I'd said I wanted her to stay. Or maybe I wanted to tell Toni that she'd been right. Whatever she saw in me at ten was real—and eventually, the church had turned on me, too.

MY FAMILY MOVED BACK to Louisiana in late 1994, a year after Toni disappeared. We found another evangelical church with light shows and a six-piece band. It was called Family Church, and I loved it even more than I had Live Oak. Every Sunday felt like a professional concert. A dozen or so singers stood onstage holding microphones, and they performed Christian pop songs in thirty-minute sets. The church employed a full-time light director, and he angled blue and purple beams across the stage while someone else projected the lyrics, and we sang as a group with our eyes closed and our hands stretched toward God. My mother and I had a few favorite songs. We liked "Lord, I Lift Your Name on High" because we got to act out its verses, lowering our arms during the line about Jesus descending from Heaven, then spreading them out to mimic the cross he died on. And we liked "My Redeemer Lives" because it had a skippy, fun beat. We hopped around in circles every time the choir sang it. We loved at least a dozen others, but our number one, all-time favorite song was "Shout to the Lord."

"Shout to the Lord," I realized later, is the kind of song that's designed to make listeners cry. It starts slow, with just a few piano notes and a soloist, then builds toward a key change that always—even now—breaks me down. At our church, a woman named Cheryl sang the solos in "Shout to the Lord," and I thought hers was the most beautiful voice in the world. Listening to Cheryl transported me somewhere, closer to God, I hoped, though I worried my affection verged on sinful. Cheryl was a straight woman with a husband and a newborn son, but she had short blond hair that I found irresistible as a preteen, and sometimes, watching her from the third pew back, I worried that the inexplicable yearning I felt was the same sin that had undone Toni.

BEFORE I STARTED GOING to Delhi, I only told my Portland friends about church when I wanted to make fun of my past. I reenacted an exaggerated version of Trana's exorcism. I laughed about Toni. I turned my memories into funny stories I told at parties in the kind of can-you-believe-it tone that hid all the pain I'd once felt in losing my faith. But the truth—as I came to remember it after I started learning about Roy—was that church had once felt like the only stabilizing force in my life. As I steered toward the Delhi Pentecost Tabernacle in 2011, I thought about Roy braving Sunday school in his pants, and I didn't want to make jokes of my memories anymore.

I DON'T REMEMBER IF my mother began using the opiate nose spray again before or after my dad slept with his office secretary in Louisiana. But I remember my parents separated and got back together every few months during my early teenage years. We switched houses each time they did. We lived with my grandparents in a two-bedroom next to the railroad tracks, then on our own in a mouse-filled home whose foundation sank and slanted into mud. We lived with my dad in a beige apartment complex ravaged by swarming crickets, and without him in a two-bedroom near the highway before we settled, temporarily "complete," into the single-wide trailer where the puppies were born. I felt alone in every place.

After my dad's friend sexually assaulted my mom, our TV was always on too loud. My dad worked late, my brother annoyed me, and my mom haunted the hallways like some kind of washed-out specter. Her skin lost all its color, and most of her clothes no longer fit. She had always been curvy—an eighteen was her goal size—but she gained a bunch of weight while I was in middle school, and she couldn't afford to buy new outfits. She spent whole days walking in circles in her nightgown, muttering to herself about my dad's infidelities or Cam and the oak tree.

Church was the only place where I felt unburdened. I spent Wednesday nights at youth group, the teenagers-only service taught by half a dozen "cool" adults. I loved the youth pastors so much, I wrote in my eighth-grade journal that they were my best friends. Brad was a goofy balding guy who loaned us bootlegged copies of movies, and Phillip worked at the Christian radio station. The youth pastor I loved most was a quiet accountant named Pamela. She wasn't charismatic like Brad and Phillip, and she couldn't sing like Cheryl, but she listened when I talked, and she called me during the week to check on me. On Sundays, she sat in the far left of the church—a football field away from my family's usual spot near the front—but I raced over to talk to her every week while the ushers passed the offering plate around.

My mother hated her.

Even when my mom was on the nose spray, she somehow roused herself every Sunday for church. She didn't linger, though. As soon as the pastor said amen, she bolted toward the parking lot, but I stayed until the ushers turned the lights off. While my mom waited in the car, listening to the end of Casey Kasem's Top 40 countdown, I went to the altar and cried with anyone who would cry with me. I prayed for God to deliver me from the life I had. I asked him to help me forget about Toni, and I begged him over and over again to make my mom go clean. Eventually, I'd stumble through the dark sanctuary, red-eyed, then I'd climb into our Camry just as Casey Kasem signed off. Every Sunday, my mom glared at me.

"Next time," she'd say, "we're leaving you here."

LOOKING BACK, THE HIGHS and lows all mix together, so I can't remember exactly when she was wan and when she was my mother. I know my mom screamed at me in front of the trailer that if my dad divorced her, it would be my fault. I know she took a nighttime cleaning job so she could buy me a pair of Girbaud jeans and brown, six-eye Doc Martens. Someone gave her a computer and an AOL free trial, and she spent weeks or months ignoring me while she chatted with a man in California. She climbed into my bed in the middle of the night and told me she hated me. She whispered it wet and low, then she left me there crying alone. She sang Eric Clapton's "Wonderful Tonight," using a hairbrush as a microphone as I got ready for my first middle school dance. She beat me with a wooden spoon. She kicked down my bedroom door, and my brother and I called her Hurricane Rhonda, a force of nature no god could stop. She taught me how to drive. She let me skip school to cry with her after Princess Diana died, and she bought me a tape of Elton John's updated version of "Candle in the Wind." I sang along, sometimes picturing Princess Di, sometimes thinking about my mother. I worried my mom would die young if she didn't stop using the nose spray. She told me she took Stadol to ease her headaches, and I believed her because I had no other options. Back then, we never said the word "opioid." There was no pharmaceutical company to blame, no worldwide epidemic that allowed me to contextualize my mom's addiction. There was only my mother, bright and joyous when she was off the nose spray, vacant and mean when she was on.

I think she stayed alert for most of my freshman year of high school, because I remember her taking me to Waffle House to talk about my first kiss, and I know she put two gowns on layaway at JCPenney so we could dress up to go see what she told me was the premier of *Titanic*. At fourteen, I was naive enough to believe that James Cameron had staged a party in Monroe, Louisiana, and I was so excited to be spending time with my mom that I didn't complain when we arrived and found that no one else had dressed up. We stayed out late that night talking about how cute Leonardo DiCaprio was, and I didn't think about Toni a single time that winter.

My parents separated again my sophomore year of high school, the year I won a part in the church Christmas play. An hour before curtain call, my mom showed up in the sanctuary, wailing like a cat in the middle of a fight. I was living with my dad then, and I didn't see my mom often, but when I heard the yowls from backstage, I knew they were hers. The director must have known, too, because he asked me to go into the audience to calm my mother down. My hair was in curlers, and I was already wearing my Martha Cratchit costume, so I tiptoed down the side of the stage, holding my hand over my face, hoping the audience couldn't tell who I was. I waved my mom over. She lumbered toward me like Frankenstein's monster, arms out and holding a crumpled piece of paper. She shoved the paper into my hands. I unfolded it and recognized my dad's handwriting. It was slanty and messy, just like mine. The first word I read was "panties." The second was "wet." I balled the paper up.

"I don't want to read this," I told my mom. I threw the paper on the ground, and my mom told me my dad had written it to someone else, a woman she called "that hare-lipped secretary."

"Mom," I said, pleading. "The play is about to start." She picked up the paper, then stormed onstage, still crying in an awful howl. I thought she might read the letter into the microphone, but instead, she ducked under the curtain and continued crying backstage. I don't remember how I got her to be quiet long enough for us to perform, but I know that after the play was over and the sanctuary was empty, my mom and my dad met my brother and me in the pastor's office. My dad looked at us stony-faced, and my mom's cheeks were black with run mascara. They told us they planned to move to a different city so they could start fresh without any ghosts.

I told them I didn't want to go. It was the middle of the school year, and I didn't want to start over. I had friends and A's in all my classes. I had this play, this church, a life. My mom hesitated, so I played the one card I knew would persuade her. I told her I was in love with my boyfriend, Jacob, that I didn't want to lose him the way she'd lost Cam.

"Fine," she said. "Stay here. Live with one of the youth pastors you love so much."

She sounded defiant, not at all empathetic or upset by the idea of giving her fifteen-year-old daughter to someone else. I don't remember if I fought her suggestion, but by the end of that night, it was decided. My parents and brother would move two hours south to Alexandria, and I would live in Monroe with Pamela.

Pamela hadn't hesitated when I called to ask if I could move in. She sounded as if she'd been expecting the request all year. "I have the room ready," she said. I was never sure whether that meant she always had a room ready for anyone, or if she'd watched my family and prepared one specifically for me. My parents moved the day after Christmas, and I spent the rest of the winter break settling into Pamela's calm. Life with her was so different than the one I'd been living. Pamela never did anything to embarrass or hurt me. When school started again, she drove me to class every morning in a new SUV she kept stocked with Pop-Tarts. At night, we ate dinner at a table and talked about what I'd learned at school, then Pamela retreated to her bedroom to read, and I went to the guest room to do my homework. Pamela lived out in the country in a brick house with a long driveway, and it was quieter there than anywhere else I'd ever been. I lay in bed for hours, listening to the crickets chirp outside the guest room window, and I wondered if my mother still turned into Hurricane Rhonda without me around.

I DON'T KNOW IF Roy ever felt the way I did at church. He had to live his entire life knowing he was an outsider, but I got to spend my teenage years convincing myself I belonged. Years later, my adult friends would laugh at the idea of me begging my mom to leave me in Monroe so I could keep attending a church. But staying made so much sense to me at fifteen. Other kids had clubs or sports to orient their lives. I had church. I assume Roy must have felt some sense of community. Why else would he have continued going to Lynda's Bible study, even after he knew that Lynda and everyone else wanted him to wear a dress?

I DIDN'T LOSE CHURCH for good until I was in college, but six months after I moved in with Pamela, my mom forced me to move to Alexandria. I begged to stay in Monroe just one more Sunday, but my mom refused. I must have seemed distant and despondent when I showed up in Alexandria that Saturday night. I know I seemed like I'd changed because I remember my mother cried when I told her I'd stopped drinking sweet tea while I lived with Pamela. I asked for water, and my mom threw a glass against the wall.

"You think you're so much better than me," she said.

MY PARENTS HADN'T YET found a church they liked in Alexandria, so in the summer of 1999, my mom suggested that she and I start our own Bible group. We spent a few Sundays reading from the book of Daniel, but our private worship didn't move me the way Family Church had. I missed the songs and the youth pastors. I missed crying until the lights went out. My mom must have known how deeply I missed Pamela because she gave up the nose spray for three months before my junior year. We danced around the living room together to Ricky Martin and the Backstreet Boys, and she splurged on a giant cheesecake from Olive Garden for my sixteenth birthday. That fall, we pored over *People* magazine's Sexiest Man Alive issue, and I pretended to think Richard Gere was hot, even though he'd just seemed kind of old to me in *Runaway Bride.* I didn't want to kiss Richard Gere. I wanted to *be* the man Richard Gere played in that movie—a freelance magazine writer who wins over Julia Roberts.

I'd wanted to be a journalist since the year I learned to read, and my mom did everything she could to help me become one. She drove me to the library to read the weekend edition of *The Washington Post*, and she saved up twenty dollars so we could print off all the Pulitzer-winning articles we could find online. When a bookkeeping job opened at the local newspaper my junior year, my mom applied for it, hoping she could put in a word for me. She'd started working when she was ten, cleaning stairwells in Bad Tölz, Germany, and she told me she wanted my first job to be more fulfilling. When the paper called her in for an interview, my mom promised to ask if they'd bring me on, too. That afternoon, she somehow returned with two yeses. We spent the next year riding to work together. Before school, I manned the circulation desk, answering phones as people called to complain about not receiving their newspaper. I worked an hour or two, then my mom let me take her car to school. After class, I went to the newsroom, where I mostly retyped press releases that came in the mail. Both positions were grunt gigs, but I relished the chance to be around journalists. I loved the smell of the newsprint and the way the cop scanner crackled in a secret numerical language. Most of the reporters weren't married, so they stayed late, tinkering with sentences, and I watched them and knew that that was what I wanted for my adult life. I wouldn't need a family, I told myself. I'd have words. A few months into the job, the editor let me write a story about Salvation

Army bell ringers, and when the article ran on the front page Christmas Day, I told my mom that the only time I'd been happier was the Sunday I gave my life to God.

WE TRIED OUT DIFFERENT congregations, but none of them felt right the way Live Oak and Family Church had. One pastor even asked for donations for a jumbo jet he hoped to buy. My mom walked up to the pulpit, mid-sermon, holding her purse close to her chest.

"My lord and savior rode around on a donkey," she told the pastor. "As far as I'm concerned, so can you."

As a teenager, I imagined I'd end up back at Family Church someday. I even drove to Monroe a few Sundays a year, and I always felt right again, listening to Cheryl sing. Later, when I told my friends that I'd left the church as a teenager, I usually told the story of a particular day, an incident that happened when I was in college. But the real dissolution started earlier. In Alexandria, I began to imagine a future for myself—an earthly one, something more tangible than a celestial mansion. No one in my family had ever gone to college, but I knew, because my grades and standardized test scores were good, that I would. My school didn't have a guidance counselor, so my mom and I searched on our own for a university. We called admissions offices across the country and asked them to send us brochures. Glossy flyers filled our mailbox that fall. We scrutinized pictures of Brown University and Boston College, and we talked as if I might definitely end up at either. We went to the website Ask Jeeves, and my mom typed, "what is the best college for an aspiring journalist." Jeeves said Columbia University in New York, but when we asked Jeeves how much a year of tuition cost, I gasped, then closed the browser. I told my mom I would go somewhere closer to home.

"No," she said. "You deserve to be in the Ivy League." I wanted to believe she was right, but I knew we couldn't afford it, so I laughed and told her the Ivy League was for other people. Besides, I didn't want to leave the South. New York seemed cold and unreachable; I hadn't even been on a plane.

Ultimately, I didn't apply to any of the fancy universities Jeeves or *U.S. News and World Report* said were worthwhile. Sometime that fall, a brochure came to our house advertising a private liberal arts school in Jackson, Mississippi. It was called Millsaps College. My mom liked that its flyers showed a bell tower and a grassy field. She told me she could imagine me reading somewhere like that. We were naive, so neither of us thought to ask if the school had a journalism major. Instead, we settled on Millsaps because it had a female president, and because we thought "private liberal arts school" sounded esteemed, Ivy League adjacent.

I sent off an application, and my mom filled out the FAFSA so I could get a Pell Grant, federal money set aside for students from poor families. In early February, a big package arrived. It was purple and stuck out of our mailbox, and when we saw "Millsaps College" written on the outside, my mother told me that schools didn't send rejections that big. She opened the package, and we spent the rest of the night screaming because Millsaps offered me a scholarship worth $25,000 a year. It didn't cover room and board, but the scholarship and the Pell Grant got me close enough. I could take out loans to pay for the rest. That night, my mom crawled into bed with me, and she held my hand as I fell asleep. Maybe I was already dreaming, but in my memories of that night, she whispered to me, "You're going to make so much more of your life than I did."

Chapter Seven

(2001–2002)

IN THE FALL OF 2001, I went to college, and my family moved back to Monroe. We were just two hours apart, separated by a flat highway and the Mississippi River, but the break felt big and immediate.

Millsaps was a Methodist college. Technically, that made it a Christian school, but we weren't required to pray or attend services. My professors talked about God in a scholarly, rather than devotional, way. We read Immanuel Kant and Friedrich Schleiermacher, philosophers who treated Christianity as something to be probed and torn apart. My religious studies professor was a Christian, but he was different from any Christian I'd ever known. The first week of class, he told us the Bible was not perfect. It was cobbled together and contradictory in places, and as proof, the professor projected sections of the New Testament onto a big screen to show us that Luke, John, and Matthew had each described the resurrection of Jesus differently. In Luke, a group of women goes to Jesus's tomb three days after he dies, and they see two men. In John, only Mary Magdalene goes to the tomb. And in Matthew, two women go, and they see an angel.

"So which is the real story?" my professor asked.

He clicked the little remote that controlled his PowerPoint presentation, and another discrepancy appeared. This one was from Genesis. Already, one chapter in, my professor explained, the Bible begins to contradict itself. In chapter 1, God creates animals before he creates humans, but in chapter 2, that chronology is reversed: God creates animals *after* he creates humans.

My professor raised his bushy eyebrows, then he clicked forward in his presentation. Jesus dies a day earlier in the book of John than he does in the book of Mark, the professor said, and in three of the four gospels, Jesus rides on one donkey during the triumphal entry, but in Matthew, Jesus rides both a donkey and a colt at the same time.

The professor seemed unbothered, but I went back to my dorm that night afraid my understanding of the world was misguided. I'd grown up believing the Bible was a flawless document, handed down by God. But if one verse undid another, how could I know which was true? And if one sentence was false, could the entire book be wrong, too?

A few weeks into the semester, my liberal studies professor assigned a chapter from *The Good Book*, a work of nonfiction by Peter J. Gomes, a theologian at Harvard Divinity School. In class, my professor explained that Gomes's book called for a contextualized understanding of the Bible, and I was intrigued. I'd read the Bible cover to cover a few times as a child, but I didn't actually understand much of it. I knew the order of the books, and I could recite at least three dozen verses by heart, but I didn't know when or where any of the Bible's characters had lived. I didn't understand which stories were metaphors and which were historical documents, meant to reflect a particular norm in a particular time. I'd always read every word without context or attribution, as if each verse were spoken directly by God.

After class that night, I took the book over to the art building, an ancient and drafty three-story lined with student work. For some reason, I was obsessed with a paper sculpture someone had built to look like both a blender and a foot. I tucked myself into a corner on the top floor, close to the blender-foot. I bent the book's front cover back, and the table of contents stopped me. Chapter 8 was titled "The Bible and Homosexuality: The Last Prejudice." I flipped past the first seven chapters and read as fast as I could.

"One would assume that the Bible has much to say on the subject" of homosexuality, Gomes wrote. "It has not."

Homosexuality isn't mentioned in the Ten Commandments, Gomes noted. It doesn't come up in the Summary of the Law, the verses that say it's most important to love God and your neighbor, and Jesus never talks about it.

I moved through the pages as quickly as I could, torn between scanning and reading carefully for proof. Live Oak's pastor had told us that God destroyed Sodom and Gomorrah because the men in those cities wanted to have sex with two visiting male angels. But Gomes explained that that wasn't exactly right. God had already decided to destroy the cities. In fact, the angels were there to warn Abraham's nephew Lot to get out before God destroyed them. My pulse beat faster as I read. Was Gomes right?

I underlined a few paragraphs, then stopped at the next section head: "The Law of Leviticus." I read the words out loud to myself and remembered that my pastor had read from Leviticus the night we kicked Toni out. He'd recited chapter 20, verse 13: "If a man lies with a male as he lies with a woman, both of them have committed an abomination; they shall surely be put to death."

The verse had seemed so unambiguous to me when I was young. God considered homosexuality an abomination. Toni was an abomination.

I closed Gomes's book, then opened it again. Why, I suddenly wondered, had God condemned only male homosexuality? Why hadn't he specified that if a woman lies with a woman as she lies with a man, that is also an abomination? I looked down the hallway, worried someone might see me, then I turned the page.

"The statements are clear," Gomes wrote. "But the context and application are not."

Gomes argued that the laws laid out in Leviticus were designed to help Jews build a nation in a foreign land. The rules were meant to protect a cultural identity. That's why the verses about sex are flanked by others about cattle and sowing fields. That's why they forbid men from wearing rounded haircuts.

I read the chapter three or four times, then I ran back to my dorm room to find my Bible. My roommate was sleeping, so I took it to the communal bathroom to reread Leviticus. I chose a stall, sat on the toilet, and flipped until I found the right book, until I saw that what Gomes had written was true. Leviticus outlawed all sorts of things my pastors had never mentioned: shrimp, disfigured edges of beards, eating fat or blood. As I read the Bible aloud to myself, Leviticus almost seemed funny. God had thought of every possible sex taboo for men—no sex with your father's brother, none with his wife, none with your daughter-in-law or your brother's wife, none with both a woman and her daughter, and definitely none with your sister, "whether she was born in the same home or elsewhere"—and yet God hadn't said a single thing about women who wanted to sleep with women.

I WROTE THE WORD "lesbian" in my journal a dozen times that fall, but I didn't tell anyone I suspected I was one. I went to frat parties and kissed drunk boys, hoping their sloppy mouths would inspire something in me. I let them fumble under my shirt, and I followed them to their bunk beds, where we twisted around and against each other. No amount of contact with a guy felt as thrilling as spotting a girl I thought might be gay. There were a handful of short-haired girls on campus, all of them seniors the year I was a freshman, but I never worked up the nerve to talk to them. Instead, I ate extra bowls of Lucky Charms so I could sit in the cafeteria long enough to watch the short-haired girls eat. That fall, I rented every Angelina Jolie movie, and I bought a poster of Sarah Jessica Parker because it showed off her abs. *Friends* was still running new episodes then, and when my mom called me every Thursday to discuss the latest one, I pretended to pine for Joey, though I secretly longed for Rachel.

After a few months, I worked up the nerve to tell one person, the liberal arts professor who assigned the Gomes book. I was too scared to say the word "gay" out loud, so I emailed it, and the professor responded with such warmth that I began to daydream about telling my mother. I wrote my mom emails that November, casually trying to explain that I'd been studying the Bible and had learned New and Interesting Things About Sodom and Gomorrah.

> *Did you know Sodom and Gomorrah were already being destroyed before any homosexual acts occurred? It's very possible that the people in Sodom were just being more wicked by basically raping these strangers (i.e. the angels who appeared to them to be strangers). Something had to have been going on BEFORE to make the angels come in the first place. No mention of homosexuality is made as to the reasoning behind the angel's need to come and destroy the nation.*

My mom never responded, and I was too embarrassed to bring it up on the phone. I read and reread Gomes's book that year, hoping I'd missed the sentence I most wanted to find. Though he'd poked holes in the stories my pastors had told me about homosexuality, Gomes stopped short of definitively saying it wasn't a sin. I spent that whole semester agonizing. I couldn't sleep, so I tiptoed outside most nights and prayed out loud in an abandoned stairwell. "*If you're there, God,*" I'd whisper, "*tell me why you made me this way. Take away these feelings.*" I waited whole nights, awake without answer or reprieve. When I did sleep, I dreamed of Gomorrah, of my life crashing into dusty dissolve.

I felt guilty and Hell-bound, but I didn't actually do anything gay beyond daydream my first semester of college. Once a month or so, I'd take the city bus north to a Barnes & Noble on the edge of town, and I'd stuff a *Curve* magazine inside another periodical, then I'd hide in a corner to secretly read about lesbians. I developed imagined crushes on the girls inside. I downloaded the albums the writers suggested, and when I listened to Sleater-Kinney and Tegan and Sara in my dorm room, I pretended I lived in Portland or Vancouver, cities where the lesbian bands lived and played music. I tried, briefly, to find a girlfriend online, but the only gay dating site was PlanetOut, and you had to pay to join. I didn't have a credit card, and even if I had, I couldn't afford the forty-dollar membership fee. My parents had only given me twenty dollars for college, a crisp bill my mom pushed into my hands in a Popeyes bathroom the day they dropped me off. I was so broke when classes started, I had to steal the three-hundred-dollar calculus textbook from the campus bookstore. I worked in the college communications department that fall, but I had to save every minimum-wage paycheck I earned to pay for my second-semester books. PlanetOut cost as much as the geology text I needed to buy. Still, I visited the site every day. If you didn't pay the membership fee, PlanetOut let you see distorted photos of all the options in your region. In Mississippi, the region was the entire South, and the options were six blurry women, but I refreshed the page every afternoon, searching for love in the blur.

That December, school let out for a month, and I vowed to go the entire break without looking at PlanetOut. I went home for Christmas and kissed an ex-boyfriend but felt nothing. That month, at a sleepover in Alexandria, I told my two best friends, Lizz and Sadie, that I was bisexual. Sadie's dad was gay, so I figured they'd be okay with it. Still, I exhaled the word, as if it were a deep breath I'd been holding in my entire life. They piled on top of me, crying and hugging me until we were all exhausted. They fell asleep still strung around me, but I stayed up all night. Saying it out loud, even the half-true version I'd told them, made it real. So I was really gay now. Whatever happened to Toni would happen to me. The sun came up and peeked through the windows in Sadie's living room, but I was crying so hard by then, I could barely make out the rays. I might lose my mom and my church. And for what? The fuzzed faces of PlanetOut?

I LASTED ALL OF January without yearning, but then, in February, I went out for coffee with Lizz one Friday night, and I saw a girl, and I lost my resolve. She was the barista, and when I ordered an Irish cream latte, she told me she liked my shirt. It was a polka-dotted, long-sleeved button-up I'd bought for a dollar at a thrift store. She asked if she could touch it. She didn't look gay, but when she reached for my arm, I knew I would remember that touch for the rest of my life. Her hands were slim, her hair was shoulder-length, and my voice cracked when I tried to speak to her. I told her my name was Casey. She said hers was Ellen, and I thought that must be some kind of sign. The most famous lesbian in the world was named Ellen; how could this girl not like girls, too?

I drank my latte slow, and as I watched Ellen fix other people's coffees, I tried to memorize everything I could about her. She was wearing Granny Smith apple–green shoes. She laughed a lot. She had brown eyes and hair that was either light brown or dark blond, and she looked tiny behind the counter. Between customers, she turned back to me, and I grinned sheepishly. Her smile was a wide, uninhibited square. I was too nervous to ask for her number when my friends and I left that night, so I wrote down my AOL Instant Messenger name, then slid it across the counter while Ellen took out the trash.

She messaged me a few days later, and soon we were sending each other long emails three times a week. We wrote about Alanis Morissette and Allen Ginsberg, and we copied whole sections of Oscar Wilde essays into our emails. We sent each other folk songs and Adrienne Rich poems. I was studying French and Ellen was translating Latin, and in between our schoolwork, I attempted to flirt with her by typing out a primitive winking emoji. We never used words like "gay" or "crush," but I didn't need language or labels to confirm the heat I felt. A month after I met Ellen, I told my roommate I was smitten with a girl.

I tried to describe Ellen, but for the first time in my life, I liked someone too much to put adjectives together. She was cuter than the short-haired seniors, more vivid than the blurry options on PlanetOut. She knew centuries-old poems and songs that seemed not to have been released yet, and, once, at a speech tournament, she performed in what I assumed was a perfect Romanian accent. I spent the little money I had buying coffees so I could see her. She looked at me over the counter with an eye contact I described to my friends as "precise," which is to say her dark eyes searched mine in a way that felt daring. She never looked away. She touched my arms when she handed over my lattes, and I could have spent the rest of the school year listening to her laugh. I sat at the closest table and tried to read my art history textbook, but the Venus de Milo seemed pedestrian compared to the teenage barista whose smile made my heart clang around my ears.

We only went out in public together once—twenty years later, I'm still not sure if it was a date. One Friday night in mid-March 2002, Ellen picked me up, then drove me across town to a fast-casual restaurant that specialized in oversized baked potatoes. She ordered tortilla soup in a bread bowl, an entrée that struck me as sophisticated, and I selected one of the potatoes. When mine showed up covered in hunks of pot roast, I felt embarrassed to be eating something so juvenile and messy. Almost as soon as we started eating, a professor from my college walked into the restaurant with her family, and I lost my appetite. Ellen and I weren't doing anything romantic. We weren't holding hands or even leaning toward each other, but I worried if the professor saw me, she'd know I was gay. I covered my potato with a paper napkin and told Ellen I didn't feel well. She drove me back to my dorm and I ran inside, terrified that everyone in Mississippi would soon know my secret.

A few weeks later, Ellen asked if she could come over after school. We sat on my twin-sized bed listening to Tracy Chapman, and I watched

Ellen's lips with a desire that felt like fear. She wore lip gloss. I'd never kissed anyone who wore lip gloss. I was too nervous to tip toward her, so we talked until the sun set and my room went black, then Ellen reached through the darkness and touched my leg.

"I want to kiss you," she whispered.

I could smell the strawberry in her lip gloss, and the sweetness of it scared me. I stuttered a few syllables, then my dorm room door flew open, and one of the sorority girls who lived across the hall waltzed in.

"Why are y'all sitting in the dark? Freaks."

The girl flipped the light on, and she started rummaging through my roommate's closet. She said she was looking for a belt. I mouthed an apology to Ellen, and the girl spun around, holding a thin black strap my roommate had bought at one of the mall stores I considered girly.

"You don't go to school here," she said, pointing at Ellen.

I grabbed Ellen's arm and pulled her toward the hallway. I didn't say anything as I walked her through the lobby. I pushed the heavy front door open, and Ellen stood in the entrance looking at me long enough to let cold air in.

"I do want to kiss you," she said.

She was a few inches shorter than I was, and looking down at her, I felt our height difference was reason enough to avoid letting our lips touch. I'd only kissed tall boys. It would feel wrong, I thought, to bend down to kiss someone.

"I can't," I told her. Everything inside me ached. I wanted Ellen more than I'd ever wanted anything, but I could feel the force of all my fears thrumming inside me. What if someone saw?

We looked at each other until someone climbed the steps and said they needed to get past us. I told Ellen I had to go. I patted her arm, and as the door shut between us, I sat down on the lobby floor and sobbed.

ELLEN WAS TWO YEARS younger than I was, but she seemed braver, and she came back the next week as if I had never turned her down. We listened to the Pink Floyd song "Wish You Were Here" on repeat, and I turned all the lamps in my dorm room on, just in case the girl across the hall came back. I don't think Ellen and I talked much that night. We mostly stared at each other, and I thought about the way my lamp made her lip gloss glisten. My mouth went dry from wanting. Sometime between our fifth and sixth listen of "Wish You Were Here," I reached for a bottle of Jones Blue Bubblegum soda. I was obsessed with Jones soda then because it seemed twee, more special than the Cokes I grew up drinking four or five times a day. Every bottle came with a unique label and a fortune typed under the cap. I twisted the top off. My hair fell in curly waves then, and Ellen reached out and brushed my bangs up as I read the fortune out loud.

"You must accept the next proposition made to you."

I grinned. Ellen touched my cheek, and I looked up at her. She was timid, more gentle than any boy had ever been with me. I thought about Hell and my mom and the demons the pastor cast out at Live Oak, and I didn't care anymore if I ruined my life.

"This so works out in my favor," she said.

Kissing her felt like melting, like dying and going to a heaven more perfect than the one I'd grown up imagining. I had worried all semester that kissing a girl would feel different than kissing a boy, and it did. Ellen's lips were impossibly soft, soft in a way that surrounded me. She touched my face, then we slipped away from each other before the song ended. I felt too dizzy to speak.

I don't remember when Ellen left, but as soon as she did, I called Lizz. I held the phone up to my computer speaker and played the Jill Sobule song "I Kissed a Girl" as loud as it would go. I didn't care if anyone on my hall heard it. I was happy. Lizz darted across campus to find me, and I told her the story four or five times. I played the song. I showed her the bottle cap, and I described Ellen's lips and hands. I didn't mention Hell or the demons I feared might have taken me over. I went to bed without brushing my teeth, and when I woke up, I ran my tongue over my lips, searching for traces of strawberry in the blue bubblegum.

I HAD TO GO back to Monroe a few days later for Easter, and I worried as I rode west that my mom would somehow see Ellen's lip gloss still shimmering on my mouth. I tried to push the kiss out of my mind for the weekend, but little things made me think of Ellen. My dad made coffee, and I couldn't help but imagine her brewing cups for customers in Jackson. My brother turned a light on after the sun set Saturday night, and I thought about the way Ellen looked under my dorm room lamp. Everything green reminded me of the shoes she wore the first night I saw her. Everything blue made me think of the soda I'd been drinking.

I went to bed early, but I couldn't sleep. I hated not telling my mother how happy I was. I wanted to throw off my covers, storm down the hall, and tell her I finally understood why people loved kissing, that all the good moments in my life added together couldn't compare to the thrill of those few seconds, that I knew what I was, and I didn't want to change it. But I didn't throw my covers off. I didn't get out of bed, and I didn't tell my mother.

The next morning, at church, I followed my mom to our usual spot on the third row. She squeezed my hand as the lights dimmed, and my heart jumped when the choir walked onstage. The spotlight swung left to shine on Cheryl, the short-haired soloist I loved. I looked at my mom, and she nodded. " 'Shout to the Lord,' " she whispered. "I requested this for you."

The keyboardist plucked the first solemn notes, and something wrenched inside me. I heaved shallow breaths. I tried to pray, but I couldn't get out anything more than "Please, God." When Cheryl hit the crescendo, I cried so hard, snot dripped down the front of my dress. I buried my face in my mother's neck.

"I need to tell you something," I said.

I realized as soon as I spoke that I might never hear "Shout to the Lord" again. I didn't want to disappear the way Toni had, but something tugged me forward. Lying was a sin, too, I told myself. My mom smoothed my hair.

"Do you want to go to the altar?" she asked.

I shook my head no. I knew the altar couldn't help me. The choir started in on another chorus, and my mom stood up.

"Okay," she said. "Let's go to the bathroom."

She pulled me down the aisle, and I felt like I was underwater. We squished into a stall. I could hear Cheryl singing in the distance, and eventually her voice gave me the courage to frame my pain as a hunch, a feeling that wouldn't go away. I didn't tell my mom about Ellen or the kiss, and I didn't tell her I knew I would never love a man. I told her the same half-truth I'd told Lizz and Sadie, even though I knew the label was wrong.

"I'm bisexual."

My mom told me she knew. She said when I was younger, back when every boy in our neighborhood was Black, her friends had asked her what she'd do if I married a Black man. Thirty-five years had passed since *Loving v. Virginia* legalized interracial marriage, but in the South, white people still looked down on it.

"I told them I wouldn't care," she said. "I'd just learn to braid Black babies' hair."

I scrunched my face in confusion. Maybe my mom didn't understand what bisexual meant.

"What I'm trying to say," she said, "is if you're going to be a lesbian, then I'll just learn to buy yeast infection cream for two."

I had no idea what she was talking about. I'd seen *The Whole Lesbian Sex Book* tucked into the sociology shelves at Barnes & Noble, but I'd never been brave enough to open it. I didn't know what lesbian sex entailed, or if it would lead to yeast infections. I looked at my mom. I waited for an explanation, but she pushed the stall door open and told me we were leaving church.

We drove away without my dad or brother. We went to Walmart, and my mom bought me a giant box of tampons, then she told me I needed to head back to college. She said she loved me. By the time I made it to Jackson a few hours later, though, she'd changed her mind. Sometime while I was driving east, she booted up the gray desktop computer she kept on our kitchen table, then she emailed me to say my professors had brainwashed me. She told me she wished I'd never moved to Alexandria, because if I hadn't, I wouldn't have met Sadie's gay dad.

"I think of you, and I want to throw up," she wrote. "Even 'Shout to the Lord' is ruined."

THE NEXT WEEK, my family went to church without me. They sang the songs I loved and talked to the people I missed, and when the preacher asked if anyone needed healing, my parents walked toward him, desperate to rid themselves of my secret. The preacher turned off his microphone. He always turned it off when people made their prayer requests. Though the altar was at the front of the church, the preacher believed there were things only God and a pastor should know. He put his hands on my mom's head, and she bent toward him as she whispered her need. I wasn't there, so I don't know what the pastor heard, but my parents told me later that after my mother said the word "homosexual," the preacher fiddled with his microphone, then his voice filled the sanctuary.

"Satan's got ahold of Casey," he announced. "We're going to pray right now. God save her."

My parents told me they closed their eyes and repeated the pastor's words: "God save her."

"Save Casey's soul. Save her and take her life immediately so she can make Heaven her home."

My dad told me he opened his eyes. He stepped away from the preacher.

"Take her?" my dad asked. "Did you just pray that our child dies? That she'll be dead?"

"Dead to this world," the pastor clarified. "But she'll live eternally."

My dad backed up, but my mom stepped forward, still praying. "God save her," she repeated. "Take her."

Chapter Eight

(April 2011)

WHEN LYNDA DESCRIBED the Delhi Pentecost Tabernacle, I'd imagined a holy fortress, the kind of vast complex I'd attended growing up. Family Church's parking lot had been as sprawling as a Walmart Supercenter's, but I could see, as I pulled close, that the tabernacle's lot was only big enough for a dozen vehicles. I steered my rental car into a space, then Aubree, Aaron, and I stepped out into the slanting sun.

I hadn't been to church in nine years, not since my Easter Sunday confession. I'd been so scared at eighteen that the pastor would cast me or a demon out, and I'd worried that Pamela and the youth pastors would stop loving me if they knew I was gay, so after the pastor asked God to take me, I made up my mind to stop loving them first. I didn't answer when Pamela called, and I threw away all my Christian CDs. My mom was right: Even "Shout to the Lord" was ruined. Eventually, I stopped praying, and I stopped feeling all wrong inside when I woke up and did nothing on Sunday mornings. I started reading *The New York Times* every weekend instead.

Aubree and Aaron circled the tabernacle with video cameras, and I leaned against the rental car. The building was tan with white trim, as generic as a dentist's office or an outlet mall in the suburbs, but that kind of facade had once seemed holy to me. Family Church was built from the same tan brick. Standing in the Delhi parking lot, I almost felt as if I were a teenager again. I still remembered the words to all the songs we used to sing, and I could hear Cheryl's voice echoing through the years. My stomach knotted up. I had told myself for nine years that God could not hurt me, but as I stood there, surveying the brick, I realized that losing church had been the most painful thing I'd ever endured. I closed my eyes. Diesel trucks and John Deere tractors motored along the highway behind me, but their rumble faded as I whispered the opening bars of "Shout to the Lord."

I'm sure I was a little dewy-eyed when Aubree and Aaron returned to say they'd captured enough. I twisted around and into the rental car, then I spent the whole drive back to Poverty Point talking about Lynda and the Bible verses that ban women from wearing pants. I still didn't understand how Christians could love a God who would condemn people for cutting their hair or loving someone, but something in me wondered if Lynda was right. What if I'd just read what I wanted to see in Gomes? What if the Bible condemned people like me?

I have tried my entire adult life to stop believing in Hell, but something always stops me. My mother used to tell me that blasphemy is the only unforgivable sin, and sometimes, when I allow myself to think that Christians have misinterpreted the Bible, that Hell isn't a place where fire burns eternal, something inside me shakes. *Blasphemy.* I can still hear the way my mother dragged out the syllables, letting the middle *s* hiss the way I imagined the serpent did in the Garden of Eden. I asked her once what the word meant, and she told me it's when you tell yourself that God and Hell don't exist. "Even if you think it only once, you'll spend eternity on fire," she said. "And you'll never burn up, you'll just feel the flames licking at your skin, and it will be so hot you'll beg Satan to just go ahead and kill you, but he won't, and you'll never fall asleep, and you'll never feel relief, and everyone you love will forget you, so they won't know you're crying, and you'll beg God for mercy, but he won't hear you anymore, and the pain will go on forever."

I've given up so much that I held on to as a kid. I don't go to church, and I don't eat TV dinners. I walk if my destination is anywhere within a mile. But no matter how much I transform myself, this early fear of eternal damnation has remained stitched into my essential makeup. I want to stop believing, but my mother's words slink back: *Even once, and the pain will go on forever.* I tell myself her vision sounds ridiculous, but then a lower, more assured voice inside me whispers back: *But what if she's right?*

I parked the car in front of cabin 7, but I didn't want to go inside yet.

I sat on the deck for a while and watched birds dive into the lake. The bugs buzzed louder as the sun sank, but all I could hear was Cheryl's voice ringing in my head. My mom's brother still attended Family Church, so I knew, from seeing his Facebook photos, that everyone I used to know still attended every Sunday. Pamela still sat in the far left corner. The pastor still moved across the same stage wearing the same expensive suits, and Cheryl still sang in the choir. Who would I be if I'd never left? I loved getting up and reading *The New York Times* every Sunday morning, but I didn't feel rooted the way I had when I was young.

The sun slid down the skyline and melted into the lake. I waited until the sky was dark and the boats across the water turned on their headlights, then I stepped inside and told Aubree I thought we should go to church in the morning.

"Roy's church," I said.

I wasn't ready to face the tan brick or the songs I assumed they sang at the Pentecost Tabernacle, but I needed to see the church that accepted Roy after Lynda's preacher kicked him out.

THE CHURCH OF CHRIST was on Delhi's main drag, just a few blocks from Hell Street. It was a split-level building with a pitched roof and a covered walkway. The tiny parking lot was jammed with pickup trucks and SUVs when we arrived at 10:15, so I parked down the road on a gravel patch in front of a house that looked vacant. I normally walk so fast that my friends beg me to slow down, but that day, I took my time strolling toward the church. My legs stung with fear. My mom used to tell me if we didn't ask forgiveness for all our sins before walking into church, God might strike us dead right there in the doorway. I didn't want to believe that was true, but as we drew closer to the building, I whispered, "God, please forgive me for all my sins."

Just before we made it to the door, I saw myself in the reflection of a dark-colored pickup. My hair was a mess, and I hadn't worn a dress in years, so I'd shaken out a pair of black dress pants and a wrinkled button-down shirt that morning. I saw now that I looked conspicuously gay. I gulped three breaths, then prayed again: *"Please don't let them kick us out."*

The door to the sanctuary was propped open, so we slipped inside, then found seats in the back pew. I looked around. The Church of Christ had the same blue-floored, water-filled baptistry that Live Oak had had when I was young, and the cherry-stained pulpit looked just like the one at Family Church, but Lynda had been right: This church was different. I didn't see instruments anywhere, and the pews were all wood with hymnals tucked into the back. Both Family Church and Live Oak had had plush rows. We never used hymnals.

At the front of the sanctuary, a sign noted that twenty people had attended last week's service, and those twenty people had contributed more than a thousand dollars to the offering. I worked the numbers in my head. Each person must have given at least fifty dollars.

Most everyone there that Sunday was old, but the couple sitting in front of us was young, and they had what looked to be a newborn baby sleeping between them in a car seat. Another young family sat just left of me, and they nodded as they sat down right at 10:30. Someone coughed, as if on cue. An assistant pastor walked up to the pulpit, then read off the prayer list, a dozen names of people afflicted by things the assistant pastor didn't mention. He prayed in the name of "our most righteous heavenly father." He asked God to grant us all everlasting life, and I thought of the mansion my mom used to tell me I'd receive in Heaven.

"Now y'all open your hymnals," the assistant pastor said. "We'll do the first, second, and fourth verses."

Everyone around us began to sing, atonally, without melody. They went in rounds, the men first, then the women right behind them. They sang about surviving through God, then they shifted to another hymn, a song so slow I couldn't make out any of the lyrics until I grabbed a hymnal myself. It was erudite but plaintive, full of phrases like "ebon pinion" and "brooded o'er the vale," and as everyone around me sang, "Let this cup of anguish pass from me," I wondered if Roy had ever sung that line.

None of the songs moved me. They didn't have the pop of "My Redeemer Lives" nor the swelling, soul-filling key change that made me cry halfway through "Shout to the Lord." The songs the Church of Christ members sang that day just droned. I wondered how anyone ever found God in those notes. The assistant pastor prayed a second and third time, again in the name of our most righteous heavenly father, then an old man with loose jowls and a hang-dog expression climbed the carpeted steps toward the pulpit. He had a bald head, a red face, and big ears that stuck out past the few tufts of white hair he still had. I realized he was the preacher.

"The lesson today is about truth and love," he said, "two of the most important words in our language."

His name was Wilford Burgess. He'd been the minister there fifteen years. That Sunday, Pastor Burgess wore a mint-green shirt under a suit the color of a latte, and he preached in a slow bass that put Aaron to sleep. I kicked Aaron and he woke up, then started snoring a few seconds later. The preacher didn't seem to notice. For thirty minutes, he read scriptures and marveled at how great love is.

"I guess you can say God thought love up, because he invented it."

It was a humble sermon, very unlike the ones I grew up listening to. Pastor Burgess didn't talk about demons, and he didn't preach about sin. He just went on and on about love.

"If you don't have love, remember what Paul says in First Corinthians? 'If I have not love, I am nothing. If I have all the wisdom and all the knowledge and don't have love, I'm nothing.' What is true love anyway? That is one of the hardest words to define, to give scripture to. When you have love, it takes on its own personality. It shows. It's like the light. You can't hide it under a bushel."

My chest relaxed, and my legs stopped stinging. Of course this was the kind of man who'd accepted Roy. Pastor Burgess wasn't charismatic, but he did seem kind, and maybe Roy needed that kind of person in his life. Maybe *I* needed that kind of person in my life. I so rarely told people then that I loved them. I spent my time working or reading, and I never went to see my family unless I was in Louisiana working on this documentary. I didn't know how to open myself to love, but I wanted to.

"Paul says examine yourselves," Pastor Burgess said. "Do you ever give time to meditate on who you really are? What you're doing, where you're going? Do you ever look deep down in your heart and say, 'Who am I? Why am I in this world?' Look to yourselves."

He lumbered down the carpeted steps, then the congregation stood and sang another song about suffering. They did all four verses. Afterward, they tucked the hymnals into the backs of the pews in front of them, and they embraced each other. I half hugged the young couple sitting next to me, then I followed a line of people toward what they called a fellowship hall. It was just one room, a kitchen with linoleum floors and six long card tables set up with casseroles and canned vegetables. Someone had brewed a big pitcher of sweet tea, and someone else had baked a pineapple upside-down cake. An ancient-looking man who said he owned a store in Tallulah called Crazy Bob's handed me a Styrofoam plate. He told me to fill it up. I spooned out some green beans and a Velveeta-covered noodle dish my mom called chicken tetrazzini. I'd gone without canned vegetables almost as long as I'd gone without church, but I took a bite of green beans, and the limp legumes tasted like every dinner my mom had ever made. I peeked at my cell phone, hoping she had called. We were supposed to meet back in Monroe later, maybe for dinner, but I didn't want to wait until nighttime to tell her that some foods would always remind me of her. My cell phone screen was blank, though. She hadn't tried to call. I put the phone back in my pocket, and I turned to Crazy Bob.

"You know," I said, "I grew up eating at potlucks like this every Sunday."

Crazy Bob faked a wide-eyed surprise. "Now you ain't telling me you had food as good as this before." He forked a big mouthful of chicken-and-Ritz-cracker casserole into his mouth. He winked at me and licked the fork clean.

"Hey," I said in a coy, teasing tone, "you haven't had my mom's manicotti."

My tape recorder ran out of batteries halfway through the meal, and nearly a decade has passed since that Sunday, so I don't remember what we talked about as we ate. But I remember I felt happy. Sometimes, when I'm around other Southerners, my good grammar gives, and I talk the way I used to talk when I was little. I say "tooken" instead of "taken," "seen" instead of "saw," and I add an extra "them" before nouns, as in "Can you hand me one of them pickles?" I'm sure I did so that day, and I'm sure I felt relieved to talk the way my brain naturally works. I know I was still smiling an hour later, because Aubree and Aaron filmed me interviewing the pastor and a woman who knew Roy.

Her name was Ann Kimble, "used to be McVay," she said. She was the older sister of Tommy McVay, the skinny man I'd interviewed on the first trip with my mother. Tommy had died a few months after I interviewed him, Ann told me. He was sixty-five. Ann didn't say why Tommy died, and I didn't ask. She sat on the front row next to the preacher, and I sat next to them.

Ann had on a yellow jacket over a yellow shirt, and her electric-blue skirt had yellow accents in it, too. I knew, from Tommy, that the McVays had grown up poor on Hell Street, and I didn't think she was rich now. She didn't talk the way I thought rich people talked, and she was missing her first left molar, leaving a hole I thought no rich person would let go unfilled. But she was wearing a pearl bracelet, pearl earrings, and a matching necklace, accessories that suggested some sort of ambition, even if the pearls were fake. She was heavyset, and her hair was short and curled the way I now realized all middle-aged women in the South wore theirs. I asked Ann what she remembered about Roy. She leaned forward and shrugged.

"Well, mostly, the only thing that I knew about her was she sat on her front porch and played her guitar."

I said I'd noticed they didn't play instruments at the Church of Christ, and the pastor shook his head in affirmation. He told me theirs was a fundamentalist congregation.

"We get our directions," he said, stumbling over his words. "If the Bible speaks it, we speak it. If the Bible is silent, we're silent. We partake of Communion every Sunday because we have a biblical illustration of that. We don't sing with instrumental music because it doesn't say anywhere in the New Testament. There's no illustration for that. There's no precedent for instruments."

I shook my head as if the pastor were making perfect sense. I could think of lots of things that aren't in the Bible that they'd used in church that Sunday, but I had nothing to gain by bringing up microphones or electric lights. Instead, I asked Ann and the preacher if they remembered where Roy sat when he came to church. They pointed to the back of the room, to the row where we'd sat during the sermon.

"Very last pew," Pastor Burgess said.

"Right on the corner," Ann added.

Ann said Roy spent most of the services writing. He kept a book in the pew next to his hymnal, and every Sunday, he listed everyone who'd attended and everyone who'd been baptized. He took notes on the sermons, too, Ann thought, but the book had disappeared long ago, and Ann wasn't sure how to find it. As Ann talked, we all looked to the back pew, and I wondered if everyone was imagining Roy hunched over a little book, scribbling notes.

"Pastor," I said, "you were talking in today's sermon about 'Who am I?' and 'What is my place in this world?' If someone asked you that about Roy—who was Roy, what was Roy's place—do you have any idea?"

"Oh yeah," Pastor Burgess answered. "She was a sister in Christ."

My pulse jumped. Everyone in Delhi called Roy "she," so I was used to that, but "sister" was a new one. Had this pastor called Roy "sister" when they talked? Did Roy mind that honorific? I still wasn't sure which pronoun Roy would have wanted me to use, but something—maybe it was my gut, or maybe it was my grandma's lead—told me to think of Roy as *he,* a brother in Christ.

"Everyone here stood ready to help her," the pastor continued. "She wasn't very talkative, but people were aware that she needed help. People at the church, I think, treated her extremely well. I think they tried to. I think Roy could have had a whole lot more fellowship with us. She wouldn't hang around and talk, and that probably had to do with her upbringing. But I never knew of anyone who said anything negative about her, and that's one of the things that's great about this church. It's very peaceful, not a lot of gossip."

As the preacher talked, I realized that he might have been the one to speak at Roy's funeral. Roy's obituary hadn't listed any survivors, but I'd seen his tombstone. It was nice, a marble slab engraved with flowers and praying hands. I asked if they knew who'd made that headstone.

"Well, she had a plot," Ann said. "It was by her mother and dad over there, the Ellises. When she passed away, we didn't know if she had enough money to buy a headstone, so I called the funeral home and said we're going to take care of it. I knew she liked pants and a shirt, so that's what I went and bought. That's what she was buried in."

"I did a graveside service," Pastor Burgess said. "It was brief. It was about Roy's faithfulness, always attending, a good person, a kind person. I believe the weather wasn't too nice. If it had been here at the church, I'd have lengthened it out a little bit."

I asked how many people came, and the pastor shook his head and said not many. "The weather was bad."

Later, I looked up the newspaper from the day of Roy's funeral and

I found that the pastor had been right: It had rained the day they buried Roy. I don't know why I didn't ask then why the church didn't move Roy's funeral inside, and I never got a chance to ask later because I never saw the preacher again. His wife died a few months after the interview, and Pastor Burgess left the Church of Christ. He died, too, in 2014. Almost everyone I interviewed during those first few trips died before I could see them again. Dorothy the historian died less than a year after we interviewed her, and Rufus the police chief died in 2012. Mary Rundell died, and Lynda Best died, and so did several members of my family. But that Sunday, I was naive enough to think that everyone would live at least until I finished the movie, so I shook the pastor's hand and told him we'd come back the next time we were in town.

Ann started to walk us out, but she remembered, as we pushed through the double doors into the fellowship hall, that she had a picture of Roy somewhere, so she led us to an office supply closet. Ann pulled down rolls of paper towels and calendars for long-gone years. She looked into a plastic bag. She moved aside Christmas decorations, and I spotted a photo album, a red one with gold lettering. Ann licked her index finger, then used it to flip through the album's pages. Most of the pictures were old family portraits, groups of three or four posed in front of a white wall. There were a few solo shots, but no one looked like Roy.

"She didn't like to get her picture made too much," Ann said.

Ann flipped another few pages, past snapshots of what looked like a beach vacation. She lingered for a moment on a page that showed the congregation standing in front of the pews, but she couldn't find Roy in the back row. She flipped slow, then fast, and finally, two pages from the end of the album, I spotted a person who looked like Roy. I pointed to the picture.

"Is that . . ." I asked Ann.

"Yeah, that's her, right there," she said. "At one of our fellowships."

In the picture, Roy was wearing a flower-print button-down with suspenders fastened over it. He had on black, plastic-frame glasses, and he was holding a paper plate that was mostly cut off by the picture's frame. Behind him, people were digging into plastic Tupperware bowls filled with macaroni or potato salad.

"I like that shirt," I said.

Ann looked closer at the photo, then she turned to me.

"Do you?" she asked. Her tone suggested she did not.

She kept searching. She pulled down boxes and other photo albums, but she couldn't find any other pictures of Roy. After a while, Ann's husband appeared and asked if we knew anything about Roy's music.

"She wrote a bunch of songs," he said. "She had a whole book full. Don't know where the book ended up, but she wrote songs and sent them to Nashville to different people."

Ann put the photos down and shook her head in agreement. "I don't know whatever happened to all of that stuff."

They were quiet, and we were quiet, but in my mind, I was thinking I knew what had happened to Roy's songs. His old neighbor, Mark King, probably had them.

Ann shut off the lights, and Aubree and Aaron filmed the hallway as we walked down it. We were just a few steps from the side door, a few seconds from leaving, but suddenly, I didn't feel ready to go. I sneaked back into the sanctuary. I sat in the back pew. I reached for one of the Bibles wedged between the hymnals, and I opened it to Leviticus, chapter 19. *"Abomination,"* it said.

Chapter Nine

(April–May 2011)

THE DAY WAS MORE than half over by the time we left Delhi for the interstate. The sky went pink at the edges, and the evening bugs came to splattery ends on my windshield as I drove toward West Monroe. Ten miles in, my phone buzzed with a message.

"Change of plans," my mom wrote. "Yr interviewing Jennifer. She worked at Delhi nursing home when Roy was there."

Jennifer was my cousin. She was only four years older than I was, but we hadn't spoken in years, maybe even a decade by then. We weren't Facebook friends, and I didn't have her phone number. I knew she'd had her first child when she was fifteen, and I'd heard that her son's father had promised, before they had sex, that he couldn't get her pregnant because he'd once peed on an electric fence. But I didn't know what Jennifer liked to do or what kind of music she liked, and I wasn't sure whose fault that was. Had she ever wanted to be close to me? Her mom, my aunt Cindy, talked to my mom every day, but I never asked for updates about Jennifer or her brother, Joey. I'd heard, in college maybe, that Jennifer was addicted to drugs—just "drugs," not a specific one—and I suppose I had stopped talking to her then. Or maybe I distanced myself years before that. I'd told myself that Jennifer and I were different, and that had seemed excuse enough to me once.

My mom sent an address and something like directions, and as I drove, I pressed myself to conjure any other memories. I could hear Jennifer's voice in my head. It was high-pitched and twangy. And I remembered that when we were kids Jennifer and Joey always opened their presents on Christmas Eve. They had a white-flocked tree, but I don't remember any of the presents they ever opened. Once, the year before Jennifer got pregnant, my aunt Cindy took her to the mall to have Glamour Shots made. When the prints came back, my mother gave me one and asked if I wanted to have ours done. I stared at the eight-by-ten and tried to cook up a response. The photo made Jennifer and my aunt look like characters from the TV show *Dallas*. They wore earrings the size of fists, and their hair was teased toward heaven. Jennifer's dress was made out of what appeared to be a red feather boa. My aunt wore matching red gloves. I looked as long as I dared, then I laughed, handed the photo back to my mom, and told her I'd rather die than let someone do that to my hair. My grandma kept one of the Glamour Shots framed on the wall in her bedroom, and because that was the only photo I'd seen of Jennifer in years, I half imagined she'd answer the door wearing that feather boa dress.

Jennifer lived in a generic, just-off-the-highway apartment in a two-story complex that looked more like a motel than a forever home. It was income-restricted, meaning everyone who lived there was poor, but the wooden sign out front said OLD OAK ESTATES, as if it were an acres-big property where rich people dwelled. I looked around as I stepped out of the car. I didn't see oak trees, only pines. Jennifer's two-bedroom was on the top floor, and as we climbed the metal steps, I recognized her eleven-year-old daughter, Olivia, blowing bubbles off the shared walkway. I'd never met Olivia, but my mom sometimes texted me pictures of her. Olivia smiled when she saw us, then she drew in a deep breath and pushed out a perfect bubble. Her hair was pulled back in a messy ponytail, and her glasses were so thick, her eyes looked huge behind them. I'd never wanted to be a mother, but watching Olivia, something new and unexpectedly maternal ached in me.

A cat, I told myself. *I could adopt a cat.*

The apartments were brick and white vinyl with teal doors, and Jennifer had draped what looked to be parts of a Christmas garland around the threshold, even though it was spring. She was expecting us, so her door was cracked open. I pushed inside. She was not wearing the feather boa, but I barely had time to notice her white T-shirt and jeans, because she rushed to hug me as if we were the kind of relatives who knew each other. When I pulled away, Jennifer waved a hand around the empty living room. She'd hung crosses on the walls, but she didn't have a couch or a coffee table.

"The carpet's clean, I think," she said. "I just moved in."

We sat down, cross-legged and facing each other, and I eyed Jennifer as Aubree angled a fancy video light toward her. Jennifer's hair was blond and shoulder length. She wore mascara and a lot of eyeliner, and the dark makeup made her blue eyes look bluer. She was thirty-two, and she looked exactly that age, I thought, still young, but a little wrinkled around the eyes.

"She rode in my car," Jennifer said suddenly.

"Who did?" I asked.

"Roy. She got food stamps, and she liked these lemon-lime sodas. It was like a throw-off Sprite."

Jennifer started to say more, but she stuttered and covered the wireless microphone Aaron had clipped to her scoop-neck tee. She leaned sideways and whispered to me.

"I don't know whether to call him a he or a she. I'm torn."

If I were doing this now, I would tell Jennifer to say "he." All the evidence I had suggested Roy would have felt more comfortable with male pronouns, but back then, in early May 2011, I was insecure and finding my way. People didn't talk as much about pronouns then, and I wasn't brave enough to be the person who went around Louisiana educating interviewees on the ways a pronoun can either empower or belittle someone. That wasn't my role as a journalist, I thought. And so, Jennifer gave me an opening, but I didn't take it. I've watched most of the video footage half a dozen times or more, and I always feel disappointed in myself. I watch and I knot my fingers together, hoping, somehow, miraculously, this time I will tell Jennifer to say "he," but I never do. After Jennifer told me she was torn, I waved away her worries and told her to use whichever pronoun she preferred. Jennifer nodded, then leaned back into the video frame. She said she'd worked in accounts payable at the nursing home when Roy arrived in 2003.

"Whenever he first got there, they tried to put him in a dress. Put her in a dress, I mean. I guess they thought that that would be normal because everybody knew Roy was really not a man."

Jennifer said the activities director, a woman named Maxine, put

Roy in the dress, then painted his fingernails pink. Afterward, Roy refused to leave his room. He didn't move or talk or eat for two days.

"He was not a woman," Jennifer said. "That's like taking me and putting me in a pair of overalls and a hat and telling me I can't wear heels again. I am a woman. That's what I want to wear. Roy wanted to live as a man. He wanted a red flannel shirt with a white T-shirt underneath. A trucker hat, that's what he always wore. It was blue and had a long bill, and he wore these cop glasses like the Unabomber."

As she talked, I wondered why I'd gone so long without calling Jennifer. She seemed cool, curious, and open-minded. She said that a few days after Roy stopped eating, Maxine gave up. Maxine went into Roy's room and removed the fingernail polish, then she brought Roy the flannel shirt and brown belt he'd been wearing when he arrived. The belt had his last name stamped into the leather, Jennifer said, and once Roy had it back, he left his room and said he wanted to go to the store.

"I took everybody everywhere," Jennifer explained. "I'm real friendly, real bubbly, you know, so we went to Brookshire's. And Roy wasn't big enough to push the buggy, he was real short. He wanted lemon-lime sodas, Cheetos, Pringles, Twinkies, Ding Dongs, and he had twenty-seven dollars. That's what they gave him on his food stamps, twenty-seven dollars a month. Not just in the nursing home, either. That's what they expected him to live on outside of the nursing home. That's what the Louisiana government gave him to live on. Can you imagine? Twenty-seven dollars a month? That's not enough money to feed nothing. And Roy had no taxable income because he just mowed yards and collected cans."

At work, I'd been trying to learn about welfare and other social services, but Jennifer understood them in a way no website had ever made clear to me. She knew the income cutoffs for everything. She knew where to apply for Medicaid and who to call if a benefit didn't come through, and she seemed to have memorized the entire flowchart of the state Department of Health and Hospitals. At one point, she recommended I call an ombudsman. She even recited the phone number.

Eventually, Jennifer leaned forward, conspiratorially. "About a week before Roy passed away, something happened in that nursing home. He fell out of the bed. Or he was pushed out of that bed."

Jennifer raised her left eyebrow. She said Roy emerged from the room with "a giant hematoma" covering his face. As she talked, Jennifer used her hand to cover her own eyes, cheeks, and lips, to show me how much of Roy's skin had turned black after the fall.

"They would not let him out of his room because he was *that* horrifying. They let him stay there seven days. Finally, they took him to the hospital, and he died the next day."

Jennifer remembered the exact date—the right date, March 8—that Roy died, and she remembered helping file the incident report after he fell out of bed March 1. She said two state workers from the Department of Health and Hospitals came to the nursing home to investigate Roy's death.

"Even if they don't have findings, the whole investigation is public record," she said. "You need to get it."

I smiled. Why did everyone in my family sound like an amateur journalist? My mom had cajoled people on the first trip, now Jennifer was pushing me, talking tough the way good editors do. She was suspicious and direct, and as she talked, I thought I must be the least naturally qualified member of my family to be conducting this probe.

Jennifer rocked in excitement. Most of the people we'd interviewed so far had been old and low-key. They didn't raise their voices or move around much as they reminisced, but Jennifer spoke with a buzzy energy. She talked fast. She waved her hands around, and she giggled after she revealed something interesting.

"I don't think he fell," she said again. "I think someone pushed him."

What Jennifer was suggesting was huge. She was saying, on camera, that she believed someone in the nursing home might have killed Roy. I wasn't sure whether to believe her. Everyone in my family has always been a legendary exaggerator. I never knew which parts of my mom's and grandmother's stories were real, and which were details they'd spun to make a tale bigger. My mom believed this was just a part of being Southern. Good Southern women added butter to their canned vegetables. They caked their faces with makeup, and they never told a story exactly as it happened. I found my mom's tendency to fudge frustrating. How could I accept any of her stories, knowing some part of them was made up?

I felt sure Jennifer had inherited some of that tall-telling, but just in case she was talking to me straight, I asked why she thought someone might have pushed Roy out of the bed. She bit her lip.

"How do I put this without it coming off the wrong way?" she asked. "When you have someone that you know is one way, but they want to live another way, it might frustrate some people. If somebody's incontinent and can't hold their own bowels, and they're not going to let somebody change their diaper, well, that would make some CNAs mad. But that's not his fault. If he don't want nobody down his pants, that's his own business."

Jennifer meant Roy, I realized. Roy didn't want anyone to change his diaper.

I'd tried to steer all my interviews away from the subject of Roy's body. Even in 2011, I knew that most transgender people didn't want to talk about their bodies, and it felt wrong to discuss Roy's physique without his permission. I wanted to talk about the kidnapping. I wanted to learn what Roy had been like, how he'd suffered and endured. But everyone I interviewed talked about Roy's body at some point. They speculated. They swore they'd seen things. Jennifer didn't do either, exactly, but what she didn't say implied as much as what other people had.

We were silent for maybe half a minute, the longest we'd been quiet since we arrived, then Jennifer pitched toward me again.

"Right after Roy died, within like a week, these three people came up from Baton Rouge, two women and one man, claiming to be his family. As far as we knew, Roy didn't have a family."

Jennifer said the strangers looked like they were in their forties, and they showed up wearing suits. They were businesspeople, Jennifer thought, or at least people trying to look like businesspeople, but they couldn't produce any proof that they'd been related to Roy. The nursing home administrator told the strangers that he could accept a family Bible, anything with Roy's name written in the lineage, as proof, but the businesspeople didn't have anything like that.

"How they knew Roy was there, that was the strange part, really," Jennifer said.

The businesspeople came to the nursing home asking for a deed to

Roy's house, the house he rented. They wanted everything inside, anything personal Roy owned.

"They wanted what you're wanting," Jennifer said, a little too knowing for my comfort.

I squirmed on the carpet. Was I really as bad as the fake businesspeople from Baton Rouge? I did want to read Roy's journals, but I wasn't willing to pretend to be his family member to get them. My intentions were good, I thought. I wanted to know Roy. I wanted to understand what his life had been like, and I wanted to find his poems so people could read them.

Jennifer kept talking, unprompted. "There was a woman in Delhi, Miss King? Is there a Miss King?"

My ears went hot. I shook my head yes. There was a Miss King who knew Roy. I told Jennifer about the long, obsequious note I'd sent two years earlier, asking Cheryl and Mark King to talk to me about Roy.

"Cheryl wrote back only one sentence," I told Jennifer. "She told me to stay away from Roy's story."

Jennifer's eyes narrowed.

"That's big red flags to me," she said. "It really sounds like there's something they don't want somebody to know."

Jennifer said Cheryl King, or at least the woman Jennifer believed to be Cheryl King, came up to the nursing home right after the businesspeople did. She told the nursing home not to let anyone have anything of Roy's. Jennifer remembered Cheryl shouting, "Roy has no family. Roy has nobody." The whole outburst seemed suspicious, Jennifer said. Cheryl and Mark had put Roy in the nursing home, but they'd never returned to visit him. Why did they care if people from Baton Rouge wanted the little things Roy left behind?

"The Kings might have something to hide, you hear me?" Jennifer said. "I have a bad feeling about them. There's evil things that happen in small towns like that. I've always heard Delhi was the gateway to Hell. Between Tallulah, St. Joe, and Delhi, they say it makes a pentagram from an aerial view. No shit, that's voodoo stuff, if you believe in it."

She sat back, eyebrows raised and arms folded over her chest. I could already imagine how good she'd sound in the documentary. She was just the tension the story needed. All I had to do was find proof to bolster her claims.

"I bet the Kings took Roy's money," she continued.

I told her I didn't think that was possible. The Kings lived in a single-wide trailer. It looked well maintained, but it wasn't fancy. And anyway, how much money could Roy have left behind to steal? Jennifer had said herself he had no taxable income, and I doubted people in Delhi were paying top dollar for a mowed lawn. Maybe, I suggested, the Kings were just trying to protect Roy.

"Protect him from what?"

"Maybe they think people are out to make fun of him, I don't know. Maybe they thought I was like the businesspeople from Baton Rouge, out to get all of Roy's stuff."

Jennifer exhaled hard, as if she were exasperated with how stupid I sounded. She looked me in the eyes, straight on.

"You've obviously connected spiritually with this person. You've came all the way across the country. You think anybody else has ever done that for him? You're going out of your way, spending money on this person, trying to figure out just a little bit of what his life was like. You think anybody else did that? For Roy? No."

She leaned back, smiled big, and told me she thought I was cool. It moved me more than I wanted to admit. I'd been telling people for the past few years that I was spending all my vacation time traveling to rural Louisiana just because Roy's life was interesting, but Jennifer was the first person to speak a truth I hadn't yet acknowledged to myself. I did feel connected to Roy. It wasn't just that he felt like some kind of queer ancestor. His life felt to me like a cautionary tale. As much as I told myself that I liked living in my Portland apartment alone and away from all my relatives, I did worry I'd end up alone and misplaced. I kept digging into Roy's life hoping some stray fact might reveal something to me. I wasn't sure what I hoped might be revealed, but I knew I didn't want to die feeling as if I'd never fit anywhere. I'd tried to hide that connection in Delhi because I feared if people knew, they'd judge me or pray their own versions of the "save her and take her" plea my pastor had once invoked. But Jennifer didn't look ready to condemn me. She was staring at me with what I had to admit was admiration. I smiled a kind of bashful grin. I felt so exposed. How could this cousin I never talked to know me so well? I haven't seen Jennifer since that evening, but a few times a year, I plug in my hard drive and watch the video of our interview, and I remember that she *wanted* to accept me. She wanted to be a part of my strange project, and what's more, she wanted to affirm that what I was doing was good and right. Occasionally, I think about writing to her. We're Facebook friends now, and occasionally she sends me a meme with an uplifting message, and I click the heart emoji, then I turn my computer off. *Thank you*, I imagine myself typing. *Thank you for seeing me.* I never write, though. It's not that I'm scared of anything in particular; I just don't know how to be close to my family. What would Jennifer and I talk about if I reached out to her? Roy? How long could we talk about him? Would I ever get to the point where I wanted to tell her about *my* life? It was obvious to me that day in her apartment that she would not reject me, but still, I hover over her name on Facebook, and I never click send.

"You're not trying to get nothing at all," Jennifer said. "You're just trying to tell a story of somebody that you're relating to."

"Yeah," I said. I think I felt encouraged. I was still squaring with my own unresolved guilt, still wondering if I was prying into someone's life when I shouldn't have been, and Jennifer's comments assuaged that nagging fear.

"We're going to go knock on the Kings' door," I said.

"Do it. Be persistent."

Jennifer said she would call one of her old nursing home coworkers for us to see if she could get what she called Roy's "social chart."

"The record that you want is right behind the nursing home in the file house. If my friend won't bring it to me, I'll go over there and break into it for you. I'm dead serious."

Aaron looked from behind the video camera, alarmed. He told Jennifer we didn't want any trouble. Jennifer laughed.

"In Delhi? I wouldn't get in trouble in Delhi, please. Bond's twelve dollars. I promise you, there's no security alarms. There's nothing. This is just a house that the nursing home rented. But they destroy stuff every ten years. And what year did Roy die?"

"2006," I said. She counted the years on her fingers, then she looked me stern in the eye.

"Okay," she said. "You got five years left."

———

THE NEXT MORNING, I lingered around the cabin, drinking coffee and watching white birds swoop across the lake. By the time Aubree, Aaron, and I ventured outside, it was noon, and the car door handle burned so hot I jumped when I grabbed it. I drove around town, trying to work up the nerve to visit the Kings. Downtown Delhi was clear of cars, so there was nothing to see but old houses and trailers whose aluminum siding peeled away in rusty sheets. A pack of stray dogs trotted down the middle of Main Street, and I wondered if the town had looked that desolate when my mom lived there.

I drove past the Kings' trailer once, then I circled back and parked on the other side of the street. A man was mowing the lawn, and I figured he must be Mark. I ran my hands over the steering wheel, and I took three deep breaths. I knew I couldn't stall any longer. We got out of the car, and whatever stinging fear I'd felt walking into Roy's church seemed benign now. I don't know what I thought Mark might do to me, but my legs shook as I watched him. Aaron started taping as soon as I closed the car door, so I know I waited three and a half minutes before I ventured into the Kings' yard. The lawn mower was loud. I waved at Mark.

"Hi," I called.

He shut the engine off.

"Hello," he said.

His voice was friendly and contained not even a hint of suspicion. He took a few steps forward, so I did, too. He was wearing a red T-shirt and a red baseball cap and the kind of wire-frame aviator glasses people in Portland wore ironically.

"I'm Casey," I said, trying my best to sound nonthreatening. "My grandma grew up on this street, and we were making a tribute video of Roy who used to live here. Miss Mary Rundell said you might have known Roy."

He took off a pair of garden gloves, then used them to wipe the sweat off his forehead. All the hair showing from underneath his baseball cap was white. He was tall and slim, save for a small, rounded potbelly, and he stood straight up without any kind of bend in his back. He held his right hand out to me.

"Mark," he said. "I know Roy. Knew Roy."

A low-riding car eased by, blasting the kind of keyboard-heavy rap music popular in Louisiana then. I asked Mark if he'd be willing to tell us anything about Roy, and he balled the garden gloves together and clenched them in his hands. He shook his head no.

"Royce was a real private person. I didn't really know a whole lot about her, except she told me she was an orphan. She was left on the steps of the orphanage at Little Rock, Arkansas. Her mother just left her there as an infant, and she stayed there for a while. I don't think she ever told me how long. When I first moved here, I didn't really see a lot of Roy because she was so busy. Roy mowed yards. At one time, she had about twenty-five yards. And she also worked at the washateria over here on this side of town for the Duckworth family. She would get up real early in the morning and go open up the washateria. A lot of times she'd stay there all day, just helping people, just watching everything to see if there was any problems with the machines."

Mark talked for a while without stopping, and the shake in my legs subsided. I didn't understand why he sometimes used the name "Roy" and sometimes called him "Royce," but Mark seemed to be the kind of Southerner who just kept talking, even though he'd said he didn't want to talk. Maybe, I thought, he'd let us see the journals after all.

"Of course, you know, she dressed like a man," Mark said. "Of course, she worked like a man, mowing all those yards and everything. She didn't really want people to know she was a woman because she felt like she'd be safer if they didn't know. I taught school over here, and the kids were always asking me, 'Who is that person who lives over next to you? Is that a man or a woman?' I'd say, 'It's a man.'"

Mark walked away from his lawn mower and waved us to the other side of his trailer. He said he wanted to show us the plot where Roy's house had sat.

"When I moved here, Roy had a lot of people who came to visit her. She was a very religious person, played a lot of religious tapes and stuff. We'd talk religion every once in a while, but I'm not real big on that myself, you know?"

Mark motioned around the yard as he talked, as if he were showing us exactly where those conversations had taken place. A ring of trees circled the empty plot that used to be Roy's. I peered up at the high-arcing branches, attempting to figure out which species Roy must have seen each day. I'd been trying for months to learn the names of trees because I'd gotten in my head that I'd never be a good narrative journalist if I couldn't describe the natural world. I'd checked out books from the library, intending to memorize every branch and shade of bark, but those guides didn't seem useful now. None of Roy's feathery leaves looked familiar. The wind blew through them, and I turned back to Mark.

"Did Roy still play music by the time you moved here?"

Mark shook his head in a way that suggested the answer was complicated.

"Royce played a little bit of music when I moved here, but most of that was over by that time. Roy told me she'd written music, though. And she told me that one of her songs was bought, I think, for three hundred dollars, by a group called the Whites."

Mark told us he thought the Whites were a country gospel group, but he wasn't sure. He said he'd collected more than four thousand records from all different genres, but he didn't own any by the band that supposedly sang one of Roy's songs. Mark pointed at his single-wide trailer, then he laughed and said he kept most of the records inside.

"Too many," he said. "My wife says, 'I'm going to throw you out, but the records might have to go first.'"

Mark looked around the yard, and I looked, too, hoping to buy myself some time to figure out a different way to ask about the notebooks. Mark seemed like a nice guy, open and affable, not at all the scary monster I'd imagined, but I worried he'd turn cold if I pushed him.

"When we moved here," he said, "some lady was taking care of Roy's affairs. But later on, the lady stopped for some reason, and I took it over. I kept the books for Roy. Every time I'd do it, I'd take it over and I'd show it to Roy, and she'd say, 'Well, nobody discussed it like this with me before,' and I'd say, 'Yeah, but I want you to see every penny.' I'd sit down and go line by line, and I'd show her everything. And God as my witness, I never took anything from Royce. As a matter of fact, I spent money on Royce. One time, right after this other lady stopped managing her affairs, Royce got in bad financial shape. She couldn't even pay her bills."

I was having trouble following Mark's stories. What were all of Roy's affairs? Which lady had been managing them, and why did she stop?

"Roy couldn't pay?" I asked.

"No. Me and my wife took about four hundred dollars, and we took care of her. Paid all her bills, got her back in shape, but that's when I told Royce, 'I got to handle your affairs.'"

Mark talked without pausing again, and he said Roy got a monthly Social Security check from the government. Mark wasn't sure why, but he thought the check had something to do with the fact that Roy stopped going to school after the third grade.

"She used to tell me, 'I'm retarded,'" Mark said. "And I told her, 'No, I'm a special education teacher, and you are just a little undereducated. You are far from retarded.'"

I winced. I hadn't heard anyone use that word in years. Mark told me he knew Roy wasn't what he called "retarded" because Roy knew how to write in cursive. I'd never heard of anyone using that as a measure of anything, but Mark repeated himself a few times. Roy couldn't be "retarded" because Roy wrote letters in cursive. Roy signed checks in cursive.

"And she kept a diary in cursive," Mark said.

Aubree shot me a look. I knew I should ask about the diaries, but my tongue stuck to the roof of my mouth, and Mark changed the subject.

"Now," Mark said. "Let me tell you what wrecked Royce, and what, till the day I die, I'm going to be agitated about. She had fourteen dogs in that house with her, and it was not sanitary, and she and I had arguments. I told Royce, 'We got to move some of these dogs. You can keep two.'"

Mark said Roy pulled out a pocketknife in response.

"She started doing her fingernails, and she said, 'No. That's my family.'"

As he talked, Mark mimicked the pocketknife action. He pretended to be sharpening a blade across his own fingernails in a menacing way. So far, everyone I'd interviewed had described Roy as either a victim or an angel, and I liked this more complicated view. I liked imagining Roy standing up for himself, threatening Mark with a pocketknife, refusing to give up his pets. I asked Mark if Roy always had that many dogs.

"No," he said flatly. "When I moved here, she had one dog, a little Chihuahua named Peanut. She had about eight cats, but they kind of went away, and that was good. Then, finally, she just had little Peanut, and I really was happy."

Mark squeezed the garden gloves as if they were a stress ball, but otherwise, he didn't seem nervous or annoyed or even curious as to why a group of strangers had stopped him midafternoon to ask about his dead neighbor. He just kept talking. He told me he often took meals to Roy, and once, he helped Roy paint his blue house white. He took care of Roy as long as he could.

"What happened was, one night, Royce had a little heart attack. She came over, and she was beating on the door. She said, 'Help me. Help me.' Honestly, I think Royce had kind of a real bad depression episode. So I had her put in the nursing home, y'all."

I coughed to buy myself some time. Jennifer was right. The Kings had put Roy in the nursing home. And if Jennifer was right about that, I thought, did that mean she'd been right about everything else? The businesspeople from Baton Rouge? Roy's death?

"And boy," Mark said, "I did not want to do that because I promised Royce I would keep her independent as long as I could. But that was it. I couldn't do it anymore."

Mark told us he went to something called the Council on Aging. He went to the welfare office and to the hospital, and he told everyone he talked to that Roy could not go home. It wasn't hard to persuade them, Mark told me. Everyone knew Roy's house was unlivable. Everyone knew Roy had no one to take care of him.

I don't remember now what I was thinking as Mark spoke. I was so nervous, and he was so talkative that I barely had space left in my brain to process the things he said. Every sentence was a big new reveal. I know that later, in the car with Aubree, and on the phone with my grandma, I questioned the things Mark told me that afternoon. Was he really the benevolent neighbor he described himself as? Or was he someone more sinister, someone who'd taken over Roy's money, then forced him into the nursing home? I couldn't decide that day which Mark was the real Mark, and I would spend years going back and forth in my opinions. But as Mark talked that spring afternoon in 2011, I don't think I allowed myself to believe or suspect him. I just let him talk. He rubbed his shoe over the grass.

"I think mostly Royce had a comfortable life. I wouldn't call it a good life, and I don't think it's a life any of us would want, quite frankly."

For the first time since we'd walked up, Mark went completely quiet. I looked around. Drivers slowed to stare at us filming this man on an empty stretch of grass. I pretended to watch the birds fly and the bees buzz flower to flower. It was eighty degrees, and I was sweaty, but more from nerves than the heat. My life had already turned out better than Roy's in some ways—I had a job and money and friends whose identities more or less matched up with mine—but I wasn't sure what trajectory I was on. I didn't have a companion. I didn't even have a pet. Maybe it didn't matter that I lived in a more liberal place. When I flew home, my apartment would be empty, and maybe, eventually, I'd also end up alone and committed to a nursing home against my will.

Mark looked as if he was waiting for a question, so I finally asked the one I'd been holding for two and a half years.

"Do you know what happened to all of Roy's old journals?"

Mark shook his head. He crossed his arms. "Mmm, uh, well, yeah, I know where some of them are. She gave a few things to me right before she got sick. One thing Royce told me is 'Anything I give you, do not sell, and do not give away.' They're in a box in that storage house over there, and they're locked up."

He pointed toward a metal shack, a square structure that looked like someone had just leaned four sheets of corrugated aluminum against each other. The roof was a piece of flat metal laid on top of the other panels, and it looked like it might blow off the next time a tornado tore through. Jennifer would have said the rickety building was the kind we could break into. The door was a thin piece of blue wood. All it would take was one good kick.

I tried to push the thought out of my mind. It didn't matter if bail was twelve dollars. My bosses would fire me if they found out I'd broken into someone's stuff for a story. And what if Mark was telling the truth? What if Roy didn't want his journals to get out?

"Can you tell me what Roy wrote about?" I asked.

Mark shook his head in some combination of yes and no. He said he'd never read them.

"It's just too personal. I know what Royce wrote was probably something that I really don't want to delve into."

Mark took a deep breath. He leaned back, and he looked me right in the eyes.

"All I know is on the front it said, 'Diary of a Misfit.'"

Chapter Ten

(May–December 2011)

A FEW DAYS AFTER I flew back to Portland, I adopted a cat, thinking I would prove to myself I could love and be responsible for someone. He was gray and white and on sale for twenty-five dollars the day I visited the shelter. A volunteer told me he'd been given up three times. She said he peed outside of the litter box and he was jealous of other cats, but I thought I could love him enough to fix his issues. Besides, the only other cat I liked was a long-haired tabby named Sue Bee, and a shelter worker told me Sue Bee had a neurological condition that made her think she had diabetes, even though she did not. Sue Bee had to be given a shot once a day—otherwise, her fake diabetes acted up. I picked the cat with litter box issues.

I named him Lafayette, after a town in South Louisiana, and I spent half a paycheck buying him a dozen toys and the most expensive cat food the pet store offered. I liked waking up to something warm and breathing, but still, I felt lonely. A few nights before my birthday, I emailed an ex-girlfriend who hadn't talked to me in three months and asked her to spend the weekend celebrating with me. She said she wasn't ready.

The day I turned twenty-eight, I pulled out my journal, a small black Moleskine, and I wondered what kind of notebooks Roy used to record his thoughts. Part of me understood why Mark didn't want to let a stranger read Roy's journals. Maybe it was wrong to pry. Maybe Roy didn't want an audience. Most of the people I'd interviewed had said they'd never really known Roy, and Mark had described him as private. But that didn't seem exactly right. Roy had told Lynda and Ann McVay about himself, or at least, they said he'd told them about himself. He'd given Mary Rundell those song lyrics about how empty his life felt, and he'd named his journal. Maybe I was intuiting something, or maybe I was just talking myself into seeing signs where I needed to see them, but I told myself that spring that people who name their journals want them to be read.

I flipped through my unnamed Moleskine, imagining what someone might find if they came looking for my diaries the way I was searching for Roy's. For the past year, I'd mostly written about being sad and disappointed. I hadn't turned into the journalist I wanted to be. I'd spent Christmas alone. Even the documentary was just sputtering along. I'd written pages and pages of to-do lists for the film, but most things remained undone. I called Maxine at the nursing home, and she swore she didn't remember Roy. I didn't believe her—how on earth could a small-town nursing home administrator forget someone like Roy?— but she hung up on me, and I felt hamstrung. Even if she was lying, I thought, I couldn't *make* her talk or tell the truth to me.

That May, almost a month after I returned from Delhi, I decided to look for the report Jennifer told me state investigators had filed after coming to Delhi to research Roy's death. I'd worked at *The Oregonian* for more than four years by then, but I'd never filed a public records request, so I asked an older reporter for help. He forwarded a short template and told me to "demand access to 2567/Statements of Deficiencies cited against Richland Manor Nursing Home in 2006, as well as any Plan of Correction filed for the nursing home that year." I cut and pasted the template into a new draft, then I sent my request to the Louisiana Department of Health and Hospitals. Half a year went by with no response. I waited so long I eventually forgot I'd even filed the request, but then, one afternoon late that fall, I found a letter in my mailbox.

> Dear Ms. Parks:
> We are in receipt of your records request pertaining to Richland Manor Nursing Home. Unfortunately, the Department's Health Standards Section has no records in response to your requests. Any records prior to 2009 pertaining to this facility have been purged pursuant to record retention policy.

I slumped into my couch. How could a health department throw away records? Maybe the documents really were gone, but if I'd been a better journalist, I would have pushed back. Maybe I would have looked up their retention policy to see if it really required them to throw away records after three years, or maybe I would have asked them to check their files again. State departments don't always throw things away on the schedule they've set out for themselves. I'd seen other journalists appeal rejections, and I could have asked one of those more experienced reporters to help me, but I was too embarrassed to admit that my first attempt hadn't worked, so I gave up.

I loved working at *The Oregonian*, but I felt like an amateur compared to the hard-nosed reporters whose stories made the front page. Back then, I worked in what we called a bureau. It was a satellite office in the suburbs, a fluorescent-lit space in a building we shared with a methadone clinic. There were a few reporters in their fifties in the bureau, but most of us were in our twenties and working our first newspaper jobs. We talked about the downtown newsroom as if it were major-league baseball and we, bench players on the farm team, were dreamers searching for the one story that would carry us out of the minor league.

I covered six communities, mostly small towns on the western edge of the county that bordered Portland. I'd spent two years filing bureaucratic updates from city council and school board meetings, but that spring, still bristling from my records request rejection, I decided to focus on feature stories. I wanted my suburban articles to feel like Talk of the Town dispatches for *The New Yorker,* so I went to water department meetings and listened for quirky quotes. I wrote about an eighty-year-old man who planned to bike eighty miles on his birthday, and I spent several Saturday nights with a group of square dancers who wanted to save the local grange in an unincorporated community thirteen miles west of the city. Those pieces were fun to report, and readers told me they appreciated having positive stories written about their small towns, but none of my articles were important enough to make what we in the bureau called "the real paper." Our pieces ran in a once-a-week edition that only went to people who lived in the most distant suburb. The paper that showed up at my Portland apartment each morning never had my name in it.

I tried to stand out. I worked overtime without getting paid for it, and I taught myself how to shoot publishable photographs. I filmed short documentaries, one about a Doris Day impersonator, another about a teenage mariachi band, but nothing I did seemed to matter to the bosses who might determine the rest of my career. I never made the weekly all-staff email where editors praised reporters, and no one suggested promoting me out of the far reaches.

At night, holding Lafayette in my apartment, I cried and wrote in my Moleskine. All I'd ever dreamed about was being a great journalist. Even when I was little and playing with Barbie dolls, I never imagined a wedding or a perfect partner. My Barbies saw Ken as a coworker, a fellow reporter out to dig for the world's big stories. I didn't know who I was supposed to be if not a great journalist, but I started to think that spring that maybe my problem was sheer location.

On a whim, I applied for a job at a newspaper in New Orleans and started telling friends I was leaving the Pacific Northwest. I even made a list of all that I'd miss about Portland—cute girls with weird haircuts, bridges and bikes, mushrooms that grow in wet forests—but when the *Times-Picayune* editor called to tell me I was a finalist for the job, I panicked and said I couldn't take it. I told him I was gay and scared of Louisiana, and when he said no one at the paper was homophobic, I stammered something untrue about wanting to get married someday. "Oregon is going to legalize gay marriage soon," I said. "Louisiana probably never will."

My stomach hurt as I hung up the phone. I *did* long to move back. I dreamed about the food and the weather and a sense of rightness I couldn't define, but I was afraid if I went home, I'd have to hide myself again. Who would cut my hair short? And if I found a girlfriend, could I ever hold her hand in public? Just thinking about it made me sweat, but I didn't want to admit that Louisiana had the power to scare me, so I made up excuses to remain on the West Coast. I told myself I'd made a moral decision. The last time I'd visited Louisiana, someone had told me with great conviction that it was illegal to recycle there, and so, for the sake of plastics alone, I told myself, I had to stay in Oregon.

Still, whatever primordial pull inspired me to apply for that job persisted, so that summer, I flew home for the Fourth of July. My family picked me up at the Shreveport airport, and as I crossed through the security gates, my mother ran at me, sobbing as if we hadn't seen each other two months before. I felt nervous in her soft arms. I couldn't remember the last time I went home without a tape recorder. Taping my family was a way of enduring them. It was a tool or a barrier, a way to turn everything that happened into a story. If my mom disappointed me, so what—that was the tension in the narrative of our lives. But I wasn't working on the documentary this trip. I was just there to be.

The temperature hovered above a hundred degrees that weekend, so we spent a day in a neighbor's pool drinking strawberry daiquiris and listening to Flo Rida and Reba McEntire. We sang and talked about nothing, or at least that's the way I remember it. One of us found a purple plastic cone, and we took turns wearing it around the pool as if it were a hat. I'd just gotten Instagram and my first iPhone, so we spent an hour posing and posting our hat photos to the app. Eventually, my mom emerged from the pool, still holding her Styrofoam cup, and she danced by herself along the ledge of the deep end while my dad grilled steaks. She put the Bee Gees on. She led herself around the perimeter, and she sang every falsetto note of "Night Fever," using the purple cone to amplify her voice.

I stayed in the water with my brother, his girlfriend, and their one-year-old son. They pushed the baby around on a yellow swim toy, and I watched from the shallow end. I opened a Corona. Without a tape recorder, booze would have to do for armor. I tipped my head back and drank half the bottle in one pull.

"Jive Talkin'" started, and my mom shuffled her hands the way the characters do during the "Born to Hand Jive" scene in *Grease*. She danced toward the grill, then twerked against my dad's leg as he flipped the steaks. She kept the melody but sang her own lyrics as he cooked.

> *I'm hungry.*
> *You're making me steak.*
> *Good eatin',*
> *Now give it to me.*

We stayed up late, drinking Coronas and playing Spades, but the next morning, my mom drifted away from us to watch TV updates about Casey Anthony, a young mother on trial for killing her daughter. The defense had rested a few days before I flew down, and all weekend, my mom waited for a verdict. I'd never heard of Casey Anthony, but once we were out of the pool, the accused mother was the only thing my mom wanted to talk about. Casey Anthony had been nineteen when she gave birth to her daughter, Caylee, my mom told me. She was twenty-two when the baby disappeared.

I thought about Roy's mother, his real mother, the one he'd never been able to find. How old was she when Delois disappeared? Was there an investigation? Did anyone ever go on trial?

My mom said Casey Anthony waited thirty-one days to report Caylee missing. Five months later, officials found the baby's bones in a wooded area half a mile from Anthony's house. Now prosecutors were arguing that Anthony had killed Caylee so she could go clubbing with a boyfriend.

"She got 'bella vita' tattooed on her shoulder after Caylee died," my mom told me. "Bella vita! As if she's the only one who ever wanted a beautiful life!"

I didn't ask my mom if she'd ever felt that way at twenty-two, if she'd wanted to stash me someplace so she could pursue the beautiful life she'd made plans for in her high school journal, but I wondered.

"What a crock of shit!" my mom yelled at the TV. "Lock her up."

I begged my mom to go to the pool with me. I told her we could live our own bella vita right now, together, in the water under the sun. We could watch my nephew splash, or we could listen to disco. We could be the kind of mother and daughter Casey and Caylee would never be. My mom sneered.

"Aren't you supposed to be a journalist? I would think you'd be following the trial, too. She killed her daughter."

I backed out of the living room. I didn't think the trial constituted real journalism, but what did I know? I'd spent all spring writing human interest pieces that few people read. Maybe Casey Anthony was more important than the square dancers or the mariachi band.

I flew back to Portland on Tuesday, the day the jury decided Casey Anthony hadn't killed her daughter. I called my mom to see if she was disappointed, but my dad answered her phone.

"Your mom's in the emergency room waiting for a shot."

He didn't tell me what she was sick with this time, and I didn't ask.

I turned my phone off, then crawled into bed with Lafayette, grateful I hadn't adopted the cat who thought she had diabetes.

I SEE NOW THAT I was casting for something that year. I was twenty-eight, too old to emerge as the young reporting phenom I'd imagined myself becoming. I remember this time as the season right before my life really got going, but when I look at my old journals, I see that I felt desperately lonely. I wrote the word over and over again. I was working, but I was lonely. I was making things, but I was lonely. I'd spent the previous three years with a woman in her forties, watching TV and eating chocolate chip cookies that she baked in huge batches. I'd felt safe with her, but bored, and once she was gone, I started looking for someone to replace her.

I think of myself as a romantic. I've spent twenty years reminiscing about that dorm room kiss with Ellen, and I once moved to California for the summer after spending one good weekend with a woman in Missouri. I'm the kind of person who would drive all day just to kiss a woman. I write long love notes and make dopey mixes heavy on songs about yearning. Maybe I inherited that from my mother. She always seemed happiest when she was dreaming of Cam, and when I was young, she and I watched endless romantic comedies together. But in 2011, I worried I didn't have time to wait for a storybook romance. The woman from Missouri had recently gotten married, and so, I thought, should I. A few weeks after my breakup, I made what I now see was largely a pragmatic list of the traits I hoped to find:

> someone I'll always want to talk to, someone who believes in
> me, someone who inspires me, someone who is good with money,
> someone who likes games, someone who makes conversation in new
> situations, someone who likes to travel, someone who likes sitcoms
> and indie movies, someone who bikes, someone who has friends
> and a life outside of our relationship, someone who will get along
> with my family

I wrote down part of a Leonard Cohen poem—"Marita please find me I am almost 30"—then pinned it to the wall behind my work computer as a reminder. Still, I felt untethered, marooned in a loneliness of my own making. I went to gay bars every weekend and kissed girls, sometimes two or three a night, but no one felt like my Marita. I waved off one woman who told me she'd never read a book, and I left another at the bar after she refused to dance to Beyoncé's "Single Ladies." I slept with someone I'd known online as a teenager, then, when she told me she loved me, I told her I was too broken for anything real. After that, I chased a British woman who refused to kiss me, and for a while, I dated a professor I knew from Mississippi, a sculptor who broke up with me every few weeks because the thirteen-year age gap between us was too embarrassing to admit to her friends. We'd reconnected and grown close after she moved to rural Washington, but she said she didn't want me to be a part of her real life. We lived four hours and a generation away from each other. Our love was best left to private weekends.

Even with the breakups, the professor met most of the criteria on my list. We rode bikes together, and we watched great movies on the floor in her bedroom. She liked Boggle. She certainly had friends and a life outside of our relationship, but I worried that no one could meet the last line on my list. I'd been out of the closet for almost a decade. I'd dated four girls seriously, but I almost never told my brother or my parents about my love life.

I wanted the professor to be my Marita, though, so that fall, after one good date, I called my mom and told her about the person I spent hours driving to see every other weekend. I tried to emphasize the good parts. The professor had a tenure-track job. She was tall and artistic, gentle with the black Labrador she'd named after a body of water. But my mom was good at prying, and by the end of the conversation, I'd admitted that I hadn't met any of the professor's friends. Later that night, my mom emailed me a list of questions.

1. *Do you find yourself hiding out when you are with her? You should be able to sing from the rooftops when you are in love and everybody should know it.*
2. *Why do you keep subjecting yourself to this? You are so smart and you have so much to offer.*
3. *Did I miss telling you something that gave you the feeling of self-importance?*

The professor was from the Midwest, but I was drawn to the idea that she had lived in Mississippi when I had. Once, a few weeks after we started dating, I asked her over Facebook Messenger if she'd liked her time in the South, and she wrote back, "To me it felt like slavery had ended about two weeks prior to my arrival in Jackson. That is some scary, sad shit."

I was at work when she replied, so I waited to respond until the end of the day, until both the bureau and the methadone clinic had cleared out. The professor was right. Mississippi did have some scary, sad truths. My college mascot had been a Confederate major, and in the fall of my freshman year, Mississippi voters overwhelmingly had chosen to keep the rebel battle insignia in the top left corner of the state's flag. Those symbols were tangible relics of the deeper, far more disturbing truths I suspected the professor was referencing. I loved reading census tables, so I knew how bad the numbers were for Black Mississippians. The year before, the Black unemployment rate there had reached nearly 20 percent—more than triple the white rate. Black Mississippians had higher rates of poverty and lower rates of college graduation, and they were far more likely than white people to go to jail or prison.

I'd once thought that leaving was the best way to deal with the things I didn't like about the South, but the older I got, the more I believed that those numbers were reasons I should return. It wasn't right to flee and forget the injustices still happening there. If I moved back, I could write stories that exposed those inequities. Why did people care so much about Casey Anthony when every year in Mississippi, Black babies were twice as likely as white ones to die before their first birthday?

I read the professor's message again, then clicked reply.

"I'm planning to move home so I can use journalism for good," I wrote.

I typed six paragraphs in a fury. I told the professor about Roy. I said I planned to press the nursing home workers to find out more about how he died. If I could expose the mistreatment Roy endured, maybe I could make life easier for other people whose bodies and identities didn't align the way other people thought they should.

I leaned back in my chair. Outside, I could hear a janitor emptying the hallway trash cans. I reread the first sentence of my email. "I'm planning to move home so I can use journalism for good." I groaned. If that were true, I would have already investigated the nursing home. I would have taken the *Times-Picayune* job and moved to New Orleans and spent my career explaining how unequal the South was. But I hadn't taken the job, and I wasn't moving home. I was a coward, and I was staying in Portland.

Back then, people didn't talk about "white privilege" as openly as we do now, but I knew I had advantages I didn't know how to name. I'd grown up poor, but I'd won a big scholarship to a private college where white students were far more likely to graduate than Black ones. How many employers had given me jobs not because my résumé was impressive but because I reminded them of some younger version of themselves? In 2011, I was just beginning to reckon with the idea that my life had been any kind of charmed, and I didn't know yet how to tell the professor I was ashamed at how little I'd done to make up for it.

I erased the email, then typed a new one, a message that left out the devastating statistics.

> *Going home now is such a hard experience. Even little things—the cigarette smoke everywhere, the styrofoam, the way EVERY stranger insists on calling me sir despite the fact that I'm pretty small and curvy—make me want to stand on a table and scream, "DO Y'ALL REALIZE IT DOES NOT HAVE TO BE THIS WAY?"*
>
> *That is all complicated by the fact that it is my home and I love it immensely. People in Portland don't tell stories the same way. They don't say hi the same way. They don't come at you directly the way Southerners do . . . On that note, I think I will leave work and go home and make some red beans and rice.*

I turned off my computer, but I did not get up. I didn't know why it bothered me so much when people in the South mistook me for a man. Roy had dealt with far worse. No one was going to push me out of a nursing home bed. And yet, when Southerners called me "sir," I felt misunderstood, like something they could not or would not puzzle out.

I looked around my office, at the Leonard Cohen poem hanging behind my computer. I was free to look for my Marita in Portland, and no one on the West Coast ever mistook me for a man. But I didn't feel like I exactly fit in there, either. People said I was too direct. At dinner parties, I talked too much. I interrupted people in a way that would have been acceptable back home but was considered rude in Portland. Maybe everyone who moves across the country to pursue life in a new culture feels this way, but I felt very alone that summer, as if I were the only one in the world who didn't belong anywhere.

I stood. I said hello to the janitor on my way out, then I drove east toward the city, listening to country songs on loop until I parked outside my apartment, saw my cat in the window, and knew I was home.

I WORKED EVEN LONGER hours that fall, not because I was ambitious, though I was, but because I was lonely. No amount of time in a gay bar made me feel loved in the ways I wanted to be. Every dance floor was filled with the kind of people I'd dreamed about meeting when I was a teenager in Mississippi—girls with spiked hair, boys in ironic T-shirts—but the rap songs blared too loud for conversation, and often I drank so much I couldn't have held one anyway. Sometimes, at the end of the party, I'd stumble toward someone, demanding to know where they were from and what pains had led them to these neon-strobed nights, but my questions never yielded deep answers. At least when I was working, I was having real conversations with people, even if they were one-sided, even if I was plumbing people for their secrets without ever giving up any of my own. I knew plenty of gay people that I might have called friends, but I didn't know how to be vulnerable with them. I worried that if I fell and broke my hip in the middle of the night, none of my supposed friends would answer their phones and come over to help me. I have no idea why that was the scenario I feared. I was in my late twenties, not my seventies, but I thought about it over and over again as I slow-stepped toward the bathroom in the middle of the night.

The problem, I eventually decided, was that I knew too many people. If I focused all my energy on hanging out with a smaller group, I thought, I'd find the intimacy I wanted. Sometime that fall, I started telling people I'd decided I wanted only six friends. Six real friends,

I'd say, friends I'll hang out with every weekend, friends I can tell my secrets. I went out to dinner as if I were auditioning people. If a conversation lingered too long in the shallows, I excused myself early, then cried the whole way home.

Looking back, I did have people in my life who would have answered that broken-hip call. I had colleagues whose family lives were as painful as mine was, and friends who longed just as sharply to talk about heartbreak and disappointment. It was me who filled our weekends with loud music and video projects. I was the one who canceled plans last minute.

Now that a decade has passed, now that I know how everything turns out, I'm tempted to go back and tinker with the meaning of everything. I want to give myself a motive where it's possible I felt none. I want to say I ran away from people and opportunities then because I was afraid of being vulnerable, but the truth is, most days, I didn't know why I did anything. I skated from thing to thing, searching for the one development that would make me happy. I wanted so much at twenty-eight. I wanted to feel safe and inspired and excited and understood and challenged and turned on and supported and dazed and comfortable, and I wanted to be a superstar at work. I wanted *This American Life* to hire me, and I wanted to know how to make perfect podcasts without even trying, and I wanted to become Kate Boo, and I wanted a girlfriend who dressed well, and I wanted the cool gays to think I was cool, and I wanted to make things, and I wanted my mother to stay awake and engaged for at least one visit. I wanted to stop myself from feeling disappointed when she inevitably slept through the days I needed her. I wanted my parents to pay off the debt they'd accrued in my name. I wanted the easy life I had in Portland, but I wanted that feeling of inexplicable rightness I felt every time I stepped out into Louisiana's sun. I wanted that feeling of "rightness" to contain not a single trace of fear. I wanted my ex-girlfriend to keep baking cookies for me, and I thought for a while that I wanted her back. I wanted to have great sex, and I didn't want to be scared of sex, and I wanted someone to love me, and I didn't want to be scared of love, and I wanted to be close to people, and I didn't want to be scared of that either. Most of all, I wanted to stop wanting, and so I went to bars, and I chugged cheap beers until my wants blurred into dull aches.

———

AUBREE AND I BOOKED tickets for another Delhi trip that December. A few days before we flew south, a friend emailed me and asked if I'd hang out with her friend Frankie, a lesbian who did improv comedy and had just moved to Portland. Initially, I told my friend I was too busy to meet anyone new. I wanted to cull the number of people in my life, not add to it. But a few days later, I reconsidered. The professor and I were broken up that week and I was aching, so I looked Frankie up on Facebook to see if she was cute.

Her interests page loaded first. She liked *Star Trek* and *The Simpsons*, hiking and a bunch of environmental groups in Idaho. I didn't appreciate any of those, but when I clicked her profile picture to make it bigger, I reconsidered. Frankie had a squinty smile and super-straight teeth. She was wearing a hoodie, a gray one pulled tight around her face, so I couldn't see what her hair looked like beyond the sweep of brown bangs that poked out from the hood, and yet, even obscured, I could tell she was cute. Even better, she seemed like an adult, the kind of person who would work an office job, not a late-night gig at a bar. She'd probably read a book, I thought. She'd probably dance to "Single Ladies."

Maybe it was magic or maybe I just wanted it to be true, but when I looked at that photo, I felt something inside me click into place. *Marita.*

"Oh my god," I said out loud to myself. "We are going to get married."

Chapter Eleven

(December 2011)

I TOLD MYSELF REPEATEDLY in my twenties that I didn't care about family, but every time Aubree and I flew south, I roped another relative into joining my crew. In December of 2011, that relative was my cousin Christopher. His mom had stopped talking to my mother years earlier for reasons I didn't quite understand, but Christopher and I were as close as I allowed myself to be with family. He was, by all measures, my coolest relative. Plus, he knew how to record audio. He played in a seven-piece band in Fort Worth, and otherwise roamed the world making strange money and looking for fun. He was a year older than I was, and we'd grown up more or less alongside each other, save for the years his family lived on an army base in Okinawa, but he seemed fluently Southern in ways I didn't know how to be. He hunted wild hogs. He dipped tobacco, and in high school, he rode and fought bulls on the small-town rodeo circuit. When Aubree and I picked him up at the Shreveport bus station, he was wearing a flannel shirt and a faded trucker hat from Texas. I was wearing the expensive jacket I bought in New York along with a pair of black boots made out of leather so thin, they'd started to rub away at the ankles. Christopher ran out of the bus station, laughing.

"Let's do this," he said. "Let's call somebody, go knock on someone's door."

"You're not nervous?" I asked.

He grinned big. Nothing seemed to scare him.

"Hell, no. The worst they can do is blow us off, but it's not going to happen. People are going to want to talk."

He tossed his duffel bag into the trunk and jumped into the back seat. I couldn't help smiling. Christopher has an easy, inviting air, and his arms are always open, as if he's waiting to bear-hug anyone who crosses his path. He can talk to anyone about anything, and his eyes are the kind of blue that somehow seems both mysterious and friendly. I've never met anyone who isn't drawn to him. Just being around him juiced me up, so I gunned it out of the parking lot, and Christopher cackled, knowing I usually drive slow.

THE DRIVE EAST TOOK about two hours, and we spent most of it talking about Louisiana. Christopher told me about Bonnie and Clyde and bass fishing, and I realized I didn't actually know much about my home state. I knew far more about Oregon. Because I'd written so many wonky development stories, I could cite the zoning codes of almost any neighborhood. I'd learned a little about every governor who'd served in Oregon for at least the last thirty years, and I could even name most of the current senators, but I had no idea who was leading Louisiana that year. My ignorance bothered me. How could I know so little about the place that had such a hold on me?

Halfway to Delhi, my phone buzzed, and when I looked, I saw my mom's number on the caller ID. I was driving, but I hadn't heard from her in a while, so I answered, and she talked without stopping or breathing.

"Are you in Delhi? Someone called about the flyer. He remembers Roy from age three and has music that Roy wrote."

LATER THAT NIGHT, AFTER we'd settled into the cabin, I pulled out my notebook and looked at the number my mother had given me. Aubree was cooking down collard greens, and Christopher was fishing off the back deck, so I tucked myself into the bottom bunk, then dialed. A man answered on the first ring.

"You callin' about Roy, ain't you? I can tell by the long-distance."

The man's name was Archie Lee Harrell. He said he'd lived next to Roy and the Ellises in a tar-paper shack outside the city limits in the

1930s. Archie didn't sound old, but the dates suggested he was at least in his seventies.

"So when you want to come do the interview?" he asked. "You want to come now?"

My stomach rumbled, hungry for whatever Christopher was catching.

"What about tomorrow?" I asked.

Archie told me to be there first thing. He lived on Edgar Street, a few houses down from where Mary Rundell had played us the gospel song eight months earlier. When we arrived the next morning, I saw that Archie's house looked like all the others on the block. It was white and single-story, and the driveway was covered but not enclosed. An American flag swayed from a pole in the front yard, high above the house.

Archie answered the door wearing a khaki jumpsuit. He smiled, and I could see he'd lost all but two of his top teeth. Still, there was something handsome about him. His hair was a wavy gray, and his eyes were so light and inscrutable they could have been green or blue or brown. He waved us inside. Both the carpet and his walls were brown, but the Christmas tree lights gave the room a green-and-red sheen. Archie pointed toward the kitchen and a set of built-in shelves that held mason jars full of vegetables he said his wife had preserved from their garden.

"That's country," he said. "Roy liked that sort of thing."

Archie eased onto his couch, a patterned beige that almost blended in with the carpet and his khaki suit. He said he'd spent most of his life living in Delhi and working on the railroad, but back in the 1930s, his parents picked cotton just beyond the parish line. They worked the plot next to Jewel's. Archie said he and Roy were small then, too young to pick or go to school, so they spent their days napping on cotton sacks at the end of rows.

"We knew Roy was a lady because her mother told us. She just never had time, working in the fields, to dress Roy in a dress. She couldn't starch and iron the clothes, and that's the way they wore them back then, so she always just put a pair of pants on her."

Archie leaned forward. He smiled his mostly toothless smile, then he nodded at me.

"Can I ask you a question? Why are you doing this for Roy?"

I laughed, nervously. How could I tell Archie what I hadn't articulated to myself? I didn't want to say I thought it was a good story. I'd told people that when I was first working on the documentary, but I'd started to think that that explanation reduced Roy to nothing more than a curiosity. I didn't want to tell Archie I'd spent a decade inexplicably drawn to a stranger I'd never met, so I said "um" and "you know," and I tried to buy myself some time as I worked up an answer.

"My grandma moved here from a place called Frog Island, and she didn't have any friends. She was really, I guess, depressed, and Roy was the first person who was kind to her. She told me the story a few years ago, and when she did, she said she wanted to know if Roy had any family, if anyone loved Roy."

I spoke slowly, as if every word was hard to get out. I didn't want to mess up by calling Roy "he" or "she" in front of Archie, so I repeated "Roy" instead of using pronouns.

"Sometimes I don't know why I'm doing it," I said. "I don't know if I'll ever find anything out."

Archie was impossibly sweet, gentle, and almost apologetic about his own existence. He listened without interrupting, and as I trailed off, he scooted to the edge of the couch.

"Well, you're going to find out some more. There'll be somebody besides me who knows something. I think it'll be nice for you to do a documentary for him. For her."

Archie blushed, and I could tell he didn't know which pronoun he should use. I didn't know if he was worried about offending me or Roy, but I thought his stumbling seemed careful and kind. He leaned back into his couch and said he wanted to tell me something. Back in 1971 or '72, Archie said, he and his wife invited Roy to go with them to Victory Full Gospel, an Assemblies of God church on the highway near the lake. Roy liked going at first, Archie said, but then the pastor decided Roy had to wear a dress if he wanted to continue worshiping.

"It hurt her feelings," Archie said. "I told Roy, 'Don't worry about what that fella says. He needs to know Jesus 'cause Jesus didn't turn nobody away.' It's wrong because Roy never has wore a dress. It just wouldn't look natural. Just like, when I die, I've told my kids I want to be buried in khakis. I don't want a suit."

Archie looked toward the ground as if he was unburdening himself of a long-carried and shameful secret. I wanted to hug him. My own grandfather—the man who carried my grandma away from Delhi—had died earlier that year, and I missed him. My grandfather and I used to chat every night online, and he was the only person who read my suburban dispatches. He even signed up for an online *Oregonian* account under the name "militaryhatspinsandpatches@aol.com" so he could post encouraging comments on each of my stories. Listening to Archie, I half hoped he'd offer to be my stand-in grandfather.

We talked for an hour, mostly about things I already knew. Archie described Roy's hair and his clothes and his dogs, then he took down my address and promised to send me anything he found. He thought he had a copy of the song Roy sold to the Whites, and he said he was sure he could find a picture that showed Roy when he was young.

Just before we left, I asked Archie if any of his neighbors knew Roy. Archie said they might, but he told me to avoid one woman who lived a few houses down.

"She don't like me at all," he said. "Never has, really. She has always wanted to be a man."

I thought I misheard him. Given how open-minded Archie had been about Roy, it seemed like a weird comment to make, but I asked him to repeat himself. Archie bent his hand limply the way straight men do when they're making fun of gay guys.

"Even though she's got three kids, she is," Archie said, letting his wrist go limp again. "She carried one woman when she was working up here at the sewing place. She was wanting to go with another woman, but that woman wouldn't go with her. She got kicked out of the coast guard. She didn't last three weeks. They found out what she was. Back then, they found out you was queer, they got you out of the army."

He laughed so hard at the thought of the army kicking out queers that he started coughing. He stepped into the kitchen to grab a tissue and some water. I didn't speak the whole time he was gone. He returned and drank a few sips out of a coffee mug, then he took to talking again.

"The first kid she had, she did it to try to prove to everyone that she wasn't. But she was. Everyone knew she was."

My ears burned and my chest hurt the way it does when I'm trying not to cry. I bit my tongue to stop myself from tearing up. I looked at the door. I worried if I stayed too long, Archie would notice my short hair and he'd puzzle me out. "Well," I said. "We better go get our next interview."

We didn't have another interview that day, but I knew I needed to leave. Archie stepped toward me, but I left without leaning in for the hug I'd wanted a few moments earlier. It was just as well, I told myself. Journalists don't hug sources. I was here to report, not find friends or a surrogate grandfather.

As we drove home, even Christopher's big smile flattened.

"But he was so sweet," Christopher said in a way that was more confused than complimentary.

WE SPENT THE REST of the week talking to the half a dozen people who answered the flyers. Most were old people who knew Roy when they were kids, septuagenarians who remembered nothing more than my grandmother did. They offered the usual tidbits about mowing grass and playing the guitar, then they pressed me to tell them what I'd learned from other people. The only interesting interview we did was with a man who said Roy told him that he'd sold a song to the country duo the Judds. I knew the Judds' music. My mom played "Grandpa (Tell Me 'Bout the Good Old Days)" and "Mama He's Crazy" on repeat back when we lived in Georgia. Both seemed bigger than the four stanzas I'd read of Roy's, more universal. They were syrupy and sentimental in a way that felt distinctly feminine, a way I couldn't imagine Roy writing. Still, I wanted the story to be true, so I spent hours tracking down the Judds' management team. I sent them a hopeful email. I waited a week. When they replied, it was with bad news: No one there had ever heard of Roy. I tried, too, to find the Whites, the country gospel band both Mark and Archie said bought one of Roy's songs, but their publicity manager said the group had never paid anyone for lyrics.

Every dead end felt like *the* dead end, but I kept pushing. We tried interviewing people at the nursing home, but Maxine still refused to talk, and the other administrators swore they didn't remember Roy. Only one woman, a nurse's assistant, agreed to chat with us for longer

than a few seconds. She told us that all she could recall is that Roy loved
snacks and liked to watch the maintenance crew mow the lawn. After
the interview, the nurse nodded toward a back corner, where a woman
was sitting in a wheelchair. The woman's skin was translucent, and she
was bent so far forward, her head touched the wall.

"She knew Miss Roy," the nurse said, then walked away.

Aubree and I walked up, and knelt close to the woman. She had
her fingers in her mouth, and when I asked her how she was doing, she
pulled them out, grabbed my hand, and laced her wet fingers through
mine.

"I need to tell you girls something," she said.

The woman didn't say anything else, so after a minute, I asked if she
remembered Roy. She patted my hand and looked at the wall.

"I can't help her. Roy Hudgins. Didn't have a place to lay down."

The woman looked around, suspiciously, as if someone might have
heard what she told us. She stuck her fingers back in her mouth, then
she pulled me toward her and used her fingers to rub her saliva up and
down my arm.

"I don't want you to get into trouble," she said. "I think about it
when I'm getting in bed every night. It's stuck. I can't get rid of it."

The skin around her blue eyes was red and thin. She pointed to her
chest. I inched closer, and my own chest hummed with new excitement.
I was so desperate to solve this mystery that I held on to the word "bed"
as some kind of proof. Jennifer had said someone pushed Roy out of
bed. Now this old lady was saying she thought of Roy in bed. Surely that
meant something. I waited. The woman bit her fingers, and I asked what
she couldn't get rid of, what she thought about every night. She leaned
forward and tried to talk, but most of the syllables that came out were
not words.

"Em pin. And so. Ah. They know. Tro. Oh. Gare and shame. And I
choo choo. Hehhhh. And I was just squalling and a balling."

She spoke quietly, and in the moment, I hoped my hearing was
just off. Later, at my computer, rewatching the footage Aubree taped,
I boosted the sound and even slowed it to half speed. I pressed my ear
against the built-in speaker, and I must have listened thirty times, hoping *this* time I'd understand the message the woman was trying to con-

vey, but it didn't matter how loud or how slow I played the audio. I never made out anything other than stray, meaningless syllables.

The woman went quiet, and I let her press a wet tissue against my hand for a bit. Eventually, she keeled forward into my wet arm, and I realized that she'd lost whatever she knew. I told her we had to go. It didn't matter how good of a reporter I became, I realized. It didn't matter how many times I showed up and let old women rub their spit against my skin. I might never solve Roy's mysteries.

All my steps felt heavy on the way out, but Christopher was smiling wide when I found him. I wiped my wet arm against his vest, and when he grimaced, I told him I thought we should get a drink.

DELHI IS A dry town, so we stopped at a convenience store just outside the city limits to buy a six-pack of Miller High Life. The cashier and three customers looked up when we walked in. One of the customers was counting two fistfuls of money, but he stopped, mid-count, to watch as I ventured back to the coolers. He followed me down the aisle.

"Where you from?" he asked.

Sometimes, when I'm out reporting, I use a different voice, one that's nicer, more obsequious than the way I normally talk. I shifted to that nicer tone before I answered him.

"Oh. My grandma grew up on Chatham Street."

He shook his head. He was still holding the money in front of his face.

"No. Where you from?"

I opened the cooler and pulled out a six-pack. I told the man my mom had graduated from Delhi High School in 1982, and he shook his head no again. He licked his finger, then counted a few twenty-dollar bills.

"Nope. I asked where *you* from."

The beer was cold, so I shifted it to my left hand.

"West Monroe," I said.

The man hesitated, and I could tell, by the way he looked at my plastic-frame glasses and wing-tip shoes, that he did not believe me. He stepped closer. He stared and waited for me to come clean.

"I live in Oregon," I said. "Portland."

I said the words as if I were confessing them. I wanted so badly to appear of this place, but this stranger had seen right through me. I didn't belong in Louisiana. I couldn't claim Delhi as mine. I looked down, and the man spun around on the heel of his cowboy boots and laughed a bit maniacally. He disappeared down another aisle, still counting his money.

THE DAY BEFORE WE left Louisiana, we drove into Monroe to buy groceries for one last dinner. Aubree and I piled the buggy with sweet potatoes and bundles of greens, and I was about to head toward the beer aisle when I heard a familiar voice call my name.

"Casey?"

My stomach felt like I'd been pushed off a building; it turned and fell. Pamela, the youth pastor I'd lived with in high school, was standing at the end of the aisle.

"Casey? Is that you?"

I couldn't bring myself to say yes. My tongue felt thick in my mouth.

"I didn't know what happened to you," she said. She sounded genuinely scared or relieved or both. I could tell my disappearance had bothered her. "Everything was so bad the last time I saw you, I didn't know if you'd killed yourself or turned to drugs or what."

I moved very slowly toward Pamela. She gasped, then sobbed so hard she had to lean on an endcap of tortilla chips to support herself. When I drew close enough, she grabbed me. She hugged me tighter and tighter until I could only breathe in shallow pulls.

"Why didn't you ever call me again?" she asked.

I'd always assumed that Pamela had been at church the day the pastor asked God to take me. I assumed she knew I was gay, and that she, like everyone else I once loved, hated me now. I hadn't called her because I couldn't bear to have her look at me the way my mom had.

"I don't know," I whispered.

Pamela's body shook, and she held on to me until Christopher appeared and asked if everything was okay. Pamela loosened her grip.

"Is this your husband? He's so handsome."

Christopher laughed, and I swallowed hard. She must not know. How could she not know?

"Um, no. He's, he's my cousin, not my husband. I'm not married."

"Oh, you'll find someone, honey. You're so beautiful. Your hair is short, but you're still beautiful. You always were."

Pamela gave me her phone number and her email address, and I promised I would call her later that day, but as soon as I got to the parking lot, I deleted her contact information. I didn't want to feel ashamed anymore. I didn't want to care if Pamela told me I was going to Hell. I'd spent a decade making myself tough, and I thought that deleting her number was proof of how strong I was.

I didn't even let myself think of Pamela again until I started writing this book. By then, I was in my mid-thirties, and though I still worried that she'd hate me once she found out I was gay, I knew that I owed her more than silence. She'd loved me. She'd driven me to school, and she'd given me the only quiet place I'd ever lived in as a kid. In the early days of 2020, I worked up my nerve to call her, but I didn't have her phone number, so I googled to see if I could find it. The first hit that came up was Pamela's obituary. She'd died in 2019, a few days after Christmas, following what the newspaper described as "a lengthy illness." She was sixty-four. I read the obituary twice and realized I *wasn't* tough. I had never been tough. I'd just run away.

WE DROVE BACK TO Delhi a few hours later. It was sixty degrees, much warmer than Portland tended to be in mid-December. I took the highway so we could keep the windows down as we drove east.

Everything hurt. My head, my stomach, my chest. I tried to put Pamela out of my mind. In the morning, we'd drive to Shreveport, to the bus station and the airport, then I'd be back in Portland, probably stupidly wishing I were in Louisiana. I wanted to make the most of our last few hours, but I felt paralyzed. We'd toured Delhi a dozen times. We didn't have any interviews lined up, and it wasn't like our conversations were yielding anything good anyway. We passed cows and horses, and Christopher played funny songs about beer runs and Seattle grunge bands, but I steered in silence. How could I keep coming here if I had nothing left to find? And why did I want to?

I wasn't sure what to do, so I drove downtown and told Aubree and Christopher we should shoot B-roll before the sun went down. I parked in front of the drugstore, and they grabbed their equipment, then darted across the road to film the abandoned swimming pool. I stood in the street, looking for something to capture. Finally, I noticed a sign for the Delhi Beautification Association. It was old and metal, missing an *i* and part of the *f.* Whoever had installed it had done so right in front of a gravel service road. I thought the juxtaposition was funny, so I set up my camera and was about to press record when a red pickup truck made a U-turn over the railroad tracks, then pulled next to me. The truck's windows were tinted and cracked open just wide enough that I could hear someone with a husky voice yelling from the driver's seat.

"People said you been asking about Roy. Is it for a personal reason?"

I froze. All week, people had been looking at me as if I didn't belong in Louisiana, and I felt sure that's what the pickup driver was suggesting, too. Anyone asking about Roy for a "personal reason" must be the same kind of misfit Roy believed himself to be. I could see a Buck Commander decal on the back window. The driver must be a hunter, I thought, someone with a gun. The window slid down, and I steeled myself. I thought of a verse from the book of Romans: "The wages of sin is death."

I saw the tattoo on the driver's upper left arm first. It looked like a seal for the local fire department, with an American flag and flames surrounding a portrait of a regal-seeming dalmatian. It was the kind of tattoo I assumed a tough guy would choose, but when the driver leaned out, I saw that she was a woman. Her brown hair was graying and buzzed short, and she was wearing a T-shirt with a howling wolf printed in the center. She never said the word "lesbian," but she caught my eye, and I knew.

"I mean, I am," she said. "Are you?"

She winked and nodded toward my video camera. "Hell," she said. "I knew Roy. What you want to know?"

Chapter Twelve

(December 2011–December 2012)

HER NAME WAS PAM, a name I thought must be some kind of omen, considering I'd just seen the Pamela I'd lived with earlier that day. The lesbian Pam—Pam Sykes—told me she'd been twelve and working the cash register at her stepfather's grocery when she first met Roy. It was 1972. Roy came in with a pack of dogs, looking to buy eggs and milk on credit, and when he got to the cash register, Pam went mute with wonder. Roy's hair was short and slicked back like a man's, but his skin was as smooth as a woman's. His hands, too, looked feminine. Pam told me she hadn't been able to name the feeling back then, but she looked at Roy and knew they had something in common.

"I asked one of the old ladies who worked in the store, 'Is that a man or a woman?' Miss May was really vague and said, 'Well, she dresses like a man and works like a man, and that's about all I can tell you.' That intrigued me even more."

Pam didn't make much eye contact with me as she talked. She was still hanging out of her truck window, and she mostly looked at the road. But after she said that, she let out a deep whoosh of an exhale, then she settled back into the cab. I asked her how old she was now, and she said fifty-one, just a few years older than Roy must have been the first time she saw him.

For reasons I don't remember anymore, we decided not to do an interview in the middle of the street that afternoon. Pam gave me her number, and I told her I'd call her the next time I visited Delhi. I figured

I'd return in a few months. She said all right, then she spun off into the distance, her wheels spitting gravel as she darted across the railroad tracks. I wondered if she was Archie's neighbor, the one who'd been kicked out of the military for being gay.

We left Delhi the next morning, and I didn't see Pam or Louisiana for another year. I went back to Portland, to the newspaper, and the professor who continued to break up with me every other week the rest of that winter. I didn't think about Pam or the documentary much because I was busier than I'd ever been at work. I could tell I was becoming a better reporter. None of my stories made it into the real paper that winter, but once or twice, the superstar narrative journalists who worked downtown emailed to say they liked something I'd written. I stayed at the bureau until seven most nights, editing videos or tinkering with words until I found the right verb. I drove back to the city after dark, buzzing off the thrill of having puzzled out a single sentence.

Everything started to slip into place for me that year. A few days after I returned from Louisiana, I met Frankie, the girl from Facebook, and I knew almost immediately that she was the friend I'd spent a year seeking. We went for a beer and ended up talking for three hours about our grandparents. Her mom's parents were from the Basque Country, an autonomous region in northern Spain, and Frankie told me that Euskara, the language her grandparents spoke, was an isolate, unrelated to any other language. She called her grandparents amuma and aitxitxa, and as she talked about eating shrimp salad and watching soap operas with her amuma, I ordered another beer just to buy another hour with her.

By the end of January, Frankie and I were hanging out three or four times a week. We watched *The Voice* on Monday nights and went for cheap oysters every Tuesday at a Louisiana-themed restaurant Frankie found. We rode bikes together. We went dancing. Once a month, Frankie watched my cat while I hung out with the professor in rural Washington, and on the weekends I stayed home, Frankie cooked bibimbap or pasta alle vongole, elaborate dinners just for the two of us. Once, she even invited me over for breakfast, and we smiled across the kitchen table, nervously eating the perfect salmon eggs Benedict she'd made from scratch.

Two of my other best friends, Claudia and Jessica, sat me down that spring and told me I couldn't keep dating the professor and spending all my time with Frankie. I told them Frankie and I were just friends, but they remained unconvinced. Friends do not eat dinner together every other night, they said. They don't share homemade breakfasts, and they don't talk wistfully about meeting each other's siblings someday. It was wrong to monopolize Frankie's time. Plenty of other girls would have loved to date her. She was goofy, and she could cook or draw anything. At queer dance nights, girls walked up to tell her how cute she was. Jessica said I had two options. I could break up with the professor for real and start dating Frankie, or I had to cut back our hangouts to once a week.

I loved spending time with Frankie, and I hadn't forgotten that jolt I'd felt when I first saw her picture. Those strangers at queer dance nights were right: Frankie *was* cute. She had hazel eyes, a mess of brown hair, and a perfect nose dotted with just the right number of freckles. Her smile reminded me of Joseph Gordon-Levitt, a dorky heartthrob whose poster I tacked to my wall in middle school. I baked her a chocolate cake for her thirtieth birthday, and she made a pineapple upside-down one for my twenty-ninth, and once, I fell asleep against her shoulder while we watched *The L Word,* but our relationship didn't feel like romance to me.

Back then, I thought only dramatic, dangerous love could be romantic. Maybe I learned that from my mother. Every story she told me about Cam was a tortured one, and she only seemed to want my father when he was cheating. Life was boring when life was good. Real love—big love—was doomed, my mom taught me. It was impossible. It was painful. Throughout my twenties, I slept with married women, mean women, women too drunk or broken to be available. Being around Frankie felt too easy. She never stood me up. She was fun, sweet, predictable, nothing like the professor I crossed state lines to chase. All my friends said that was a good thing—"The professor is not good for you," one friend texted me every single week of March—but easy wasn't thrilling. It wasn't agonizing the way my mom made me believe love should be, so instead of asking Frankie out, I asked her to watch my cat while I whiled away the weekends in the professor's art-filled house.

I might have continued making that mistake forever, but a few weeks after my birthday, the professor broke up with me for good. I moped around for a few days, but then, in June, *The Oregonian*'s managing editor called to tell me my big shot had arrived. Starting mid-month, I'd cover North and Northeast Portland, the city's most diverse neighborhoods. After five and a half years in the bureau, I was finally moving to a job downtown.

I started my new beat on a Tuesday, the day Frankie and I always went for dollar oysters. She texted me the night before to suggest we celebrate by biking to the Louisiana restaurant together. At 6 p.m., I ran downstairs and found Frankie outside *The Oregonian*, leaning against the pearl white Bianchi she'd assembled herself. I grabbed my blue Kona, and we pedaled east, uphill and over the river.

The sun was shining when we left my office, but just before we hit the Broadway Bridge's highest point, it started to rain. Normally, Portland rain wouldn't be worth mentioning. "Rain" is the city's perpetual state. The sky skews dark, and the streets stay wet eight months a year, but most of the time, the rain there is only a drizzle. That afternoon, it stormed the way it does in Louisiana. The rain banged down in pelting sheets, and the wind shoved my bike back and forth.

By the time we reached the restaurant, Frankie and I were so soaked, I had to go to the bathroom and wring my shirt out in the sink. I looked at myself in the mirror, all messy-haired with rain, and I told myself it was time to be happy. I'd finally earned the job I wanted, and now this nice girl was in my life. I didn't need to choose bad romance anymore. I didn't need professors or broken women. All I had to do was walk into the restaurant and decide to be happy, normal. I shook my hair out, then I went.

OUR CLOTHES WERE STILL wet when we left the oyster bar two hours later, but Frankie insisted on biking me all the way home. She followed me up the stairs, and we watched another episode of *The L Word* still wearing our itchy, damp work clothes. We sat so close to each other that the sides of our hands touched. Frankie says I put my arm around her "woodenly," but I don't remember that. I don't remember either of us moving until 8 p.m., until the light streaming in from my picture window dimmed as the sun arced close to the river, and Frankie remembered she hadn't brought any bike lights. She stood. She went to the bathroom, and when she returned, she was wearing her helmet. I didn't know it then, but she told me much later, she'd decided in the bathroom to kiss me. I thought we were going to hug, but when we tipped toward each other, our lips caught. It was a clumsy first kiss, probably the most awkward one I've ever had, but a few days later, we kissed again, then we kept kissing until finally, a month later, after she'd returned from a trip with her mother to the Basque Country, we agreed to call each other "girlfriend."

THAT SUMMER, MY PARENTS came to visit me in Portland for the first time. I spent the week before their trip worrying, looking at my beloved apartment the way I suspected my mother would. The hardwood floors were scuffed. The tile around my sink had turned black with the kind of mold every century-old Portland apartment has. And the crown moldings I thought of as jazzy looked ancient in a bad way when I imagined my mom staring up at them.

When I pull out pictures of that apartment now, I can see that it was the kind of place you can only have when you're single and in your twenties. I kept Christmas lights strung along a curtain rod all year long, and I never once hung drapes. I had a Polaroid camera, and I used it to take photos of every person who visited, then I hung those pictures above the crown molding. I had several dozen, just enough to wind around two-thirds of the room. I left the remaining space empty, open spots for future visitors. I did have a sectional couch I'd spent a whole paycheck purchasing. It was locally made and cornflower blue, and its silhouette was a mid-century modern style I associated with classy people, but behind that beautiful couch, I hung a huge, unframed David Hockney poster that showed California's littered Pearblossom Highway. The only framed art I owned was a mixed-media piece titled *Catalog Portraying the Lesbian Lifestyle*. The work included images of twenty or so "required objects" for lesbianism, everything from a box of Dyke cigars to a set of dildos in three sizes. All my plants looked a little funky. The cactuses had gone crooked creeping toward the sun, and the dracaenas were burnt and barely alive. But I was happy in that apartment. I had a heavy wooden desk where I wrote stories, a double IKEA bookshelf full of my favorite novels, and an old card catalog I'd bought from a man who picked all the local thrift stores clean of their best items.

The night before my parents flew in, I ran my hand along the card catalog drawers, and I hoped my parents wouldn't notice the other piece of odd furniture in my living room—an end table a friend had made me out of three different cabinet doors. It was useful, a place where I set my books and glasses down, but it didn't look like something my mother would ever allow in one of her immaculately decorated rental homes.

My parents flew in mid-July. My mom complained about the three flights of stairs she had to climb to reach my apartment, and when I suggested sushi or Thai food for dinner, she pretended to gag. "Can't we eat something American?" she asked. I took them to a pub. Frankie biked over to meet us, and as she walked toward our table, I held my breath. My mom had only ever met one girlfriend, a very sweet army brat I went out with in college. My mom hadn't met the professor or anyone else I'd liked in Portland, not even the newspaper designer I dated for three years. I clenched my fist anxiously, but when Frankie ordered a beer and a corn dog, my mom flashed a thumbs-up.

"Thank God you eat normal food."

My parents stayed a week. We were good when we were drinking, happy when we were out, but the mornings were tougher to navigate. My mom swore she was allergic to cats and walked around holding her nose when Lafayette was in the room. She complained about having to go downstairs to smoke. And she did notice my silly cabinet-door-table. Every time she walked past it, she started singing the theme song from *The Beverly Hillbillies*.

I only took my parents to a restaurant I liked once. It was a vegetarian place, which I knew was a risk, but I persuaded my mom to try it by telling her they served baked Brie, her favorite food. She spent most of the dinner grumbling about the fact that Portland restaurants don't serve drinks in Styrofoam or with nearly enough ice. After the baked Brie arrived with a few too many fancy additions—hazelnuts, thin slices of an apple variety she'd never tried—she pushed her plate aside and started playing Candy Crush on her phone.

After a few days in Portland, I took my parents on an overnight trip to see the Pacific Ocean. I thought it would be an easy win—my mom had always loved the beach when we lived in Georgia—but when we got there, she refused to walk to the shore. She said the beach was too cold and the water too far away from the parking lot, and she was right. The Pacific Ocean is nothing like the Atlantic. That far north, the water is too chilly for swimming, and you have to wear a jacket most weeks of the year. But it's beautiful, and we'd driven three hours to see it, so I didn't want to just sit in the car.

"I'm walking down there," I said.

My dad went with me to see the sea lions sunning themselves against the surf, but my mom stayed behind. He and I spent maybe twenty minutes on the beach, taking pictures of the sea lions and each other. We laughed a lot. We posed goofy, and we talked in high-pitched silly voices, but I couldn't stop thinking about my mother waiting in the parking lot. I wanted my family to be proud of me. I wanted them to love what I loved, or I wanted them to at least experience what I loved. Instead, my mom was sitting in the car, probably bored and mad at me. I told myself I'd been insensitive. I shouldn't have picked an activity my mom didn't feel comfortable doing. My dad and I headed back to the parking lot, and I made up my mind to apologize, but when we reached my car, the interior smelled like cigarettes, so I plopped into the driver's seat, sulking without saying a word.

Later that night, after we'd eaten dinner at the only restaurant my mom would consider, we somehow locked ourselves out of our hotel room. The front desk worker had already gone home, so we had to wait an hour until a locksmith showed up. A breeze blew off the ocean, and my mom's teeth chattered. Even in the summertime, the nights are cold on the Oregon coast. The temperature dropped to fifty-seven degrees while we huddled outside, and my mom looked at me as if even the weather were my fault.

"I can't believe you live here," she said. "I'm never coming back."

I DON'T REMEMBER the rest of the trip. I took my parents to the airport, then I avoided talking to my mom for several months. My dad called every few weeks or so to tell me my mom was in the hospital again, but usually, I made excuses to get off the phone. Years later, my dad told me that he'd felt like he was on an island back then. No one wanted to talk about my mother's hospital stays, and so he had endured them alone. I could reject his calls and live my life pretending, but he had to spend his life walking up and down the fluorescent halls of her anguish. All his money went to hospital bills, and all his clothes smelled slightly antiseptic. He didn't tell me any of this then, but I'm sure I wouldn't have listened even if he had. After that beach trip, I turned distant and cold.

Frankie told me recently that I seemed tough in my twenties that I came back from the beach and griped about my parents only eating American food, but I didn't act hurt. Later that week, I told a friend over instant message that I was glad my parents were gone.

"We have nothing in common," I typed.

"You have nothing in common with your parents? How is that possible?"

I wanted to believe I was angry, but I understand now that I wasn't mad. I was embarrassed. I felt rejected, and I hadn't thought it was possible to feel that way in Portland. I expected to be hurt in Louisiana, but Portland was my place, a city where I felt safe and empowered to be myself. I used to think that the only thing distancing me from my parents was my sexuality, but I realized during that trip that being gay was only a part of it. It didn't matter if my parents met my girlfriend, or if they stopped believing I was going to Hell. There were things we'd never have in common, ways I'd always feel like I didn't belong. I couldn't show them my life if I didn't take them out to eat sushi or Indian food. I didn't play the Frank Ocean or Kendrick Lamar albums that were my favorite records that year because I knew my mom would plug her ears and call it noise. And even though my mom read constantly, I didn't talk about books I loved because I didn't want my parents to remember that I was more educated than they were. Those gaps made me feel horribly alone. I'd thought when I was younger that if I found my city, my place in this world, all my wounds would magically heal. I wouldn't feel rejected. I wouldn't be a misfit. But after my parents left, I realized I was wrong. My hurts had traveled with me.

For weeks after, I moped around my apartment, somehow believing I was the only person in the world who'd ever drifted apart from her family. I think I felt that way, in part, because Frankie's family was tight-knit. Her parents hadn't just tried sushi, they loved it. She and her mom liked the same old movies, and her whole family texted all day long on a group they'd labeled "Saturday Fun Bunch." I thought something was uniquely wrong with me. But in the years since, I've realized that Portland was a place full of people who'd fled somewhere else. All my friends had their own Louisianas haunting them. They came from Tucson or Gainesville, the northeastern suburbs or some tiny midwestern town no one's ever heard of, and they told themselves they didn't miss those places. Usually, their parents didn't visit Portland. Instead, once a year, my friends dragged themselves home, where they pretended to be less queer, less educated, and less citified versions of themselves. They posted iPhone photos on Facebook, beaming shots that showed them drinking outside their favorite childhood hangouts, then they flew back to Portland, the Xanadu where we told ourselves we could be free.

ALL FALL, I TRIED not to think about my parents. I hung out with Frankie, and I worked on an article about a sixty-one-year-old professional wrestler who'd found the daughter he'd abandoned when his career first took off. He wanted his daughter to see him perform, so I was writing about the comeback he was trying to stage. The wrestler and his daughter were transplants from New Orleans, and I played up my accent when I was interviewing them, but off the clock, I rarely thought about Louisiana. I went camping and started making my own chia seed pudding, activities I never would have done in the South. I went back to the beach with Frankie, and we shivered along the shore, but neither of us complained about the cool air swooping off the Pacific Ocean. I was happy in a way that leaves no room for longing, which meant I spent very little time that year wondering about Delhi.

I'd told Frankie on our first hangout that I was making a film about Roy. Aubree and I had raised eleven thousand dollars through Kickstarter to pay for plane tickets, but a year had gone by, and I hadn't booked another trip. One night, Frankie asked me why.

I didn't think I was avoiding the project because of my parents. We weren't talking, but I wasn't so hurt that I was ready to give up on the film I'd spent three years trying to make. I wasn't sure what to tell Frankie, so I blurted out an answer.

"I'm worried I won't accomplish anything. What if I get down there and nobody will do an interview?"

I hadn't actually given it much thought, but I realized after I said it just how afraid I was that I'd never finish the documentary. I'd spent so much money flying down, and I didn't have a whole lot to show for it. What if I never found Roy's real parents? What if Mark kept refusing to share Roy's journals? What if I wasn't supposed to read them?

I don't think Frankie understood back then how much of a pessimistic self-doubter I am, but she knew what to say.

"Has that ever happened? Have you ever gone down and not learned anything?"

Usually when I'm wallowing, I don't want to be cheered up. I wanted to tell Frankie that I'd failed every single trip. But she was right: I hadn't figured out everything I hoped to, but I always discovered *something* when I went to Louisiana.

By the end of the night, I had a plane ticket. I emailed Pam, the lesbian from the pickup truck, and asked if she was still willing to be interviewed. I suggested we meet at her house. When she wrote back she said she'd love to talk, but only if we met in a parking lot. Her house, she said, was off-limits for now.

"After my mother dies," she wrote, "you can come by."

THE PARKING LOT PAM chose was in front of an abandoned brick building on the highway. A faded sign hanging on the front said it was THE HUMAN HOUSE, open Fridays and Saturdays, nine to four, but we pulled up mid-morning on a Friday, and it looked long closed. The only vehicle in the lot was Pam's, the idling red truck that had scared me a year before.

I pulled into a spot, and Pam stepped out wearing a gray T-shirt, hiking boots, and baggy men's Levi's. She was short, maybe five feet even, and heavyset. Her brown hair had gone gray at the temples, and it looked like she'd just had it cut.

"Welcome back to Louisiana," she said, pronouncing it *Looz-ee-anna,* the way my dad does. "Y'all proud to be here?"

Christopher and Aubree had come along again, and they answered in unison: "Absolutely. Of course."

I asked Pam why she'd chosen this spot. She pointed to the building next door, an Anytime Fitness that looked like it had just opened. It was the first new business we'd seen in three years, so I craned my neck to get a better look. The building was squat and nondescript, with a strip mall stucco facade and a tiny, pitched roof.

"That's where I met Roy."

Back in the 1970s, Pam said, the building had been Pickett's Grocery, the store her stepfather owned. The town had three groceries then, including a Jitney Jungle on the other side of The Human House, but most people went to Pickett's because her stepfather allowed people to buy things on credit.

"You had the little old ladies with their mink coats on. You had the farmers with their overalls and no shoes. Black people came here. Mexicans came here. We even had a few Japanese."

Pam told us she started working the register in junior high. Roy was a regular shopper then, but unlike the farmers and the ladies with the mink coats, Roy didn't speak when he reached the counter. His eyes were bright but sad, and when Pam tried to talk to him, he just muttered a few words.

"I always wondered what's wrong with that person. Why is their life so miserable that they can't talk to people?"

Pam looked down at her baggy jeans, then back up at me. She kept her hands in her pockets.

"I found myself comparing myself to Roy over the years," she said. "I kind of keep to myself. I've always kept my hair short. I dress like a man. It's somewhat embarrassing when you're with your family. I'm sure it's embarrassing to them. It's been many a time right there in that grocery store when kids would come in and say, 'Are you a man or a woman?' And I'd go, 'Uh, I'm a girl. I guess.'"

I know people who exist between genders, people who would relish the chance to say "neither" when asked "man or woman," but that kind of liberation hadn't yet reached Pam at the tail end of 2012, and I understood how badly those questions could hurt. They were more of a statement than a question, a judgment that said something's not right. I hadn't grown up with a Roy the way Pam had, but I remember the first lesbians I ever saw, and I remember the wave of recognition and relief I felt as those low-voiced, short-haired women crossed my path. *So I'm not the only one.* Even my friends who reject the binary seem to long to fit somewhere. Most have adopted "they" as their pronoun, an agreed-upon nomenclature for the in-betweens. They have their own purple, yellow, white, and black nonbinary flag, and they even have a collective nickname—enbies. Pam didn't have a flag or a word yet. She only had Roy.

"I can remember wondering," Pam said, "wanting to ask Roy, 'How is society going to treat me, growing up different?'"

Pam looked at the video cameras, then back at me. She told me she'd gone to Roy's house once, intending to ask him. Pam was maybe fifteen or sixteen, and Roy was in his fifties, and he'd come by the grocery store earlier that day with a pack of dogs circling him. He left carrying an armful of Cokes, and most of the dogs followed him out, but a few minutes later, Pam noticed a white-and-brown hound mix still waiting by the coolers. The dog wasn't bothering anyone, but Pam had been looking for an excuse to talk to Roy outside of the store, and this seemed like the only opportunity she might get.

"So," Pam told me, "I asked one of the older ladies where Roy lived so I could take the dog back home." A cashier who'd worked there for years told Pam to drive up Hell Street looking for a "little bitty wood-frame house."

"So I loaded the dog up in the front of my truck, and I took it to the house."

Pam puttered north. She inched toward Roy's intersection, and she gripped the steering wheel so tight her hands hurt. What was that feeling in her chest? Curiosity? Envy? She parked her truck in front of Roy's house. A ring of mutts crowded the tiny half porch, and a few other dogs were sniffing around the yard. Pam stepped out, grabbed the hound out of the cab, then set him in the grass. She watched the dog for ten minutes, hoping if she lingered long enough, Roy would come out and talk to her, but he never did. Eventually, Pam climbed Roy's steps, opened the screen, and knocked three quick raps on his front door. The porch dogs looked up. Pam waited. She knocked again, but Roy never answered.

I'd been hanging spellbound on Pam's every detail. In my memory, my mouth is hitched open, but Aubree wasn't videotaping me, so I have no way of knowing for sure. I thought Pam was going to reach some climactic high, that Roy would step onto his porch and tell Pam everything she needed to know about living this kind of life. When Pam made it to her actual reveal, the blood drained out of my head. I could almost feel her disappointment reverberating through the years and into my chest, or maybe that was my own disappointment I was feeling. We'd both ginned up the courage to knock and ask for answers. We'd both found the door shut.

Lately, Pam said, she'd been thinking about all those dogs she saw that day. Back at her own house, the house I could not visit, Pam said she had as many dogs as Roy had had. She owned some of the dogs and was fostering the others until a local rescue group could find them homes. She'd named a yellow mutt Emmylou and a black one Crystal Gayle. The poodle was Rosie. And the crazy dog, a Pomeranian Pam affectionately called "crackhead," was Zoey.

For years, Pam told me, the dogs had been her only companions. She hadn't kissed anyone since Y2K, and she couldn't remember the last time she'd had sex. She lived with her mom, Geraldine, but that was just a spatial formality. They shared a living room, a kitchen, and a tiny television set, but they did not share details of their lives.

"So why do y'all live together?" I asked.

I had barely survived that week in July with my mom. I couldn't imagine a lifetime. Pam exhaled a long, slow breath.

"Because I made a promise."

Pam dragged her hiking boot over the concrete, then she cleared her throat. She told me she hadn't expected to live in Delhi this long.

"Even from the time I was three or four years old, I knew I was different," she said.

Back then, Pam told us, she'd begged her mother to let her keep her hair short. Her mom never relented, so Pam spent her childhood in ponytails she hated. She stole her brothers' cowboy boots every chance she got, and people joked that she was in a tomboy phase. They didn't understand, she told us. She didn't want to grow into her feminine side. She wanted to *be* a cowboy.

Pam's stepdad was the only person who accepted her as she was. Her real father had disappeared when she was a baby. He'd moved away to Singapore or Nicaragua; her mother never knew which. But Joe Tatum, the man her mother fell in love with at a livestock auction, more than made up for the man who'd left for someplace foreign. He drove Pam to the Little Grill Cafe every Saturday, and on Sundays, he took her deer hunting with the boys. He taught her how to shoot. He let her do everything her brothers did.

The year after she met Roy, Pam kissed a girl for the first time, but she didn't tell anyone, not even Joe. The girl was a classmate, a tall butch teenager who, confusingly, was also named Pam. They called each other Big Pam and Little Pam, on account of their heights, and one morning, while everyone else was in class, the Pams met in the bathroom, then slipped through a back door to a small, secluded patio. They didn't make any confessions or even conversation, Pam said. There was no need to. Once they were outside, hidden, they kissed sloppy and long.

As soon as Little Pam—my Pam—got her driver's license, she took Big Pam on a date. Delhi had a movie theater back then, but cinema darkness wasn't safe enough, so Pam borrowed her mother's station wagon, then drove Big Pam out to an uncropped field. They parked on a turnrow and kissed until their lips blistered.

I couldn't help but laugh. That was the most redneck gay story I'd ever heard. I could almost picture it as a country music video, two Stetson-topped women barreling down dirt roads, kissing in a field while the sun set. I would have loved to have made that kind of music video, but country music, of course, wouldn't have allowed the love story of two butch women to invade the charts.

I asked Pam if she'd been scared that someone in Delhi might hurt her if they found out. She smiled kind of smug and smooth.

"No, I was always a badass little dyke. Nothing scared me. I'd pull out my gun and shoot the shit out of them."

She angled her body so it was out of the frame for a moment. "Don't put that on camera," she said, "because I have shot at people before, and they probably remember it."

Pam laughed at her own bravado. I assumed she was faking confidence. If she wasn't scared, why had she driven so far out of town to kiss

Big Pam? Why would she only meet me in the parking lot of an abandoned building? I didn't push her, though. I understood that pretending to be brave is sometimes the only way to survive the South, so I laughed, and I pressed on with the interview.

"What happened next?"

"We stayed together five years," Pam said.

They kept sneaking around until Pam's mother overheard her talking to Big Pam on the phone one night. When Pam hung up the phone, her mother marched toward her, angry and unhinged.

"She promptly slapped my face and told me to get the hell out of her house," Pam said. "That's when I left."

Pam told me that she realized back then that moving out of her mother's house was not enough. She would have to leave the whole town behind. The day she loaded her truck, Joe hugged her a little longer than usual. He told her to remember what he'd taught her at the grocery store: It doesn't matter how a person dresses, what color they are, or how they were raised. All customers are customers and deserve respect. Pam knew Joe wasn't really talking about customers. Leaving Delhi meant leaving the grocery store, but she assumed it was his way of telling her he accepted her, even if her mother didn't.

Pam moved to Monroe in 1981. She must have been living there when I was born two years later. The way she described it, Monroe was the big city. It was the escape. Pam went there expecting to earn a college degree, but she didn't stay enrolled in school for long. Monroe had a gay bar and parties and women. Pam lasted a semester, then she dropped out to revel in that freedom. She still regretted that decision, she told me. If she'd finished college, she might have become a veterinarian. Instead, she worked the graveyard shift at a sweet potato factory. She stood for eight hours straight, manning the machines that turn root vegetables into waffle fries, then she slept through daylight. All her jobs had been that way. She'd met her last girlfriend working the late shift at Walmart in the 1990s. Pam stocked dog food, and Lana sold shoes. Their aisles were close enough that they could see each other, and one night, Lana wandered over. They talked a few minutes, and talking felt so good, Pam decided to try for more. She earned less than six dollars an hour, barely enough to pay for a date, but she asked Lana if she could buy her a hamburger after work. That night, and every night after, Pam drove Lana around town in her cherry-red pickup. They rode down highways and gravel roads, talking until they were too tired to form words. Eventually, they moved in together.

They lived together for eight years and might have gone on forever, but in the spring of 1998, Joe had a stroke. Pam drove home to Delhi one afternoon to take him to physical therapy, and on the ride home, he started crying.

"I didn't understand what was wrong with him," Pam told us in the parking lot. "He was like, 'I don't know what I'm going to do. I can't take care of your mom anymore.'"

Geraldine was only fifty-eight, but Joe told Pam she had heart problems and weak legs. She had even fallen out of bed a few times. Joe begged Pam to promise that she'd take care of her mother when he died. Pam and her mother hadn't spoken more than a few words to each other in nearly twenty years, but Pam loved Joe, so she promised to do what he asked.

"A few days later," Pam said, "Joe had a massive heart attack and died."

Fifteen years had passed, but Pam started crying when she talked about Joe's death. Her voice broke, and she covered her face with her hands. After a few minutes, she wiped her eyes and told me her mom bought a double tombstone, one side for Joe, and the other already etched with "Geraldine." She told Pam she'd join him soon, and afterward, Pam felt like she didn't have a choice. If her mom only had a few months left, she had to make them easy ones. A week after Joe died, Pam said goodbye to Lana. She bought a two-bedroom house on three acres of flat land a mile north of the Delhi city limits, and she and her mother moved in that May.

The double tombstone, it turned out, was premature. A decade and a half later, Geraldine was still living, and Pam had almost forgotten what it was like to be in control of her own life. She knew her mom wouldn't want her to date women, so she didn't. Instead, Pam worked the night shift, and she spent all day at home. She cooked for her mother, usually something microwaved or boiled, then she cleaned the house and occasionally drove into town to pick up her mom's prescriptions. Those were the only plans she made.

"So that's where I'm at in my life," Pam told us. "I'm fulfilling that last promise."

Pam didn't look at me or Aubree or Christopher for a while. I was glad she didn't. I was worried if she looked at me, she'd see that I pitied her and hated myself. I didn't even need to wonder if I would make a similar promise to my father. I knew I wouldn't. I wouldn't give up a girlfriend or a job or a life to move back to Monroe to share a house with my mom. I wouldn't take care of her. I wouldn't spend my thirties and forties waiting for her to die. I didn't want Pam to know any of that because I didn't want her to know how selfish I was. I wanted Pam to think I was a good person, the kind of woman who loves her family so much, she spends her vacation days working on a documentary for them.

"What happened to Lana?" I asked.

"She moved to Seattle."

A train rushed past, and Aubree called cut. While we waited for the engines to chug forward, I imagined Lana out west, living free and unafraid. Did she miss Louisiana? Did she walk down the street unabashedly holding a woman's hand the way I held Frankie's?

The train pushed east until it disappeared. Pam cleared her throat.

"You know," she said, "I've decided there are places I want to see, things I want to do. When my mother dies, I'll go."

Pam told us she wanted to buy a travel trailer. She planned to go to Gatlinburg, Tennessee, then all the way to Wyoming to the Grand Tetons. She'd see every national park.

"Someday."

I wanted to tell Pam that she didn't have to wait. She could go now, leave her mother the way I'd left mine, and she could find her own Frankie someplace out west. Life would be easier. She could find a day-time job and rent a house on a street where no one asked if she was a man or a woman. Maybe she could even go to Seattle and reunite with Lana. She wouldn't have to depend on dogs as her only companions.

But I didn't tell Pam any of that because even as I allowed myself to think it, I knew that no city cured loneliness. It didn't matter that I lived in the lesbian capital of the United States. It didn't matter that I had a girlfriend and the downtown newspaper job I'd spent so many years wanting. I was missing something, in Portland as much as I ever had in Louisiana, and no amount of running could change it.

Chapter Thirteen

(December 2012)

SOON AFTER I STARTED working on the documentary, people began telling me they thought I should put myself in the film. Aubree said it needed a narrator, someone to link all the interviews together, and Frankie agreed, but I didn't want to be in front of the camera. Every book I'd ever read about journalism said the best reporters were invisible. I worried my bosses would think less of me if they saw me making myself the story. Plus, I didn't want anyone to suspect I was only curious about Roy because I was gay. I didn't even know how Roy identified. Maybe he was gay or maybe he was transgender or maybe he lived as a man because his parents made him dress that way when he was young. Whatever the truth was, I told myself, it had nothing to do with me.

People in Delhi saw through that.

The day after we interviewed Pam, I called another woman I hoped to film. When I told her what the movie was about, the woman asked me why I was interested in Roy. I started to tell her what I'd told Archie—my grandmother grew up on Hell Street and wanted to know more about Roy's life—but the woman cut me off.

"I get why your grandmother's interested, but that's not what I asked. I asked why are *you*. Nobody's that nice to their grandma. Why are you, personally, interested in a morphodite?"

"You're breaking up," I said, pretending I couldn't hear her. "My service is bad. I'll have to call you back."

I hung up, turned my phone off, then tucked it into my back pocket, just in case.

After I got off the phone, Aubree, Christopher, and I piled into the car, then we set out to do more reporting. We'd flown down close to Christmas again, and all the tiny houses were lit up with red and green bulbs. On Main Street, First Baptist was playing "O Little Town of Bethlehem" in the same key it had three years earlier when I visited with my mom. Delhi hadn't changed much since that first trip. Hot Wings Heaven was still closed, and barber shops still dotted the main drag. The highway and all the potholed streets looked the same, too, but I felt different somehow.

I thought about my mom as I looped around town. I still couldn't believe Pam had given up her life to take care of her mother. I hadn't even called my mom this trip to tell her I was in Louisiana. She was in the hospital again, and anyway, she and my dad had moved to Tyler, Texas. Their house was only three and a half hours away from Delhi, so I could've driven over, could've even stayed until Christmas, but I didn't plan to do that. Instead, I drove my mom's old streets, and I imagined the girl she had been. I stopped at the squat brick house Golden and Rita Mae used to own, and I cruised past the wood-frame hulk my grand-parents rented in the 1970s, then I steered toward the house my mom was living in when Cam died. I don't know if Aubree or Christopher wondered why I started each trip with these meandering drives. Aubree usually shot footage from the window, and Christopher sat in the back seat, napping or eating a PayDay candy bar for breakfast. I'm not even sure what I hoped to accomplish. I'd seen all these houses before. I'd looked them up on Google Maps, and I'd taken my own photos, too. But I had to see them, in person, every trip.

Eventually, after I'd driven by all my mom's places, I pulled into the library parking lot, then called a woman Archie had told me might be willing to talk. Her name was Lou Rogers. Both she and her husband had lived on Chatham Street, and she knew my grandma's sister, Shir-ley. Lou sounded hesitant when she answered, but after we'd talked for twenty minutes, she gave me her address and told me to come over.

Lou lived in Epps, a tiny community north of Delhi, and the drive up was long and country. Half the homes we saw were barns. We passed a donkey and a Shetland pony, and I had to swerve three times to avoid bumping into slow-moving tractors.

Epps is about half the size of Delhi, but the two places have a lot in common. They both have slightly more Black residents than white, and both have among the lowest median incomes in the country. In 2012, an average woman in either town earned just above $12,000 a year. I got the feeling, driving up, that the entire region's best days were behind it. In Epps, as in Delhi, most businesses looked forever closed. Their exteriors were so decayed that I could only make out the name of one, Ruth & Reds, an Italian place whose faded sign showed a Native American waiting outside a teepee for pizza.

The streets on the west side of Epps were named Honeysuckle and Magnolia, but Lou lived in the east, an area where most roads were named by numbers. I turned left on the one she'd told me to look for, a single-lane asphalt strip filled in with gravel. Lou and her husband didn't have a paved driveway, but they did have a lot of land, so I parked on a patch of dead leaves next to a pickup truck. Their house was a big wood-frame that looked like a cabin but wasn't one. As we unloaded all of our equipment and walked toward the house, I could see Lou waiting in the doorway. She was in her sixties, and she kept her hair cut short and blown back in a way that seemed more utilitarian than stylish, but I could tell she'd been beautiful once. Her skin was smooth, her eyebrows perfectly shaped, and she was trimmer than most people we'd interviewed.

"No pictures!" she called from the doorway. "No pictures."

She covered her face, and I explained to her that the project was a documentary.

"Can't you do me like they do on *America's Most Wanted*?" she asked. "With the blacked-out face and the voice distorted?"

We followed her and a yipping black Chihuahua inside, toward a living room filled with plants and Christmas lights. The cameras were off for a while, so I don't know how we persuaded Lou to go on with her real face and actual voice, but she doesn't look uncomfortable in the footage, and she didn't seem to hold anything back. Once the cameras were on, Lou gracefully lowered herself somewhere near the middle of the couch. "Casey, sit next to Lou," Aubree suggested. "I want you both in the shot."

I sat down, but I scooted as close to the edge as I could. I knew I might be ruining the perfect framing Aubree wanted, but I didn't care. I didn't want to be in the movie.

"So," I said to Lou. "Do you mind introducing yourself?"

Lou took a deep breath, clasped her hands together, then looked at me as if there were no video cameras in the room. She told me she'd gotten married and left Hell Street when she was sixteen, but she'd tried, for a while, to keep in touch with Roy. They went to the Church of Christ together for many years, and she even sat next to Roy in the back pew. Some weekends, Lou and her husband would drive over to play checkers or guitar with Roy, but they'd stopped doing that years ago. Lou said she felt guilty about that now.

"I think that's why Roy got so bad," she said. "You can imagine her having to go to the doctor. She just didn't go. And nobody was there to say, 'Something's wrong. Come on, let me take you to the doctor.' We should have been. But we had our own family."

Lou picked at a piece of fuzz on the couch. She said she and her husband had both tried, later, to check on Roy, but they waited too long. By then, Roy had stopped bathing, and his dementia was so advanced he didn't remember either of them. After Roy went into the nursing home, Lou went up there to visit him, but when they sat down at a table, Roy didn't recognize or even seem to notice Lou. He babbled on in words that were barely words, and Lou found it too unbearable to witness. Roy was a songwriter, Lou reminded me, someone who'd always known how to string a perfect sentence together. She never went back to see him a second time.

"Then," Lou said, "the man wouldn't let us have the pictures after Roy died."

Lou looked down and twisted her wedding ring around her finger. She shrugged in a way that suggested she was annoyed but resigned.

"What man?" I asked.

"Roy's neighbor. Mark King."

For years, Lou explained, Roy had kept pictures of her and her husband tacked to the walls of his house. Some of them were old photos, snapshots from the 1950s and '60s, pictures of Lou and her husband when they were kids. After Roy died, Lou heard that Mark King had taken most of Roy's stuff, so she drove down to Chatham Street to ask for the pictures. Cheryl King answered the door.

At first, Lou said, Cheryl was friendly. She knew Lou because she'd taught one of Lou's daughters PE at the junior high. When Lou asked if she could have Roy's old pictures, Cheryl said yes. She disappeared into a back room, but when she returned, Mark was with her. He said he wasn't sure he was willing to hand over any of Roy's things. He told Lou to give him some time to think.

"So I waited a month or two," Lou said. "Then I went back."

The second time Lou visited, Mark didn't let her inside. He stuck his head out of the screen door and told her he'd decided he wanted to keep Roy's old photos.

I didn't understand, so I asked Lou why Mark decided to keep the photos.

"I don't know," she said. "They were nothing to him."

Lou and I looked at each other. She clasped her hands back together.

"Now, the journals would have really been interesting," she said. "I would have loved to have gotten my hands on those."

Lou was probably the least dramatic person we interviewed for the film. Her words didn't jump up and down the way my relatives' did, and her accent sounded muted in comparison. She didn't gesture much when she talked, and she didn't reposition herself on the couch even once. But she smiled a tiny bit when she mentioned the journals, and that was enough to make my hands burn with some kind of nervous excitement. Christopher and I had started thinking that maybe Mark was bluffing. Maybe he didn't have any of Roy's stuff. But Lou—steady-voiced, even-keeled Lou—was offering me something like proof. The journals were real. Mark had them. My mystery was solvable. All I had to do was persuade Mark to let me see Roy's diaries.

"What did they look like?" I asked.

"They were thick spiral notebooks. Probably started when my husband was a little boy. Roy had lots of them. I think she wanted people, after she was gone, to know what kind of life she led. Why else would she have kept them? I know she didn't plan on them ending up like they are now. I think she did it for a purpose, for people to know what it was like living like that. But as it turned out, we won't ever know."

Lou's mouth turned ever so slightly into a frown. I told her I had asked Mark about Roy's journals, and he'd refused to share them.

"It doesn't seem right to make this documentary without including Roy's own thoughts," I said.

Lou unclasped her hands. Her eyes lit up, then she sprung off the couch.

"I've got a Bible of hers that's got her name wrote on it," she said. "She's got a lot marked in it."

Lou disappeared down a hall. She returned a few minutes later holding a red King James Version Bible just slightly bigger than my hands. She sat down on the couch and set the Bible between us. I stared at it for a while before I picked it up. The leather felt cool in my hands, and I felt a kind of power, holding something Roy had held. I knew how personal a person's Bible could be. My mom had always used hers like a journal, and so had I, back when I lived in Louisiana. The Bible was a place where I could reveal myself, where I could confess and struggle and seek mercy. Holding Roy's Bible, I realized I must have gotten rid of mine at some point. I didn't remember when or how, though. I couldn't even remember what my Bible looked like. I know I used to have strong feelings about the different editions, but I couldn't recall which one I'd preferred. Did I like the New International Version because it was readable? Or had I hated it because it seemed dumbed down compared to the stately King James? How had I forgotten something that once seemed to matter so much?

I pushed back the cover of Roy's Bible, carefully, as if it were an artifact on loan from a museum. Inside the front flap, Roy had stamped his name and address. I smiled. I had always thought only rich people had stamps with their names and address on them. My family never lived anywhere long enough to memorialize our address in a stamp, and I wondered if Roy felt the kind of pride I knew I'd feel if I ever owned one. A stamp meant you were somebody, you belonged somewhere, even if it was just a shotgun house on Hell Street.

I flipped the pages slowly at first, looking for some sign of Roy, but he hadn't marked much in the earliest books. Lou scooted closer toward me, so I moved faster, turning pages ten at a time until I found something, tiny blue marks scratched alongside verses. It's hard to explain what I felt when I first saw Roy's handwriting. It was better than the stamp and almost better than seeing the photos Ann McVay had given me on the first trip. These lines were Roy's lines, marks he made with the same hand he used to play the banjo that lured my grandmother across the street. I ran my finger over the grooves his pen left behind, and I felt like I'd discovered some kind of portal to the past.

Roy's handwriting was small and slanty. Most of his letters were capital letters, though occasionally a lowercase *h* would slip in between a capital *C* and *R*. In the book of Isaiah, he used a pink pen to make notes about the Devil and the king of Babylon. He underlined New Testament verses about love. He highlighted the ones about sin. Roy wrote throughout his Bible, but no book was as marked up as 1 Corinthians. He'd underlined and highlighted verses, and he'd penciled questions alongside the edge. His letters were so tiny and messy in chapter 11, I had to hold the Bible close to my face to decipher each one. This was the chapter Lynda had told us about, the one that suggests women shouldn't cut their hair. Roy had underlined the verse Lynda had recited to me the year before—"But if a woman have long hair, it is a glory to her: for her hair is given her for a covering"—but in the margins, he'd written a cursive commentary: "Power is not a hat or a covering."

Was Roy pushing back against the Pentecostals? Lynda and Archie had talked about Roy as if he were a victim, someone who'd been shamed and pushed out of the church. I believed them because that's what happened to me. Even after I started to believe that Leviticus didn't mean exactly what my pastor said it did, I didn't dare write any challenging notes in my Bible. I didn't send the Gomes book I read in college to anyone at my church. I just disappeared. I somehow still didn't have the strength to tell Pamela or anyone else from church that I was gay and no longer believed there was anything sinful about that.

I read Roy's words again—"Power is not a hat or a covering"—then I turned to chapter 12, a passage that suggests Christians are supposed to be unified. Roy had covered the page in penciled thoughts. Along the bottom, he'd written "divers," "different," "schism," and "division." He'd underlined a dozen words, and next to verse 23, a line that says we must bestow more honor on those we think to be less honorable, Roy had written "ME?"

The question mark looked crooked and unsure. I knew that feeling. I'd pushed it away long ago, but I remembered what it felt like to sit in the pew and listen to the preacher and wonder if the unconditional love he promised was meant for me.

I wanted to sit with that page for the rest of the afternoon, but Lou looked up, so I flipped forward to the end of chapter 15. Roy had used red and blue crayons to highlight the page. I scanned through it, and every verse seemed to be about bodies or flesh: "God giveth it a body as it hath pleased him." "It is sown a natural body." "How are the dead raised up, and with what body?"

The verses might have depressed anyone living in a shell they felt was wrong, but Roy, again, had written his own thoughts along the bottom of the page. No one takes their body to the afterlife, he'd noted. No "body" is forever.

"FIRST BODY FLESH, SECOND BODY SPIRIT," he wrote. "We shall be changed."

I read the words out loud to Lou, and she took her glasses off, then gazed at me.

"I think she was hoping for a better life, after," Lou said.

After. How many years had I spent waiting for "after"? I'd never dreamed of a different body, but as a kid, I thought constantly about that mansion my mother promised me. Even though she told me we wouldn't know each other in Heaven, I pictured my mansion as a place where she and I would live together, happy in a way we never seemed to manage on earth. She would be clear-brained and free of ghosts, and I would be the kind of daughter who didn't disappoint her.

I didn't dream that way anymore. I suppose I'd pinned my hopes on Portland instead. But when I was young, I didn't believe there were paradises on earth. I thought Heaven was heaven and earth was Georgia or Louisiana. It didn't occur to me to long for anywhere else. I didn't want to spend time in Germany the way my mom and grandma had, and I didn't apply to any of the good journalism schools Ask Jeeves recommended because I couldn't even picture myself in New York. On earth, at least, I belonged in the South.

My freshman year of college, I made a zine dedicated to showcasing all the ways movies and national newspapers pegged the region wrong. I was proud of my home—not in a "Don't tread on me," Confederate flag way, but still proud. Southerners were resilient and evolving, brilliant in ways I believed people in other regions could never be. We had the best food. We invented country music and jazz and the blues. Everyone had something interesting to say, and anyway the South was warm. I didn't want to live anywhere cold or distant.

I can't remember when moving started to feel inevitable. Maybe it was in college, maybe just after. Maybe I began looking for a new paradise after I realized I was gay and would probably never reach Heaven. Or maybe "inevitable" is a story I told myself after I'd already left. Leaving was achieving something, I reminded myself once I'd rented my apartment in Portland. It would have been a failure to stay home, would have been proof that I was stuck, unable to propel myself beyond the place that shaped me. I didn't need to spend my life waiting for some fantasy "after." I could be whole and happy on earth. All I had to do was leave Louisiana.

I looked down at Roy's Bible again. I thought of Pam, hoping for her own better life, after. I worried she'd never buy that camper, that she'd stay in Delhi, waiting without end the way Roy had. What kept him in Louisiana? By Pam's logic, Roy could have moved after Jewel died in 1958. He could have tried Nashville. He could have gone west to Oregon. Transgender men had been reconstructing their bodies in Portland since the early 1900s. Roy could have given himself the chest he wanted people to believe he had. But Roy didn't leave. He stayed and hung his hopes on the hereafter.

Maybe he hadn't known back then that a new body was an option on earth. Maybe he didn't have enough money to leave. Or maybe Roy stayed for the same reasons I drove to my mom's old houses every time I came to Delhi. Maybe he walked down Chatham and felt Jewel's presence. Maybe he was longing for something so unreachable that the land itself felt like his best connection.

Someone coughed, and I looked up from the Bible. Lou's husband appeared as a silhouette in the doorway. He nudged forward just enough that I could make out his face in the glow of the Christmas tree lights. He had a camouflage hat pulled low across his brow, and he was wearing the kind of light green plaid shirt that most men in north Louisiana wear to church. He was tall and toothless, brawny but bent in a way that suggested he'd spent his life working physical jobs. Lou said his name was Roy, too.

"Hey," Lou said, waving her husband in. "I couldn't figure out why Roy's name was Hudgins. Where'd that come from?"

"I think it came from the people that she come from before she went to the Ellises," Roy Rogers said. "When they came here, they dressed Roy as a boy because they thought somebody was huntin' them. But I don't think anybody ever looked for her."

Lou turned to me to explain her husband's comments.

"Roy always thought that she had been kidnapped or taken when she was a baby."

I felt strangely relieved. This, too, felt like proof. Everyone else we'd interviewed had told a different rendition of Roy's origin story. They said Roy was abandoned. They said he was too poor to wear dresses. One person said John wanted a boy, and another said Roy had been in a farming accident that left him confused about his gender. No one else had confirmed the story my grandmother had told me a decade earlier. But I believed Lou and Roy Rogers were good sources. They'd known Jewel and John Ellis. Roy Rogers had even worked on the ice truck with John, and he told me that John was a loner who never had company. They had known Roy as a child and as an adult, and if they said he was kidnapped, then I believed them. Or rather, I wanted to believe them. Believing them meant believing my grandma, meant believing that the years I'd spent working on this film were years rooted in something real. But there was one detail that never made sense to me in the kidnapping story.

"It's weird," I said. "It's weird that they'd go through the trouble of changing her into a boy but not change her last name, too."

"I know," Lou said.

The three of us looked at each other. I couldn't make eye contact with Aubree or Christopher because they were hidden behind a wall of film equipment, but I wondered if they were feeling the same mix of relief and skepticism I was.

Roy Rogers cleared his throat, then he stepped deeper into the living room.

"Some terrible things happened to Roy," he said. "She deserves to be in Heaven."

I asked him what he meant by terrible things, and Lou interrupted.

"Just being raised like she was."

"Not having a family?" I asked.

"Yeah," Lou said. "And everybody knowing she was female but dressed like a man. That was just common knowledge all over town."

Roy Rogers cleared his throat again, and I could tell those were not the terrible things he meant.

"She went to school in Delhi," he said. "Some boys I know, all of them are probably dead by now, they took her down and pulled her clothes off. And looked at her."

Aubree was running two cameras that day—one on Roy Rogers and one on Lou and me—so I can see exactly how I reacted in the moment. I just stared straight ahead. I remember that Roy Rogers's accent was so thick, I thought I might be misunderstanding him at first. But as he talked, or as I started to understand what he said, my mouth slowly fell open. Lou didn't move. She kept her hands in her lap, and her face looked as placid as it did the whole time I was interviewing her. But I look stunned.

"Roy never went to school another day, and I don't blame her," Roy Rogers said. "I hated those boys for doing that. I'd of shot them if I had a gun."

Lou bent over and laughed. She told her husband not to say things like that, but he waved her off. He said he'd been too small back then to help Roy, but he'd thought about it for seventy years, and he still wanted to shoot the men those boys became.

"They did Roy terrible that day at school. They laughed. They thought it was funny. But it wasn't funny. Ain't nothing funny. It broke Roy. It killed her."

Neither Lou nor I said anything. In the video footage, my mouth hung wide open for several minutes. Eventually, somehow, Lou and Roy Rogers changed the subject back to the things they loved about Roy. They said he cooked pones of cornbread for them, and when he lost at dominoes, he'd get so mad, he'd throw the pieces out the window. They told me, as Mark and Archie both had, that Roy sold a song to the gospel group the Whites.

"They paid her five hundred dollars for it, I remember that," Roy Rogers said. "She had a lot of songs in those books the man wouldn't let us have."

"Poems and her whole life history," Lou said. "Mark has her three-wheel bicycle, too."

"He ain't going to let you have it," Roy Rogers said. "He might sell it to you. It might cost you a couple hundred, but it'd be worth it if you got it."

In the video, I have my hand over my mouth for some reason, and my eyes are darting back and forth as if I'm seriously considering whether I should pay Mark for the journals. Eventually, Lou said she had to go buy a new heater for their bathroom, so we pulled ourselves off the couch, then said goodbye.

LATER THAT NIGHT, Aubree, Christopher, and I drove back to West Monroe to see my grandma. She and her sister, Shirley, were smoking in the carport when we arrived. Shirley looked exactly as I remembered—a little plump, radiant, with blue eyes and silver hair—but my grandma must have lost thirty pounds in the year since I'd seen her. A black-and-white button-down shirt hung off her frame as if she'd borrowed it from a large man. And her face was so slim that her ears seemed to have doubled in size. The only thing that hadn't changed was her hair. She still had it styled in a kind of medium-length crew cut. It reminded me of the way butch lesbians wore their hair.

It was late when we arrived, 9 p.m., and my grandma was sitting on a pillow wedged into the seat of a plastic chair, but she seemed eager to talk. I collapsed into one of the folding chairs that faced the row of space heaters she kept blasting, and she motioned for me to sit up straight.

"I wanted to tell you something," I said. "Lou Rogers has gone and asked Mark King for the journals twice."

My grandma tipped forward, eyes big and wide. She gripped a plastic cane she'd kept propped against her chair. "Wait, Casey," she said. "You gon' have to start over. She did what now?"

I repeated what I'd said. Lou went to ask for Roy's stuff, but Mark wouldn't let her have it. My grandma tilted as far forward as the cane would allow. When she spoke, her voice was quiet in a way that unsettled me. She never spoke softly.

"It angers me," she said. "It angers me that he won't share the scribblings of Roy. Roy poured his heart out on paper when he was lonely. It's sore on them to keep it."

"Roy *was* lonely," Shirley said. "Wasn't he, sis? He sat and he wrote all the time."

"I don't think Mark has what y'all think he has," my grandma said. "He went and took them, right? They're not his. He stole them. I know the King family. They think they're better than everybody else. He's running around telling y'all he did this and that for Roy. My guess is no, that is not true. Didn't he tell you one time it was just thrown up in the shed? How ugly of him."

"Sis," Shirley said. "You want my take on it?" Shirley's voice was peppier, more dramatic. She spoke the way my grandma usually did. "I think that he did go in there and get it, but I think over the years, he's probably destroyed it, and he's ashamed to tell you he didn't keep it."

My grandma grabbed a cigarette, then slid the pack toward her sister. Shirley nodded at Aubree's video camera and asked if her husband, George, was going to see this footage. "George doesn't know I smoke," she said. "And I don't want him to see this and find out."

I shrugged.

"Who knows when I'll actually finish it. At this rate, I could be dead and gone before it's finished."

"Honey," my grandma said, "if you're waiting on those journals, I don't think you're ever going to get them."

She dropped the cane. She lit the cigarette she'd been holding, and I sank lower into my plastic chair.

"So what do you think I should do?" I asked.

"I think you should leave it alone."

Leave it alone. Somehow, without knowing it, my grandma had used the exact same words Cheryl King had written three years earlier. *Leave this story alone.*

How could my grandma expect me to give up now? She was the one who'd started me on this journey. Maybe she'd grown impatient, or maybe she'd realized she'd sent me in search of something that couldn't be found, but I knew, as soon as she told me to drop it, that this wasn't just a story to me. I sat up straight again so she'd pay attention.

"Grandma," I said. "I can't."

Chapter Fourteen

(April 2013)

CHRISTOPHER AND I WENT back to Delhi a few months later. We planned to stop by Archie's house, and we'd told Pam we'd spend a day with her in the woods, but mostly, we went down that week to try to talk to Mark.

This time, I called Mark and asked if we could come over. He picked up on the first ring. He owned a landline, not a cell phone, but he must have had caller ID, because he answered by saying, "Casey?" He talked to me that night on the phone as if we were relatives or old friends. He told me he'd gone sale shopping in Vicksburg earlier in the day, and now he was looking into his genealogy online. I didn't tape the call, so I don't remember the exact words Mark used, but he talked for a while about the Cave Theater. I'd seen the theater on Broadway, and it was charming, one of the few remaining relics of the bustling town my grandmother must have seen when she first rode into Delhi. The Cave was built in 1946 in an art deco style that had already begun to fall out of fashion elsewhere. Back when my grandmother moved to town, the theater screened movies for five cents a ticket, and she'd told me once that she'd thought the world was ending the day the Cave increased admission to a dime. The theater didn't show movies anymore, Mark said. It had been closed for more than forty years, and Mark told me he was angry because city leaders had promised to restore it. They'd collected donations and won grants from the state, but decades had passed, and the Cave still sat as empty and unmaintained as all the other buildings near the railroad tracks.

Driving toward Mark's the next morning, I wondered how people felt, living in a place whose best days were behind it. In Portland, residents complained that too many people were moving to the city. Every month, it seemed, a new apartment building went up on a vacant lot, and the neighbors warned that we were running out of land. Meanwhile, in Delhi, whole acres sat empty. It seemed like they'd never be developed again.

I didn't feel nervous as I steered toward Mark's. Christopher and I joked about alligators and Garth Brooks songs, and eventually, we started talking about Roy's journals. Mark had told me a year earlier that he'd never read the diaries. He didn't want anyone else to read them, either, so I wasn't sure why he'd kept them.

"If he honestly wants to protect Roy," I told Christopher, "if he doesn't want random people just showing up and knowing all of Roy's private thoughts because he doesn't know what Roy would have wanted, then I understand that. I don't think we necessarily have a right to know just because we're nosy."

Christopher nodded. "I agree with you," he said. "But I think you have to be willing to be ballsy at the end."

I've worked with lots of journalists who push and demand that sources reveal everything they know, but that method has never come naturally to me. At *The Oregonian*, I started most interviews by telling people I understood that they didn't owe me anything. This was either my journalistic superpower or the fatal flaw that would prevent me from becoming the great reporter I wanted to be. I was patient, and usually that patience led people to open up to me in ways they never did with reporters who rushed through interviews, but editors said I was too passive. I lay back when I should have pressed people. I waited too long to ask the key question.

I parked the rental car on the side of the road a few trailers north of Mark's. Christopher and I pulled out our video cameras and the boom pole he used to hold a microphone above the shot, then we walked together down Chatham Street toward the intersection where our grandma once lived. A woman with long white hair was sitting in a lawn chair on Mark's porch. I said hi. I told her my name was Casey, and she said she was Cheryl, Mark's wife. Her voice was tiny, meek, friendly, but not inviting. I stopped walking toward her after she spoke. I don't know why I hadn't expected to see Cheryl, or why I suddenly felt anxious. Lou Rogers had said Cheryl was nice, but Cheryl and I had never spoken in person. The only time we'd communicated was when she wrote me in 2009, telling me to leave Roy's story alone.

I stood in the gravel driveway, a little paralyzed with nerves, until a swarm of bees swirled around me. I shrieked, and Mark stepped out of the trailer and into the buzz with me. He was wearing the same red baseball cap he'd had on the last time I saw him.

"They won't sting you," he said.

Cheryl stood and stepped into the swarm. The sky was clear blue, but she looked up and squinted as if a storm were coming.

"It's supposed to get rough Wednesday," she said.

"How bad?" Christopher asked. "Just thunderstorms?"

"They're predicting severe. And the wind's going to be high."

Mark pointed to a brown, two-door Oldsmobile Cutlass Supreme parked in the yard. I don't know much about cars, but it looked like a classic. The nose dipped in a way I'd never seen before, and the body reminded me a little bit of a Cadillac. Mark said he planned to cover it before the bad weather moved in, but still, he worried we might see hail.

"If we do, Cheryl's going to be mad because that's her baby right there. I could have sold that sucker four hundred times, no joke. The record, I think, is five or six offers in one day. They stop right there and say, 'Hey, when you going to sell me your car, Mr. King?' I say, 'Oh man, I can't sell that car. It's my wife's. If I sell it, she's going to get the police up here on me. She's going to put me in jail.'"

Mark said Cheryl wanted him to be more forceful, wanted him to tell people flat out that if he wanted to sell it, he'd hang a sign in the window, but he preferred a more jovial approach.

"You better know how to deal with these Black guys," Mark said. "I don't mess with Black guys. I had some tomato plants out there last year, and two Black guys walked by and said, 'Mr. King, I want to get a tomato.' I said, 'Go right ahead, man. I got plenty.' If I tell them, 'No, you don't get any, thief,' they'll come over the next night and chop them all down."

Mark laughed as if his monologue were funny. I had no idea how he had gone from talking about the weather to calling Black guys "thief," but I was used to that kind of casual racism because some of my family members talked that way. I felt uncomfortable and appalled, and yet I knew the South did not have a monopoly on racism.

When Oregon became a state in 1859, it did so with a caveat: No Black people, not even "mulattos" with one white parent, could move there. Oregon was the only free state admitted into the union with a constitution that forbade Black people from living, working, or owning property there. When African Americans did arrive, in the 1940s, to help build ships for World War II, they found that most landlords wouldn't rent to them. For decades, real estate agents and city policies kept Black residents penned into one part of Portland—the North and Northeast neighborhoods I now covered at *The Oregonian*.

Most of my stories that year were about gentrification and the ways city and state policies had harmed generations of Black residents. Local leaders had used urban renewal to force African Americans out of North Portland. Now white people were moving in, and I myself was complicit. When I finished this trip, I planned to move into the two-bedroom house Frankie was renting in what was once Portland's Blackest neighborhood. She'd chosen the house because it was the only place she could find when she first moved to Portland. She didn't know anything about the neighborhood's history or the future that developers were actively plotting. But she knew now. We'd considered finding a home in a different neighborhood, one that wasn't gentrifying, but we couldn't afford one, and anyway, the neighborhood Frankie lived in felt more like home than any other place in Portland. Over the years, I'd found that most Black Portlanders have some connection to Louisiana, a link that can be traced back to the train lines that led out of my home state during the Second Great Migration. People in Frankie's neighborhood talked like I talk. One of her neighbors even sold gumbo out of a food truck. I wanted to live near him. But I knew, because I'd written articles explaining, that my moving there would push Black residents out—maybe not immediately, but someday. As I and other white people moved in, the rents and property taxes would go up. Coffee shops and white-owned bars would replace Black-owned businesses whose owners never could secure the loans they needed to maintain their buildings. Some Black people wouldn't be able to afford to stay. Others would eventually look around and decide that the neighborhood they'd loved no longer felt like home. Somehow, they would become misfits on their own streets.

All of that to say, it didn't matter that I'd never heard white people in Portland casually say the things Mark was saying without a wisp of fear in broad daylight. Real racism was more than a stray sentence. It was more than stereotyping, and in Oregon, as in Louisiana, it was baked into everything.

When Mark finished talking, Cheryl nodded at me, then she spoke in the same meek voice she'd used earlier.

"I remember your mother, Rhonda. I taught her PE."

"Was she any good at it?" I asked.

"Yeah, she was pretty good. She did a lot of tumbling and so forth. She was a cheerleader."

I'd seen pictures of my mom in the red Delhi Bears cheerleading uniform, but I'd never been able to imagine her jumping and turning flips on a field. She liked to dance, but as long as I'd known her, she'd shied away from everything else physical. She always made my dad drop her off at the front of a parking lot, and she never joined in when the rest of us played badminton in the backyard. She tried to persuade me to avoid physical activity, too. I was very small when I was young—I still remember my mom throwing me a party in second grade because I'd finally made it to forty pounds—and she worried if I moved around too much, I'd lose what little weight I had. When I was eight, she forged a doctor's note, excusing me from PE for the rest of elementary school.

"Well," Mark said, interjecting. "There it is, right there."

He motioned toward a patch of grass just beyond the Cutlass. A blue tricycle stood in the yard. It looked like the three-wheeled bike every person we'd interviewed had described. Roy's bike.

"That was her baby," Mark said. His hands were on his hips, and he looked proud in a way I hadn't seen before.

"Oh my god," I said.

I'd pictured this bike for so long, and it somehow looked exactly like I'd imagined and also like something else entirely. It was a rusted, step-through tricycle with red and white "Free Spirit" decals peeling off the frame. Later, I looked it up and found that Free Spirit was a brand of adult tricycles that Sears sold in the 1970s. The bikes came with a basket attached to the rear, but Roy must have added a second one to the front, because his bike had two. It was originally a three-speed tricycle, but Roy's derailleur was gone, and the shifter cable that changed gears was cut and tied in a knot around the front basket.

"At one time, she was upset because she couldn't fix it," Mark said. "Royce was pretty good with fixing stuff. She really knew her way around a lawn mower, but this mechanism in the back is pretty tricky."

Mark said his dad, a retired army sergeant who ran the motor pool in Germany during the Korean War, came over and helped Roy work on the bike. They repaired it a few times, but after the brakes went out, Roy just used his feet to stop.

I bent down and examined all the parts. Frankie volunteered as a bike mechanic, and she'd taught me a few things about the chain and the gears. I didn't know nearly as much as she did, but what I did know suggested Roy's tricycle was no longer operable. I peered at Mark.

"What made you keep the bike all these years?"

"Okay," he said, beaming. "In a minute, I'll show you something Royce wrote, and after you read it, you will see why I keep Royce's stuff. Would you like me to get it now and let you look at it?"

I told Mark that would be great. He held up a finger, then walked toward the trailer. Once he and Cheryl were inside, Christopher whispered to me.

"So you know what I'm thinking about?"

"What?"

Christopher started to say something, but the screen door whacked open, and the Kings stepped back out. Christopher shuffled to the other side of the yard.

"Cornbread," he said.

"Cornbread? I thought it was going to be something . . ."

"Related? Yeah, I'm sorry."

I furrowed my brow. Christopher tends to say silly things, so I wasn't that surprised by his random cornbread comment, but I was slightly annoyed. We were finally seeing Roy's bike, and he wanted to talk about food? I knew he was doing me a favor, recording all the sound for free, but I wanted him to take the unpaid job seriously. I cut my eyes at him.

Mark held up a stack of eight-by-ten flyers printed on heavy, yellowed cardstock. He was still smiling the big proud grin he'd flashed when he first nodded toward Roy's bike. He flipped one of the flyers over. It looked like an advertisement for the Cave Theater.

"Royce loved the Cave Theater, like everybody else did in this little town," Mark said. "They'd mail these to you if you wanted to be on the mailing list. You could pick them up so you'd know the week's shows. See? Real neat."

Mark handed me one of the flyers from November 1966. Rock Hudson was starring in *Blindfold*, and Sophia Loren was in *Lady L*. Mark pointed to a sentence Roy had written along the top left corner: "Keep this to show your grandkids something different."

It was the same handwriting I'd seen in Roy's Bible, just a little messier. Mark turned the flyer over, and I could see that Roy had covered the back with a big, loopy cursive.

"I can read it to you," Mark said. He held the flyer close to his face, and he read slowly:

> *I am the dead talking, and don't throw away all my foolish*
> *books, papers, and things because if you do, I shall come back.*
> *You'll see me some night when it's dark, standing over your bed.*
> *Then you must explain why you threw my things away.*

Mark lowered the flyer and explained that Roy had told him that once, after Jewel died, he'd seen her ghost standing at the end of his bed. Jewel's ghost didn't say anything, Mark said. She just stood there at the end of Roy's bed and looked.

He raised the flyer back up, then finished reading what Roy had written:

> *If you keep all my foolish things, you shall have good luck. If you*
> *throw them away, you shall have very bad luck for my curse shall*
> *be on you.*

Mark laughed a good-natured chuckle. I knew he must have read the note before, but he reacted as if he were reading it for the first time.

"I'm not worried about a curse, but I told Royce I'd keep her stuff, and obviously you see she meant it, so I do. I never have sold anything of Royce's, and I'm not going to. I've been able to sell this bike probably a dozen times. This bike never is sold. It stays with me, and if I can keep it past when I'm gone, I'll try to get my granddaughter to keep it 'cause I don't plan on any of Royce's stuff going anywhere."

Mark didn't mention the journals, but I suspected this was his oblique way of telling me he wouldn't be giving or selling me those either. He seemed happy to show me the flyers, though. He leafed through his stack, looking for other notes. Roy mostly used the backs as scorecards. He'd written the results of a dominoes game on one—Susan, 105. Roy, 45—and tallied a card game on another, noting that he'd beaten Jimi, 4 to 3.

"Aha," Mark said, pulling out one flyer that had been ripped in two. The bottom half was missing, but the top showed that in May 1963, the Cave was hosting a midnight screening of Elvis Presley in *Follow That Dream*. Roy had gone through the listings with a red pen, noting which ones he wanted to see. He'd marked *Guns of the Black Witch* as a maybe and *The Adventures of Huckleberry Finn* in CinemaScope as a no. Next to *Too Late Blues,* a John Cassavetes film that stars Bobby Darin as a struggling jazz musician, Roy had written, "Song by Roy Hudgins." Mark motioned for me to turn the flyer over. Roy had written, then crossed out, a few lines in blue ink:

> It's to late for me to think about living.
> Old father time, my life I'll soon be giving.
> I'm wearing out the souls of my shoes
> and singing these To Late Blues.

Underneath, in black ink that he hadn't crossed out, Roy had penned an addendum:

> Sept. 1979
> I'm still living
> OLD
> FAT

AND
WRINKLED

Mark handed me the pile, and I scrutinized each flyer. On another, next to a May 1965 screening of *The Back Door to Hell*, Roy had written, "The front door to hell is on Hell Street." Roy was wry, I thought, funny in ways people didn't often describe when I asked about him. I nosed through the other flyers, but I didn't see anything else beyond a few dominoes scores.

"I used to go to the Cave Theater," Mark said, "and for twenty-five cents, I got to see two motion pictures, a cartoon, the commercials, and still have enough money to buy a Coke. We had a cry room. That was so nice. The babies got to cry, and the mamas got to take them to the cry room, and you wouldn't hear them. To be truthful about it, they had an upstairs like a balcony area, and that's where the Black people sat. They didn't sit in the bottom with us. That was a rule. I never saw a Black person sitting down in the bottom, all of the years I went. I was like seven, eight, nine, ten, eleven, twelve. I never saw a Black person. We went in the front door, and they had a little side door. They had stairs. They went up to the balcony and watched the movies in the balcony. I don't know if they really cared that much. I imagined, truthfully, it probably irked them. But I never saw any problem with it."

Mark shrugged, then ducked into his trailer to look for more of Roy's stuff. Christopher shuffled back over to me.

"I don't think we need to pressure him," he whispered.

I looked at the flyers. They weren't the deep, revealing tomes I wanted to read, but they were something. Mark seemed to be opening up. Maybe patience was the best strategy for now.

"Yeah," I said. "I think this is enough. He didn't have to give us this."

"That's what I was going to talk about when I talked about corn-bread earlier. But I botched it."

Christopher laughed and did a little dance. I was grateful he was with me. In some ways, Christopher and I are very different people. He plays concerts and picks up other gigs when he needs money, and he lives part of the year on a sailboat in Panama. He never seems to need to control life. He just sways along with whatever forces rock him. I like to control everything. I spend most of my waking hours working, and at night, when I'm trying to fall asleep, I fret about every dollar I've spent. It didn't occur to me to use my vacation time to relax in Panama or anywhere else. *The Oregonian* gave me three weeks off each year. I spent them working on this film.

However different our personalities are, though, I sometimes think that I have more in common with Christopher than I do with anyone else. Some nights, after a few beers, we talked about our mothers. He understood how complicated my relationship with my mom was because he had the same strained connection to his. We backpedaled through their histories, trying to sort out exactly when they'd been damaged. I suppose any of my cousins might have been able to relate in the same way—all our mothers suffered from something unnameable—but I never felt comfortable hanging out with any of my other cousins. One was in prison. Another, a rodeo rider, had died the year before at thirty-two. I hadn't seen Christopher's sister in years, in part because I'd heard she'd joined a Christian cult and didn't like gay people. But Christopher is the kind of guy I would have wanted to pal around with even if we weren't related. In Delhi, after we'd interviewed people, Christopher and I talked about documentaries we'd seen or new albums we loved. We never tired of hearing other people's stories. I turned those stories into articles, and he channeled them into songs, but we were both always listening.

Being with him is the one time I ever feel like my two worlds exist in the same place. I can be Southern, descended from my grandmother, but also worldly in a way that doesn't appeal to my other relatives.

Mark emerged from the trailer holding several dozen records. He handed three Hank Williams albums to Christopher, then he held up a few others, one by Mickey Gilley and another by Flatt and Scruggs. These were Roy's favorite records, Mark said, the ones he spun over and over again on a big box player.

"Royce would ask me sometimes, 'Am I playing my music too loud?' I'd say, 'Look, Royce, I love country music. Play on.'"

Mark looked down Chatham toward a group of young Black boys playing basketball without a hoop. He held up a Merle Haggard album for me to see.

"I thought it was kind of funny she'd play it around here because people would go down the street playing something *unknown*. I don't like rap much. And Royce really didn't like it. She didn't even see it as being music, and neither did I. We agreed on a lot of stuff."

Mark's words surprised me. I hadn't realized how much of myself I had projected onto Roy. I loved rap, so I assumed Roy would have loved it if he ever heard it. It's good storytelling, full of the same kinds of rhyming techniques Roy used in his own music. But what if Roy did think rap was unknown noise? Did that mean he'd also said the kind of breezy racist things Mark and my relatives did? Did he grumble when the other white people left Chatham, leaving him with only Black neighbors? For years, I'd been thinking that my grandmother was wrong to cast Roy as an angel. Real people aren't perfect, I wrote in my journal. But that afternoon, I realized that I, too, had turned Roy into what I wanted him to be.

Mark scanned through the records one last time, then he carried them back into the trailer. Christopher fiddled with the audio recorder knobs, and Cheryl stared at me.

"I appreciate you letting us come to your house multiple times," I told her.

"You're quite welcome."

She said it matter-of-factly, almost stern. She wasn't mean, but she wasn't Southern friendly.

"I know you don't know me," I said. "I know you don't have any reason to trust me, so I appreciate that y'all are going out on a limb and letting us see this stuff."

Cheryl laughed.

"I know I don't," she said. She crossed her arms, and she softened her voice. "Just do it right."

Mark reemerged from the trailer, and I repeated what I'd said to Cheryl. I thanked him for letting Christopher and me come over.

"That's okay," Mark said. "You've made your big promise that you won't portray Roy in any bad light, Casey, so if you can help anybody else from being bullied and mistreated like that, good. That's one reason I became a special ed teacher, because I wanted to make sure special ed kids were not bullied. And boy, I fought some battles on that line."

My legs shook. I wanted to tell Mark why I kept returning. Maybe he wouldn't even care that I was a lesbian. After all, his brother Keith, the man who'd taken my mother and me to see Roy's tombstone four years earlier, was gay. Maybe Mark already suspected that's why I was interested in Roy. But I hadn't even articulated that connection to myself, so I stuttered as I tried to explain what about Roy's life interested me. Watching the video now, I can see that I was just starting to piece together my own role in the project.

"I definitely have no interest in portraying Roy in a bad light," I said. "My grandmother told me about this when I was a teenager. I'm about to be thirty now, so that's twelve years."

I said a few mumbled words that didn't add up to a sentence. I almost hoped Mark would interrupt me, but he didn't.

"I have never wanted to be a man or dress as a man, but I felt different growing up in Monroe. My grandmother told me that everybody in town loved Roy. I don't think that's as true as she wanted to believe it was. But I think she told me that because it was her way of accepting me, and showing me that she grew up somewhere where people are different. At the time, it was really antithetical to what I thought about Louisiana. I thought everybody would bully you if you were any kind of different. I couldn't believe there was a place where you could be different, and people would love you and accept you. That's really how I got started on it."

I took a deep breath. Telling Mark I felt "different" was as close to coming out as I'd ever done in Delhi. I searched his face for some sign of judgment, but I didn't see any. My legs started to shake a little less, and my voice grew more confident.

"Ultimately, the longer I've worked on it, the more I've wanted to show that Roy was a complete person. Not just show that Roy was 'a woman who dressed as a man.' To me, at the end of the day, that's the least interesting part. That one thing can't be a whole person's life. The more interesting part is Roy playing music or riding a bicycle or working. I just want to find things that make Roy a real human and not just limited to one tiny thing. People aren't that way. They have hopes and dreams and feelings and interests and annoyances."

I was sputtering out. Two birds were fighting over a worm mid-air right next to me, and they were squawking so loud it distracted me. I wanted to tell Mark that everyone I'd interviewed seemed to remember Roy as some kind of victim or novelty. I wanted them to remember Roy as a person. I didn't get the words out right, but he seemed to understand what I meant.

"Well, you're right," he said. "Royce was a multifaceted person. She could write. She loved her country music. One of her favorite things she ever did was go to the Grand Ole Opry. She went to Nashville with some folks before I moved here. At least she told me she did, and I believe she would tell the truth."

I felt rattled, revealing so much of myself and my hopes for this project, so I saw Mark's mention of Nashville as an opening to change the subject.

"Do y'all travel much, now that you're retired?" I asked.

"No," he said. "We're pretty much stuck here."

He told me that he and Cheryl used to go to Las Vegas. They'd stayed at Mandalay Bay and a casino called Paris. Once, they even climbed the fake Eiffel Tower and looked down at the Bellagio fountains. It was beautiful, Mark said. But now both his and Cheryl's parents were old and in need of care. He and Cheryl didn't go to Las Vegas or anywhere else. Instead, they took his dad out to run errands every Monday, then they took Cheryl's mom out on Thursdays. Sometimes they drove over the Mississippi River to Vicksburg. It wasn't the Bellagio, but it was something to see.

All of a sudden, Mark remembered one more thing. A picture. He rushed back into the trailer, then returned holding a four-by-six snapshot from the late 1980s.

"Roy decided she was tired of white, so we decided to paint her house blue. I guess we worked probably three or four days."

Mark handed me the photo. I'd never seen Roy's house before. It was double-wide and made of wood, just like my grandma told me, and it had a little half porch. In the picture, two bikes and one plastic chair filled the porch, but as I looked at it, I imagined a circle of kids squeezing together to listen to Roy play music. I pictured my grandma climbing each of the three stairs, then finding a spot on the corner. This was where she said her life began.

Mark and Roy were both holding yellow cans of blue paint in the picture, and they were standing in the yard next to a wooden swing. I've always wanted a swing like that. When I was young and dreaming of my heavenly mansion, I always pictured a porch swing. My parents never owned a house, but when I left the South for *The Oregonian*, I told my mom I planned to earn enough money to buy a home with a swing. My dreams were fruitless, though. Few homes in Portland have porches, and my parents had ruined my credit so badly, no bank would let me finance a house. For now, until I moved into Frankie's rental, my hundred-year-old apartment would have to do.

"You know," Mark said. "I can let you have this picture if you'll send it back to me."

I couldn't believe what he was offering. Lou had said Mark wouldn't even let her look at Roy's old photos. Now Mark was going to let me take one back to Oregon? Maybe my long, patient approach to reporting was paying off.

"Really?" I asked. "You wouldn't mind?"

"That's fine, but please send it back because it's the only one I have of us working together. It's precious to me."

I slid the photo into the flat part of my camera case, then I told Mark and Cheryl we should be heading out. It was nearly 4 p.m., and neither Christopher nor I had eaten anything all day. The water tastes so gross in Delhi, we hadn't even had a glass of it before leaving the cabin that morning. I turned off my camera, and I started breaking down the tripod.

"Wait," Cheryl said, more forcefully than she'd said anything all morning. "Before you scatter . . ."

She held up an old camera.

"Do you want a picture of us?" I asked.

"Yeah," she said. "In front of the bike."

It seemed only fair. We'd spent hours pawing through Roy's stuff. Christopher slung his arm across my shoulders. We posed in front of Roy's tricycle, smiling. Cheryl took three photos, and when she lowered her camera, I saw that she was smiling, too.

Christopher and I walked back to the rental car, and once we reached it, he let out an exhale so long I assumed he must have been holding it in the entire interview.

"That bike," he said. "When I look at it, I want to see Roy on it. I feel the absence of this commander of this bike."

Christopher, I supposed, had his own reasons for working on the film. He spent hours each night playing his guitar on the back of the cabin's porch, writing songs the way I imagined Roy used to. Christopher had lived in all the little towns around Delhi when he was young, and even though he lived just a few hours away in Texas now, he treated each visit as his own kind of homecoming. I was so invested in my narrative—my fears, my deductions—that I sometimes forgot that this was Christopher's journey, too. He was returning to his mother's hometown. He was giving up weeks every year to learn about a stranger.

I made a U-turn, and we passed Mark and Cheryl's trailer. They were still standing in the yard, and they waved as we drove by. Christopher rolled down the window, stuck his hand out, and waved back.

"I really respect them," he said. "If I had lost someone and I had so many of their belongings, it would be hard for me to be like, 'Yeah, come on by.'"

We drove toward Main Street, and we talked about the notes Roy had written on the back of the Cave flyers. Roy didn't want Mark to throw his stuff away. That had to count for something, Christopher and I thought. Why would Roy want Mark to keep all his things if he didn't want people to see them?

"This wasn't just Roy writing this stuff down so it would be lost or in a box somewhere," Christopher said. "I feel like that's worth noting to Mark. Let's just keep building a rapport with him."

We made a plan. We'd come back to Delhi a few more times. We'd stop in and say hi to Mark. We wouldn't ask him for the journals until he trusted us. It was a slow approach, but that afternoon, Christopher and I figured it would take another year at most.

"We're closer than we've ever been before," Christopher said.

A FEW WEEKS LATER, at home in Portland, I scanned the photo Mark let us borrow, then I mailed it back to his house. I wasn't expecting a reply, but later that week, I found a package in my apartment mailbox. Mark's name was on the return address. I carried the package upstairs to my apartment, wondering what it might be. It was too light to be Roy's journals.

I sat down on my couch, then slid my finger under the tape to open the package. Inside, wrapped in a gallon-sized ziplock bag, was a letter and a bundle of photographs.

"These pictures should be helpful to you," Mark wrote. "Look on the back of each picture. Roy wrote some information on most."

The photos were all at least thirty years old, and the edges on some were torn, but they didn't smell musty the way pictures sometimes do if they're stashed in a box. A few had sticky backs. Others still had tape on them, and I wondered if Roy or Mark had kept them in an album. I picked up the top photo. It showed Jewel Ellis standing next to a truck in 1949. She was tall and dark-skinned, and her hair was pulled back into a bun. Roy had written "Indian" on the side of the picture. Underneath, he wrote "mama."

Maybe, I thought, it didn't matter who gave birth to Roy. He had a mother who loved him, at least as long as she could. I looked through the rest of the stack so slowly an hour passed before I reached the end. Mark had sent three photos of Jewel and one of John. I'd never seen pictures of either of them, and it was thrilling, adding details to the people I'd imagined. Jewel appeared stone-faced in every image. John was white, short. He was wearing overalls and holding a hammer in the 1948 snapshot Mark sent.

There was a photo from 1983, the year I was born, that showed Roy in his sixties riding the blue tricycle I'd seen at Mark's. In another, a wallet-sized picture from 1968, Roy steered a riding lawn mower across a yard. He wore rainbow suspenders in an undated image, and ball caps in several others. He was sixty-six in the snap that showed him hoisting a giant sweet potato he'd grown in his yard, and seventy-two in an image that showed him standing outside the flooded Bayou Macon.

I barely looked at that last one, because when I picked it up, I saw that underneath, Mark had included a photo of Roy at eleven years old. The picture was black-and-white and tiny, no bigger than a yearbook photo. In it, Roy's hair was slicked back. His face was smooth. He wore a button-down shirt, a nice one, the kind a guy would wear for a professional portrait.

Mark must have arranged the photos, knowing I'd see the best ones last. Underneath the eleven-year-old shot was a picture of Roy at fourteen, standing in front of his first truck. He looked lanky and cavalier, very much like a teenage boy.

The final picture was from 1952, the year my grandmother moved to Hell Street. Roy was posing in a field, holding a guitar whose strap was just pieces of string knotted together. It looked like the kind of shot you'd see in a country music magazine. Roy's hair was gelled into a pompadour, and his jeans were cuffed high enough to reveal new cowboy boots. This was the boy my grandma watched and spent her lifetime remembering. He was handsome, beguiling.

"Oh my god," I whispered to myself. "Did she have a crush on him?"

Chapter Fifteen

(2013)

THE SUMMER AFTER I started high school, my mom told me I was old enough to find out who my future husband would be. She had a surefire trick for predicting the future, she said, a practice she'd learned from Rita Mae's mother. All I had to do was boil an egg, scoop out the hard yolk, and fill the empty space with salt. I had to eat the salt-filled egg, then go immediately to sleep. I couldn't read or drink water or talk to anyone. I couldn't even brush my teeth. Whoever I dreamed about that night was the man I'd marry.

My mom told me all her sisters had done it. Aunt Cindy had dreamed about Stanley, her second husband, and Christopher's mom had dreamed about a soldier. Both of the men she married served in the military, and if that wasn't proof enough, my mom said, Aunt Ann had dreamed about five different men, and already, she'd been married four times.

"Who did you dream about?" I asked. "Dad? Cam?"

My mom shook her head in a way that suggested her dreams were secret.

"It's your turn. Let's go boil your egg."

We huddled around the stove, watching the egg rock gently around the pot. After ten minutes, my mom pulled the egg out with her bare fingers, then peeled it without waiting for the shell to cool. She cut the egg in half, and I reached to eat the yolk, but she slapped my hand.

"Only the white part."

She loaded the hole with salt, then she held the two pieces together, as if the egg had never been cut. She told me to eat it in one bite. I stuffed it into my mouth and grimaced as it slid down my throat. It tasted like gulping the ocean. I started to complain, but my mother put her finger over my lips. She ushered me toward my bedroom and closed the door before I could ruin the experiment. I tried to think about guys other girls liked. I pictured football players and the star of the cross-country team. When I grew bored of picturing them, I thought about Leonardo DiCaprio, scrambling around the *Titanic*. The next morning, my stomach hurt. I hadn't dreamed about the runner or Leonardo DiCaprio. I hadn't dreamed about a guy at all.

"Did you sneak into the bathroom and drink some water?" my mom asked in a voice that was more accusing than curious. "It worked for everyone else."

"I didn't. I ate the egg, and I went to sleep."

We tried again later that week, but I still didn't dream about a man. I ate four or five salty eggs in one month, but every time, I woke up with a swollen tongue and zero revelations.

"I guess I was wrong," my mom said after the fifth attempt. "You aren't old enough yet."

THE FIRST TIME I saw Frankie's picture, I felt that flash I suspected my mom's sisters must have had in their egg dreams. Even though I hadn't met Frankie, even though I was dating the professor, I felt this overwhelming sense of recognition. *This* was my person.

In past relationships, I'd always needed space. I never let anyone sleep at my apartment on weeknights, and I didn't leave a toothbrush at theirs. Even after I'd posted my "Marita please find me" note at work, I resisted hanging around anyone too long. I liked to spend at least half the week alone. If I did stay over at a girlfriend's house, I woke up early to dash across town toward my own shower and ceramic coffee mug. But Frankie was different. I never grew tired of her. I begged her to spend the night—every night—at my place. When I woke up in the morning, it didn't bother me that she was there, wild-haired and curled around Lafayette. I liked watching her iron her Banana Republic button-downs before work, and I peered through the blinds in my kitchen as she scurried toward the bus stop across the street from my house, later than she would have been if she'd slept at her own place.

I felt safe with Frankie. Our relationship wasn't fiery, but it was easy and fun, and I wanted my life to be easy and fun. I moved in with her a year after we started dating, a month after Mark King sent me the pictures. It was the summer of 2013, my fourth year working on the documentary, and I'd finally started to see just how different my life would be from Roy's or Pam's. I wasn't stuck in the South. I wouldn't end up alone. Maybe something would always be missing, but I could patch those holes by creating a new and better life. I knew, soon after Frankie cleared half of her bedroom closet for me, that I wanted to ask her to marry me. Same-sex marriage wasn't legal in Oregon yet, but a nonprofit had begun collecting signatures to get it on a 2014 ballot. I didn't want to wait that long to propose, though. I was too happy, too relieved to discover that I even could feel happy. It felt wrong to wait on the law to catch up with my heart.

I don't think I worried, initially, that the ballot measure might fail. Portland was lesbian paradise. Everywhere Frankie and I went, we saw short-haired women living their lives together. There was no official count that I knew about—the census didn't record that information—but some days, it felt like lesbians outnumbered straight people in our neighborhood. They were at the gym, the bank, my office. Every morning, I waited at the bus stop with two butch women wearing sensible shoes. Another half dozen boarded before we'd reached Broadway Street, a mile south of our house.

Something happened, though, after I decided to ask Frankie to marry me. That August, I began reporting a story about a lesbian couple who'd tried to buy a wedding cake in the Portland suburbs earlier that year. The lesbians were the same age I was—thirty in 2013—and they'd moved to Oregon from Texas, hoping the West Coast would accept them in ways the South never had. When Rachel Cryer and Laurel Bowman decided to get married, they knew which cake they wanted to serve at the ceremony. The year before, they'd ordered a "raspberry fantasy cake" for Rachel's mother's sixth wedding. The cake was a two-layer, white butter batter, baked with raspberries and topped with white chocolate. Rachel and her mother had spent many years estranged, but they'd decided that serving the same cake at their weddings would help them bond, so they made an appointment at Sweet Cakes by Melissa, then headed over to sample the raspberry fantasy one February morning. Melissa Klein wasn't there when Rachel and her mother arrived. Melissa's husband, Aaron, met them instead.

"What are the names of the bride and groom?" Aaron asked.

Later, in court, the two sides testified that Rachel giggled. "It's two brides," she said.

The Kleins said they had agreed, after Washington legalized same-sex marriage in 2012, to "stand firm" if a gay or lesbian couple asked them to bake a cake for their wedding. The Kleins ran a Christian shop. Their pastor prayed over the bakery when it first opened, and Melissa listened to religious music as she decorated cakes.

"I think we may have wasted your time," Aaron told Rachel. "We don't do same-sex weddings."

At work one afternoon late that summer, I printed off the complaint one of the lesbians had filed with the Oregon Bureau of Labor and Industries. It was short, two pages, and light on details, but something about the spare sentences moved me. "I am a thirty year old female in a same-sex relationship who requested a cake service for my wedding." "I am aware that Respondent provides wedding cakes for weddings where the persons getting married are not of the same sex."

I grabbed a highlighter, printed off the bakers' response, then took the two files up to the third floor, where reporters sometimes ate their lunches. I read through the Kleins' arguments, highlighting the parts I hoped to include in my article, and I started to feel uneasy. The bakers told bureau investigators that they'd only done what the state itself endorsed. They were refusing to acknowledge a marriage that Oregon voters had chosen to prohibit.

I put my highlighter down. My head throbbed. I had always thought of Oregon as the antidote to the South, the place where I could be free. I'd forgotten that it had banned gay marriage the same year Louisiana and Mississippi had.

In 2004, when I was a junior in college, more than a dozen states took steps to prevent same-sex couples from getting married. I didn't have a girlfriend then. I wasn't even sure I would ever want to marry, but when Louisiana held its vote that September, I drove the two hours home from college to log my dissent. I waited in line behind a group of men wearing Confederate flags as pants, so I didn't have high hopes as I drove back to Mississippi. Later that night, I checked the results online. Seventy-eight percent of Louisiana voters had approved a state constitutional amendment banning same-sex marriage and civil unions.

I told myself it didn't matter. I lived in Mississippi, not Louisiana. But that November, as John Kerry and George W. Bush fought for the presidency, Mississippi lawmakers proposed their own constitutional amendment banning gay marriage.

On election day, after my post-colonial lit class let out, I drove through a thunderstorm back to Louisiana to vote. The line to get into the precinct was so long, it wound around the parking lot twice. I stood in the rain behind a middle-aged couple, and we made small talk for a while. They asked me where I went to school and what I wanted to become. Eventually, they brought up the amendments.

"It's what the people want," the woman said. "It's what we good Christians want."

She told me she hoped all heathen homosexuals stayed away from her children, and I had to bite my lip to keep from laughing. I was twenty-one, and I had no interest in spending time with anyone's kids. We moved forward, closer to the precinct, and I looked at myself in the reflection of one of the car windows. My hair was buzz-cut short, angled into a little mohawk, and I was wearing checkered Vans slip-ons with mismatched socks. How could this woman not realize I was gay? At the very least, I looked liberal.

"They want to take the Bible out of everything," she said. "If they want to separate church and state, I want my mail on Christmas and Thanksgiving. I want them to have to work on Christian holidays."

I nodded along without disagreeing—nodding along, I'd learned working at a weekly newspaper called the *Jackson Free Press*, was a fundamental journalistic skill—but later that night, as I drove through darkness toward Mississippi, I wondered what this woman's pastor had taught her. Thanksgiving isn't mentioned in the Bible. It's not a Christian holiday.

I made it to Jackson just as the first returns trickled in. All my liberal friends were waiting at a restaurant called Hal & Mal's for election officials to call the races, so I drove straight there. I jammed into a diner booth filled with every gay person I knew in town.

Maybe I ordered a drink. Red Stripe, the only beer I liked then. We called ourselves the Queer Young Adult Network, but most of us had nothing in common outside of our shared outsider status. One of the girls was a jock who played basketball, a sport the rest of us never watched. Another loved Korn and System of a Down, nu metal bands I couldn't stand listening to. There was a computer programmer, a Chaucer expert, and a thirty-five-year-old woman who'd tried to kiss all of us. I can't remember most of their names, but that night, they were my force field. We linked arms and looked up at the TV as the news host announced that the results were in.

I'm not sure what I was expecting. Defeat, probably, but not a resounding rejection. Jackson always felt more liberal than West Monroe, and I was young and stupid enough to think that meant all of Mississippi was more liberal than all of Louisiana. I thought it would be a close race, maybe the kind that warranted a recount.

It wasn't. Eighty-six percent of Mississippi's voters approved the amendment banning gay marriage. I looked around the table at the jock and the computer programmer. The thirty-five-year-old started to cry. Eighty-six percent of Mississippi had voted against us.

A decade and a half later, I sometimes lose sight of how gutted I felt that night. Same-sex marriage is legal in every state now—so legal that my brother chides me when I call it "gay marriage." "It's just marriage," he tells me. "You don't need a qualifier." But after that night in Mississippi, I eyed everyone with suspicion. Had the gas station worker voted against me? Had the grocery store clerk? At red lights, I looked at the cars idling next to me and knew that most of the drivers had likely waited outside a precinct in the rain to make sure I never married a woman.

Mississippi's initiative passed by the largest margin in the country, but eleven other states voted the same way that night. Michigan and North Dakota banned same-sex marriage. Ohio and Montana did, too. And in Oregon, the one place I'd imagined would accept me, more than a million people voted to change the constitution so it specified that marriage could only be between a man and a woman.

Sitting at work with my highlighter uncapped, I thought that the bakers had made a solid, scary point. Oregon voters had already decided: They didn't want me to marry Frankie.

After I read those documents, I started eyeing people in Portland the way I had in Mississippi. I decided not to look for rings in person because I didn't want to tell a clerk I was hunting for a men's band in size four and a half. Frankie wouldn't want a woman's ring, I knew. She wouldn't accept a diamond. She wouldn't even like a rounded band. Searching online felt safer, but even after I found the one I wanted—a silver palladium circle that would sit flat on Frankie's ring finger—I stalled. If she said yes, we'd have to order a wedding cake. What if a baker turned us away? I didn't want to become front-page news.

I left the ring in my Etsy shopping cart, unpurchased, until mid-September. Later, in my journal, I wrote that the night I bought Frankie a ring was the kind of evening I hoped we spent the rest of our lives having. We'd planned to make habanero hot sauce and tacos from scratch, but I stayed late at work, and we were both too hungry by the time I made it home. Frankie opened a bottle of Txakoli, a slightly sparkling Basque wine, and I dumped a box of macaroni into boiling water. We ate dinner on the couch. We stayed up late drinking until we were tipsy, watching and rewatching a video where a gay man proposes to his boyfriend in a Home Depot in Salt Lake City.

The gay man had choreographed an entire flash mob featuring their friends and family dancing down an aisle. He'd enlisted his own parents, as well as his boyfriend's, and when they bopped through the frame, dorky dancing to support their sons, I started crying. I wanted that. Not the Home Depot spectacle, but parents willing and able to help me propose to a woman even though it was not yet legal. I was so moved—by the parents, by the man proposing in a state that banned gay marriage in 2004—that I sneaked off to my computer and bought the ring while Frankie was brushing her teeth. By the time it arrived in late October, I knew how I wanted to propose.

In high school, every time I ate one of my mother's salty eggs, I tried to imagine the moment a man would ask me to marry him. I pictured fireworks and rings floating in glasses of champagne, but none of those clichés ever moved me. The proposal remained as much of a mystery to me as the man did. With Frankie, I didn't need to brainstorm. We'd first bonded over seafood and sea creatures, so I knew I wanted to propose on the coast. I knew, too, that I wanted to ask in late November.

Thanksgiving had always been my family's worst holiday. Some of the bad things that happened aren't my stories to tell, but we spent one in the lobby of a mental hospital. My parents separated one Thanksgiving, and on another, my boom box accidentally picked up the cordless-phone conversation my mom was having with a strange man. She told the man that my dad had thrown her across the trailer and burned her nightgowns in the front yard. Neither of those stories was true. My dad had spent the entire morning at Walmart, and all my mom's nightgowns were folded in her bottom drawer. But the man believed her. He called her "baby," and he sighed in a way that suggested he loved her. I unplugged my boom box just as he started to tell my mom all the ways he'd make her feel better.

I'd tried, as an adult, to reclaim Thanksgiving. My first year in Portland, I ruined a pumpkin pie by using salt instead of sugar. The next, I attempted to make banana pudding, but every batch came out wrong in a new way. The pudding burned once and didn't congeal another time. The last attempt—the one I took to a friend's house for dinner—had more tears than bananas in it. The next year, I volunteered to work. Someone had to listen to the cop scanner every holiday, and for the next five years, I was the Thanksgiving girl. While my friends shared Tofurky roasts and green bean casseroles made with chanterelle mushrooms, I sat close to the scanner, listening for holidays worse than mine. I didn't mind the shift. The pay was double, and the crime briefs tended to distract me. I figured I'd spend all my Thanksgivings transcribing dispatch calls, but the year Frankie and I started dating, she asked me to go with her to Boise to celebrate with her family instead.

We spent the 2012 holiday in Idaho the way I assume Americans everywhere do. We woke up early and watched the Macy's Thanksgiving Day Parade. We played board games. We shared a big turkey and half a dozen caloric sides. I walked around all weekend, dazed by every detail. I'd never seen the parade. I'd never gone a whole holiday without crying. I hadn't even eaten Thanksgiving dinner at a table before. My family always sat on the floor, crowded around a big TV to watch whatever football game was on.

Frankie's family augmented the American traditions with Basque ones. On Thanksgiving morning, we took sol y sombra shots, which they made with a mix of anisette and Canadian whisky. The shots were sharp-tasting, a little too bitter and a lot too sweet, but I felt warm as soon as I swallowed mine. Frankie's mom spent hours baking and rolling a dessert called brazo gitano, a kind of oversized jelly roll she filled with lemon pudding. And on Black Friday, we drove downtown to wander the Basque Block, a street lined with restaurants that served tiny bites of food called pintxos. I ate skewered anchovies and at least a dozen fried balls of béchamel and cod, then we tiptoed across the street to the Basque Center bar for a round of Bud Lights.

At the end of the weekend, Frankie's mom covered their long table with leftovers, and everyone listed the things they were thankful for. When my turn came, my voice gave out as I tried to speak. I didn't want them to know how I'd spent my holidays before, but I did want to tell them that I wanted the rest of my life to be different.

"I've never had a good Thanksgiving before," I said. "I'm thankful for this one."

I KEPT FRANKIE'S RING in a drawer at work until mid-November. Her family had been such a huge part of why I wanted to marry her that I decided that fall I wanted to ask for their blessing before I proposed. I'd imagined asking in person, but we couldn't make it to Boise for Thanksgiving in 2013. I didn't want Frankie to know I was going to ask, and I didn't yet have any of her family members' phone numbers, so I waited until Thanksgiving morning, until Frankie looped her parents and her siblings into one big video chat to take the early-morning sol y sombras. While they were distracted, comparing recipes, I sneaked a second one, hoping the whisky would embolden me. I downed the shot and reached for Frankie's cell phone.

"Hey," I said, a bit too peppy and slurred. "Can I talk to your family alone? I want to ask them about Christmas presents for you."

I'm a terrible liar—usually Frankie can spot even the tiniest exaggerations—but that day she handed me the phone, then turned back to the turkey she was basting. I carried her cell to the bedroom we used as an office. My heart was beating so hard, I could feel it knocking behind my eyes. I looked into the phone. Frankie's parents were sharing a screen in Boise, and her brother and sister were on, too, squished into frames with their significant others. I can't remember what I told the six of them that morning, but I remember that both Frankie's mom and I were crying before I finished.

Asking for permission was a dorky, gentleman's move, the kind I'd never imagined myself making. I felt vulnerable in a way I hadn't experienced before, but it was worth it, I thought. I wanted every Thanksgiving to be as good and easy as the one we'd spent together. I wanted in-laws and forever access to those fried balls of béchamel and cod.

"Of course," her mother said. "We love you."

I hadn't talked to my mom in a few months, but I tried calling her that night. She'd want to know that I was going to propose, I thought. She'd want to start planning a wedding. I knew my parents wouldn't be able to help me pay for anything, but I thought my mom would have ideas. Maybe she'd want me to eat one last boiled egg, just to make sure. My hands sweat into my cell phone case as I waited for her to answer, but she never picked up.

I woke up the next morning to the pinkest sky. It burned through our curtains and cast a pastel shadow across Frankie's thin shoulders. Usually, she doesn't talk much when she first wakes up, but the sunrise roused her from a dream, and she squinted and smiled at me, then said she needed to ask me something.

"What kind of wedding cake do you want one day?"

It was a funny question. She never talked about weddings, and I didn't think she suspected I was about to propose. I kissed her cheek.

"Anything but raspberry fantasy."

We took my beat-up Toyota Matrix, but Frankie drove as we headed south toward a part of the Oregon coast called Cape Perpetua. The drive was nearly three hours, and I spent most of it aiming my video camera out the window. I turned the lens toward Frankie, and she crinkled her nose in protest, but I didn't stop filming.

"What if one day I want to remember the trip we took to the coast for Thanksgiving?"

She doesn't love to be documented, but she's used to me taping everything, so eventually, she turned back to the road and shrugged. We listened to a Janelle Monáe album, and when it ended, I switched to the Bee Gees, my mom's favorite group. I imagined calling her later that night to tell her Frankie and I had listened to "You Should Be Dancing" right before we got engaged.

We made it to the ocean around 3 p.m. The ring box bulged in my Patagonia pocket, so I kept my left arm glued to my side in an attempt to hide the square lump. Frankie had been telling me about Cape Perpetua since we first met. The cape had tide pools, she told me, pockets of water the Pacific Ocean's receding waves left filled with sea creatures. Her family used to visit the pools every year when she was young, but I had never seen one. That afternoon, we climbed over big black rocks and piles of barnacle-covered mussels, then Frankie motioned toward a dark basin in the distance.

I thought the pools would be the color of the ocean, but they swirled with neon hues. We bent close to the water, and Frankie pointed out purple urchins and bright orange sea stars. She told me the green anemones would close around my finger if I poked their centers, so I reached through the water, brushing past the hard-shelled starfish, to touch every one. The anemones were squishy, water-squirting creatures, and I laughed so hard mashing them that I accidentally stepped into the water. I fell back against the barnacles and shook my foot dry.

I wanted to propose near the water, but when I looked around, I saw an elderly couple circling the adjacent pool. My blood went hot. Old people don't like gay people, I thought. If these old people see me propose, they're going to judge me or attack us. They're going to ruin what might be the most important moment of my life.

Frankie stepped back from the pool and peered down at me as if she wanted to know what I was thinking.

"I wish those people would leave," I told her.

"Why?"

The wind stung my face. I told her I wanted us to have the cape to ourselves. We lingered for twenty minutes, touching all the sea anemones until every one had closed up, but the elderly couple never disappeared. My stomach hurt so badly I could barely stand. Eventually, I stopped looking at the sea creatures and stared at the couple, willing them to leave.

All these years later, I mostly feel sad for my younger self. I spent all my big happy moments worrying someone else would spoil them. The first time I kissed Ellen, I couldn't stop thinking about Hell. And that day by the water with Frankie, I spent more time thinking about the elderly couple than the woman I hoped to marry. My chin quivered, and Frankie drew closer to me. I asked her if we could walk away, down a slope to a spot no one could see.

"What's the matter?" she asked. "Are you hungry?"

I shook my head no and sat on a boulder. Frankie kneeled in front of me.

"I just have something for you," I said.

Every dream I had about proposals always involved a great speech. The man would know what to say to me, I thought as I lay in bed, waiting for the boiled egg to work its magic. He'd recite a poem or find the kind of happy-ever-after verbs no one else had ever thought to use. Once I made up my mind to do the proposing myself, I sketched out a few lines I wanted to say. I walked around our neighborhood the week before Thanksgiving, practicing. I don't remember those lines now, in part because I didn't remember them that day on the rocks. I struggled to get the ring out of my pocket, and by the time I did, Frankie looked like she knew what I was going to do. I don't think I even asked her to marry me. I handed her the box and started crying.

"We had a good Thanksgiving," I said.

She must have said yes, and we must have kissed or cried or celebrated in some way, but I'm ashamed to admit that I don't remember those moments. We called her family members from the parking lot, then I tried to call my mother. The phone rang until an automated message said my mom's voicemail was full. I called my brother, and I squealed, and we laughed about how artless my proposal had been. I tried my mother again. I called her the next morning from the hotel we were renting on the beach, and I called her as we drove back to Portland. I must have told my father, but I don't remember the conversation. All I remember about what I'd imagined would be the biggest day of my life is dialing my mom's number over and over again, listening to a robot tell me she had no space available.

Chapter Sixteen

(2014–2015)

FOR HALF A DECADE, I scratched out the same New Year's resolution in my journal: Finish this documentary. I wrote it in black ink in 2012, blue in 2013, and a slanty green the year after that. Every January, I drew a little box where I planned to mark the film's completion, and every December, I looked at the unchecked square and told myself I needed a few more months.

I'd thought, after Mark sent me the photographs, that he would give in on the journals soon, but every time I asked, he told me he didn't feel right turning over Roy's thoughts. Without the diaries, I tried to find other ways to finish the film. I wrote to the health departments in Arkansas and Missouri to see if either state had a birth certificate for Roy, and I combed an old newspaper database for clues, but none of my searches yielded anything. Occasionally, I logged on to a Facebook group dedicated to remembering the olden days of Delhi, and I asked if anyone knew Roy. Their replies were genial but empty: "Sweet woman always heard she had a bad childhood." "All us kids would pile up on her porch 'n visit early 70's." "Sweet lady." "I remember her mowing yards."

In 2014, for the first time in five years, I didn't book a single trip to Louisiana. The flights south were expensive, and I suspected there was no one left in Delhi for me to interview. I'd contacted at least a hundred people, a tenth of the town's white population, and I'd run down every rabbit hole those people suggested. I'd interviewed a few Black residents, too, but as far as I could tell, Roy mostly talked to other poor white people. The Black people who lived on Chatham said they'd seen Roy, and they'd smelled what they described as "the aroma" that emanated from his house, but they'd never said anything more than hello to Roy, and he tended to say less than that.

"We never really knew what went on in that small house," a young man named Dequantae McDowell told me outside of the single-wide, white-and-yellow trailer he shared with several family members. "It had been going on for so long, and no one understood."

Dequantae said he and a bunch of neighbors stood out in the street and watched the day Mark King took Roy to the nursing home. Dequantae told me the story in April of 2013, ten years after Roy had left the street for good, but Dequantae said he remembered every detail.

"Once they actually got her out of the house, buses, truckloads of cats came out of that house. And they weren't your typical, everyday, run-down-the-street cats. I don't know what those cats were bred with, but they were some strange-looking cats. I would not be caught dead with one of those cats in my house. But she was drawn to them. The way she acted toward them, you would think they were all accounted for. She knew them by name."

Were those anecdotes enough to drive a movie? Aubree and I applied for half a dozen grants that year, and in every application, I took the depressing facts I'd gathered and pieced them together into something like an arc. I described the kidnapping the way my grandma had. I wrote about the porch concerts and the animals Roy hoarded, and I hinted at the scandalous ending my cousin Jennifer believed happened in the nursing home. But none of the organizations handing out money to filmmakers chose us for one of their awards.

I gave up for a while. I told myself if grant makers didn't see the value in my movie, maybe it had no value. I stopped trolling through Newspapers .com, and I spent my vacation days on actual vacations. Frankie and I went to Nashville and the San Juan Islands, and I documented every delicious thing we ate on our trips. Hot chicken and raw clams, prawns fresh from the ocean. Oregon legalized gay marriage on my birthday, and that summer, the paper got a new editor, a two-time Pulitzer winner who told me I was "fucking awesome" and my articles were "fucking beautiful." He believed in me in ways the previous editors never had, and he gave me time to write the long narratives I'd always wanted to write.

"It was a super good year," I journaled in late December. "But the big albatross is the movie. How can I ever finish?"

Though the grant makers didn't believe in my project, I knew that plenty of people did. The mayor of a suburban town I'd once covered for *The Oregonian* called me every few months to ask if the film was finished. People who'd donated money to the Kickstarter campaign wondered when they'd see it, and my relatives continued talking as if we would all attend the Oscars together someday. The truth was, even if Aubree and I had won one of those awards, even if someone had given us a lot of money, I probably would have stalled out in 2014. After five years, I still didn't know whether Roy had been kidnapped. I didn't know if he'd really sold any of his songs, and I didn't know how he felt about his own life. I kept returning to the same sources, as if *this* time, I'd find the newspaper article that would render everything clear. I loaded Final Cut Pro, and I moved scenes around, hoping the right documentary arc would suddenly appear, but every time I watched the footage through, something seemed to be missing.

The longer I wrestled with a draft, the more I came to believe that one more trip to Louisiana might crystalize everything. Plus, Frankie had never been. We were planning to marry in August 2015, and it felt wrong to spend forever with someone who'd never seen my hometown, so I bought us tickets south for a long weekend in February, six months before our wedding.

At the airport, Frankie loaded up on gifts to take to my parents. She'd only met them once, over corn dogs at the pub in Portland right after we started dating, and she wanted to make a good impression, so she bought hazelnuts and marionberry jam—Oregon specialties—for my mother, and she picked out six local beers to take to my dad. As our plane descended into Shreveport, I imagined the scene my mother would make. Usually, she stood at the edge of security, sobbing and shaking and clasping her hands together as if she had waited her entire life to lay eyes on me again.

"She's probably going to cry a lot," I told Frankie as we deboarded the plane.

I pretended to be embarrassed by the thought of it, but the truth is, I'd come to see my mom's showy tears as a kind of ritual, the first signal that I was home. Her smeared mascara sealed something inside me. Tears meant she loved me.

Shreveport Regional Airport is small, so we reached the lobby in a few minutes. I looked around, but I didn't see my mother. There was another family, holding helium balloons and hugging as if a million years had passed since they'd last seen each other, and I thought, at first, that maybe my mom was waiting behind them. She wasn't. I thought maybe we were supposed to meet at the baggage claim, so Frankie and I took the escalator down to the basement level. My mom wasn't there, either. Finally, I spotted my dad, sitting and scrolling through his phone. I called his first name. *Alan.* He looked up, smiled crooked, then walked toward us. He grabbed me in a sideways half hug.

"Your mom wants Mexican food," he said, taking my book bag off my shoulders. "We need to stop and get some."

I must have asked why she wasn't there, but I only remember flashes of that night. My dad, Frankie, and I ate fajitas at the Mexican restaurant. We ordered chips and queso to go for my mother. When we got to my parents' house, my mom was asleep in a recliner, so my dad put the cheese dip in the fridge. The next morning, my mom was still sleeping in the same spot. She woke up mid-afternoon, just long enough to reject Frankie's hazelnuts with a silent sneer, then she microwaved the queso until it liquefied in its Styrofoam cup. She carried the chips and dip back to her recliner, but she fell asleep almost as soon as she started eating. I remember walking into the living room and finding her frozen, hunched over the bag with one arm in the air and a chip hanging out of her mouth. The queso had hardened again.

"Is she sick?" Frankie asked.

I shrugged. I was sure my mom was on pills, but I was too embarrassed to tell Frankie that. I'd told her a little bit about my childhood, but I worried if she knew too much, she'd pity me. Back then, I couldn't think of anything worse than being pitied by someone I loved. I thought real strength meant living as if nothing had ever shaped or broken me, and so I walked away from the living room as if the woman sleeping with a chip in her mouth had no bearing whatsoever on my life or well-being.

Frankie and I puttered around the house for a bit. I wanted Frankie to have what I thought of as a quintessential Louisiana experience—not

Louisiana as I had lived it, but Louisiana as a movie might render it—and so I suggested we go out and buy a king cake, the cream-cheese-slathered cinnamon rolls that bakeries sell in February and March to celebrate Mardi Gras. Every king cake has a tiny plastic baby hidden inside, and whoever finds the baby has to buy the cake next season.

"Hopefully you'll get the baby," I told Frankie. "Then you have to come back next year and buy a cake for us."

My dad wanted to get out of the house, too, so he offered to drive us to a place he said made the best king cakes. He grabbed his keys, scooped up the Shih Tzu he'd recently adopted from a rescue shelter, then headed toward the car. I looked back at my mother before we left. She was still sleeping, chips in hand.

We were gone for maybe half an hour, but when we returned, Frankie found an entire bag's worth of Dove chocolate candy wrappers in the bathroom trash my dad had emptied that morning. Frankie didn't speculate, but I did: My mother must have eaten several dozen pieces of chocolate while we were gone. I looked at the recliner. She was still passed out exactly where we'd left her, but the chips were on the floor. She'd probably spilled them, I thought, on her way to eat the candy. My dad's dog charged toward the chips, but he picked her up before she reached the scraps.

"Let's go outside," my dad said. He was talking to his dog, but I followed them out anyway, still carrying the king cake. The temperature had notched above sixty degrees, and my dad was wearing shorts. I took off my jean jacket, then sat on the grass next to him. We didn't talk about my mother. We never talked about her when she was on pills. I don't know if it was too painful or just too familiar to make new conversation about, but we always found ways to avoid it. We could have talked about ways to help her, but instead, that afternoon, we talked about shrimp. My dad told me he'd learned how to do a Louisiana boil in the backyard using an old camping stove and a propane tank. He'd bought a seasoning mix and three pounds of shrimp, along with a pound each of corn, potatoes, and mushrooms. He had smoked sausage, too, but he wasn't sure if he should cook it on the stove before throwing it into the pot with the vegetables. After a while, we decided sautéing it was best, so Frankie and I headed inside to cook the meat while my dad set up a burner. When we stepped back inside, I saw that my mom was standing in the middle of the living room. She was wearing a threadbare cotton nightgown, and her hair stuck out in chunks. She was fifty years old, but she looked at least seventy.

"I got new boobs," she said.

My mother had had her breasts removed a few years earlier. She'd told me two different stories about why doctors had taken them. First, she said that a brown recluse spider had bitten her when she and my father lived in Oklahoma after I graduated college. As proof, she regularly emailed me photographs that showed her right breast turning black with rot. Later, she told me she'd had breast cancer. I never found out which story was true, and I never asked my dad or brother if they had any theories, but I know something real must have happened. Her breast was bruised and oozing black in the pictures she sent, and doctors don't perform double mastectomies for no reason. I never believed she had cancer, though. Wouldn't she have lost her hair? Wouldn't she have called me to complain about chemo or radiation? She posted funny dispatches on Facebook every time she came down with shingles or kidney stones, updates that inspired her friends to leave a flurry of encouraging messages, so I know she wouldn't have wasted a good hospital visit. She would have posted photos from the oncology ward. She would have listed her room number and asked her friends to call. Wouldn't she have? I could have pressed her for more details, but I didn't see the point. She was an excellent liar, and I suspected she'd talk her way around any holes I pointed out.

"Wanna see them?" she asked.

She didn't wait for an answer. She lifted her nightgown up over her head. She showed us her entire naked front. Frankie closed her eyes and backed away, but I saw the ragged, purple scar my mom had had etched across her stomach since 1988, when she had her gallbladder removed. I saw the skin that had gone loose and empty when she lost a hundred pounds while I was in Portland. And I saw her new breasts, firm B cups, scabbed from construction, nipple-less.

"Mom. Put your nightgown down."

Frankie didn't react. She's unflappable, or at least, she always seems unflappable. She stood on the edge of the living room as if this spectacle were one she'd seen a dozen times. I kept sneaking glances at her, waiting for her to look as distraught as I felt, but she gazed off to the side of my mother as if the wall were suddenly very interesting.

"But they're perky," my mom said, lifting her left boob up. "You don't understand because you've always had perky breasts, but mine, they hung down and bowed to the moon."

"Well, you've had kids. You breastfed. It's natural. Put your night-gown down, and you can show them to me later, okay? Frankie doesn't need to see everything you got."

My mom snorted. She huffed and let her nightgown fall back over her frame.

"Aren't we about to be family?" she asked.

She put her hands on her hips, sassy as if she'd just made a great point. I stared at her in a way I hoped she recognized as disapproving. She sank back into her recliner, then twisted around to turn up the electric heating pad she'd been lying on. I told her we were doing a shrimp boil, but she didn't say anything as Frankie and I passed into the kitchen. By the time we finished the sausage, my mom was asleep again.

She didn't wake up until the next morning, until Frankie and I were packing our suitcases to drive to Monroe to see my grandma. Around 8 a.m., I carried my bag through the living room, and my mom flung herself out of the recliner. She was still wearing the same nightgown. Her left eye was completely closed, and the rest of her face sagged sallow in a way that looked as if her skin might slip completely off. Later, in my journal, I wrote that she'd looked "an evening away from death," as if that were the kind of thing people said about their fifty-year-old mother.

"I have something for your wedding," she said. "Go into the computer room and grab the box at the foot of the bed."

The computer room was just a spare bedroom where my parents kept everything that didn't fit somewhere else. The room did have an ancient desktop sitting on an iron Singer sewing machine table, but it was also filled with unhung wall sconces, half-used rolls of Christmas wrapping paper, and a stack of homemade quilts my mom had owned since before I was born. I looked around and saw the cardboard box she wanted me to take. The box reeked of something floral, and when I opened it, I saw different colored soaps, all stamped with a fleur-de-lis.

There were two antique teacups in the box, mismatched ones that looked as if they'd been part of fancy sets at some point. One of the cups was lavender with scalloped edges and a heart-shaped handle. The other was white and gold-rimmed with a kind of pastoral scene painted on the side. I set them back on top of the soaps, then grudgingly carried them to the living room.

"What are these?" I asked.

"They're for your wedding. The soaps will go into the teacups, kind of like a sachet, then we'll give them out as favors to your guests. Are you planning to invite any of my cousins?"

I'm sure my face gave away how ugly I thought everything inside the box was. When my mother looked up, her expectant smile fell into a frown. I can't remember if I took a breath or tried to find a nice way to tell my mother there was no way I was giving out soaps and teacups. Frankie and I didn't like girly things. We wanted to hand out mix CDs and coasters stamped with an Oregon fern Frankie had drawn.

"The fleur-de-lis is a Louisiana thing," I told my mom. "Frankie has no connection to it."

"But you're the bride!" my mom choked out.

She bent over and cried so hard and silent, I worried she had stopped breathing. My stomach thudded. I knew my mother had been planning my wedding in her head since the moment she first held me. She used to tell me when I was little that she'd make sure my ceremony was better than hers. It wouldn't be rushed, as hers had been, and I wouldn't throw up on the preacher. The reception would be catered, not a potluck, and I'd go on a real honeymoon—somewhere that required plane travel. I knew how much my mom had adapted over the years. She'd given up dreaming of the groom, and she'd even accepted that I didn't plan to wear a dress. But I realized, watching her cry over the box of soaps, that she'd held on to a few of her expectations.

"Mom, there are two brides. It's not just about me."

I don't remember how we resolved that conversation. I think we may have yelled at each other. I was still angry that she'd never answered the phone the night I proposed to Frankie, and I think I may have told her that morning that she had no right to collect things for my wedding because she hadn't been present when I needed her to be. Maybe I cried, too. I wanted my mother to help plan my wedding. Portland didn't have a ton of cool formalwear stores, so Frankie and I had talked about going to San Francisco to look for wedding outfits, and we'd agreed that we wanted to take our mothers with us. In fact, I'd suggested San Francisco instead of another city because my mother had always longed to go there. It feels uncharacteristically girly of me, but the few times in my life I ever pictured getting married, I always imagined my mother would help me find an outfit. I wanted her there, drinking champagne, vetoing the ugly ensembles and thumbs-upping the good ones. I wanted her to taste cakes and choose the flowers with me. I even wanted her to give out wedding favors if that was important to her, but I wanted it to be something we did together. I wanted her to know me well enough to pick something other than teacups. I wanted her to answer the phone. I wanted her to wake up when I flew down, and I wanted her to live until August.

I'm sure I wasn't brave enough to tell her any of that, but I don't know what I did say. I don't remember if we hugged goodbye or if I stormed out. I only remember that as I drove toward Monroe, I told Frankie that I didn't want my mom to go to San Francisco with us.

Frankie seemed disappointed. She wanted to take the trip, and she wanted her mother to go. I wanted to have the kind of dependable mother Frankie had, but I didn't tell her that. Instead, I suggested we lie to mine.

"We'll tell her we canceled the trip, but then we'll still go to San Francisco with your mom. We just can't put any pictures on Facebook."

Frankie was silent. She shook her head no. She didn't want to lie to my mother, and she didn't like how quickly I'd suggested it. I can't remember the exact words Frankie used—my ears were ringing in anger—but I felt as if she were saying she didn't want to marry the kind of person she'd suddenly realized I was, the kind of daughter who yells at her sick mother, the kind of person who lies.

"What choice do I have?" I asked. "You saw her. I cannot take that person on a trip."

I deserved to go to San Francisco, I thought. I wasn't going to let my mom take that away from me. But Frankie, I knew, might never understand. She didn't have to lie to her parents because her parents wouldn't disappoint her. They might even offer to help pay for the trip.

My parents weren't like that. My parents used my name to take out illegal credit cards. They cheated on each other and lied to me. How could I owe them an honesty they'd never given me?

Frankie and I didn't talk about this conversation for another five years, but I thought she was judging me that day in the car. I often thought she was judging me when we expressed different ideas about family. We didn't fight often, but family was the one subject that reliably turned our sweet words sour. Usually I ended conversations like that one by accusing Frankie of thinking she was better than I was. She usually told me that I was projecting, that she didn't think of me as a bad person just because I was different, but I never allowed myself to believe her—not later, once we were married, and definitely not that day in the car.

I PRESSED ON TOWARD Monroe, mostly quiet and clenching my jaw. The highway was a long, repetitive stretch of brown. All the pine trees had dropped their needles, and I worried Frankie would think my home state was ugly. We'd spent Christmas at her parents' house two months earlier, and I hadn't been able to stop taking pictures of all the snowy mountains that rose in the distance at the end of their block. Boise was blue skies and desert sand and so many different shades of green. When the sun set, it spun the valley with shades of pink and purple I hadn't known existed.

West Monroe appeared as a McDonald's and a twenty-four-hour tobacco shop. I pushed past the Western-wear store that's shaped like a barn, then I turned left down the street toward my grandma's house. When we arrived, she was sitting in her usual spot, in front of the space heater in her plastic chair in the cluttered carport, but she looked much thinner than she had the last time I'd seen her. She told me she weighed eighty-five pounds. All the fat had gone off her arms, and her lavender nightgown hung loose and tented from her shoulders. We sat in the carport for an hour, talking about things I no longer remember, until my grandma reached for her walker and told us she needed a nap. Frankie and I were still on edge from our car conversation, plus, we were hungry, so I suggested we go out for a late lunch while my grandma slept. We'd only eaten a few slices of the king cake, so I left the rest of it on the kitchen table, the one my grandma and I had been sitting at when she first told me about Roy.

"You should have some," I told her. "It's good. It'll help you gain weight."

My grandma shook her head no. "That's yours. I wouldn't enjoy it."

"Just try it," I said, bending down to kiss the shock of her gray hair. She shook her head no again. She told me to "leave it alone."

Crawfish season had opened a week or two earlier, and I was still hoping to show Frankie the version of Louisiana I'd idealized, so I took her to my favorite seafood restaurant, and we split three pounds and a round of beers. They were light beers, Bud Lights or maybe Coors, but they lifted my mood enough that I suggested I take Frankie on a tour of my old haunts. If we're going to get married, I told her, you should see where I lived. The trailer was too far out of town, so I opted for some of the closer-in spots my family had rented.

I'd told Frankie that I grew up poor, but working-class poverty looks different in the South than it does in Portland, and I thought Frankie seemed unsettled as I drove her around. Most of the low-income housing in Portland looked indistinguishable from other homes. One subsidized complex was so beautiful I'd even googled it, thinking I might want to live there, before I realized it was income-restricted and my newspaper job paid me too much. In Monroe, some of the poor neighborhoods were just dirt roads dotted with dented trailers. A few were missing walls, and people had pushed sheets of aluminum up against the sides, makeshift barriers whose gaps revealed the insides of the homes. I drove down one street lined with squat two-bedrooms and abandoned car parts, and we passed burned-out homes where people still lived.

I took Frankie past the rotted wood-frames, then we wound along the Ouachita River levee toward the house I lived in for most of middle school. I slowed to a stop in front of it, but we didn't get out. There was no shoulder to park along, no sidewalk to stand on, either, and anyway, I didn't want to get too close to that house. It looked fine enough. It was airy and white, the nicest place my family ever lived. The roof was a bit buckled, and the foundation slanted, but someone had planted a few flowers along the front, and they'd decorated the concrete stoop with ceramic vases. I stared at those steps, and I felt something clamp, then cascade inside of me. It was just a house, I knew, a rental that dozens of other families had probably inhabited, but I looked at it and I felt twelve years old again. I remembered walking up the steps after the Point of Grace concert. I remembered the wild, unhinged look in my mother's eyes, the way she rushed at me with her fists. I knew she'd been on the opioid nose spray long before we lived there, and maybe her problems started somewhere else—with Cam, in Delhi, perhaps—but I told myself that this house was to blame. This house was the reason I lost her.

The front window was my window, the hole I crawled out on the nights when my mom didn't sleep. If I was gone, she couldn't find me and force me to eat half-cooked meat. She couldn't ask me to bleach the tub or kill one of the mice that ran across our kitchen counters. And she couldn't crawl into bed and whisper the ways I'd disappointed her.

I turned back to Frankie. I'd never told her any of those stories. I didn't plan to ever tell her those stories, in part because I barely ever let myself remember them. It was enough, I thought, for her to see the neighborhoods, for her to picture my Louisiana as something real.

A car pulled up behind me and honked, so I drove on. Frankie worked in river restoration, and I wanted her to see the Ouachita, but as soon as we pulled close to it, I felt embarrassed. The river was brown, and the bank around it was covered in trash. The sun was setting, and I tried to shoot a picture as pretty as the ones I'd snapped in Boise, but no matter how I adjusted the settings, everything came out brown.

We walked back to the car, and my phone buzzed in my pocket. My grandma's voice on the other end sounded frantic.

"Casey? I need to tell you something."

"What? What is it?"

My throat froze and felt thick. My grandmother must be calling to say my mom died, I thought. What if the last thing I said to my mother was something mean about those teacups?

"Just tell me, Grandma. What is it?"

She cleared her throat, lowered her voice to an apologetic whisper.

"I just took a small piece, okay? Naturally, I didn't want you to know, but a baby fell out. I used my finger and tried to push the baby back inside, but it won't go back."

I laughed and leaned against the car in relief. She'd gotten into the king cake.

"Grandma, it's fine. The baby just means you have to buy the cake next year. Frankie and I will come back, and we'll eat one together."

The line was quiet, then I heard my grandma spinning her thumb across a lighter. She inhaled. She let herself laugh a tiny bit.

"Ooh. That baby is an ugly little shit."

I drove back to my grandma's house, and the three of us stayed up late, talking and folding plastic grocery bags. My grandmother had been appalled to find out that Oregon had banned them, so she wanted to send us home with the two hundred she'd been saving from trips to Walmart and the commissary. She ironed each bag flat with her palm, then folded it like a T-shirt. I told her I didn't need them—we used cloth bags—but I nestled them into my suitcase anyway.

I took Frankie to Delhi and Vicksburg. Then, on Sunday night, we drove back to Shreveport to catch our plane home the next morning. My mom was still asleep, but she'd moved from the recliner to my parents' king-sized bed. She'd burned herself so badly on the heating pad, my dad told me, that the skin on her back had turned black. I looked into their bedroom. She was lying facedown and naked. The dark, burnt square around her spine reminded me of the pictures she used to send of her breast, and I wondered, again, what had led to her mastectomy.

I can't remember how I forced myself to walk away. I really believed that would be the last time I saw my mother, and yet, I don't think I lingered long. I handed my dad the car keys, then he drove me and Frankie to the airport. By the time we landed in Portland, I'd already willed myself into forgetting the weekend. The journal entry I wrote that night is about an immigration story I planned to start writing the next morning.

Once I returned to the West Coast, I forced myself to work on the documentary. I always fill my hours with work when I'm sad, and the trip home had left me anxious to put Roy's story behind me, so I rented a cabin for a week and wrote a whole new script. I drew an arc of our journey, making little notches to note each development. I wrote "Mark says no" along the rising action and "Lou gives us the Bible" as we neared a climax I hadn't yet found. By the end of the week, my script remained unfinished. I read somewhere that directors plot out films on index cards, so when I returned home to the house I shared with Frankie, I bought packs in different sizes and colors, and I taped them to the wall in our second bedroom. I spent weeks filling in the cards with potential scenes, but the structure still felt wrong in ways I couldn't pin down. I left the index cards up, though, reminders of the work I needed to finish.

In late March, Frankie and I went to Boise for her brother's wedding. My mom called, and I ignored it, but she called again as Frankie and I were driving toward the rehearsal dinner. When I answered, my mom's voice came through clear.

"Casey. I know I've disappointed you. I know I've hurt you. I wish I had reacted better when you first told me you were gay. I wish I hadn't slept through your visit, but baby, I am going to be different. I dumped all the pills down the toilet. I told your daddy to have them cancel my refills. I am going to come to your wedding, and I'll even ride a bicycle if you want me to. I'm so sorry, baby, but I'm going to be the mother you deserve from now on. I promise, baby."

I wish I had better documentation of how I felt, listening. I remember I cried. I know I wanted to believe her, but I was reluctant. I don't remember anything else, and I didn't record much about that conversation. By then, I'd stopped telling my friends about my life. All my emails from that week are about work, and most of my journal entries are, too. I wrote only a few sentences about the call, tiny ones in red ink.

My mother called saying all the things a person might want her to say, if only I could trust they weren't the product of a manic lucidity. I want her to be a part of my life, but I'm scared. I don't believe this clear-eyed promise will last.

Chapter Seventeen

MY MOM AND ALL her siblings have always told me I was reading full books by the time I was three. They may be exaggerating—in fact, I'm not sure any of them have ever told a story straight and true—but all my earliest good memories involve books. In elementary school, my mother left me at the public library for hours at a time, and I worked my way through the kids' section into the young adult stacks. I loved the way the spines of The Baby-Sitters Club turned the shelves into a pastel rainbow, and I spent one summer reading every Choose Your Own Adventure book three or four times, always opting for a new path once I'd flipped back to the front. For a while, my favorite books were *Hatchet* and *Island of the Blue Dolphins*, stories about young people cast into solitude by tragedy. I suppose I was meant to feel sorry for the main characters, but I read those tales seething with jealousy. I didn't know how to fish or hunt, but I longed to disappear. I wandered around the woods by my house, pretending I, too, had lost my family and every modern comfort. Back home, my parents were probably fighting or my mother was sleeping off a squirt of Stadol, and the daydream calmed me.

Maybe everyone who grew up in the 1980s was similarly obsessed with lost or abandoned children. Back then, missing kids seemed to appear on TV all the time. Baby Jessica fell down a well when I was four years old, and *Home Alone* came out when I was seven. All the parents I knew talked about the disappearance of Adam Walsh as a cautionary tale, and my mother never missed an episode of *America's Most Wanted*.

Still, as a kid, I felt that my obsession was unique. I thought I was the only person in the world who dreamed of slipping out of my life and into something else.

Because I couldn't actually steal away to an island in the Pacific Ocean, I wrote stories, mostly cheap riffs on the narratives I loved, and my seventh-grade language arts teacher encouraged me by giving me books from her own collection. She sneaked all of S. E. Hinton's novels to me, and she loaned me thick nonfiction collections about journalism. I kept writing "lost in the woods" fantasies until one day, after class, my teacher handed me a smooth paperback called *The Face on the Milk Carton*. The book was about a high school student who suddenly learns that her parents kidnapped her when she was three years old. I read it in an evening. Afterward, I decided that a kidnapping was an even better fate than disappearing, and I started searching my family members for proof that I, too, had been stolen. Yes, I had my mother's nose and my father's lips, and my brother and I were practically twins, but maybe, just maybe, I thought, I belonged somewhere else.

Of course, now I see that I wasn't unique. My mother taught me how to yearn and disappear. Maybe she was cooking dinner, or maybe she was helping me with my homework, but most of the time, she seemed as if she were only half in my world. Her eyes had a far-off look, and she usually kept a novel propped open where she could see it. She'd answer any questions I asked, but she looked past me, and I knew she was somewhere else, as gone in the plots of her books as I often was in mine.

NO ONE ELSE IN our family read, but they did like to tell stories. The first time my grandma told me about Roy, I sat at her table practically fizzing with excitement. I had been waiting to write about a stolen child since I was twelve years old, and my grandma had handed me the most exciting kidnapping saga I could imagine. Later that week, I drove to the West Monroe public library and read *The Face on the Milk Carton* again. Janie Johnson, the book's main character, makes sleuthing seem so easy. She stumbles onto her parents' secret one day in the high school cafeteria after she recognizes a picture of herself on the back of a friend's milk carton. The milk carton says the girl is missing. By the third chapter, Janie's in full detective mode. She hits up a local library, scrolls through the microfiche, and finds a *New York Times* story that reveals almost everything. The book ends on a cliffhanger and drags on through a five-part series, but when I finished the first installment, I felt sure I could crack Roy's case quicker than a fictional high school student had solved her own. Microfiche? I'd spent hours spinning the wheels of the archives in college. I could settle Roy's tale in an afternoon, I thought. All I had to do was find one article, one faded headline.

Solving a mystery is not that easy, it turns out. I did go to the library, and I did load spools of old microfilm onto the machine, but no amount of spinning revealed the answers I sought. Most of the small-town papers only reported on the comings and goings of the rich. The Delhi paper had recorded all of Miss Mattie Smith's visitors, but they'd never written about the plight of poor families. The only crimes the newspaper covered were allegations of Black residents drinking in public, racist dispatches that marked the only time Delhi's Black residents appeared in print at all. I scrubbed through the 1920s, alternating between national and local newspapers, but I couldn't find a single article about a stolen baby. A few hours in, I just felt dizzy.

For a while, after my grandmother first told me the story but before I began interviewing people, I talked about Roy at parties. I reenacted the deathbed confession my grandmother had reenacted for me. She hadn't been there when Jewel pulled my great-grandmother down into the bathtub, but she'd been across the street, watching and waiting for word, and Rita Mae had eventually recounted the whole tale. I loved thinking that I was carrying on some family tradition, reenacting what all the women before me had already reenacted. The story was good, juicy, dramatic, and I tried to tell it with the exact same lilts my grandmother had used. The rain came down in sheets that night, she told me, and Jewel confessed right before her spirit lifted toward the pearly gates. The story had all the action I'd ever hoped to find in a library book. But I'm a journalist, not a novelist, and eventually, sometime in my early twenties, I realized I needed to do something more than recite what my grandmother had told me. I had to find proof.

Could any one document have answered all my questions? In the early days, I didn't know what I wanted to know or why I wanted to know it, and so I searched for pieces of paper as if they might solve all my unspecified riddles. When Aubree and I found a copy of the 1930 census that showed Roy was five years old and living with Jewel and John half an hour west of Delhi at the start of the Great Depression, we celebrated. The census made our story feel certain. Roy was real, Jewel was real, and they'd been living not too far from Hell Street. It felt like the start of something. The only way to make our way forward, we figured, was to work backward, and so we set out to find Jewel's obituary, hoping it would yield the clues we needed to trace Roy's life back to the beginning.

In December of 2011, Aubree and I drove to the Monroe public library, then we parked ourselves in front of the microfilm machines. My grandmother hadn't remembered the exact date, but I assumed, based on the story she'd told me, that Jewel had died in the mid-1950s. Aubree and I pulled all the reels from that decade and divvied them up. We must have scanned for hours. I pushed through 1953 and 1954, and when I finished 1955 without any evidence of Jewel's death, I started to worry. My grandma told me she remembered the night Jewel died. She watched her mother leave the house in the rain, and she was there when her mother returned. But my grandma left Delhi in 1955 when she married my grandfather. Jewel couldn't have died any later, I thought.

Aubree and I didn't have anything else to do, so we kept searching just in case. Finally, sometime long after we should have stopped for lunch, I loaded a spool of *Monroe Morning World* newspapers from February 1958. I twirled past articles about stock shows and the stock market until I reached each day's obituaries. My eyes started to blur, but then, near the end of the month, on page 4-D, I spotted Jewel's name.

> *Funeral services for Mrs. Mary Jewel Ellis, 65-year-old Delhi resident, will be conducted today at 2 p.m. at Gay's Funeral Home Chapel in Delhi. The Rev. Clyde Yates will officiate with interment in the Delhi Masonic Cemetery by Gay's.*
>
> *Mrs. Ellis died yesterday morning in a Monroe hospital. She is survived by her husband, John Ellis, Delhi, a daughter, Miss Lois Hudgins, Delhi, and three nephews. Pallbearers will be Earl and Herschel Henson, Donald Castle, Curtis McVay and Elsie Fulford.*

It had to be her. John's name was listed, and a bastardized version of Roy's birth name was, too. But the date couldn't be right, I thought. In 1958, my grandma lived in Fort Huachuca, Arizona. She couldn't have stared across Hell Street as her mother walked toward Jewel's deathbed.

"Maybe Jewel just got sick the night your grandma remembers," Aubree suggested. "Maybe she had a long illness."

I shook my head, wary. What if the story my grandmother told me was just something she'd made up or misremembered? What if there was no bathtub confession? What if I'd spent all these years trying to solve a mystery that didn't exist?

I hadn't read any mystery novels since I was in middle school, so maybe I was expecting an unreasonably clean arc. Janie navigates many twists and turns in *The Face on the Milk Carton*, and the main characters in both *Hatchet* and *Island of the Blue Dolphins* feel conflicted once they're rescued. Good authors embrace the mess, but I hadn't yet learned how to do that, and so I worried that this one discrepancy might ruin the whole film.

Eventually, Aubree nudged me and pointed toward the back of the library, where a sign spun in the air announcing a genealogy department. Aubree suggested we go ask for help. We'd been filming ourselves looking through the archives, so we picked up our tripods and carried the equipment back to the genealogy room. When we walked in, two library workers nodded, but they didn't seem to take note of the cameras. It's striking to me now how calm everyone remained in the face of our film equipment. Every time I see a camera on the street, I duck or cover my face, but the people in the library, and people in Louisiana generally, tended to act as if they'd been filmed a million times.

The genealogy department looked like the rest of the library, only slightly better lit. Shelves of old books led up to two round tables, and a studious-looking woman wearing a red sweater and a red cross necklace sat at one of them. She said her name was Lora Peppers. She'd worked at the library for more than a decade, helping patrons sort through their family histories. When I asked if we could film her for our documentary, she said "sure" as if appearing in films were a routine part of her job.

Aubree set up the equipment, and I tried to quickly explain our project, but my words came out in disarray. I told Lora about the kidnapping and the country music. I told her we were making a movie and the only documents we had were the 1930 census and two obituaries, and she nodded along, somehow making sense of my mush. I slid the printout of Jewel's obituary across the table.

I still thought the one piece of evidence I needed was a stolen baby article, and I figured maybe I'd missed it because I didn't know the right newspaper to search. If I could trace Jewel's life back, I thought, I could figure out where she was living when she took Roy. The obituary didn't give any clues about Jewel's past homes, so I asked Lora if she could help me find Jewel's birth certificate. Lora rested her chin on her hand, and she read the obituary very slowly before she answered. I think she was doing math, trying to figure out when Jewel was born, and when she realized that it must have been in the late 1800s, she shook her head.

"You're not going to find a birth certificate for Mary Jewel or her husband. They are too old. They did not require birth certificates until after 1915, and even then, it's kind of sketchy. If they're born out at home in the country, they're not going to go traipsing into town saying, 'By the way, my daughter was born yesterday, and here's the information for the government.'"

It hadn't occurred to me that Jewel's birth certificate might not exist. None of the mystery novels I loved as a child ever ran into dead ends. Sometimes they spun in cul-de-sacs, but the proof always existed somewhere. I wasn't sure how we could trace Jewel if she had no verifiable beginning.

Lora looked at me, waiting, so I tried to think of another way she could help us. I peered down at my notebook and saw the few sentences I'd written while interviewing Mark. He'd said that Jewel had found Roy at an orphanage. She hadn't stolen him, she'd adopted him. That seemed implausible. Both my grandma and Mark had sworn that Jewel was Native American, and Roy had written "Indian" on one of the three pictures he left behind of Jewel. Roy was white. As far as I knew, the U.S. government didn't allow Native American women to adopt white children in the early twentieth century. In fact, the government spent decades taking Native children from their parents. They forced them into boarding schools, where teachers cut off their braids and required them to learn English, and they made them convert to Christianity. Later, in the 1950s, government officials launched what they called the

Indian Adoption Project, a program that took Native children from their parents and gave them to white families. I couldn't imagine anyone in Arkansas agreeing to defy government norms by giving a white child to a Native woman. Still, I knew I needed to chase down every rumor, so I asked Lora if she could help find adoption records. She adjusted her wire-frame glasses and told me adoptions weren't her specialty.

"But it's my understanding that those adoption records are gonna be sealed. Shut tight. And if what you think might be true, that she was stolen, there's not going to be anything."

I must have looked disappointed because Lora offered to send one of her coworkers to track down John's obituary for us. Jewel's obit hadn't answered any questions, but I was desperate, so I told Lora that would be nice. She walked us around the stacks, pointing out old books on North Louisiana until her coworker, a middle-aged man with a long dark pony-tail, reappeared with a printout from late May 1959. I read it out loud:

> *John Ellis, 68, died in a local nursing home Wednesday*
> *morning. Funeral services were held at 3:30 Thursday from the*
> *Westside Baptist Church of Delhi, the Rev. W. A. Dearman*
> *officiating. Interment followed in the Delhi Masonic Cemetery*
> *by Young's Funeral Home of Winnsboro. Survivors are a step-*
> *daughter, Mrs. Delores Hidgins, Delhi; a brother Milford Ellis,*
> *Lake Providence; a niece and two nephews.*

I read it twice more, but John's obit didn't make sense to me, either. According to the census, John was already sixty-nine in 1930. He couldn't have been only sixty-eight in 1959. Maybe it was a misprint. The obit, after all, had gotten Roy's name exceptionally wrong. Or maybe, I thought, Jewel had replaced the original John Ellis with a second John Ellis. I know that sounds more like a young adult mystery plot than a real life story, but I felt that day in the library that my theory was wholly possible. I held out the obit and shook it at Aubree.

"I really think there must be more than one John Ellis."

"Or," Aubree said, "it could have been a misprint on the census."

I turned to Lora. "Did that happen? Did people get wrong informa-tion in the census?"

"Yeah," she said. She sounded nonplussed. "Imagine, a census taker from the government knocking on your door way out in the country say-ing, 'Okay, what's your name, where were you born, how old are you?' And the person is thinking, 'That's none of your business.' In a lot of cases, they didn't really keep up with their birthday. Life was hard. That just wasn't that important."

The man with a ponytail appeared between the stacks. He said that most census workers back then weren't especially qualified for the job. No one wanted to walk across dusty wide counties, prying into people's business, so government officials pulled drunks out of saloons and forced them into the jobs. Lora Peppers nodded.

"I have heard that one census taker got real tired of going door to door, so he bellies up to the local bar, sits down with his records, orders him a drink and says, 'Okay. Who lives down the road?'"

I sank into my chair. I had felt so sure of the information we found in the 1930 census. I'd thought if only we could find a few other docu-ments tracking Jewel or John, we'd be able to solve the mystery of Roy's beginnings. The government releases census information only after a seventy-two-year embargo, and Aubree and I had even set up a count-down, waiting for the 1940 census to come out in 2012. That suddenly seemed pointless.

I shuffled through my papers, looking for anything that might be a real clue, but I had nothing. My dates might be wrong. The records might not exist. And Roy's journals, the notebooks that might answer all my questions, were locked away in Mark's storage. Lora must have known I was struggling, because she reached her hand closer to mine. She didn't touch me, but it seemed like she was trying to comfort me somehow.

"If you know where she was stolen from, there would of course be newspaper articles at the time about it. You know, 'We're hunting for this girl who was taken from her parents.'"

I didn't want to dive back into the dizzying microfilm, didn't want to scroll through years and states, searching for an article that might not exist, but I wanted Lora to feel helpful, so I nodded.

"If I could find that," I said quietly, "that would be a goldmine."

Lora lowered her voice to match mine. "But you don't know where, and you don't know when."

AT TIMES, MY SEARCH felt like those labyrinthine Choose Your Own Adventure books. If you choose to pay seventy-seven dollars to subscribe to Ancestry.com, turn to page eighty-three. If you go to Face-book, hoping to find Milford Ellis or Herschel Henson or the niece or two nephews listed in John's obituary, turn to page eighty-six. If you choose to give up, close this book, enjoy your life, and try to forget your failure.

Aubree and I did all of those in the years after we met Lora Peppers. We ran into dead ends, then we started back again. We subscribed to Ancestry, spent days searching, then let our membership lapse until, months later, we again decided that we could puzzle out what the genealogist had said was impossible.

Somewhere on Ancestry, there are at least three family trees we made for potential Jewel Ellises. If Jewel's obituary was correct, her first name was Mary, and she was sixty-five when she died in 1958. That meant she had to have been born sometime around 1893. Aubree and I didn't know where Jewel was born, but we plugged every possible fact into Ancestry's search engine, hoping the internet would spit out the one piece of information that might solve our mystery. It never did. Even with those parameters, Ancestry found dozens of Mary Jewels born around the right time. We found Mary Jewels in New York and Oregon, and we briefly congratulated ourselves for finding a Mary Jewel Clampitt who was born in North Louisiana in 1894, but then we found a death certificate that showed *that* Mary Jewel had died when she was only five.

At some point, Aubree and I thought to look in the Louisiana death index for Jewel's maiden name, and we found one. But "Jones" only complicated our search. Once, while tabbing through Ancestry in the Monroe library, my computer froze after the site tried to give me results for "Mary Jones."

Eventually, after years of seventy-seven-dollar searches, we found two promising leads. A Jewel Jones was born to a woman named Mary in Elmo, Texas, in 1892. And another was born two years later in Oklahoma. According to the 1900 census, the Oklahoma Jewel was part of the Chickasaw Nation. By 1910, she was living in Mulberry, Arkansas.

I wish I could say that finding that Jewel had solved even a piece of the mystery, but our trail ran cold. On Ancestry, the Chickasaw Jewel just disappears after 1910. Her mother and her brother stayed in Mulberry, but by 1920, Jewel was no longer living with them. Where did she go?

I tried clicking and typing in new searches, but I never could trace the Chickasaw Jewel Jones to Delhi. If she met Roy and John Ellis in Arkansas, I don't know when or where. I don't know if she told Roy to meet her by a fence post, and I don't know if she found him at an orphanage. All I know now is all I knew when I first started: A woman named Jewel raised Roy.

I must have worked on the documentary for six or seven years before I realized why I was so taken with Jewel. I was at home in Portland, looking for the millionth time at the photographs Mark King had sent me. It was 2015, a few months before I got married. I was studying a picture of Jewel from 1949, the one Roy had labeled "Indian." Jewel was tall in the photograph with dark skin and gray hair pulled loosely back. Her face was square and stern, more handsome than beautiful. Underneath the picture, just left of where he'd written "Indian," Roy wrote "mama." That word unraveled me. "Mama." It felt so full of affection, brimming with a familiar love. Maybe it didn't matter if Jewel stole or adopted Roy, I decided. What mattered is that she wanted him and she loved him enough to keep him.

I suppose anyone who knew the bare facts of my life would have diagnosed me as someone who had "mother issues," but I didn't tell people back then how I felt about my mom. I mimicked her one-armed dance. I told stories about the time she tried to drown a statue of Jesus in our toilet, and I recounted the way she told off that preacher who wanted a jumbo jet. I turned her life into funny narratives, and once, in college, I told Ellen that I planned to write a book about my mom someday. But those stories didn't reveal how I really felt. I didn't want anyone to know that I longed for my mother to love me in a steady, stable way. I didn't even talk to Frankie about my mom until we were in Louisiana and I could no longer avoid the subject. But I think I was drawn to Jewel, especially when my grandmother first told me about her, because I wanted the kind of love I assumed Roy had. Roy wasn't an accident Jewel had made a few months after the love of her life died. He was a decision, carefully plotted and carried out.

Of course I wanted to believe my mother when she called in the spring of 2015 and said she was going to stop taking pills. It felt like she was saying that she'd taken stock of her life and decided, finally, to choose me. But months passed before I believed it. It was only later, after she showed up to my wedding, free of pills and eager to walk me down the aisle, that I came to see that conversation as the turning point, the day my mother returned to me. By then, I'd lost hope of ever finishing my documentary, but the failure didn't sting the way I'd expected it might. I had my mother. What story could compare?

Chapter Eighteen

(2015–2016)

WE WENT to San Francisco. We did not take my mother. Three months had passed since she called me, promising to be different, but I hadn't let myself believe her yet. Instead, I avoided her calls and booked tickets to meet Frankie's family in the Bay Area. Our plane took off for Oakland around 7 a.m., and at 7:07, the Supreme Court of the United States ruled in *Obergefell v. Hodges* that same-sex couples had a constitutional right to marry. *We* had a right to marry—not just in Oregon, but anywhere. Idaho, if we wanted. Louisiana.

We didn't have Wi-Fi above the clouds, but when our plane landed, Frankie's phone buzzed with the news. Soon we were all crowding around her tiny screen, reading Justice Anthony Kennedy's words out loud in the lobby of the Oakland airport:

> *No union is more profound than marriage, for it embodies the highest ideals of love, fidelity, devotion, sacrifice, and family.*

Frankie's parents cried, and they kissed our cheeks and held us in hugs that seemed to last forever. We somehow made it out of the airport and emerged into what looked like a sea of rainbows. It was Pride weekend in San Francisco, and everywhere we went, people were celebrating. Our cab driver, a man with wrinkled skin and an eastern European accent, greeted us by asking if we'd heard the good news. He drove us to a grocery store, and when I paid, the cashier handed me a small rainbow flag along with my change. Even the churches were calling the decision a victory. The large, ornate chapel down the hill from our Airbnb lit its windows with rainbow-colored gels, and the four of us trekked down to take pictures of our illuminated history.

It was a perfect weekend. We toasted the decision with champagne and four or five rounds of raw oysters, then we went to a Giants game and walked along the Embarcadero, and the sun was shining hot enough to burn us. Frankie's mom and I were obsessed with beet juice, so we kept going out to buy more. That Saturday, as I swigged a ruby-red gulp, I watched sailboats bob over the bay, and I knew that I wouldn't have done any of the things I loved if my mother had come. She would have complained about San Francisco's hills. She wouldn't have tried oysters or beet juice, and she definitely would not have sat through nine innings in a stadium where the drinks cost north of ten dollars.

What my mother *would* have liked was the parade, a celebration *The Guardian* called "the most jubilant Pride festival in living memory." Nancy Pelosi and Laverne Cox were in the line-up, and so was Jim Obergefell, the man whose name was on the Supreme Court decision. I kept wondering what my mom would have thought about everything. Would she have whistled at the Dykes on Bikes? Would she have cat-called the men who strolled around wearing nothing but cock rings? I know she would have danced to the brass band that blew loud and happy for hours on end. And I suspected she would have cried when the PFLAG marchers drifted by, wearing tie-dyed shirts and carrying signs that said they loved their gay sons and lesbian daughters. My mom had never lived anywhere that had a PFLAG chapter, and I wondered, as the marchers drew close, if things might have been easier if she'd known other parents with gay children. Maybe she could have told them, instead of me, that some days she wanted to throw up, thinking about me kissing a girl. Maybe they could have pushed her to accept me sooner.

San Francisco's PFLAG group was so big, it took them two whole minutes to march past us. I reached for Frankie's hand, and I looked back at her mom and dad. They were crying. Frankie's parents are Catholic, and I suspected that they, too, had had a hard time when she came out, but they were here now, flanked by naked men and topless lesbians, waving their own tiny rainbow flags. Frankie's dad kissed her cheek, then he kissed mine, too.

"We should be out there," he said.

I didn't wind up looking for an outfit in San Francisco. We spent a day at a custom suit shop, picking out fabrics and buttons for Frankie's outfit, but I was too embarrassed to try on clothes in front of her parents. I adored them. I just felt like I'd be betraying some lifelong dream I'd promised to my mother. Instead, I ordered a white jumpsuit online. It had one strap, pockets, and an overlay of lace that made it fancy enough for a wedding. I tried it on at home, one evening after work, in a cramped hallway where we kept all our board games and the only full-length mirror we had. Frankie zipped me into it, then we stood in front of the mirror together. The jumpsuit was baggy in the chest and long in the legs.

I stared at myself, and I knew the experience would have felt different in a real shop with my mother. We would have had champagne, and my mom would have cried and told all the sales clerks stories I didn't want them to hear. She would have found a jumpsuit that fit me. At home, Frankie and I stood, sober and silent, frowning at my baggy form. Eventually, one of our three cats sauntered by on his way to the litter box and broke whatever spell we were under. Frankie disappeared and returned half a minute later with safety pins. She would fix this, she said. She pinned the jumpsuit in a few key places, then she waved her hand as if to say *voilà*.

"We can get it tailored," she said. "We can make it fit."

THAT YEAR WAS A particularly bad one for my parents. My dad got fired from his exterminating job for a reason he never quite explained, and he spent what little savings he had trying, but failing, to open his own bug-spraying business. My mom didn't work. She hadn't worked in years, not since I was in high school, and even as their bank account slipped toward zero, she didn't offer to look for a job. She was too sick, she said. By July, they were out of money. They couldn't cover rent, so they moved out of their house in Shreveport, stashed their stuff in storage, and went to live with my brother in the one-bedroom apartment he was renting in Washington, DC. Frankie and I had a two-bedroom house with a yard, but my parents never asked if they could live with me, and I didn't offer. I told myself I didn't ask because my parents were allergic to cats, but that was just a way of rationalizing the truth. I didn't want them to live with me. I didn't want to see my mom if she went back on pills, and even if she stayed clean, I didn't want her nosing around, judging my eating habits. I felt guilty, imagining my brother sleeping in his living room while my parents took his bedroom, but I waved that guilt away by telling myself that my brother was the good child, the one who started working when he was twelve to help pay rent, the one who would move home and take care of my parents when they grew too old to fend for themselves. I wasn't good like him. I would never be good like him.

My parents didn't have enough money to fly to Portland for our August wedding, so I bought their tickets, and my brother paid for their week-long stay in a hotel near the airport. They flew in early that week, and my stomach ping-ponged as Frankie drove me to the airport. What if my mom hadn't kept her promise? What if her voice slurred, and her eye drooped, and she looked as old as she had when we'd seen her in February? We got to the airport early, so I dragged myself through the parking lot, then walked circles around the lobby, waiting. My stomach hurt. My hands sweated, and when my mom finally rushed past the glass doors, I felt like I was letting go of a breath I'd held in my entire life. She looked fifty again. Young. Her eyes were clear, and she ran toward me, and I cried the way she usually did at airports. We held hands all the way to baggage claim, and I knew, before we'd ever picked up her suitcase from the carousel, that everything would be okay that weekend.

Frankie and I took our parents to some of our favorite restaurants that week. We ate roast chicken and Italian chopped salads and Belgian waffles topped with Brie. We didn't have a regular, catered rehearsal dinner, but we did buy everyone sandwiches at Bunk Bar, a hip-but-casual restaurant a few blocks from our house. Afterward, we went to a karaoke bar, and my mom and I stayed up late, taking shots of Patrón and singing "Stayin' Alive" in high-pitched squeals. I was drunk before 9 p.m., but my mother kept ordering tequila, pushing the shots toward me, then pouting if I refused to drink them. I can't remember how I made it home. A crack of thunder scared me awake at 4 a.m., and I groaned, then curled toward Frankie.

"I'm going to be hungover on our wedding day."

Frankie's parents had rented an Airbnb in a neighborhood a few miles west of ours, so she left early that morning to get ready with them. My dad dropped my mom off at our place around 9 a.m. She labored through the doorway, smiled meekly, then sat on the edge of my couch.

"Are you hungover, too?" I asked.

She shook her head no, but I poured us both tall glasses of water anyway. She didn't touch hers. For a while, we sat in the living room, close to each other but not talking. It was raining, and we were supposed to have our wedding ceremony outside, so every few minutes, I stood and looked out of our picture-frame window to see if the clouds were starting to break. They weren't.

"Soooo," I said, collapsing onto the other side of the couch. I wasn't sure what to say next. I tried to remember the last time my mother and I had been alone together, but I couldn't think of anything recent. Maybe it was that first trip to Delhi, before I started bringing Aubree along, before my mother stopped going with me.

"Should we play music?" I asked.

My mom shrugged, and I wasn't sure what else to suggest. I hadn't expected us to feel so awkward around each other. When I was young, we had so much fun getting ready for my school dances. Back then, my mom applied my makeup. She fixed my hair. She jigged around my teenage bedroom, forecasting all that the evening would hold. I'd thought that the morning of my wedding would be like those high school nights. I'd pictured her singing into a hairbrush, dancing to the Bee Gees, maybe even pulling me close to match her disco sway. But she didn't dance the morning of my wedding. She sat on the edge of my couch and made herself small in a way I'd never seen her do before. When she spoke, her voice was timid.

"What do you want to do with your hair?"

I pulled my bangs straight up. My hair was much shorter than it had been in high school. Back then, my mom had used hairspray and curling irons and bobby pins to give me fancy updos. But now the sides were close to shaved, and the top was only three inches long. The best I could do was maybe form it into the kind of fancy mohawk the singer P!nk wore at awards shows. My mom was the queen of wielding hairspray, but when I suggested P!nk's style, she shrugged and said she didn't know how to do that.

My best friend, Hayes, came over later that morning, and my mom suggested that the three of us go out to have our nails done. It was the only festive thing she'd suggested, so I consented, even though my nails were short and I hated polish. We drove to a salon, briefly excited, but we both seemed to deflate as soon as we walked into the shop. I felt uneasy, and I think my mother was embarrassed because I was wearing a brown flannel shirt and a Wyoming baseball cap. She kept asking if I was "comfortable" in those clothes.

"More comfortable than I am in this shop," I said.

Neither of us spoke as we browsed through the shelves of polish. Hayes picked something pink and daring, and I chose a clear overcoat. My mom frowned.

"You don't even want a French tip?"

Later, at my house, Hayes flat-ironed and sprayed my hair into the mohawk. Hayes zipped me into my jumpsuit. My mother stood six feet away from us the entire time. Maybe she was nervous, but I kept hoping she'd pull closer to me. She didn't tell me I looked beautiful. She didn't pose for any pictures with me the way we used to before high school dances. She just stood six feet away, silent and bunching her hands together.

My dad picked us up mid-afternoon in an economy car my brother rented for the day.

Frankie and I had only fifteen thousand dollars in savings, so we'd planned the cheapest wedding we could. Frankie designed all the invitations and place settings. I spent months mixing a seamless playlist to avoid hiring a deejay. We didn't pay for a wedding photographer, either, but I could see, as my dad pulled up to the park we'd rented for the ceremony, that my friend Beth, a photojournalist at *The Oregonian*, was waiting in the street with her Canon. Beth shot rapid-fire as my mom leaned in to kiss me. Only later, after my mom had gone back to DC and Beth had invited me over to look at the pictures, did I see that I'd bent away as my mother reached for me.

I walked up and down the block. Eventually, I spotted Frankie. I know straight people think it's bad luck to see each before the ceremony, but Frankie always calmed me, and I wanted to hug her before our parents walked us down the straw-covered path we'd deemed an aisle. I waved her over. I wasn't wearing my glasses, so the trees and the crowd were both fuzzy, but Frankie was clear when she stood close enough to hold. She held on to me, and I felt rooted, assured.

"Are you ready?" she asked.

I walked toward my parents, and my mother looped her arm through mine. She and I were close to the same height, so our arms linked naturally together, but my dad was six foot one, half a foot taller than I was, and I kept losing his arm as my mother tugged me toward her. She cried as we slow-stepped toward the front. Of course she cried. She cried when she was happy or sad or tired or amused or praising God or asking God to perform some workaday miracle like opening up a parking spot right by the entrance to the mall. She almost always cried dry. I knew she was really feeling something when she let tears streak her makeup. But that afternoon, she cried the same scrunched-face, tearless cry I'd seen in mall parking lots. She must have been happy, but that cry told me she was not rocked.

People say weddings are the happiest day of a woman's life, but I mostly felt nervous. I was disoriented without my glasses, and the people who came up to congratulate me appeared in a blur. I only ate a bite or two of the paella we served and none of the oysters we'd spent all year dreaming we'd have. Our first dance was clumsy, and a few hours in, I got mad or hurt because people started leaving before the good rap songs played. I've forgotten almost everything else. Did Frankie and I dance together after our first bumbled attempt? Did we whisper anything to each other? Did we kiss in a dark corner? I only remember one or two details vividly, and the one I remember most is my mother's speech.

She started to speak into the microphone, and people clinked their spoons against their wineglasses a little too long for her liking.

"Shut upppp," she said, feigning annoyance. Everyone laughed. When she started again, she sounded formal and rehearsed. She'd written the speech on her phone, and she held it close enough to read.

"I'm standing before you tonight with overwhelming pride and joy. Casey, I love you so . . ."

The speakers hummed with feedback. My mom shot the microphone an appalled look that was exaggerated and hilarious. Everyone laughed at their tables, and my mom bent in half, laughing, too. When she stood back up, she put her phone down. She looked at me and Frankie.

"Casey, you have truly been the sunshine of my life from the moment you were born. As a little girl in pigtails, as a little girl in fifth grade getting kicked out of class for correcting the teachers on their grammar, to the beautiful woman who sits before me. I adore the fact that you've always dreamt big and you have chased your dreams into reality. Frankie, Casey and I have spent a lot of hours talking about heartbreak and finding true love, and we spent a lot of hours at the Outback Steakhouse over Sydney's Sinful Sundaes."

At this, she turned away from me and Frankie. She put her hand on her hip all sassy-like, and she riffed for the crowd.

"Whenever she broke up with a dud, that's where we wound up," she said. She pointed to her butt, then winked. "And now you know why I'm so big."

Outback had been the fanciest place my mom and I could imagine in the 1990s. We saved up to go there or the Olive Garden for holidays, and we pieced together the cheapest menu items into what we considered an epicurean feast. At Olive Garden, we ate way too many breadsticks, then ordered the pasta e fagioli because it came with unlimited refills. At Outback, my mother always asked for a plate of lemons so she could mix her own lemonade using the sugar packets on the table. We'd fill up on the brown bread Outback gave out for free, and we'd split the six-ounce sirloin—the smallest steak the restaurant sold. All of that was just a preamble for the dessert we went there seeking. The Sydney Sinful Sundae was vanilla ice cream rolled in toasted coconut and topped with hot fudge, whipped cream, and a single strawberry sliced into thin pieces. My mom and I shared one after the first boy I kissed dumped me a week after the homecoming dance. We split another later that year when a boy from church told me he only saw me as a friend. My mom took me to Outback for every heartbreak in high school, and as an adult, I never drove by one without thinking of her, but we'd never gone out for sundaes when a woman broke my heart. I didn't tell her that Ellen, the first girl I kissed, chose a boy over me, and we didn't slide into an Outback booth when the professor dumped me over and over again the year I met Frankie. Now, I supposed, my mother and I would never have a reason to go for a breakup sundae. I was getting married. I'd never feel heartbroken again.

My mom finished her speech. She stepped toward her table and grabbed a glass of champagne. She line-danced her way back into the spotlight.

"I would say congratulations, but I am truly a hick, so I am going to say ayyyeeeeeeee."

She held her champagne high in the air. The crowd ayyyyeeeed back. She swigged, curtseyed, then sat down again.

FOR MONTHS AFTER, PEOPLE came up to me to tell me how much they'd loved my mother. Everyone seemed to have shared a cigarette with her. Everyone said they'd watched her nasty-dance to "Da' Dip" or "Wobble" or "Back That Azz Up." I didn't smoke or dance with her, but after the wedding, my mom and I started talking on the phone every few weeks. That December, for the first time in a decade, I spent Christmas with my parents. Frankie and I went to DC for a week, and we did the kind of family activities I'd loved doing with her parents. We played games and painted ceramic mugs at a shop below my brother's apartment. We hung stockings and watched old movies. My mother loved going to tea shops, so I took her out for scones and cucumber sandwiches on Christmas Eve. A few days later, she went out to eat mussels with me. I'd never seen her eat anything as adventurous as mussels. I was smiling so big and stupid in the restaurant, I could hardly stand to eat. My mom didn't complain about the texture or the taste, and she dipped bread into the broth until every drop was gone. Later that week, after I'd told my mom that Frankie and I wanted to try the Asian-fusion restaurant Momofuku, my mom even went with us. She mostly stuck to the Southern fried chicken the restaurant served, but she tried a few pieces of kimchi, and even though she winced as if she'd eaten something disgusting, I was happy. She was trying to understand me—not the me she'd spent her younger years believing I'd become, but the real me, the me who liked fermented foods.

The weather hovered above seventy degrees on Christmas, and my mom told me she'd just started a new job keeping the books for an interior design company. I remember going to bed one night that week thinking that 2015 had been the best year of my life. It wasn't illegal to be gay anymore. I was married, and my mom was no longer on pills. I was thirty-two, and I thought I'd spend every year after that one happy. But the plot of a life is never a straight line up. It arcs, bends, and some-times turns back in on itself.

Chapter Nineteen

(April 2016)

IN THE SPRING of 2016, I found out that Aubree and I had won a spot in the Crossroads Film Festival in Jackson, Mississippi. We hadn't finished our full-length documentary about Roy, but we'd submitted a shorter cut, one that focused on Pam Sykes, the lesbian who'd called to me from her pickup truck. The film is mostly about Pam's relationship with her mother. At the time, I thought that plot just made good narrative sense—films need tension, and Pam and her mother had tension—but I'm sure I was working out some of my own demons as Aubree and I spliced together clips. It's a sad movie, a glimpse of the life I might have had if I'd never moved or if my mother had never accepted me. Editing it made me feel grateful for my mom in new ways, and when the film festival's organizers asked me to fly down to Jackson for the weekend, I asked her if she wanted to go with me. Aubree couldn't attend, and Pam could only come in for one night, and I wanted to make a weekend of it. Plus, my mom and I had been talking since Christmas about taking a trip together. She wanted to go to Las Vegas to see Celine Dion, and I did, too, but for some reason, we'd never booked tickets.

"Look," I said, when I called her. "I know it's not Vegas or 'My Heart Will Go On,' but it is a weekend we can spend together back home in the South."

I offered to pay for my mom's airfare, but she told me she'd earned half a dozen paychecks since I last saw her. She wanted to buy the ticket herself. I smiled on the other end of the line. My mom really did seem like a new person.

We flew in a few days early so we could spend time with my grandmother. The weather was nice, mid-sixties and rising, so we rolled our windows down to let the air in as we drove from the airport to my grandma's house. I kind of shrieked in happy recognition when the wind rushed past me.

"Do you smell that?" I asked.

Oregon's air was thin and clean, neutral in a way that seemed empty. Louisiana smelled like honeysuckle and fish, like afternoon rain evaporating off hot pavement into a haze of cigarette smoke. It was a thick and briny scent, a little bit rotten, but it felt right to me.

"That's the paper mill," my mom said. "The funky stank of home."

The carport door was hiked half-open when we coasted up to my grandma's house. I peeked underneath and saw that both she and my aunt Ann were wearing cotton nightgowns even though it was the middle of the day and neighbors could see their bare legs. I ducked under the door, hugged them both, then watched as my mother let herself into the house.

When my mom reemerged ten minutes later, she was wearing a nightgown, too. Hers was sleeveless, hot pink, less threadbare than the ones her sister and mom were wearing. No one commented on what I now realized was the carport uniform, and I never asked why they spent so much time in their nightgowns. I didn't change into my own pajamas—a pair of baggy shorts and an oversized T-shirt emblazoned with the Portland basketball team's logo. My aunt, my grandma, and my mom lit a round of cigarettes, and I sat in my usual spot ten feet away.

They talked about essential oils for a while. Aunt Ann was taking classes online to become a certified distributor, and she'd set up vaporizers around the house, each one pumping out lavender or peppermint to calm everyone down. As they smoked, my grandma folded over herself. She looked withered. She didn't have any teeth in her mouth, and I realized I had no idea whether she'd worn dentures or if she'd lost her teeth since Frankie and I visited the year before.

At some point, I held up my phone and started shooting video. My grandma said something, I'm not sure what, because I started recording just after she said whatever she said. It must have been upsetting. Afterward, my aunt sat slumped with her hand covering her face, and my mom lurched forward with an unlit cigarette.

"You say that every time, Mama," my mother said. "We worry about you."

Her voice was thin and breaking. My grandma poked a finger in the air.

"Well, y'all better start worrying because I'm hurting."

My grandma's voice was gruff. She'd always been mean when I was young, but I'd forgotten that because I'd spent so many good years talking about Roy and the olden days with her. She hadn't used this tone, at least in my presence, since before I came out. But I could tell by the way my mom reacted that my grandma always spoke that way to her. My mom picked up her cigarette. She tried to light it, but when she flicked the wheel, no fire came out. She started to cry—a wet cry with real tears that made her voice quiver in a way that unsettled me. I'm sure I'd thought about my mother as a daughter before, but in that moment, I felt something clearer, more tender. *Oh*, I thought. *You too are a daughter who longs for her mother to love her.* I wanted to hug my mom, but I didn't want to anger my grandma, so I stayed in my seat, filming. My mom tried the lighter again, then she caught her mother's eye.

"Mama, I call you every minute that I'm not at work."

"Rhonda, stop that. Stop it."

My grandma stood. Her nightgown had bunched around her waist, so she pulled it down and shook her head at my mother. She hobbled toward the house, still telling my mother to stop crying. After she was gone, my mom and aunt each smoked one more cigarette, then they went inside to take naps that lasted the rest of the day. I walked around the block a few times. I drank three bottles of water and read the Matthew Desmond book *Evicted* until my aunt's vaporizer ran out of peppermint oil. Sometime midafternoon, my grandma called my name.

"Casey, come get in bed with me," she croaked.

I shuffled back to the bedroom. My grandma was a tiny lump under a pile of quilts. She'd lined the bed with her essential supplies—a walkie-talkie, the remote, a Maglite, and a Dove chocolate bar—so I pushed them aside, then lay on top of the covers next to her. Only her eyes peeked out, but she spoke to me from beneath the blankets.

"Have you learned anything new about Roy?" she asked.

"I got some pictures from Mark King," I said. "I've been meaning to show them to you."

I didn't have the originals anymore, but I'd scanned the photos into my phone. I scrolled past cat pictures until I found the image I wanted to show my grandma. Roy was supposedly twenty in the shot. He was standing in a field with one leg propped on a wooden chair. His hair was slicked back, and his arms were filled with a guitar. It was the brooding photo that had made me wonder if my grandma had had a crush on Roy. I handed her my phone, and she tucked it under the covers with her, then she sighed.

"This is what I remember."

"This is the person who came over and invited you?" I asked.

"Honey, yes. If you could just see what I saw as a young girl, all the kids on this shaky front porch, listening to him play the banjo. You either loved country music, or you went in the house and shut the doors and windows because you could hear it all over the neighborhood."

She sighed again. She asked me if I'd ever heard the Rod Stewart song "Maggie May." The mandolin solo at the end sounded like the songs Roy used to pluck on his banjo, she said.

"Promise me we'll listen to it later," she said.

I promised, then my grandma wiggled her way out from under the blankets, and I scooted closer to her so I could see the photo again.

"He looks like a country music star," I said.

"He does. Look at his blue jeans rolled up. That was very popular back in that day. Wonder what was in his head."

She touched the screen in a way I thought seemed full of longing.

"Roy was a fairly decent-looking man," she said.

I wanted to ask if she'd had a crush on Roy. I knew I was running out of time, but I couldn't bring myself to say the question out loud because I worried it would remind my grandma that I was gay. I don't know why I feared that. She obviously knew and had known for fifteen years or maybe more, and she'd never said anything mean to me about it. But I worried if I suggested she'd had feelings for Roy that I'd be suggesting something big and scary about her own identity, something I suppose I hoped was true. It was that hope I was protecting, I realize now. It was a vulnerable longing to see myself in my grandmother. I worried if I spoke that hope aloud, she would destroy it, and I would feel alone again the way I had when I was young. My grandma must have sensed what I was thinking because she changed the subject suddenly.

"You could have your pappaw's ring," she said. "It's in my top drawer."

"What?"

"As an inheritance. You can have his gold ring."

Almost everything else was already spoken for, she said. The cast-iron pot would go to her sister, Shirley, and half a dozen other people had laid claim to an old paint palette my grandma used back in her crafting days. She told me I could have a stack of months-old HGTV Magazines and a roll of pennies from 1983. She tried to give me an old bra, my grandfather's tie, his ring.

"You might need your bra," I said. "Why don't we wait?"

She burrowed deeper under the quilt until only her eyebrows and her gray spikes were showing.

"Honey. You wait too long and there'll be nothing left."

THE NEXT MORNING, my mom was up and dressed by seven. She seemed to have slept off whatever nightgown blues she'd had the day before, and she told me she wanted to get on the road as soon as possible. We stopped in Delhi for lunch on our way east, and she didn't seem nervous the way she had the last time we'd gone to the drugstore lunch counter. She even asked me to take a few photos with her under the pharmacy's sign.

We meandered around Vicksburg for a bit, and by the time we made it into Jackson, it was late afternoon. I scanned the news on my phone as we sat in early rush-hour traffic. When the *Clarion-Ledger*'s website loaded, I gasped. That morning, the Mississippi Legislature had agreed to pass House Bill 1523, a law that would allow anyone in the state to discriminate against gay, lesbian, or transgender people. I can't remember what I said to my mother, but my face must have given my feelings away. If I got sick in Mississippi, a doctor could refuse to treat me. Waiters could kick me out of restaurants, and shop owners could ban me, too.

I wasn't surprised exactly. This kind of state-sanctioned discrimination often follows civil rights wins. The spate of 2004 referendums banning same-sex marriage were, in part, a response to Massachusetts legalizing gay marriage earlier that year. Mississippi's bill felt like the same kind of reaction. We'd won the right to marry, and President Barack Obama's Department of Education had just moved to expand protections for transgender students. Now conservative states were fighting back. North Carolina had already passed a similar bill in 2016, one that banned transgender people from using bathrooms that correspond with their gender identities. I assumed other Southern states would follow.

I told myself I was only in Mississippi for the weekend. Whatever happened there wouldn't govern my normal life. But I felt sick. Jackson is where I went to college. It's where I first kissed a girl. I still had lots of friends in town, and I'd always thought that I might live there again someday. That dream was dumb, I realized as I read the article out loud to my mother. I couldn't live in Mississippi again. I wasn't brave enough.

A woman on my mom's flight had suggested we have dinner at Hal & Mal's, the restaurant where I'd watched the 2004 presidential returns with my gay friends, so she drove straight there. When we climbed out, my mom wrapped her arm around my waist, and we teetered through the parking lot together, our hips too wide to let us walk straight.

"We look like the Monkees," I said, laughing and slinging a foot over hers the way Davy Jones does in the opening credits of the TV show. My mom let go of me at the front of the restaurant. I grabbed the door handle, but she stopped me from tugging it open.

"What if someone kicks you out?"

Her brown eyes were impossibly big and terrified. I knew she'd felt bullied growing up, but I didn't know if she'd ever studied a room and wondered if someone might cuss her out or beat her up or tell her God would banish her to Hell forever. I considered, for a moment, telling her about the time a security guard had kicked me out of the mall in Columbia, Missouri, for holding a girl's hand. He'd followed us all the way to the entrance. He'd yelled that the mall was a place for families, and we had desecrated it. Another time, in rural Oregon, a woman had screamed at me and trapped me in a campsite bathroom after she saw me kiss my girlfriend on the cheek. I wanted to tell my mother that I knew how to endure. I'd survived those experiences, and I'd survived my mother's own anger long ago, and I would survive whatever else happened to me, too. I suspected those stories would scare or hurt her, though, so I faked a cocky smile as I opened the door.

"It's just a few days," I said. "Then I'll go home and be gay as I wanna be."

We searched for a table inside, and I reminded myself that life in Portland was easy. Our governor was a bisexual woman. The speaker of the house was a lesbian. Once a week, the middle-aged straight guy who sat next to me at work made a point of telling me he believed in gay rights. "And how's your wife?" he'd ask me, apropos of nothing.

My mom and I sat in a booth near the middle of the room. She kept fishing out the sugar packets and rearranging them nervously. I wasn't sure how to calm her, so I checked my phone for new messages. No one had texted me. When the screen went dark, I stared at myself in the reflection. I looked especially gay, I thought. My T-shirt was a guy's shirt. My hair was slicked. Every other woman in the room was wearing makeup and the kind of hair that requires tools and products. If anyone was wanting to kick out a lesbian tonight, I was the obvious choice.

My mom and I read through the menu, commenting on what sounded good or gross, and when our waitress walked up to take our order, I laughed in relief. She was a trans woman I'd known in college.

"I don't think we're going to get kicked out," I whispered.

My mom ordered red beans and rice, and I chose hot tamales, the skinny, ground-beef-filled kind that people only make in Mississippi. They're different from the tamales you order at a Mexican restaurant. There's no masa, only cornmeal, and the tamales are served wet in a spicy sauce.

The waitress brought our dishes out fast, and she lingered as we ate. She said she was saving up to leave Mississippi. I told her I was glad I'd left, but I knew, even as I said it, that wasn't exactly true. I forked a bite of hot tamale onto a saltine cracker and into my mouth.

"Actually, I miss it," I said. "Parts of it, anyway."

"I miss the South, too," my mom said. "They don't even have Walmart in Washington, DC. You have to walk to the grocery store, then carry all of your groceries back. I want to pull my car up to the front and use a buggy inside. And I sure as hell don't ever want to see snow again."

The waitress's face fell, and I could tell she was thinking about the legislature's anti-gay bill.

"Y'all want to trade places?" she asked.

Just before we paid, the waitress told us that the Human Rights Campaign was hosting a lip-sync battle at the bar next door. They were raising money to fight the bill, so my mom suggested we go.

We wandered over ten minutes later. The bar was dark and loud, and as my eyes adjusted, I saw three gay Black teenagers leaning in to hug two white lesbians, both of whom looked past retirement age. One of the lesbians stepped back to show off her three-piece suit. It was black and double-breasted, and she was wearing a gold tie underneath her vest.

"I'm crossdressing," she told the teenagers. "I'm hoping to get arrested tonight."

I didn't know the woman or the boys, but watching them made me miss my old life in Jackson. I thought of the Queer Young Adult Network, the way we'd stuffed ourselves into a booth the night Mississippi voters decided we couldn't get married. Before the network, we'd had a group we called the Quilting Club, though none of us knew how to sew. Every weekend, we'd crowd around a dinner table or a recorded episode of *Queer as Folk,* and we'd talk the way we couldn't in public. I remembered that I used to read them the emails my mother wrote me after I first came out. They cried with me. They held me until I forgot I was losing my family. I didn't have that kind of intimacy in Portland. The city was so flush with lesbians, they drifted in and out of my circle without comment. I felt suddenly wistful.

I didn't know if Roy ever knew any gay or trans people. I didn't know if he saw himself as a member of any group. As far as I could tell, he never had any role models to show him how one moves through life as a misfit. And I didn't think he had a quilting club or a bar like this one. He might not have even known other people like him existed. When I was young, before I found my own real-life people, I learned about myself by trawling the internet for clues. I read online journals and excerpts from gay books, and when I was old enough to drive, I rented movies about gay and transgender people. But Roy learned how to be himself without the internet. *Stone Butch Blues* didn't come out until the 1990s, and I'm not sure how Roy would have found a copy even then. Delhi didn't have a bookstore. Louisiana's newspapers did run stories on Christine Jorgensen and Billy Tipton, but those articles were sensationalized and judgmental. In 1953, a Monroe columnist described Jorgensen as "Miss—er, Mr.—er," while a Shreveport reporter went with "shem." And when Billy Tipton, a jazz musician who was born about a decade before Roy, died in 1989, Louisiana papers reported his death under headlines that said HE WAS A SHE and JAZZ 'MAN' LIVED A LIE. Mark King told me once that Roy subscribed to the Monroe paper, so maybe Roy saw those articles. If he did, I can't imagine he felt any less alone. The newspapers only confirmed what preachers told Roy, and what lawmakers were now telling gay and trans people in Mississippi: *You are not human to us.*

My mom kissed my cheek, then pointed toward the bar. I knew which cocktail she would order before she even suggested it. Her favorite was a potent mix she called "Walking with Jesus." It had two kinds of schnapps, both rum and vodka, and a glug of blue Curaçao topped with Sprite. The drink made my head hurt, but just the thought of it inspired my mom to dance toward the bartender in an ass-shaking version of the waltz. I ordered a beer, and when our drinks arrived, my mom sipped her lethal Jesus cocktail through a tiny straw. She closed her eyes in exaggerated ecstasy.

"Mmm, so good. You sure you don't want one?"

The lights dimmed, so we sat down at the first table we could find. My mom pushed her drink toward me, but I waved her off, swigged my beer, then turned my phone on to record. A trans woman took the stage in a tan sheath dress bedazzled at the shoulders.

"I'm Blossom," she said, then kicked the air as the opening notes of Shania Twain's "Man! I Feel Like a Woman!" played.

My mom jumped up and sang along. She kept swishing her hips toward me, bumping my chair with her butt, until I stood and danced, too. Blossom zoomed and hopped across the stage, and the song's lyrics suddenly seemed progressive to me.

Oh, oh, oh, go totally crazy, forget I'm a lady
Men's shirts, short skirts, oh, oh, oh

How had I never realized when I was young that this song seemed to defy all the gender rules the South had taught me? I felt so moved by its transgressive lines about men's shirts that I grabbed my mom's hand and sang loud with her. Later, I googled "Man! I Feel Like a Woman!" and found that Shania Twain had written the lyrics after seeing men transform themselves into women for a night on the town at Toronto's gay bars. But I didn't know that yet in Mississippi. Even as I sang along, claiming the lyrics for myself, I wondered if Blossom and I were just hearing what we wanted to hear in lines meant to convey something else.

The song hit its peak, and Blossom snatched the wavy blond wig off her head. She stood in the spotlight, allowing the crowd to look at her for a minute straight. Tears ran tracks through her makeup. I remember my blood felt charged with electricity. I wanted to be as brave as Blossom. My mother roared, and I tried to scream, too, but my voice gave out.

A retired accountant named Charlene performed next. She told the judges she was wearing every bracelet she owned, shining silver she hoped would infuse extra life into her performance of "I Am What I Am" from *La Cage aux Folles*.

"I was with Dee for twenty-nine years," she said. "We married the first day it was legal. We made it thirty-nine days before she died."

My mom looked at me. She was crying, and I felt overwhelmed to be experiencing this night in Mississippi. This was the place where I'd begun to hide myself. This was where I'd told the Quilting Club all the things I couldn't tell my mother. Would I have stayed in the South if my mother hadn't rejected me? Would I still have those friends? I scanned the room and didn't recognize anyone. No, I thought. My friends had fled, too.

Charlene started with a slow vogue, her hands working out the beats. I wondered what Dee looked like. *Thirty-nine days*. Frankie and I had already been married longer. It didn't seem fair that Dee had spent most of her life in love with, but not legally bound to, Charlene. I felt grateful or in awe, and I didn't want to forget the night, so I took notes on a napkin. I described Charlene's fingerless fur gloves and the purple embroidered smock she wore over a black dress. I wrote down a few lyrics from the song: "My world, and it's not a place I have to hide in." "Don't want pity." "One life."

I finished my notes, then whispered to my mom, "I wish I worked for *The New York Times*. This would be such a good story."

"Stop working," she said, reaching for the napkin. "You're home."

When Charlene finished, one judge cried. Another, who deemed Charlene the long-lost love child of Liza Minnelli and Stevie Nicks, told her, "Girl, you shop like a drag queen." I glanced over, and my mother was laughing. I relaxed into my chair.

Six or seven people performed after Charlene. Mom and I catcalled Daniel, a man with perfect abs and no shirt, as he strutted through "Free Your Mind." We laughed at a lanky restaurateur's goofy performance of "Only the Good Die Young," and we snapped along as a baby-faced Iraq War veteran mimed a Backstreet Boys song we used to sing together when I was in high school.

Someone must have won, but I don't remember the crowning. When the show was over, the bar stayed dark. Ed Sheeran's "Thinking Out Loud" started playing, and my mom stood.

"Dance with me," she said.

No one else was dancing, but my mom didn't care. She jerked me to my feet, and she draped her arms around my waist, and we drifted between the tables. My mom hadn't held me that way since I was young. I remember I kept thinking of the word "envelop." I was five or seven in her soft arms, helpless, loved, safe even though the legislature had just decided I never should be as long as I was in Mississippi. My eyes burned and my nose started to run. I sniffed. I didn't want to cry in front of my mom or the gay people I didn't know, so I tried to distract myself by cataloging details. My mom smelled like cheap soap and blue Curaçao with a hint of menthol. Her earrings were big double loops. I saw Charlene in the corner, and I wondered if she'd ever told her mother about Dee. Did Charlene and Dee ever dance in public? My mom drew me close. I wanted to hold on, but I felt overwhelmed with emotion and I didn't want my mother to know that, so I broke away.

"I need a beer," I said.

My mom watched me walk to the bar, then she continued dancing by herself. I turned away. I pretended to study the options. Red Stripe. Miller High Life. Blue Moon. I took my time paying. I smoothed every dollar bill before handing it to the bartender, and I drank a few sips before counting out a tip. I told myself if I drank I wouldn't cry. I'd be more fun, and my mother wouldn't know how many pains I held inside. I held my beer up, then downed half the bottle. When I returned to the table, my mom was hugging Blossom.

"I don't think it's a crying song, but I was bawling."

The music was loud, so I could just barely make out what my mother was saying. I heard her tell Blossom that she'd had her breasts removed, that she'd had to learn what it meant to be a woman without them. They hugged again, then my mom grabbed my hand and pulled me toward a homemade photo booth. A trans woman in a sequined dress and matching headband was shooting photos of the contestants there.

"Can we get a picture?" my mom asked, posing as if she were one of the night's stars.

The photographer waved us into the frame. My mom turned her head in the way she knew photographed best, and she cheesed the way she always did after a Walking with Jesus. I was too self-conscious to smile, so I struck what I thought was a casual stance—hand on my head, far-off gaze.

"You are so lucky," the photographer told me. "It's been twelve years, and my mom still doesn't accept me."

The photographer looked down at her dress. The lightboxes were making the sequins shimmer. Her boots were knee-high. She ran her free hand through her brown hair, then she sighed.

"I may be a boy the next time you see me."

"Honey," my mom said, reaching for the photographer's elbow. "I was an asshole for a long time. She'll come around."

I finished my beer. My brain was woozy, washing between words and the photographer's sequins, but I told my mom I needed another drink. Again, I took my time at the bar. Again, I smoothed my bills. When I found my mother again, she was outside joking with a group of ancient lesbians. They formed a circle around her, and I hung back for a few minutes and watched. I'm usually shy in crowds. I'm meant to write the world down, not star in it, but my mother glowed when she was around other people. She didn't just talk, she performed.

"Of course, I'm going to be honest with you," my mom told the lesbians. "Because I'm straight, I had to vote for the guy who sang 'Free Your Mind' because he has got the nicest ass I've ever seen."

The woman in the three-piece suit high-fived my mother.

"Sweetie, that's the whole point. You do what *you* need to do," she said.

Her name was Debbie. She was a lawyer, and I thought she was sexy in a Holland Taylor sort of way, if only Holland Taylor were butch.

"I'm sorry," my mom continued. "I'm very open-minded, but I'm not quite into carpet yet. Men's asses just do it for me."

I know much of my mother's bravado was a mask, a ruse she kept up in public but dropped at home, but I loved watching. I wrote my little napkin notes, knowing I wouldn't want to forget the night, knowing already that notes would not be enough.

My mother and Debbie lit cigarettes. The stars were shining without light pollution or cloud cover, and I made a note of that on my napkin: "*Stars brighter in Mississippi.*"

I don't know if my mother told the lesbians we were visiting, or if they just knew because they knew every gay person in town and they didn't know me, but Debbie asked where I lived.

"Oregon," I said, almost proud of myself.

"Oooh. You ran."

My mother interjected.

"She ran from her mother."

"No," Charlene said. "She ran from the stigma."

"No," my mom said. "She ran from her mother."

I have no idea what I was thinking, but I taped the conversation, so I know what I said next.

"I work at a newspaper in Oregon."

It was a strange reply, one neither Debbie nor Charlene commented on. My mom changed the subject. She said she'd heard from some drag queens that there was a good after-party in a bad part of town.

"So are we going or what?" she asked.

The lesbians demurred. It was after eleven. They'd partied enough. My mom was undaunted, though. She pulled a huge puff, then she asked a second time, and the lesbians agreed to go as soon as they finished their cigarettes. They all smoked slow, and eventually, they started talking about the anti-gay bill again. Debbie said she was annoyed.

"I liked knowing my neighbors and all that bullshit. Then we saw the news and realized, 'Oh god, they are coming for us.'"

It pains me to listen to the tape now. My mother is so cool, so at ease with everyone, and I keep piping in with awkward, robotic reporter questions. I sound emotionless, direct, not at all cool. I think I must have felt overwhelmed with longing and fear. I wanted to dance with my mother. I wanted to have friends like the ones I'd had in college. But I didn't want to stand in front of the mirror every morning wondering if my hair looked too gay.

"Why don't you leave?" I asked the lesbians. "This kind of thing doesn't happen in Portland."

"Fuck that," Debbie said. "Winter only lasts six weeks here. My house is here. My people are here."

"Yeah," Charlene said. "I get to have my state. And they got to take me."

My mom high-fived the lesbians. I looked up at the stars and back toward the bar, where six gay people were dancing and talking close. I loved Mississippi. I wished I were brave enough to stay. Instead, I stared at Debbie and held up my napkin, too dumb with envy to do anything but take notes.

Chapter Twenty

(2016)

I NEVER SAW MY grandmother again. One night that September, my mother called me while I was out at a bar. It was a hip spot, one that specialized in hamburgers and spicy margaritas, and I think I was there waiting to see a local indie band play. All evening, the bar had been streaming 1990s hip-hop songs. A Tribe Called Quest had flowed into the Notorious B.I.G., and Lauryn Hill was playing when my phone rang.

Usually, I ignored my mother's calls. I liked to talk to her when I was ready, not when I was out at a bar blasting loud music, but I knew she was in Monroe with my grandma, so I answered. The song changed as I said hello. Lauryn Hill dissolved into Rod Stewart.

"Y'all are not going to believe this," I said. "The bar I'm in right now just started playing 'Maggie May.' Remember how grandma said the mandolin part sounds like Roy's music?"

My mom was so quiet, I thought she must have butt-dialed me. Finally, I heard a long, low moan, then my mother, whispering.

"Casey, she's gone."

MY MOM AND HER siblings held the funeral a few days later. I didn't go. I only had a week of vacation left that year, and my mom wanted me to spend it with her after the funeral. She told me that she and Aunt Ann planned to clean out my grandma's house, and they needed help. I felt awful missing my grandma's funeral. I'd spent seven years flying back to interview her; how could I not be there for her memorial? But I owed my mother, I thought. She'd gone to Mississippi with me. She'd given up pills. If she needed me to clean my grandma's house, I could do it.

I flew in the last week of September on a morning that was ninety degrees when I landed. It had been below fifty in Portland, so I was wearing a sweatshirt and a jacket, layers I stripped off in the airport parking lot. I turned on one of the dark rap stations that stream in North Louisiana, then I headed toward West Monroe listening to a song about OxyContin and promethazine. No one was in the carport when I drove up. My aunt was asleep in my grandma's bed, and I found my mother on the couch, wrapped around her childhood Mrs. Beasley doll. I kissed my mother's forehead. I told her I loved her, and she buried her face in Mrs. Beasley's blond hair.

"Baby, I need to sleep for a while."

I took a few steps back, but I didn't leave the room. Was my mom grieving or was she on pills? I couldn't tell. The grandfather clock chimed on the hour, then the house was silent. The only thing I could hear was my aunt's CPAP machine whirring one room over. I missed my grandma's voice, the slow way she said "naturally" at the beginnings of sentences, like "Naturally, I'll make biscuits and gravy for you children."

The quiet felt too depressing to sit in awake and alone, so I walked to a park half a mile away. My dad used to grill boudin sausages in that park when I was young. We spent whole days sitting there, eating meat and playing cards. I'd always known that trails circled the open acres, but my parents had never wanted to travel more than a few feet into the woods, so I'd never explored them. I looked at my watch. It was 1 p.m. I figured my mom and aunt would sleep for a while, so I had plenty of time to see the woods now. I chose the longest path, a paved two-mile loop. It was flat and flanked by thin trees whose leaves were starting to brown. Someone had gone through with blue chalk and graffitied the asphalt, scratching out mostly misspelled Christian messages. I spotted "babtist" chalked near a pond, and "Jhon 3:16" etched close to a suspension bridge. I posted photos of the phrases on Facebook, and my seventh-grade language arts teacher—the one who'd given me books—messaged me to say it was "ugly" to make fun of my hometown. I felt ashamed, but I left the pictures up for my Portland friends to see.

I kicked a stone into a small pond, angry. I'd wanted to solve Roy's mysteries before my grandma died, and I'd failed. I had never failed at journalism before. I'd written stories that weren't as good as they should have been, and I'd gotten a couple of facts wrong here and there, but I'd never started something and not finished it. I should have worked faster. I should have asked Mark again for the journals. I should have hired a private investigator to comb the Arkansas records for some trace I might have missed.

I told myself then that I was angry at myself because my grandmother had died without getting the answers she'd asked me fourteen years earlier to find. But did those answers matter to her as much as they did to me? Usually when my grandma and I talked about this project, she preferred to talk about herself. And I listened. I treated her life story as something worth recording. Maybe I couldn't have finished this story while my grandma was alive. As long as I was working on it, we had something to talk about, and so I'd stretched my reporting as long as I could. Still, I'd wanted to finish because I'd wanted to show her I could. I'd wanted her to be proud of me.

The afternoon was hot and sticky, and I was covered in mosquito bites by the time I slouched back to the house. My mom and aunt were still sleeping, so I tiptoed into the big bathroom, intent on soaking in my grandma's Jacuzzi tub. I shut the door. I opened the cabinet below her sink, and the smell of her soap unraveled me. My grandma used Dove or Caress, soft feminine bars that belied the tough-as-nails woman I knew when I was young. She dried the pink soaps after every bath and slipped them back into their boxes to retain their scent. I pulled a half-used bar of Dove out of its box, sniffed it, then sat on the side of the tub, lost with aching. I wouldn't eat her biscuits again. I wouldn't listen to her talk about cotton and country music. I probably wouldn't even come back to this house. The carport would just be the concrete box of my memories. I turned the faucet. I dropped the Dove into the rush of water, then I lowered myself into the stream, crying and fumbling for the bar that smelled like her.

My mom and aunt woke up around 9 p.m. I don't think they spoke to each other inside the house. They just went straight to the carport, still wearing their nightgowns. By the time I followed them out there, they were cackling like cartoon witches. I hadn't seen either of them drink or take anything, but they laughed as if they were under the influence of something other than grief. Every once in a while, I'd make out a word like "seatbelt" or "clary sage," then they'd howl so loud and high-pitched that their words vanished.

Around 11 p.m., my mom asked my aunt if she wanted to dance. They went into the living room, turned on the Bee Gees, and swept the bottoms of their nightgowns around as if they were fancy dresses. They danced solo through "More Than a Woman" and together during "Guilty," Barry Gibb's duet with Barbara Streisand. It was their favorite song. My mom hung her arms around my aunt's shoulders, and my aunt circled my mother's waist. They pressed their cheeks together, and I filmed them for a while as they whirled around the living room.

"Casey," Aunt Ann said, as my mother led her around the glass coffee table. "I two-stepped with Charlie a week and a half before he died. And you know what he said?"

Charlie was my older cousin, a rodeo cowboy who'd died in 2012 when he was thirty-two and I was twenty-nine. My brother said Charlie died after drinking a bottle of vodka. My aunt said a medication he was taking did something to his heart. She buried him in Delhi, and I hadn't seen her in anything but a nightgown since. She didn't smile often, but thinking of Charlie as she danced, she allowed her mouth to curve up.

"He said, 'Oh, Mom. Look at that. You still got it.'"

For a moment, my aunt looked happy, even though her son and mother were both dead. She held an arm in the air, and my mom grabbed her hand and spun her. When the song ended, they kissed on the lips. My mom pointed to the carport door.

"Smoke?"

I went to sleep soon after, but around 3 a.m., they woke me up, yelling that someone was outside trying to steal my grandma's Crown Victoria. I padded out to the kitchen and looked through the window, but I didn't see anyone. The car was sitting in the driveway. My aunt handed me a tiny monitor. I guessed it was some kind of security camera, but it looked cheap, more like a toy than a real gadget. She said it made a noise anytime someone crossed into the driveway. It had beeped several times, and that's how she knew someone was trying to take the car. I peered into the monitor, but all I saw was a grainy black.

"There's no one out there," I said.

"There was, Casey. I heard it."

My mom went to take a shower. I held the monitor and watched it for ten minutes. Eventually, a raccoon crossed through the frame, and the monitor beeped. I handed it back to my aunt and told her I was going to bed.

"Wait," she said. "Will you sit with me while I smoke one cigarette?"

I sat outside while she smoked half a pack. Eventually, I made it back to bed, but my aunt woke me up again around 6 a.m. to tell me the cops were on their way. I thought, at first, that my mom must have taken pills and fallen or crashed a car the way she used to do when I was young. I asked my aunt if my mom was okay.

"Your mom's in the carport, baby. We think Jennifer's boyfriend came by last night and tried to take grandma's car."

I threw the covers off. My stomach hurt from staying up most of the night.

"I told you that was a raccoon. We saw the raccoon together on the monitor."

"This was later, Casey. You weren't up."

My aunt said the cops would be there in ten minutes, so I changed into a pair of jeans and my least-wrinkled T-shirt, then I went to sit in the carport with my mother. She was wearing the hot-pink nightgown she'd worn when we visited my grandma earlier that year. My aunt came out a few minutes later in the blue nightgown she'd been wearing all week. They smoked, and my aunt talked about collecting stamps, and my mother stared at the ashtray between them. It was filled with the Virginia Slims my grandma smoked the week she died. I tried to smile at my mother, but her eyes looked vacant. I worried she'd taken something.

Ten minutes later, a female officer knocked on the carport door. My aunt stood, seemingly thrilled, then walked up to the cop and tried to hug her.

"Ma'am," the officer said. "I don't do hugs."

"But I recognize you, honey," my aunt said.

"Yes. I've been to this house many times."

I smiled at the officer in a way I hoped communicated that though I was related to these women, I was not a part of whatever they had going on. I was normal, fully dressed, not at all alarmed about the raccoons and the Crown Victoria. The cop did not return my smile.

My aunt shrugged and moved back to her plastic chair. The officer asked what was going on, and my aunt told a long, unintelligible story about my cousin's boyfriend. My aunt said she wasn't afraid of the boyfriend because she'd worked for Homeland Security. The officer looked at me, as if seeking affirmation for my aunt's story, and for a moment, I felt a kinship with the uniformed woman standing at the carport's edge. I, too, was trying to wrest stories from these unreliable narrators. I, too, had come away with more questions than answers. I raised my eyebrows. No, I tried to say with my eyes. I did not think my aunt had worked for Homeland Security.

The cop left without writing a report, and my mom and aunt both went to bed. I was exhausted, but I can't sleep during the day, so I texted Frankie about the carport spectacle, then I went to my grandmother's bedroom to clean out her chest of drawers. It was tall, five feet or so, and made of cherry. My grandma didn't organize anything in it. There was no one drawer for underwear or night clothes, just things stuffed wherever they fit. The top drawer was a mishmash of old coins, long socks, and medical files. I pulled out a beige sports bra and found it wrapped around a ziplock bag with two sheets of loose-leaf paper inside. I pulled the pages out. I hadn't seen my grandmother write much, but I knew the loopy big lines were hers. On the top of the page, right along the edge, she'd written "gone to see your daddy I hope." On the side, she'd scrawled in big, wide letters, "I love all of you very much and always will even from the grave."

I didn't know if she'd shown this to anyone. It didn't look like a legal document. There was no notary stamp, no lawyer signature, just a list of things written crooked across the page. She'd left Cindy something called a "salt box pickle" and told my uncle Tracy he could take "all items in the hallway." As far as I knew, my grandmother hadn't spoken to Christopher's mother in several years, but she wrote that she could have anything she wanted "from above the cabinets." To my mother, she left a list of kitchen supplies, a bun warmer, two soup spoons, "and anything you desire except what I gave the other girls." The only child my grandma hadn't left anything to was Ann, an omission that seemed charged because Ann had been living with her since Charlie died.

"As for the rest of the items," my grandma wrote on the second sheet, "work it out evenly."

I didn't think I needed anything. I tucked the will back into the ziplock bag, then I set it in one pile, and the sports bra in another. I pulled out a single diamond earring, six rolls of dimes, and several pairs of unworn socks. I found three or four nightgowns tucked into a corner, so I yanked them out, smoothed them into nicer folds, then set them on the end of my grandma's bed. The only thing I found that I wanted to keep was my grandma's old passport. The leather wasn't cracked or folded, but I knew it was old because it didn't look anything like my passport. When I opened it, I saw that she'd applied in 1969, just before she went to Germany. The picture was a full studio portrait, not the tiny mug shot passports use now. In it, four of my grandma's five children crowd around her. Cindy, I realized, must have been old enough to apply for her own documents by then. I stared for a while at my mother. She was five in 1969, and she looked wild-eyed and misbehaving in the picture. Her head was cocked in a way that suggested she did not want to be sitting in this dress on this bench with her mother. My grandma was staring into the camera, seriously, if not angrily. Looking at it, I remembered that Aunt Cindy had told me once that my grandma never said "I love you" when they were young. She didn't hug. The only time my grandma touched my mother, Cindy said, was when my mom was having an asthma attack. Cindy believed that my mom was so desperate for love that she had learned how to make herself sick. By the time they moved back to Delhi from Germany, my mom could have an attack on cue. Cindy thought it was my grandmother, not Cam or the rape, that led my mom to pills. I never got up the courage to ask.

The passport was green with a red and blue stamp marking their departure out of Washington, DC. My grandmother had told me years earlier that she felt bad that Roy had never traveled the world the way she had. She'd been to Europe, and she'd lived in three or four states. But she'd ended up back in Louisiana, living in the same place Roy did. Had my grandma wanted that? Did she return because it was easy or because it was home? Had she ever missed the air or the accents? Maybe, I thought, she'd returned because she'd proven to herself that she could leave.

I sat on her bed. I'd already been to more places than my grandmother ever had, and I still had years left to travel. I could visit Thailand or Spain or one of the countries in South America. I could go anywhere, and yet, when I thought of airplanes, the only place that called me was this one.

Why did Louisiana tug me home? It was hot and full of bugs, and the graffiti artists couldn't spell. My relatives all seemed a little bit crazy, and I'd promised myself since I was young that I would live a different life than the one they had. And yet I kept coming back with new questions to answer. What penned my mother and her sister into nightgowns? Why had my cousin died young? Did something happen on Hell Street or Frog Island that determined the rest of my family's lives? And what happened to Roy?

I barely remember the rest of that week. My mom and aunt didn't spend much time awake, so we never cleaned the house together. I was exhausted and more than tired of cigarette smoke as I flew back to Portland, but I knew something had changed for me. Vacations weren't long enough. Like my grandma, I'd proved to myself that I could leave the South. Now it was time to go home.

Chapter Twenty-One

(2017–2018)

IN MY MEMORIES, the night in Mississippi and that afternoon in my grandma's bedroom feel like Big Moments, twin catalysts that propelled me toward a new life, but memory has a way of speeding through the particulars. I did leave Louisiana intent on finding a way home. I waited a year, though, to come up with a plan, mainly because I was scared to quit my job. By 2016, I was earning fifty-eight thousand dollars a year at *The Oregonian,* and I was mostly writing about whatever I wanted. I knew if I left, I might never have that again. The newspaper had gone through four rounds of layoffs in my decade there. The staff had shrunk from four hundred reporters to ninety, and most other newsrooms had endured similar cuts. A new job might not exist. I wanted to write about the South for a national audience, but I didn't have any connections with editors, and I didn't possess the skills to write the deep pieces I loved most. At night, I outlined all my favorite articles and knew, vaguely, that I needed to learn how to imbue stories with academic research and deep historical context, but I didn't know how to find that research or thread it through a story's narrative arc. That fall, I read about a mid-career master's program at Columbia University's journalism school, and I felt the kind of Big Moment buzzing I'd felt in Mississippi and Louisiana.

The application terrified me. Columbia is an Ivy League school, and I had long ago realized that the education I got in Louisiana was inferior to the ones my friends had earned elsewhere. Every night, Frankie and I watched *Jeopardy!* together, and she rattled off most of the answers while I sat quiet and waiting for a hip-hop category to appear. I couldn't name most of the country's past presidents, and I didn't know when the Civil War started or where. I didn't think I had anything smart to offer Columbia, but when I sat down to write my application essays, every sentence came easy. I wrote about knocking on strangers' doors in Delhi, and I recounted the trip my mother and I took to Mississippi. "I can find good stories," I wrote. "But there are questions I can't answer on my own."

I scrolled through the online course guide, bookmarking electives in the sociology and history departments. There were dozens of seminars on race, and classes on Reconstruction and poverty. The program was only nine months long, a stint that seemed far too short to track the South from the cotton fields to my grandma's carport, but I typed out a list of all I hoped to study, then I sent in my application.

A few months later, in March of 2017, I was in a strawberry field reporting on undocumented workers when my phone buzzed with the email notification. The dean had emailed me a congratulations that twinkled with digital confetti. I read the message quickly, then shut off my phone. All around me, men were digging through chemical-covered crops to earn a living, and I knew that after I left them, I would go home and tell my wife that I planned to quit my cushy job so I could spend a school year studying. I felt horribly spoiled. One of the men winked at me, and I thought of the stories my grandma used to tell me about her father, how he'd saved a few coins each month to buy her weeks-old newspapers from a man in town. My grandmother never graduated high school, and now I was going to the Ivy League.

THAT YEAR, MY BROTHER left DC for Miami. My parents went to Tampa, and I moved into a 290-square-foot basement apartment with a view of six New York City dumpsters. Frankie and I decided it didn't make sense for her to leave her job, so she stayed in Portland as I began to make my new life above the trash cans.

Most of my classmates came from other countries. They'd been journalists in Finland and Brazil, Pakistan and Colombia, and now, one year after the election of Donald Trump, they'd flown to New York to learn about America. I can't remember if it was the first or second week that we started talking about opioids. Everyone in journalism seemed to be suddenly fascinated with Purdue Pharma and the working-class white people who guzzled pills and carried Trump to the White House. Every week, a new opioids article came out, and each one seemed to take place in a Walmart parking lot or a long-dead rural town. The main character was always slumped over a steering wheel or hoarding Oxy-Contin after a factory accident. They never seemed like real people to me, just two-dimensional portraits to pity. My foreign classmates called it an "epidemic," and my throat burned with a dozen things I was too embarrassed to say. What if your mother only sometimes seemed like an addict? What if one day she slumped and the next she danced through Walmart bright and alive? What if she'd never worked in a factory? What if she hadn't voted for Trump? What if the "pain pill" was a nose spray that existed before OxyContin did? What if she'd promised you that she wanted to live?

Early that fall, a professor came to my Wednesday seminar to talk about a civil rights–era study known as the Coleman report. The study, which analyzed equity in education, was seven hundred pages and full of facts about schools and neighborhoods and state funding. The professor told us that more than sixty thousand teachers and six hundred thousand students filled out surveys in the fall of 1965. Their answers showed that the most important factor in determining a child's future was not their school, but their family background. For instance, the professor explained, a child who grew up with encyclopedias at home was more likely to go to college.

After class, I walked back to my apartment thinking about the encyclopedia set I used to see at Publix, the grocery store my mom shopped at when she was cooking for the rich old lady in Georgia. The crisp volumes were navy with gold lettering and embossed numbers on the spine. I used to stand at the end of the checkout, staring at the books while my mother shopped. Sometimes, I'd reach for one, then I'd sit on the grocery store floor, reading about albatrosses or transcendentalism until a clerk asked me to put the volume back. I begged my mother to buy a set. I can't remember how much they cost, but I remember the way her eyes sank when she told me we couldn't afford them.

Sometime after my dad returned from the Gulf War, a local storage facility announced that it was auctioning off the things dead soldiers had left behind. One private first class had stashed an encyclopedia set in his storage unit before he left for Saudi Arabia. No one had come forth to claim it, so the auctioneer set the price at ten dollars per book. I told my mom I could be happy with just one. I loved the T volume I'd been reading at Publix, so maybe I asked for it. Sometime that weekend, though, my mom told me she'd talked to my father, and they had found a way to buy the whole set. I never knew, when I was young, what my parents did to pay for the encyclopedia. I only remember my father bringing the books home, shrink-wrapped in several boxes. They were bright red, and as we unwrapped them and placed them on the bottom rung of a bookshelf otherwise filled with my mother's favorite romance novels, my mom told me that all the world's knowledge was contained within the encyclopedia's uncracked spines. For years after, I rushed home from school, snatched a volume from the line, then retreated to my room to take notes.

Walking across the Columbia campus, past the stately brick buildings that looked to me like knowledge itself, I thought maybe the professor who'd visited my class had been right. Maybe those auctioned encyclopedias had delivered me to the life I had now. I called my mom when I reached my apartment.

"Hey," I said. "How did y'all pay for that encyclopedia set?"

My mom told me to hold on. She turned off the talk show she'd been watching, and she went out to the closed-in area she called a lanai. I'd never visited her in the new home, but she'd sent me a video tour, so I knew that the lanai had wicker furniture and glass walls that looked out on a lush Florida yard. She'd even laid a carpet down on the concrete.

"It wasn't me," she said. "It was your daddy. He sold all of his comics."

I remembered the comic books. They were the only thing my dad owned when I was a kid. Every weekend, he'd pull out crates full of Spider-Man and Batman comics, all covered in plastic. He never read them. Mostly, he stared at the covers with a scrutiny I never saw him give anything else. I remember I wondered back then if he was drawn to comics because most of the superheroes were orphans. My dad's parents were alive, and I occasionally saw them, but they hadn't spent much time with him when he was young. My dad was an only child, and his parents liked to work, so mostly, he spent his childhood alone and reading about other lonely boys who acquired special powers. He'd told me once that he'd been attracted to my mom because she had everything he didn't. She had a huge family, three sisters, a brother, and two parents who were always around. I see now that I did the same thing with Frankie.

"Was he sad to sell them?" I asked my mom.

"Baby, you were so smart. You longed for those encyclopedias."

"But was he sad?"

"Shit," my mom said. "After we got them for you, you only wanted to read about women. At one point, you were interested in Mary Todd Lincoln, but I told you that bitch was crazy. They had to physically move her out of the White House. She was nuts. But you would secretly go and read more about her. I wanted you to read about Benjamin Franklin and Thomas Edison. I wanted you to enjoy reading the things I had read so we could talk about them, but that did not interest you. You really only liked to read about women."

I laughed and told her that should have been her first clue that I was gay. She said she hadn't thought to look for that then. She was too busy worrying I'd end up nuts like Mary Todd Lincoln.

"People don't go crazy just by reading about crazy people," I told her.

"Well, I couldn't take any chances."

Back in high school, my mom said, Cam Milton had given her a 1979 Susan B. Anthony dollar just before he died. It was her prized possession, a silver circle with ridged edges, and she kept it tucked into a secret compartment in her jewelry box. She'd never shown it to anyone, not even my dad, but after I started reading about Mary Todd Lincoln, she pulled it out in hopes of encouraging me toward Susan B. Anthony instead.

"Did it work?"

"Oh my god. You were obsessed with it. You decided you had to have it, so you stole it from my jewelry box. I tore your ass up. It's the only thing I have of Cam's, but you just kept taking it. You said you needed it for 'research.'"

I asked her what happened to the dollar, and she told me she still

kept it hidden in her jewelry box. She pulled it out once a year, usually on Cam's birthday, when she was sad and thinking about him. She
sighed, and I didn't say anything for a bit. I looked down at my desk.
I had three hundred pages of *Coercion, Capital, and European States* to
read before bedtime.

"Hey," I finally said. "You do know Susan B. Anthony was gay,
right?"

THE MOST FAMOUS CLASS in my master's program was a book-
writing course that met every Monday for eight hours. The class had produced something like eighty published books—good books, real books,
books I could buy at the shop across Broadway. One of my mentors, the
New York Times journalist Andrea Elliott, told me I had to apply.

"It's probably the best class I've ever taken," she wrote. "People fight
to get in."

I'd only ever imagined doing Roy's story as a movie. Everyone we'd
filmed had such great accents, and even my best sentences didn't compare to the lilts and long gazes Aubree and I had taped in Delhi. But I
trusted Andrea, and I thought, worst case, if I got in, I could use the
class to plot out an outline for the movie. When the application opened
in late November, I told the professor about my grandmother and the
kidnapping, and I tried to paraphrase all that I'd learned in the years
since.

> Some called Roy a morphodite or hesheit. Nurses forced him to
> wear a pink sweatsuit after they discovered his female anatomy.
> But a devout Baptist cooked Roy dinner every Christmas. A
> Pentecostal fought a pastor who refused to let Roy worship. The
> roughneck barber shaped Roy's crew cut every week without
> question. The people in Delhi weren't the two-dimensional
> stereotypes we see in the news. They had their own stories of
> longing and isolation. They understood Roy because they thought
> of themselves as misfits in the bigger world beyond.

Three hours later, the professor wrote back.

Dear Casey,

Is there really enough material available on Roy to sustain a book of 80K or more words? And, other than his sexuality, what was significant about Roy's life? Anything?

Also, do you have access to Diary of a Misfit? That seems extremely important.

Sam Freedman

My stomach fell. In two paragraphs, the professor had pinpointed all the problems that bedeviled me. No, I did not have Roy's journals. No, I did not know how to sustain a book. And no, I didn't know if anyone would be interested in the person I'd spent nine years researching. I closed my laptop. I texted a friend—"my life is over, and this documentary is never happening"—then I collapsed onto the pull-out IKEA sofa I was using as a bed, and I cried for two hours straight.

Sometime late that afternoon, I reminded myself that nearly eighteen years had passed since I sat with my grandma at that wobbly kitchen table. No amount of time had weakened my interest in Roy. I had to believe other people would find his life as interesting as I did. I crawled from the couch to my computer desk, bleary-eyed, and I typed without thinking.

I thought about Roy when my college security guard slipped Focus on the Family tapes under my door. I thought about Roy when my pastor went in front of the church and prayed "save her and take her," hoping I'd ask forgiveness for being gay, then die immediately. And I thought about Roy when I fled the South for Oregon.

I tried to describe the complicated feelings I felt about home. I told the professor I had made peace with Louisiana while reporting the documentary, and I intended to spend the rest of my career going home. The line about peace wasn't exactly true, but I wanted it to be. The professor replied the next morning, admitting me to the course.

"So," my mom said when I called to tell her the news. "Does this mean *The Diary of a Misfit* is going to be a book I can actually buy?"

"Well, I have to write it first. And sell it. Then, who knows? People might not be interested."

"I'll whoop their ass if they're not interested."

I laughed, and when we hung up, I tucked my phone into my down coat. I was thirty-four, and I felt, for the first time, that I had the relationship with my mom I'd always wanted. I never rejected her calls. We talked about our failures and our ambitions, and we watched *The Bachelor* together, texting every adjective we could think of to describe the loathsome leading man.

"Pond scum," my mom dubbed him. "Him and that hooch with no drawers on. if you are ever on the finale of the bachelor and you choose not to wear panties . . . make sure your dress isn't see through. Your mama does NOT want you to show your hiney on national tv. Put some drawers on. Just saying."

She sent me pictures of her home office, and I texted shots of Harlem and Morningside Heights. She told me she couldn't wait to come to my graduation. She'd been stopping people in Walmart to boast about having a daughter in the Ivy League, and the only thing she could imagine that might be better was going for a frozen hot chocolate at Serendipity 3, an Upper East Side restaurant that's famous for its desserts, and bragging to someone there.

Some nights, we talked for a whole hour. She told me things no study unspooled, and I took notes as if I were in class. That November, when I went to Shreveport, my mom persuaded a friend to let me stay for free so I didn't have to spend my savings on a hotel room. She even wired sixty dollars to my bank account—"money for dinner," she texted. I felt guilty taking it. My mom hadn't given me money since she'd pressed that twenty-dollar bill into my hand in the Popeyes bathroom the first day of college.

"Are you sure?" I texted back. "I don't need money. Frankie's working, and I saved a bunch before I quit my job."

A few minutes later, my mom texted a picture of the paycheck she'd received that morning. The interior design company had paid her two thousand dollars for two weeks' work. "Can you believe it? $25/hour. The biggest check I've ever gotten."

IN EARLY 2018, my brother and his girlfriend decided to get married in Miami during my spring break. Mom and I texted all February about the things we hoped to do together. We were going to drink Pinot Gris by a pool, and we were going to hail a cab to South Beach, where we'd order the biggest tropical drinks the strip served.

Frankie and I flew to Miami mid-March. I texted my mom from the air—"Wine? Pool?"—but when our plane landed, I found my mom at the baggage claim, tired and cranky. She wanted to eat a hamburger she'd seen on the Food Network, but the restaurant was closed, so we drove in circles until my mom agreed to settle for a different hamburger restaurant. Afterward, my parents dropped me and Frankie off at an Airbnb we'd booked, and my mom promised we'd rendezvous by a body of water the next morning.

I texted when I woke up, but my mom didn't reply until late afternoon. By then, Frankie and I had already made plans to go to the beach with Christopher.

"But I'd really like to see you," I texted my mom.

"I'd like to C U 2," she wrote.

I texted when I got back from the beach, and again the next morning, but by Friday afternoon, the day before the wedding, I still hadn't seen my mom since the hamburger restaurant.

"I guess I'll see you at the venue?" I texted.

I woke up Saturday paralyzed with dread. My brother married a beautiful woman with beautiful relatives. They were tan, lithe, and long-haired, and they all fit exactly right in dresses. I wanted to look like them. Christopher and I were in my brother's wedding party, and I'd spent more than I could afford on a jumpsuit in the same gray tones as Christopher's suit, but when I tried it on a few hours before the ceremony, I saw that I did not look beautiful. My face was boyish and plain, a little pale, and slightly speckled with acne. I hadn't gotten my hair cut since I moved to New York, and it was at an awkward, in-between length I had no idea how to style. Frankie spent an hour drying and gelling it into shape, but every time I looked in the mirror, I felt ugly. I'd gotten over the shame of being gay a decade earlier, but every once in a while, I still felt like I'd failed at being a woman. I tried smiling at my reflection. Frankie told me she thought I looked great, but I waved her away. I shut the door. Alone in the bathroom, I thought of my mother. I knew she'd always believed that her weight kept her from being beautiful, but she knew how to dress and live as a woman. I wished that I had paid better attention when she tried to teach me how to use mascara in junior high. I wished my hair were long. I opened the medicine cabinet and searched through the toiletries other Airbnb guests had left behind, but I didn't see anything that would make me magically pretty. Finally, desperate, I plucked my phone from the back of the toilet, and I texted my mother.

"Can you bring a little makeup for me? Nothing too crazy."

I couldn't remember the last time I'd felt so vulnerable. I had spent twenty years telling my mother I did not believe in makeup, assuring her I was happy and proud to be myself, and here I was, weak and begging her to turn me into the thing she'd always wanted me to be.

"I sure will. I'll just bring my makeup bag."

Maybe I wanted to feel as close to her as I had all semester, or maybe I was finally ready to be open about how I felt, but I texted back the most honest thing I'd told her in years: "I feel insecure. In how I look."

I waited in the bathroom for a while, but my mother never replied. Finally, Frankie asked if she could use the shower. I took one last agonizing look at myself in the mirror, then headed outside to wait in the sun.

When we got to the venue, I picked up my mom's makeup bag, and I realized I'd made a huge mistake. What she called a bag was in fact a small suitcase. It was leather and opened up to reveal what seemed to be several drawers full of makeup. She had at least fifty shades of eye shadow, all lined up in little squares, and more lipsticks than I dared count. The bag was heavy the way my backpack gets when I carry a laptop. I handed it to my mom, and she told me to stand in front of her with my eyes closed. I obeyed but peeked to see what she was digging out. I saw her grab powder and a brush and a few of those eye shadow palettes. She fished out brown mascara and black mascara and another mascara with an ultra-thick wand before she found the one she wanted, a thin tube labeled brown-black. She produced a few things I'd never seen before, then she told me, again, to close my eyes.

She worked on my face for half an hour, brushing and blending until I felt sure I'd never want to open my eyes to see what she'd done. I imagined huge streaks of blush and maybe black eyeliner swooping up toward my bangs. She rubbed something that felt like lipstick across my eyebrows, and I stepped back, but she told me to calm down. Finally, after she'd gone over my entire face with a blush brush, she pointed me toward a mirror, and I cracked one eye open.

My mom was smiling bigger than she had all weekend. Somehow, she had made me look exactly like myself, only better. She hadn't used any daring colors of eye shadow, nor any red streaks of blush. She'd just smoothed me out.

"What did you do to my eyebrows? They look amazing."

"Goof Proof," she said, handing me the tube I'd assumed was lipstick. "It's an eyebrow pencil. It's so easy even you could do it."

I wish I could describe the look on my mom's face. She gazed, dopey and proud, and I could see for the first time in my life that she did not want me to be any other daughter. She looked at me as if she really saw me, as if she thought I was beautiful the way I'd always hoped someone would find me beautiful. I was so moved, I started to tear up, but my mom snapped her fingers in my face.

"Don't cry. You'll ruin your makeup."

BOTH OF MY PARENTS drank too much at the reception. The bar was self-serve, and after my mom downed a few plastic glasses full of orange juice and I don't know what, she was out on the empty dance floor, twerking alone to Gloria Estefan. She came back to our table long enough to eat three bites of paella, then she was gone again, leading herself in a Tim McGraw slow dance. By the time everyone else was gearing up to conga, my mom exhausted herself, and she pulled me to the back of the covered plaza.

"I have something for you."

She snaked her hand into her bra, then held out what looked like an oversized quarter.

"I don't understand," I said.

She held the quarter closer to my face, close enough that I could smell the notes of orange and rose in her Ralph Lauren Romance perfume, and I saw that it wasn't a quarter. It was the 1979 Susan B. Anthony dollar Cam Milton had given her before he died.

"I want you to have it," she said, pressing it into my hand.

"Why? I'm not going to read about Mary Todd Lincoln anymore. It's your prized possession. You shouldn't give that away."

My mom closed my fist around the dollar. She told me she didn't need it anymore. I ran my index fingers around its ridges, and when I looked up again, she'd left me for the dance floor.

I watched for a while, then I checked my email on my phone. The book professor had written to tell us that Jennifer Finney Boylan, a trans woman who'd written the memoir *She's Not There*, was coming to our class to speak. I couldn't believe it. That book had changed my life. A decade and a half earlier, during my junior year of college, my mom had seen Jennifer Finney Boylan on *Oprah*. She'd bought *She's Not There* a few days later. I don't know what exactly about the book swayed my mother, but after she read it, she started to accept that I was gay. She even sent a copy of the book to me at college.

I ran toward the dance floor, still holding my phone open to my email.

"Guess who's coming to my book class?" I sputtered, pushing the phone into my mom's hands.

My mom grabbed my arm, and we rushed off the dance floor together so fast I scuffed my oxford wingtips. When we reached our table, my mom slammed a cup of spiked orange juice, then she read the email again.

"You have to let me FaceTime into the class," she said. "You don't understand. For me, Jennifer Finney Boylan is up there with Barry Gibb."

I hesitated. I was sure my mom would cry if she FaceTimed Jennifer Finney Boylan. She'd want me to hold the phone up so she could say something to Jennifer. She'd tell secrets I hadn't shared. My classmates all knew I was gay, but it seemed like a theoretical gayness. They hadn't met Frankie, and I'd never told them about my pastor or my mom or any of the ancient pains I carried around. To them, I was the workaholic who penciled in detailed edits on everyone's stories. I was quirky, Southern, maybe a little aloof. If they saw my mom, they might know more than I wanted anyone to know. I told her I would tape the talk for her.

"Oh, no," she said. "I want to watch it live. I want to tell her what she did for my life."

———

TWO WEEKS LATER, the day before Jennifer Finney Boylan's talk, I texted my mom. It was Easter Sunday, so I sent a series of rainbow emojis, reminding my mom that Easter was my coming-out anniversary.

"JFB will come to my class around eleven," I typed. "Should I Face-Time you then?"

She didn't reply, so I tried calling her late that evening. She didn't answer. I called her the next day before class, then during class from the bathroom, but her phone rang without end the same way it had when I tried to tell her I was engaged. I hung up, sure she must be taking pills again.

The professor did not allow cell phones in class, but I tried to position mine in such a way that I'd see if my mother called. Jennifer Finney Boylan spoke for an hour, and when she finished, my heart thudded. I was mad that my mom was letting me down again, but I believed she really did want Jennifer to know how much she'd changed our lives. When the professor opened the discussion for questions, I waited for a few of my classmates to talk, then I raised my hand.

I can't remember the exact words I used. I know I told Jennifer and my entire class about my freshman year of college. I told them my mom had written emails that said thinking of me made her want to throw up. I think I told them about the preacher and maybe the security guard who'd forced his way into my dorm room to tell me I was going to Hell.

"But then my mom saw you on *Oprah*," I said.

After that, I just cried. I felt painfully exposed, but mostly I felt surprised. I didn't know I was still upset about the preacher or the emails my mother sent. I thought I was a well-adjusted lesbian, a confident woman with a cache of silly stories I told about the years the South spent hating me.

When class ended, I approached Jennifer and apologized for crying. She told me it happened all the time. Back in 2003, when Jennifer came out, we didn't have a ton of queer role models who made it onto shows as mainstream as *Oprah*, so a whole generation of people looked at Jennifer the way I did.

As we talked, I remembered something Pam Sykes had told me on one of my trips to Delhi. She'd said she wanted to ask Roy what her life would be like. How are people going to treat me? As a teenager, I read

Jennifer's book searching for the same answers. We were different, of course. Jennifer was trans, and she lived in the Northeast, but she was a lesbian, and she'd survived coming out.

When we finished talking, Jennifer offered to call and leave my mom a message. I dialed my mom's number for the sixth time that day, then we waited until her answering machine picked up.

"Hi, Ronni. This is Jennifer Finney Boylan, and I got the chance to be a guest in Casey's class here at Columbia. Well, I bet you're proud of your daughter and everything she's doing up here. I was just so blown away by our conversation. We talked about *She's Not There* and *Oprah* and the long journey we all take to open our hearts. Thank you for a great daughter and all the work that you've done in the world."

We hugged goodbye, and as I pulled away, my phone rang. My caller ID said it was my mother, but when I answered, my dad spoke.

"Your mom's in the hospital. It's serious this time."

Chapter Twenty-Two

(2018)

I KNEW FROM MY dad's tone that this hospital visit was unlike all the false alarms and forced emergencies he'd called to report in the past, but I didn't run immediately to my apartment or the airport. I went back to class. I sat at my desk. I looked straight forward until my eyes and ears and everything else burned, then I stood, whispered a version of the news into my professor's ear, and left.

I must have walked across campus. I must have eaten dinner and called my father back. I must have booked a ticket. The tape in my head is spliced with scenes spaced far apart, so all that comes back are borderless vignettes. I can see Jennifer Finney Boylan on the phone with my mom's answering machine. I can see the M60 bus barreling over a bridge toward LaGuardia, and I can see my brother, waiting outside of security in the Tampa airport. He was supposed to be at the hospital. I was supposed to have taken a taxi to meet him and my dad at my mother's bedside.

"Is she dead?"

I asked the words before I thought them. My brother put his hand on my back and told me we should walk. I asked again, "Is she dead?" My brother took a step to the left, and in the distance, I could see my father, folded. Did I walk toward him? I only remember suddenly being in his arms, collapsed and heaving. My brother's wife handed me a stiff tissue, and for months after, I woke up in the middle of the night thinking of the hummingbird printed on it. I wiped my nose with its beak.

My mother had been dead thirty minutes or an hour, I no longer remember which. "While you were in the air," my dad said. There was no reason to go to the hospital, so we went to her house, to the lanai I'd promised her I'd see someday. She'd described it as something fancy, proof that her life had taken a sharp turn up, but I saw now what no wicker furniture could conceal: The lanai bore a striking resemblance to my grandmother's carport. I lowered myself onto the concrete and listened as my brother called my mom's sisters. She didn't make it, he told them. Her esophagus was torn. She went into surgery and never woke up.

I didn't ask a single question. I always ask questions—it is my central, and perhaps most annoying, trait—but I couldn't bear to know any details because details would have made it real. As long as I didn't know how my mother died, as long as I didn't see a body, I could pretend she was on vacation somewhere. I could pretend I would see her again.

I called my thesis advisor. I waited for Frankie to arrive. I made hash browns with American cheese, and I lay on the carpet and watched my dad and brother, grown men sharing one recliner, sob into each other. One of us brought up the Bee Gees. When Maurice Gibb died, my mother sat on the end of her bed, sobbing, for three days. Maurice had also died after an emergency surgery. He was fifty-three, the same age my mother had been earlier that morning. Was she still fifty-three? Would she always be fifty-three?

"At least Barry Gibb is alive," I mumbled from the floor. "She never had to live in a world without him."

The pain I felt was too deep to put words to, and even now I can't describe it. I wasn't shocked, exactly. As a kid, I had always expected my mother would die young, and now she had. But the timing felt wrong. She'd been doing better, I thought. Her voice sounded clear every time we talked on the phone, and I'd just seen her two weeks before. She had a job and a lanai. She wanted to watch me graduate. I couldn't bring myself to reckon with the hole my mother's death had suddenly carved inside me, so I closed my eyes and imagined her dancing.

The last night I saw her, in Miami after my brother's wedding, she grooved in the street because it was her first time drinking Hennessy. One of my brother's neighbors, a man under house arrest, had sent his girlfriend for a bottle, and when the man screwed off the top, my mom shimmied across the road and asked for a taste. She said, "Can I try that?" and "What did you do to get an ankle monitor strapped to your leg?" He said, "Cocaine. One shot or two?" He eased the liquor into a red Solo cup. My mother swallowed it in a gulp. A teenage boy played rap songs from a car parked in the street, and my mom held up the empty cup, then leaned. She said it burned. She asked for a second shot. The headlights were a spotlight, and when the man tipped the bottle, my mom drew me close. We drifted over the gravel. She said she was finally happy, that she was working and living and trying new things. I believed her because I wanted to. She had eaten Korean food and mussels in DC; now she was tasting Hennessy. When my cab pulled up at the end of the night, she ran after me. "Wait," she said. "There are things I've never told you."

Lying on my mother's floor in Tampa, I wondered what she'd wanted to say. I'd laughed or winked that night in Miami. I'd finally allowed myself to believe that my mother would last. We had time, I'd thought. We finally had time. "Call me," I'd said, but she never had.

I sat up, and I remembered that she'd told me on our first trip to Delhi that she'd been drawn to Roy because he kept a journal, just like she and Cam had. It was a hobby my mom had passed down to me when I was young. She bought me my first diary—a denim-covered book with a girly clasp—the summer before I started fourth grade. My parents moved too often to hold on to much, so I'd lost that journal years ago, but suddenly I suspected that my mother probably kept her old diaries. I crawled toward the recliner.

"Do you have any of mom's old journals?"

My dad told me to check the closet. My mom kept shoeboxes on the shelves, and he thought he'd seen leather-bound books in one of them. I made my way to their bedroom, still on my hands and knees. I pulled down a Keds box full of empty pill containers, then I reached for a bigger box that must have once held boots. I'd never seen my mom wear boots. She liked flashy, bedazzled sandals, the kind I once told her I assumed a mermaid would buy as soon as she got legs. The shelves were high, so I hit the box until it fell into my arms. Inside, I saw three wide books with padded covers. They didn't look like the journals I kept or the marble composition books I imagined Roy used, but I felt desperate, so I told myself these books must hold some answers.

The first was a yellow scrapbook my mom had kept for most of her childhood. She'd taped in pictures of her sisters trudging through the snow in Germany, and she'd left comments throughout in the same loopy handwriting she used to use to fake doctor's notes to get me out of PE. She'd described a Charley Pride concert and a meeting of the Beta Club, and then, on one red page, she'd written in the center, "Because you are afraid to love, I am alone." I flipped through to the end, but I didn't see any other hints about her loneliness. Who had been afraid to love? Cam?

I wanted to reach through time and space to tell the teenage version of my mother that she wouldn't feel that way forever, that she'd find love and have kids, and she wouldn't be alone. But what did I know? Maybe she never shook that feeling. I'd never been able to. I'd been so sure when I met Frankie that she was the cure for my lonely aching. I'd buried all my pain in her, and I'd even pretended my pain had never existed. I'd wanted to be happy and normal, but something still haunted my edges. Maybe my mother had felt the same way.

The second book was mostly pictures, and the third was a Thomas Kinkade fill-in journal called Mother's Memories to Her Child. She'd answered seventy pages of questions about her childhood and mine. She'd loved the livestock show and playing Chinese checkers, and her favorite thing to wear was overalls—"cotton or denim." She wrote about her parents and the first job she ever had. She washed steps when she was ten. At night, she hid in the bathroom so she could read.

"I feel like I grew up with you," she wrote on one page, ostensibly to me. "I always loved the times you made me laugh, cry, think, and dream like no other person in my life."

I had spent a decade and a half wishing my mom loved me the way I assumed Jewel had loved Roy. I'd held on to the bad things—the times my mother hit me, the way she'd once whispered "I hate you" into my ear as I lay in bed—and I'd mistaken her pain and addiction for a lack of love, but holding the little book she filled out, I knew that I had what Roy had with Jewel. Maybe I was an accident, and maybe I couldn't heal my mother, but that didn't mean she hadn't loved me. It didn't mean she didn't want me.

I skimmed forward and backward until I landed on page 46 and an entry titled "My first broken heart."

Cam Milton. His death remains my biggest break.

I sank into the carpet, then I lay there under a curtain of my mom's nightgowns, turning the word "break" over and over in my head. Had she always been broken? How did her esophagus tear? I assumed that pain medication was somehow involved, but I wasn't ready to ask my dad if I was right. A few years earlier, a friend of mine at *The Washington Post* had written an article that said white women in their fifties were dying at greater rates than ever before. We'd gone out for sushi while he was writing it, and I remember feeling a sense of dread. He'd profiled one woman in Oklahoma, and I'd wondered, but didn't ask, if that woman's children had also suspected their mother would die early.

I closed Mother's Memories to Her Child, and as I reached to tuck it back into the box, a letter fell out. I recognized it as one she gave me when I was sixteen and she was thirty-five. It was two pages, typed in Comic Sans and filled with misspellings and missed commas, the kind of grammar mistakes my mom hated, the kind of mistakes I'd never seen her make.

Dear Casey,

I am writing this to you for so many reasons that I barely know which one to begin. As you know, I have been very depressed lately and I have had some thoughts that are less than healthy. But I am writing to you because I have the most trust in you than anyone in the whole world. I have been half out of my mind in despair. Not because of any one thing exactly but with so many things weighing so heavily on my mind, I guess it's been like that old favorite pair of blue jeans, you see the wearing and tearing on a daily basis, but decide it is okay to wear them one more time because well they're not ripped and then one day you go to pull them on and the seams in the rear end just sort of tears wide open. Does that make sense? I hope so because it describes exactly how I've been feeling lately. The only thing is I've had this almost uncontrolable urge to help that seam rip open. And for that I am sorry. (one very big reason for writing)

I know that my depression has put you in the position of being embarrassed greatly and it has made you make excuses for me. I know it has caused you to pity me and probably even has probably brought shame to you. For all of these things Casey I am sorry more than you'll ever know. I am so proud of you and of the woman you are on the verge of becoming (reason 2) almost envy the children you will one day have, because they are going to have one hell of a mother. You are probably the smarted person I know and I may not always let you know that I think you are so smart and that I value your opinion very highly.

This next part is where I am asking you to let me able to trust you more. I don't want you to repeat any of this to anyone. I put the vial of Stadol in your room this morning because I feel like it will be safer in your room than anywhere else. I realized this morning that if I don't reach down and grab myself by the bootstraps, I may not make it out of this depression and haze. The past week, you have shown me so much love and support that I don't know where I would be without you. When you've laid with me while I just cried for no reason this week and just have listened to me babble, you have made more difference than anyone has ever made in my life. I now really know that I can make it and that if I need help you will be there to try and support me and for that I thank you (reason #3 and main 1) I'm giving you the stadol because I want you to see that you can trust me and that I am going to try to get myself together. I promise to you that as of today I will never try to or even think through to try and plan to physically harm myself again. I won't be in the bed as often when your friends come over. I know they may find the fact that I really have legs hard to believe. (God that sounds like a title for a Jerry Springer show). I don't want to spend so much time in bed and I don't want to be depressed any more. But most of all I don't want to die, I want to Dance!

I promise to you that now I've realized that I will do everything in my power to pull myself together. I love you so much Casey. Please forgive me.

I'm older now than my mother was when she wrote that letter, and when I first read it after she died, I felt an immense amount of empathy for both of us. I'd always told myself that I was a bad daughter. I didn't answer the phone when my mom called, and I didn't do anything to stop her from taking pills. I didn't love her in the ways she needed to be loved. I didn't even know what those ways were. Now, when I read this letter, I want to tell my teenage self that I wasn't a bad daughter. I want to forgive myself for the things I didn't do. I want to go back and tell that teenager it's not her responsibility to solve her mother's addiction. But who else did my mother have? Was it my fault that she didn't have a better life? In an alternate reality, one in which Cam lived and my mother never went to the park and met my father, a reality in which I never arrived, maybe my mom would have gone to college and become someone stable. I've spent more than a decade tracking my family's problems back to the roots, and I still don't know who to blame. Is everything a function of poverty? Would my grandma have been more loving if she'd never picked cotton? What if her dad had never left for Washington? Was Louisiana itself—a state built on oil and bigotry—to blame? At Columbia, I read three dozen books about the South. I took a whole course on American poverty, and I read countless papers on cotton, and I still don't understand why exactly my mom lived and died the way she did.

I DON'T KNOW HOW long I lay there in my mother's Florida closet. I must have eventually crawled out. Frankie must have arrived. I fell asleep, or I didn't; I don't remember. Suddenly, it was daylight, and I was in a pool. I dunked myself and stayed below the surface long enough to turn my brain black. My memories stutter forward after that. A classmate sent flowers. My advisor ordered groceries. I turned my phone off and asked Frankie to tell my best friends to stop texting me. I wanted to live in my memories, and every electronic ping tugged me out of the past.

One afternoon—I can no longer remember whether it was the second or third or fourth day—my dad, my brother, and I sat in the lanai and discussed a memorial. None of us could afford a funeral. My dad owed something north of ten thousand dollars for the medical bills my mom had accrued, and my brother had drained his savings to pay for the wedding. I hadn't worked since I moved to New York, and I was down to my last two thousand dollars. My dad wanted to cremate my mom because it was cheaper and because, he said, that's what she wanted. I'd never talked to her about it, but I could imagine her hating the idea of being penned into a plot somewhere. She was too restless to linger. Still, I wanted a marker. I hadn't seen her before she died, and now we weren't having a funeral, and it felt as if she'd disappeared. How could someone whose presence had loomed so large in my life leave behind no trace?

I don't think we settled the discussion—my dad eventually had her cremated after we left Tampa—but I remember I walked around the neighborhood alone for a while after we talked. I thought about the cemetery in Delhi, the one Keith King had shown us on our first reporting trip. The last time I went down, Christopher and I stopped by the cemetery to visit Roy's grave. I parked on the gravel next to the same half-broken gate my mother had parked next to in 2009. I needled between the plots, careful not to step on the tombs marked "Moreland" and "Lancaster." Then I made my way over the uneven ground to the back right corner, where a towering live oak tree shaded Roy's grave.

No one ever left flowers there, and I'd never seen a single other person in the cemetery, but that time, Christopher and I spotted a square end of concrete sticking out near Roy's headstone. I could tell by the way the concrete slanted into the ground that it was the corner of something bigger. Grass and mud covered the rest of whatever it was, so Christopher and I bent down to work it free. We pulled out tufts of grass, and we used sticks to chisel the mud away. Eventually, we uncovered a rectangle slab grooved with letters. It was, we realized, a homemade headstone.

Delhi is a poor town, but its cemetery is filled with what I imagine must have been expensive memorials. Many of them have attached vases, and a few include personalized benches. The markers nearest Roy's have marble finishes, and the inscriptions include little pictures of hearts and flowers. I'd never seen a headstone like the rudimentary one Christopher and I unearthed that day. All we could make out was "Jewel E," letters carved into the concrete in the same handwriting I'd seen in Roy's Bible.

"Do you think Roy made this?" I asked.

Christopher frowned. "Can you imagine that?" he asked. "Not having any money and just taking a brick and carving your parents' name into it with a knife or a screwdriver? I'd cry the whole time."

Jewel's sinking headstone felt like a metaphor. I'd asked everyone we'd interviewed if they knew anything about her, but few people remembered Jewel, and hardly any artifacts from her life remained. She'd existed once, but then she'd slowly slipped back into the earth. Walking around Tampa, my mother lost to the ether, I knew that what happened to Jewel could happen just as easily to her. Neither Jewel nor my mother had lived what historians would have called a remarkable life. Few people in Delhi had. But their lives were important, to me, if to no one else.

Maybe none of the books I read at Columbia explained what happened to my family because they weren't written for or about my family. I'd started to think of Roy and Jewel as ancestors in the same way I thought of my grandmother, and as I walked around my mom's old neighborhood, I decided I owed it to all my people to write them back into existence. I needed more than my own words, though. I needed my grandma's memories and my mother's journals. I needed the unreliable census and the tapes Aubree and I had recorded on Hell Street. But what I needed most, I knew, were the notebooks Mark had repeatedly told me I couldn't see.

Maybe I knew then that if I found Roy's journals, I'd grant myself permission to keep working on this project. If I kept working on it, I could spend years replaying the videos I made of my mom and grandmother. I could live in the recorded world where they were still smoking in the carport, as electric as the space heaters they cranked year-round. I'm not sure any of my thoughts were exactly clear, but by the time I reached my mom's lanai, I'd convinced myself that I had to return to Delhi. I had to ask Mark one last time to let me see Roy's diaries.

Chapter Twenty-Three

(2019)

I HALF EXPECTED TO find my mother crying in the terminal when I flew into New Orleans a few months later. She wasn't there, of course. I was the one who sobbed my way past the stalls selling beignet mix and Tabasco sauce. I cried all the way to the rental car place, until I got a car, rolled down my windows, and blasted "Cruise," a Florida Georgia Line hit I'd always hated but now found irresistible. I'd started listening to country music after my mother died, and I'd let my accent ease back into the twangy vowels I'd once tried hard to flatten. I don't know if I was performing a charade or tapping into some truer version of myself, but I didn't care. I missed my mom, and I ached a tiny bit less when I let myself go redneck.

Technically, I'd returned to Louisiana to work on a story for *USA Today*. I'd started freelancing for national newspapers and magazines after I graduated from Columbia, but I planned to extend this reporting trip to make one last push for Roy's diaries. I was scared, but amped up. Maybe, I thought, I would finally reach a conclusion. I drove out of the parking garage so fast, the wind turned my hair curly. I stuck my head out the window and inhaled as long as I could. Even the interstate smelled like fish and cigarettes. I pulled my head back into the car. My mom might not have been waiting for me, but I felt her there in the funky stank of home.

———

A FEW DAYS LATER, after I'd finished my *USA Today* story, Aubree flew into New Orleans. Aubree had moved to Los Angeles a few years earlier to work as a director and cinematographer, and it had been a while since we'd seen each other. We stayed up late the first night, drinking at a hotel bar, and Aubree told me they'd realized in the years since we first started the documentary that they were transgender and nonbinary. They looked happy, younger somehow, relieved of a burden I hadn't known they were shouldering. They'd married their long-term girlfriend, and a documentary they'd made about intersex people had won some awards and was screened all over the world.

We left New Orleans for Delhi late Friday afternoon, intending to ask Mark King one last time if we could read Roy's journals. I'd made something like half a plan. I'd texted Pam Sykes, and I'd rented the cabin Aubree and I had always stayed in, but I hadn't called Mark. I wasn't even sure he'd be in town. I'd googled his name, and I hadn't found an obituary, so I was pretty sure he was still alive, but otherwise, I was just gunning north, hoping this was the weekend I solved my mystery.

The drive to Delhi from New Orleans is a four-hour arc from Louisiana through Mississippi and back again. The sky was dark by the time we made it to town, and Delhi doesn't have a ton of streetlights, so I couldn't make out the shape of the place as we cut down Main Street toward Poverty Point. I assumed nothing had changed because nothing about Delhi had ever changed in the years I'd been visiting, but the next morning, Pam texted and asked us to meet her for brunch at a Mexican restaurant that had opened next to the grocery store. Aubree and I only had two days in town, but I told myself meeting up with Pam was a good first step. Maybe she had a better plan than I did. I said we'd be there at eleven.

Pam was close to sixty now. She'd let her hair grow long in the back, and she'd left her job at the sweet potato factory for a night gig manning the police department's dispatch line, but I could tell, when I saw her across the parking lot, that something bigger had changed. She smiled in a way I hadn't seen her smile before, and she'd tucked a stuffed pink unicorn into the dash of her truck.

"What is this about?" I asked, waving toward the unicorn.

"I'm in love," Pam said. "I'll tell you about her later."

I figured the unicorn wasn't the "her" Pam meant, but I'd learned over the years that I had to let Pam unspool at her own pace. She'd open up when she was ready. I nodded, then we went inside to plot. We'd decided earlier that week that we'd all go to Mark's together, and when we sat down in the booth, Pam told us she knew what she wanted to say. She believed Roy's story could help people. Somewhere out there, in other small towns, there was probably a misfit who felt alone in the world, she said. That person needed to know Roy existed. If we could just explain that to Mark, Pam thought, we'd be reading Roy's diaries by the end of the day.

We polished off plates of cheese enchiladas, then we headed back into the sun. Pam revved the engine in her pickup truck, but I waited to start the rental car. I'd had a decade to prepare for this moment, but still, I didn't feel ready.

"We are doing this for a good reason," I told my reflection. "If we don't do it, Roy won't have a legacy."

Aubree hooked a wireless mic onto my lapel and asked me what I thought the value of a legacy was.

I knew "legacy" sounded cheesy, and maybe the word didn't even capture what I meant, but I had come to believe that it was my responsibility to tell Roy's story. Some journalists call this "giving voice to the voiceless," but I've never liked that phrase. Most people aren't voiceless. They're just made to feel powerless or invisible. Roy had a voice. He wrote songs, and he kept journals, and once upon a time, I'd lived my life sustained by the sheer fact of his existence. As far as I knew, his words had never left Hell Street, but I had a power now that Roy was never able to claim, and I believed that if I forced myself to be brave one last time, the world might finally hear his voice.

"Well," I told Aubree. "It's important to remember that people existed."

It was a lame explanation, nothing close to what I felt, but I was nervous and bumbling with my words, so I left it at that. I pulled onto Main Street, hoping Delhi's lone stoplight would catch me before I made it over the train tracks. I needed just three more minutes, I thought, to puzzle out what I'd say to Mark. The light stayed green, though, and I made it to Mark's faster than I wanted, all my words left unrehearsed. I parked, as I always did, across the street and a few feet up so that Mark couldn't see me from his window. I turned off the car, and I let out a big, deep breath. Every big-time journalist I've ever met has told me they hate knocking on people's doors. Calling strangers never gets easier, and most reporters have to psych themselves up before they dial a new number. I suppose we fear rejection. I once spent a summer in counseling, practicing with the therapist as she pretended to repeatedly turn down my interview requests, but even that hadn't inoculated me. I feel sick every time. It's usually easier to approach a source you've interviewed before, but I'd talked to Mark half a dozen times, and I still felt sweaty and shaky as I sat outside his trailer.

We stepped out of the car, and I shook all my limbs around. The trailer looked dark, but the Kings' Cutlass was parked outside, so I assumed they were home. Pam bounced up behind me.

"Are you nervous?" I asked her.

She shook her head.

"Not really."

She eyed my shaking legs, laughed, then said she'd knock on the door. She swung her keys around as we walked up the steps. I remember standing on Mark's deck for a long time, waiting for him to answer the door, but the tape recording from that day shows that only twenty seconds passed. Pam knocked, the screen door flapped open, and Mark stepped out.

"Casey?"

Mark said my name the way my relatives say my name. He dragged out the *a,* and he added an extra syllable in the middle. The lilt of it comforted me. I asked Mark how he was doing, and he shrugged. I hadn't seen him in probably six years, but he looked like he hadn't aged. He was still skinny and fairly wrinkleless, and his hair was the same shade of white it had been the first time I knocked on his door. I thought he was even wearing the same red hat he'd had on the last time I interviewed him.

"We're still working on our project about Roy," I said.

I was trying to sound friendly, but my nerves hadn't abated, so I stuttered. Mark took two steps back and put his hand on his chest the way someone does when something shocks them.

"Goodness, gracious. I didn't know that. Well, I wish y'all hadn't found me here. I wish I wasn't still living here, but unfortunately I am for a little while longer."

"Do you think you might move?" I asked.

My voice was timid. I barely knew Mark, but I didn't want him to leave Delhi. So much in my life had changed, and Mark's continued existence on Chatham Street felt like something I could depend on. Maybe it's because I moved so often as a kid, or maybe I'd co-opted my grandmother's memories for my own personal origin story, but I couldn't think of anywhere on earth that felt more like home than Hell Street. As long as Mark lived there, I thought, I had some right to return.

"Well, you know," Mark said. "I'm hoping one day, I don't know when."

He clapped his hands.

"I hate to tell you, folks, I can't talk right now. I've got my brother up at the dryer. He's drying clothes. He's got one step in the nursing home, and one step in life."

"You mean Keith?" I asked.

I'd met Mark's brother on my first trip to Delhi. He'd answered the phone when my mom tried to call the Kings' landline, then he'd taken us to the cemetery. I remembered he'd told me and my mother, as soon as we'd stepped out of the car, that he was gay, and I'd been both embarrassed and hopeful. I'd thought I'd spend more time with him, that he'd tell me what it was like to be gay in Delhi, but I'd never mustered up the courage to tell him I was gay, too. I hadn't seen Keith since that first trip, and I'd never talked to Mark about him, but I knew Keith was too young to have one step in the nursing home. He was my aunt Ann's age, late fifties at most.

"Yeah," Mark said. "Keith's in bad shape. He's in a walker right now. He's got, Lord, everything but cancer, I think."

I was still in that stage of grief where I compulsively mentioned my mother's death to everyone I saw, and as soon as Mark stopped talking, I told him my mom had died a few months earlier.

"Yeah, I heard that," he said. He looked down and ran his tennis shoe over the deck.

"She was only fifty-three," I said.

Cheryl opened the screen door. She must have been listening from inside.

"What a shame," she said.

I'd only seen Cheryl once before, and I hadn't looked at her long enough then to remember later what she looked like, but I tried to take her in now. She was wearing a fleece jacket with the Olympics logo embossed on the front, and her hair was pulled back in a long white ponytail that she'd topped with a matching Olympics hat. Cheryl hadn't talked much the other time I met her, but she seemed genuinely sorry my mother had died. I wanted to ask her to tell me again about the days when she taught my mom junior high PE, but Mark spoke before I could.

"I gotta go pick up Keith, y'all. We got to go and get his clothes out for him and make sure we can get him on back to the house over there."

I felt foolish. Why had I insisted we fly down without any sort of plan? I wanted to back off the deck and hide from Aubree and Pam, but I knew if I didn't ask one more time, I might never have an end to this story.

"We're just here for the weekend," I said. "Any chance we could stop back by?"

Mark let out a low, long whistle. He looked at Cheryl, then he turned to me.

"Where y'all at?"

I told him we were staying in one of the cabins on the lake, and Mark widened his eyes to show he was impressed. I'd never thought of the cabins as fancy, but compared to the trailers on Chatham Street, I suppose they were. Mark said he'd always wanted to see inside one.

"Cheryl and I might run up tomorrow and visit with y'all there."

Mark's answer felt like a victory, but he must have sensed something in my reaction, because as soon as he said he'd stop by, he turned to Pam and issued a caveat.

"Now, like I told Casey, I know she wants it, but I don't even look at them. I've got some of Royce's old books. Some of them I laid out behind the storage house one day because they smelled terrible. I was going to let them air out. And lo and behold, it wasn't supposed to rain, but it did. Some of them got wet, and I threw them away because I couldn't deal with them. But I put a few of them that were still in an okay condition in a box."

Pam asked Mark if he'd seen any song lyrics, and Mark shook his head no.

"There wasn't nothing like that. It was just a journal of day-to-day misery. Royce liked this place about as much as I do."

Cheryl closed the screen door, and Mark inched toward it. Aubree and Pam were both smiling, but I felt like Mark had already given me the answer I'd come seeking. He was not going to let us see the journals.

THE DAY WASN'T EVEN half over, but we couldn't think of anything to do in town, so the three of us drove to a part of the lake I hadn't seen yet. It was the nicest spot, a wooden pier with a view of big houses, and we walked out to the end and sat on two posts for a while. Pam told us that her mom had moved to a nursing home. For years, Pam had said that she couldn't date anyone until after her mother died, but she'd decided that the nursing home was distance enough.

"So I met someone."

Pam smirked, and Aubree and I smiled, goofy and big. As long as we'd known Pam, she'd been living in a kind of bardo, waiting for her new life to begin. And now, suddenly, it had. Pam told us that the "someone" was a redheaded woman from a few towns over. They'd met through Pam's dog groomer, and the first time they hung out, they'd saved a bunch of puppies from drowning in a culvert. Afterward, they'd driven out to this pier, and they'd talked for a while in the dark.

"It was very easy to talk to her freely and openly about the things that affected me in my life, being different, a lesbian, a dyke, or whatever, and I found that very enjoyable," Pam said, mumbling as she said all the words for gay. "She's very adamant about being open. Me, I just been kind of doing my own thing, hiding in the closet. And I was fascinated that someone could be so open. If I was going to be in a relationship with this person, I knew I was going to have to learn how to be open the way she is."

The woman had urged Pam to buy a rainbow flag, and she'd bought her that unicorn I'd spotted earlier in the truck. Those totems would have been small gestures in Portland—in some neighborhoods, they wouldn't even be cause for a second glance—but I knew how big a risk flying a pride flag in Delhi might be.

"Are you scared to be out here now?" I asked.

"Out here?" Pam asked, looking down at the pier.

"Not out on this dock, but in Delhi. Can you imagine going to the grocery store and saying 'my wife'?"

Pam was quiet for a few moments, then she shook her head. No, she said, she couldn't imagine telling people in Delhi she was dating a woman. She hadn't told her mother she'd fallen in love, and she hadn't told anyone that she'd gone online and bought a ring.

I raised my eyebrows.

"A ring?"

"Now that it's legal in some states, we talked about maybe doing it in the Vermont mountains."

It took me a minute to understand what Pam was saying. The Supreme Court had legalized gay marriage four years earlier, but Pam still thought she could only get married in liberal places like Vermont.

"It's legal in every state," I said.

"I know it's legal in Vermont."

"You do know it's legal in Louisiana, right?" I asked.

"No, not really," Pam said. "It's like Mississippi, they don't recognize it."

I told her, again, that she could legally marry a woman anywhere in the United States, but I knew the law was only words on paper in some places. Who in Delhi would agree to host the ceremony? What caterer would consent? I wouldn't have tried to plan a gay wedding there. Hell, I'd spent my whole *USA Today* reporting trip in New Orleans trying to hide my wedding ring because I feared my sources would find out I was married to a woman. I told myself I didn't want to make anyone uncomfortable. I wanted to be safe. But at night, alone in my hotel room, I was embarrassed by my shame. I'd been out of the closet for seventeen years, and I still felt like hiding every time I visited Louisiana. It didn't matter that most of the people I loved there were dead. The state itself had an inexplicable hold on me. I wanted to tell myself that it was just a place, that its people were just people and their judgments held no real bearing on my life. But my fear felt reflexive, like something I couldn't control, and I didn't know what to do with that. How can a place be so right in some ways and so limiting in others? How could I barrel down the interstate, free and connected in a way I never felt in Portland, when I still hid such an essential part of myself?

My phone buzzed in my pocket. I snaked it out and saw Mark had left me a voicemail. In the video footage Aubree shot, I look remarkably calm, but that seems crazy to me now. Yes, Mark had said he would come by the cabin the next morning, but I hadn't really believed him. I thought he'd make up another excuse when I called, but instead, here he was, calling *me*. Why didn't I jump around celebrating as if the voicemail itself were a huge win? It had to be good news, didn't it? Mark could have ignored us if he didn't want us to know anything. Maybe I was afraid to get my hopes up again, so I didn't even smile. Instead, I turned on my speakerphone and played the message for Aubree and Pam.

"Casey, Cheryl and I'd like to come talk to y'all now, if you're not busy. Call me back and see if we can go ahead and have our talk today and get that done."

My eyes widened a bit. I can't remember how I felt in that moment, but I know that I called Mark back, and we agreed to meet at the cabin in fifteen minutes. As soon as I hung up, I let myself hope again. I sped around the lake. Mark knew what I wanted, and he'd called and he'd asked to talk sooner. Maybe he wanted money for the journals. I'd been against paying for them when I first started, but now I felt desperate to read Roy's words, and I was willing to give Mark whatever he wanted.

MARK AND CHERYL made it to the cabin a few minutes after we did. Aubree led them on a tour of its two bedrooms, and Mark marveled at how high the ceilings were.

"You won't feel cramped in these," he said. "But it's probably hard to heat and cool it."

We sat at the kitchen table, but none of us brought up Roy. We talked about people we knew who'd died in the past few years, and eventually we talked about records. Mark had two thousand albums and another nine thousand 45s, mostly country singles and what he called

"Black music." He said he loved Ray Charles and Stevie Wonder. I told him I'd just bought a steel drum record from Trinidad. We both paused for a second, and I knew it was time. Music had been the impetus of this whole project—it was Roy's banjo that lured my grandmother across the street in 1952—so it seemed the best way to transition into the question I knew I had to ask one last time.

"When we first started this," I said, "one of the ladies who used to live on Chatham Street said she had a tape of Roy singing, but she lost it in a divorce."

I'd tried to get this tape. I'd spent two whole years bugging the woman on Facebook, and I'd begged her to ask her ex-husband for the tape. She'd strung me along for several months. She'd promised to reach out to him, but eventually, she'd told me to give up. Her ex had thrown the tape out.

"A tape?" Mark asked. "Wow. I never heard Roy play and sing except maybe a couple of times when we first moved there. After that, we didn't hear it anymore."

That tape was lost to time, but I knew the journals weren't. Roy must have wanted some kind of legacy. Why else would he have written songs? Why would he have sent them off to the Judds or the Whites or the other bands no one remembered? Why would he have typed "YOU CAN'T GET TO HEAVEN BY GOING THROUGH HELL" for Mary Rundell all those years ago? People write, I think, because they want to be understood and remembered.

I cleared my throat and tried to look at Mark as plaintively as I could.

"We definitely understand that y'all want to protect Roy, but the longer we've worked on this story, the more I've thought that it doesn't make sense to do it without hearing Roy's own perspective."

Mark laughed a deep, almost sinister, laugh. It scared me. He laughed like he'd been waiting for me to ask this question, like he'd suspected I had bad intentions, and I'd proven him right. I didn't want to keep talking, but I knew I had to. I couldn't tell Roy's story, I said again, unless Roy got to tell part of it himself. Mark shook his head no.

"Just knowing Royce, she was a private person."

My chest seized up. Maybe Mark was right. He'd known Roy way better than Pam or my grandmother had, and so he was probably the closest I'd ever get to understanding how Roy might have responded to my inquiries. I swallowed hard.

"I was kind of the same way until they came along," Pam said, pointing at me and Aubree. "Now I'm like, 'Wow, I'm sharing my story, and it's not hurting anything.' Hopefully these stories that we're telling today will inspire someone, if nothing else, to continue on with their life. That's one reason that I'm truly inspired by all this because that's my goal, to be able to help someone. I'm a misfit. Maybe I could help change somebody's way of thinking about misfits. Roy, we had a lot of similarities in our lifestyle, the way we dressed, whatever. Seeing this person in this town, doing what she does, and living how she does, that gave me a little inspiration to say 'I'm not going to change for everybody. I'm going to be like I'm going to be.'"

I knew Pam was braving something big. She didn't use the words "gay" or "lesbian" or "transgender," but "misfit" said enough. She was coming out to Mark and Cheryl. She was telling them the very secret she'd just told me on the dock she wasn't ready to share, and she was doing it just so I could read Roy's journals. I felt painfully moved, but I didn't join in with my own confession.

I suspected the Kings already knew we were queer. We all had short hair, and we were wearing the kinds of boots lesbians wear—heavy shoes with wide toes and soles suited to hiking. I suspected the Kings wouldn't judge me if I did tell them I was gay. They were still taking care of Keith, after all. How homophobic could they be? But I didn't tell them. Instead, I told Mark that Roy was the kind of person the world should remember. Every day, newspapers and magazines chronicle the lives of powerful people, but I'd spent a decade returning to this small town because I believed that regular people deserved the same thing.

Mark listened without interrupting. When Pam and I finished our spiels, he put his hands on the table. He tried to let us down gently.

"Royce didn't want her stuff to be given to anybody else," he said.

I told Mark he didn't have to give me the journals. We could just look at them together. He shook his head no.

"But if we go over what she's written, we are kinda giving it. Do y'all believe in karma? Cheryl and I have a lot of bad luck. We have bad luck with our family. I would really feel funny about the karma."

I didn't feel bold, just out of options, so I asked Mark one more time if he could imagine any situation in which he'd show me even part of the journals. Cheryl shook her head no, more vigorously than Mark ever had.

"It's karma," she said.

She cut her eyes at Mark in a way I'd seen my mom do with my dad hundreds of times. It was a look that said "Back me up on this." Mark seemed to take the hint.

"Y'all, I just don't feel comfortable," he said. "I'm worried about doing that. Royce, one thing is, she said she'd curse ya. She said, 'You have this. If you give it away, you're cursed, I curse you.'"

I remembered the curse that Roy had written on the back of one of the Cave Theater playbills Mark had shown me a few years earlier. But did the curse apply to showing people Roy's stuff? I didn't think so. I'd taken a picture of the playbill, and I'd read it so many times, I had the words memorized: *If you keep all my foolish things, you shall have good luck. If you throw them away, you shall have very bad luck for my curse shall be on you.*

I waited a beat, shook my head, then reminded Mark that I'd seen the playbills.

"It said if you throw my stuff away, I'll curse you," I said.

"Well, all right," Mark said. "I just feel kind of spooky about that."

Cheryl folded her arms in a way that suggested she was ready to leave. I assumed she was the one who didn't want us to see Roy's journals, but it didn't matter who or what the reason was, I realized. I'd asked the Kings repeatedly for nearly a decade, and they had remained resolute. They weren't going to give me Roy's journals.

"Okay, then," I said. "Well."

Mark stood and Cheryl stood, so I stood, too. We talked about the weekend as if we were people who might see each other again, but I felt very sure that some chapter in my life had suddenly come to an end. I walked them to the door. We didn't shake hands. Pam was late for the night shift, so she followed Mark and Cheryl out. When they left, I turned toward Aubree's camera and grimaced. I'd tried everything, I thought. The project was dead.

Aubree turned the camera off, and we stood in the middle of the cabin, unsure of what to do. I realized we'd probably never stay there again. Outside, the sun was setting in pink and purple bars, but I felt too defeated to look at something pretty for the last time. I grabbed a beer from the fridge. The cabin's walls were covered in posters advertising bass-fishing spots, and I studied them for a few minutes, then I sat on the floor. I tore the beer's label away.

When I was young, I used to pray every time I wanted something. My mother taught me that desires are meant to be spoken, so I used to whisper my wants. I asked God for toys and TV dinners, straight As, and blank VHS tapes I planned to fill with Christian music videos. I hadn't made that kind of request in nearly two decades, not since I came out, not since my preacher asked God to take me. I no longer asked any celestial being to give me things, and I wasn't even sure if I believed in heaven anymore, but something in the cabin quieted me that evening. Something told me to ask. I didn't feel close to God anymore, though, so I shut my eyes and prayed to my mom and grandmother.

"If y'all are up there, can you talk to Roy?"

I suppose I wanted them to broker some kind of celestial deal. I wanted permission, a sign that I hadn't wasted a decade searching for something that shouldn't be found. I didn't want to put this story out there unless Roy got to tell part of it.

I prayed in fragments, half sentences that were both pleading and apologetic. I didn't say amen. I opened my eyes, and when I looked up, I saw headlights sweeping across the cabin wall. No one drives that deep into the park by accident, and there weren't any cabins farther in than ours, so I knew what those headlights meant. I jumped up. I stashed my beer outside on the deck, then I ran to the front door. I knew before I opened it that Mark would be standing on the other side.

Chapter Twenty-Four

(2019)

I OPENED THE DOOR, and Mark strolled in as if our afternoon talk had never happened. He was holding three trash bags, one black and two white, each bulging with the kind of square corners I knew had to be notebooks.

"Y'all," he said, "these things are in pretty bad shape, but you can look at them if you want to."

Cheryl appeared holding gloves and disinfectant. In the video Aubree shot, I look absolutely nonplussed, but I remember I was working hard to appear that way. I wanted the Kings to feel like this moment was no big deal, like they weren't risking a curse to betray a friend, so I didn't even ask them why they'd changed their minds when they'd been so certain of their "no" an hour earlier. Instead, I trailed Mark through the living room. Every second felt like a lifetime, but I can see in the video time-stamps how quickly the whole thing unfolded. Less than a minute after I opened the door, Mark was kneeling on the cabin floor, wearing a pair of brown gardening gloves, and digging into one of the bags. I was standing, nervously shifting from one foot to the other, making small talk as if this moment were one we'd all planned and anticipated together.

"Wow," I said, looking at the bags. "There's a lot of them."

I started clearing my laptop and battery chargers off the kitchen table so Mark could spread the journals out, but he didn't move from the spot he'd claimed on the ground. With absolutely no ceremony, Mark pulled out a faded green notebook from 1992, and he started reading silently to himself.

"I told you," he said. "Royce, by gosh, she wrote in cursive. And you can read it. It's good cursive."

I was standing a few feet away, so I bent toward Mark to look over his shoulder at a page from May 1992, and there they were—the words I'd spent a decade imagining. Roy had covered the top half in big, loopy black letters, and he'd penned an update later in the day with red ink.

> *It wasn't bad here last night, and we didn't get any rain. The high was 91 degrees, but I cut the church yard and finished my yard. I put a partition on the shed and put the two old pieces of lawn mowers I had in it. Now, I got a little more room in the junk room. Well, that's how my day went. I'm sure tired tonight, but I'm sure glad I was able to do what I did.*

Mark chuckled, but my heart sank. Had I really spent a whole decade waiting to read about lawn mower parts?

Mark flipped a few pages, then he set 1992 on the floor and dug out a Mead notebook marked "1984, The Complaints of a Misfit." He laughed again.

"Complaints! I guess that's the reason Royce and I got along so good. Both of us are negative."

Mark kept hauling journals out of trash bags until eventually they encircled him. I tried to count them, but I was too hyped to tally past twenty. I'd always imagined Roy wrote in the marble composition books I used to use in elementary school, but his diaries were one-subject notebooks, the spiral-bound kind my mom used to buy at Walmart two for a dollar. They were mostly teal and blue, a little bit moldy and rusted along the metal spines, and Roy had used a Magic Marker to name and date each one. Aubree and I had started calling our project "Diary of a Misfit," but as I looked over Mark's shoulder, I saw that he had gotten the names of Roy's journals just slightly wrong. Roy had named his 1980 diary "Life of a Misfit," and he called the 1978 edition "Day by Day Life of a Misfit." I smiled, dazed at what was unfolding in front of me. I was grateful Mark had remembered wrong—his title was punchier, more memorable than the ones Roy himself had chosen.

Mark didn't settle into any one journal for long. He'd pick one up, read a random sentence, then set it aside. Occasionally, he lifted one so

I could see. Some of the ink had run down the pages, but mostly, Roy's words were legible. Even standing a few feet away, I could make out whole paragraphs detailing the heat and the rain.

"I'm telling you," Mark said, "sixty percent of it's probably weather. Royce had to work outside, so she was really interested in the weather."

Mark placed three journals next to my feet. My Blundstone boots were muddy, and I worried if I moved, some of the mud might flake off onto Roy's notebooks. I don't know why that scared me. Most of the journals were covered in a brown silt Mark told me might be dog excrement, but still, I didn't want to add my dirt to the time capsule. I watched as Mark emptied out the other trash bags. As far as I could tell, Roy had written every year from 1972 to 2001. Once Mark had them spread out the way he wanted, he sat down in the nest of journals. He plucked one from the pile.

"This one's 1993," he announced. "'Life of a Misfit by Roy D. Hudgins, *the* Misfit. *Heat gets worse every year.*' How about that? 'Heat gets worse every year.' I didn't think that."

Mark raised an eyebrow, and I wondered if he was suggesting Roy had noticed global warming before the rest of us had, but I didn't know how Mark and Cheryl felt about climate change, and I didn't want a political discussion to jeopardize the night, so I just nodded. Mark jumped forward a few pages, then he beamed when he spotted a sentence about himself:

> The Kings went to Walmart today, and they got me a big sack of bird seed.

He held up the journal so Cheryl could see it. It was waterlogged and missing a cover. The pages were wrinkled, and at least half the sheets appeared to have burnt edges. After Cheryl looked at it, Mark set the journal down next to my feet. I wanted to touch it. I'd dreamed of this exact moment since 2009, and in my dreams, I always read the notebooks, but that night in the cabin, something stopped me. Maybe I was waiting for clearer permission. Mark had said we could look at the diaries, but I wasn't sure yet what he meant by "look." I left the journal near my feet.

Mark picked up an avocado-green 1987 edition, set it down, then opened the 1974 journal and skipped through until he found an entry Roy wrote in August after President Richard Nixon had resigned.

> *A day to go down in history. No man could stand under what they put on him. They saw all his mistakes, but they didn't see any of the good things he did. The people voted Nixon president. We no longer have a free country.*

Mark furrowed his brow. He said he'd have to read that entry again sometime. Already, Roy was starting to become real in ways I hadn't expected. "We no longer have a free country" sounded like a populist rallying cry, the kind of pessimistic thing a rural Southerner would absolutely say in 2019, and yet, I was surprised to see Roy express it. I'd projected so much of myself onto him, I realized, that I'd assumed we'd agree on everything.

Mark thumbed through two other notebooks, then he settled down with the 1998 edition. It was a thick purple notebook, and Roy had shaded all the white letters on the front cover with a pink highlighter. Mark's lips moved as he read silently to himself for three or four minutes. When he found an entry he wanted to share, he stood and read it out loud.

> *I went to Fred's and bought a boiler and a few things. I tried to find some jeans, but the jeans they have in Delhi now is those big-legged jeans. Don't want any of them. I don't know what I'm going to do for jeans. I guess I'll have to try to get to Rayville or Monroe. My little dog I call Little Bit is having puppies. I don't know how many she will have yet. I cleaned the church this evening. I went to bed.*

Mark kept skimming, but the entry unlocked something in me. Did Roy mean bell-bottoms or women's jeans? People had told me he was only five feet tall, which might have made him too short for most men's pants, but I assumed he'd always shopped in the men's department. If he had, I wondered how he felt, straying to that side of the store. When

I was younger and skinnier, I shopped in the little boy's sections at Target and J.Crew. I loved the striped T-shirts and plaid button-downs I discovered there, but I always browsed as if I were under surveillance. Even in Portland, I waited until the departments were empty, then I slipped between the aisles and pretended to shop for someone else, an imaginary son I prepared myself to describe. When I found a piece I liked, I crouched someplace private and held it against my frame, measuring, without daring to try it on in the women's fitting room. Had Roy sneaked through stores? Was it even possible to sneak in Delhi? I hadn't worn boys' clothes in several years, not since my hips grew too wide for guys' tapered silhouettes. Still, I could feel that old fear rising inside me. I missed the T-shirts, but I did not miss shopping as if I were committing a crime.

Mark read for ten minutes or so, mostly entries about the weather, and eventually, I worked up the nerve to reach for one of the diaries near my feet. I chose the oldest one, a busted-up 1974 edition that no longer had a cover. It felt dusty in my hands. Along the top of the first page, Roy had scrawled, *"Bury me in a pair of my pants and one of my blue shirts."*

I was looking for permission, some kind of proof that Roy *wanted* me to read these diaries, and I latched on to that directive as the evidence I needed. Didn't "bury me" have an implied "you" lingering just before it? If Roy didn't have any friends or family, who did he think would bury him? The sentence suggested to me that not only did Roy expect someone might read this journal, he expected they'd read it before he was in the ground.

When I looked up for affirmation, Mark nodded in a way I found inscrutable, so I turned back to the notebook, then read down the page. Underneath the burial instructions, Roy had written a kind of introduction. I read the words out loud, wondering if Mark and Cheryl heard them the way I did.

> *Roy Delois Hudgins, better known as Roy, born April 19, 1925, to the best of my knowledge. This will be a day by day record of my life as I live it in the year 1974, if possible, as long as I live, anyway, or as long as it's possible for me to write. Five foot, 170 pounds, hair light, almost white, eyes kind of hazel or*

streaked, skin light, speckled and red, no money, no family, no friends, no sense.

Would Roy really have taken time to introduce himself if he thought no one would ever read these journals? I never wrote my name in my diaries. I never described what I looked like or when I was born. Later in the night, as I read through other notebooks, I saw that Roy had written introductions like that for every journal. In 1979, the preface covered the whole inside cover.

> *A misfit, says Webster's Dictionary, is something different, something that don't fit, something odd, well that's me.*
> *In this book, if it be the Lord's will and nothing happens, will be my life as I live it day to day, what I do, what happened each day in my life, and my thoughts from time to time, for this book will be my companion to talk to for 1979, or as long as I live and am able to write in 1979.*
> *My name is Roy Delois Hudgins, and I'm ugly, short, fat, and getting old. I'm a female dressed in men's clothes. I live alone with two dogs and a bunch of cats, and I'm very, very stupid.*

It feels insufficient to say I felt sad reading the introductions. I'd imagined that Roy might have been lonely or depressed, and Mark had told me repeatedly that Roy thought of himself as stupid, but something about seeing those adjectives strung together in one paragraph made my stomach hurt. *Ugly. Fat. Stupid.* Roy hadn't used a single positive adjective to describe himself. Even when I was a teenager, when I felt most rejected by my mom and the church, I'd held on to some vision of myself as worthwhile. Maybe I was going to Hell, but I was smart. Maybe everyone I loved would turn against me, but I could write. I knew Roy had good traits. Every person I'd interviewed had listed at least a couple. He could play the guitar. He wrote songs. He was good at dominoes, and he was kind to children. Why didn't he see any of that good in himself?

The Kings didn't seem in any rush to leave, but I didn't know how much time I had with the journals, so I skimmed. Mark was right: Most of them *were* about the weather. Roy noted every time he mowed a lawn, and he complained about both the heat and the cold. My mom would have loved that. She wasn't happy unless the air was a perfect eighty degrees. Suddenly, I wished she and my grandma were in the cabin, reading with me. My grief caught in my throat, but I tried to swallow it down. This was supposed to be a happy moment, a moment Aubree and I had worked and waited for. I couldn't spoil it by missing people.

I leafed past the spring and summer of 1974, then I stopped on a paragraph Roy wrote in October at 10:45 p.m. on a night he described as "dry, hot, and dusty."

> *I just listened to Let The Bible Speak over T.V., and they really let me have it with both barrels. Our preacher did the same thing this morning. The way I dress is wrong, and I'll have to agree with them, but there seems to be nothing I can do about it. Unless God works some kind of miracle in my life, there's just nothing I can do about it on my own. Does God want one of his children to be miserable and unhappy? Unless God's undeserved mercy forgives me I haven't got a chance. I would feel as miserable in women's clothes as a man would in a dress. that's a real man*

I used to ask myself questions like those. Why would God want me to be unhappy? Why would he make me this way? I hadn't thought like that since I was a teenager, not since Ellen kissed me, and I stopped caring, but Roy was nearly fifty when he wrote this, and I wondered, as I read it, how I would have felt if I'd stayed in Louisiana. Would I have continued to hate myself? Would I have spent my life waiting for a miracle that never arrived? I looked up from the journal, and Mark shrugged.

"Roy went to that church for a long time," he said. "I don't guess they were too bad on her, or she wouldn't have been able to stand it."

Cheryl had been sitting silently in a leather chair, but she scooted to the seat's edge after Mark said that. Her hands were clasped together, and her jaw was set in a way I found angry.

"You don't pinpoint a person for what they wear when they go to church," she said. "She was like she was, and if she wanted to go to church, you don't say anything about it. That hurts."

Cheryl looked at me for a moment, her mouth pursed firm, and I suddenly felt like I understood her in a new way. She'd told me no for so many years, I realized now, because she loved Roy. She'd seen other people harm him, and she wanted to do whatever she could to protect him, even in death.

I nodded. I told Cheryl I agreed with her, then she relaxed a bit into the chair. None of us talked for a minute, but I worried I was running out of time, so I turned back to the journals. Roy's words surrounded me. I wanted to spend whole weeks reading through them, but Aubree and I were flying out the next day, and Mark said I couldn't take the diaries with me. I kept picking up notebooks and turning the pages, hoping my eye would catch on the word "kidnap." I assumed the answers I wanted must be in one of them. But which one? I shuffled through three or four, and eventually, I recognized a pattern. Every notebook ended with what Roy called his year in review. Most of the reviews chronicled all the ways Roy had suffered that year, and even the good ones read morose.

"*This year wasn't too bad,*" he wrote in 1981. "*In fact, it was a pretty good year. A few unpleasant things, like my dog Angel dying and the time I turned the table over on the kitten and had to get somebody to kill him for me, and my cat Slim dying, and all my aches and pains and complaints and self-pity.*"

Every journal also included an index of what Roy titled "hard-to-spell words that i may be using from time to time." It was a miserable list that started with the word itself:

Miserable, mental, spiritual, bicycle, medicine, unusual, usual, lightning, arthritis, physical, afraid, experiences, emotionally, attacked, degrees, pessimist, nervous, exist, energy, slept, severe like in storms, porch like front porch, phobia, air conditioner.

I read the words out loud, and Mark put his finger on his chin as if something had just become clear to him.

"That makes me wonder," he said. "If Roy had all those words written down, she didn't want somebody at some time to see that she was ignorant and didn't know how to spell. If she wanted to make sure she spelled things right, then she expected somebody would read that."

I felt the slightest speck of hope bloom inside me. I'd waited ten years for Mark to say he thought reading these journals was a good idea, and here he was, saying it. I didn't exactly agree with his logic, but I didn't tell Mark that because I *wanted* to feel good about reading Roy's diaries. So I read on, searching for my own version of permission. I suspected I'd never know what Roy wanted, but as I flipped through the diaries he kept in the 1980s, I thought I found a bit of evidence. Every year, Roy pasted photographs of himself onto the pages. In one, a tiny square shot of his face in 1982, Roy wrote, "That's old me." That caption was something, wasn't it? It seemed to be directed to someone, an unknown reader. I set the notebook aside, then gazed for a while at a Polaroid dated 1980. In it, Roy was standing in front of a white wall wearing a blue button-down tucked into jeans held up with a studded belt. He stared forward the way someone would when posing for their driver's license. I don't know if he was smiling or not, because he'd taken a Sharpie and blacked out his mouth. If the birth date listed on Roy's tombstone was correct, he was fifty-five in this picture. His hair was all white, but I thought I spotted something youthful in his eyes. Maybe it was the plastic-frame glasses. I'd long worn the same kind.

I didn't allow myself to acknowledge it that night, but of course I was still looking at Roy searching for signs of myself. The glasses were such a small connection, the kind of frames every hipster wears at some point, but I latched on to them anyway. I felt sheepish searching for those similarities. Why did I need Roy? I was thirty-five. I was married. I had a good career, and I knew plenty of gay and trans people. I told myself that night that I didn't need Roy the way I had when I was eighteen, but I understand now that I was still looking to him as a North Star because none of the people I know now are from my place. They didn't grow up with the same funky air and long-stretched vowels. They didn't know my grandma, and they'd never faced the wrath of a small-town Louisiana preacher. I've filled in a lot of my own blanks over the years, but Roy was the first queer community I ever imagined for myself. Two decades later, holding his notebooks, I still felt the simple but keen-edged curiosity I first experienced at my grandma's kitchen table. I wanted to know him.

Mark and I sat on the floor together for two hours. We read through dinner and the last bit of twinkling light, but time moved so much faster than I wanted it to. I knew I'd never be able to read every entry. I knew I'd miss things. Somehow that hurt as badly as reading nothing. Now that I held Roy's words in my hands, I wanted to take my time with them. I didn't even care if the entries were bombshells; I wanted to read every detail, every weather report and any other mundane item Roy saw fit to record. At some point, after I'd realized that I couldn't read fast enough, I started taking pictures of pages. I told myself to calm down and savor the sentences I did get to read, but I couldn't, not really, because I knew each page was just a piece of Roy's bigger story. I felt desperate. I sped through the journals the way I'd once zipped through microfilm at the Monroe library. I kept hoping I'd see one sentence that answered everything, a personal confession to make up for the newspapers' lack of coverage of stolen babies. I didn't find the exact line I wanted, but eventually, I thought I found an answer in the middle of Roy's 1974 year-end review.

> *Rejected at birth and rejected every sence, a born loser, a born complainer, that's me. Old fatso, ugly, fat, and I can't spell the other word.*

"*Rejected at birth.*" Mark was right. Roy must have thought he'd been given up for adoption. That didn't necessarily mean the story my grandmother told me was wrong. Roy was supposedly only three or four when Jewel took him, young enough that he may have forgotten his own origins. Maybe Jewel kidnapped Roy, then told him she'd adopted him. But if my grandma's story was the real story, I thought, if Jewel *did* steal Roy, this entry seemed to suggest he never knew it. I looked up from the notebook and wondered how the stories we tell ourselves shape the people we become. Did Roy think he wasn't worth loving because his birth mother gave him away? Would he have felt worse if Jewel had told him his real parents abused him? And what stories had I told myself? I'd grown up knowing that my mother never meant to get pregnant with me. She'd only turned to my father because she was so distraught about losing Cam. On good days, I told myself I was an accident. On bad ones, a mistake. But as I read Roy's end-of-the-year review, I felt newly lucky.

My mother kept me. She gave up college so she could have me. She married my father, and she stayed. Whatever else she did wrong when I was growing up, I knew she wanted me.

I ran my index finger over Roy's words. *"Rejected every sence."* The page was brittle, crinkled in the way paper turns after it gets wet. I imagined Roy settling down on New Year's Eve. Maybe he sat at the wooden desk I'd seen in the pictures Ann McVay had shown me. Maybe he was drinking Coke from a glass bottle. I imagine he must have been hurting, but his handwriting didn't look especially anguished. The ink was faint from lack of pressing. I touched his words again. He hadn't borne down on the notebook, so the lines hadn't left any tangible imprint.

I used my phone to take a few pictures of the page, then I set it aside and opened a rusted notebook with burnt edges and a yellow cover. On the front, Roy had written in black capital letters, "THE LIFE OF A MISFIT 1979 DAY BY DAY ROY D HUDGINS." I thought I didn't have enough time to read the entire journal, so I flipped to the back page to see how Roy had summarized the year. As always, I found, he'd written a New Year's Eve wrap-up, but this one struck me as a little more existential.

> In the '70s, men became women, and women became men, and the men let their hair grow longer than most women. I no longer stand alone in the fact that you can't tell the women from the men. The men tried to look as sloppy and ugly as they could. 20 years ago if we saw a man that looked like most of the men today looks we'd call him a bum and probably hide from him. And women, well, they decided they wanted to be like men.
>
> Of course, I'm one to be talking about such things, but my problems started when I was a kid. And I know that there are jobs that men do that I can't do, even though I've always wore men's clothes and had to work like men. It was never because I thought I could handle everything and do everything men could do. It wasn't really because I wanted to be equal with men. I was raised up confused and mixed-up and stupit. I mean, I am stupit. Good by.

Over the years, people had repeatedly told me that Roy dressed like a man because Jewel and John forced him to as a child. My grandma said Jewel wanted to hide Roy's identity. Other people told me John wanted a son. When my grandma first told me this story, I'd accepted her explanation, but as I met more transgender people, I'd changed my mind. I thought people in Delhi were just uncomfortable with the idea that maybe Roy was trans. But reading Roy's diaries left me even more unsure. Did "raised up confused" mean Jewel and John forced him into an identity he might not have sought on his own? Or did this paragraph mean Roy had known since he was young that "female" didn't fit him?

I snapped a picture of the page, then I closed the journal. The entry didn't solve my mystery, and it deepened a suspicion that had long nagged at me. If I'd come to Delhi when my grandmother first told me about Roy, I could have met him. And if I'd met Roy, it's possible he wouldn't have liked me. He complained often in his journal that the country was drowning in sin, and as far as I could tell, he never reached any kind of peace with his identity. I certainly couldn't imagine him stuffing Pam's pink unicorn into the basket on his tricycle. In April 1984, on what he believed was his fifty-ninth birthday, Roy noted that the only things he hated were sin and *"maybe myself because I am like I am and I can't seem to do anything about it."* If Roy hated himself, would he have hated me? Would he have hated Pam? Would he have shooed us off his porch if we'd come a decade earlier with our questions and short haircuts?

I couldn't bear to consider that possibility further, not on the night I'd long waited for, so I reopened the 1979 journal and read from the beginning. In January, Roy wrote that he was thinking about going back to the Pentecostal church. He wanted to stop smoking, and he'd gone to the altar at the Church of Christ, but praying there hadn't worked. He was still smoking. Later that month, Roy wrote that Ann McVay had had her phone taken out.

> I guess she'll be moving soon. I won't have anybody to talk
> to. She don't come around much anymore, but when something
> unusual happened and she heard about it, she usually called and
> told me, and I'd do the same with her. It was just having someone
> to share with once in a while.

Ann had told me back in 2009 that she stopped talking to Roy because his pets made his house smell bad, but I ached in a new way, reading Roy's account of the end of their friendship. Ann had told me the story in a matter-of-fact tone I'd found cold. Roy didn't write particularly anguished sentences—even when he was depressed, his writing was spare—but I could feel how lonely he must have been. His best friend had stopped visiting him, and all he had left to hang on to was the occasional phone call. Then Ann had taken those away, too.

Mark and I looked through the journals for another half hour, occasionally reading a few lines out loud to each other. All told, the Kings spent four hours in the cabin that day. None of us ate dinner, but when I asked if they were hungry, they shook their heads no. Maybe they felt the way I did, too moved to eat.

After I finished 1979, I moved on to the avocado-green 1987 edition. Just as I opened it, Mark closed the notebook he'd been reading, and my heartbeat sped up. I was running out of time. Soon, I figured, Mark would want to go home. I didn't want him to see that I'd noticed him closing his journals, so I bent my head deeper into the notebook, then skipped forward to the paragraph Roy wrote on his sixty-second birthday.

> *I went to church today like always. I got three birthday cards from church today. Mrs. Alred give me one, and Carolyn Perry sent me one. She wasn't at church today. She's sick with a cold, and Ann Russell give me one tonight with 10 dollars in it. And she bought me supper tonight. I didn't want her to spend lots of money on me, so I got a small hamburger. That was nice of them to think about me like that. And Jo called me this morning and sung happy birthday to me. I wish I had a car and a driver's license. I could drive out to see them because I've been here nearly all my life, and I'm afraid I wouldn't be happy anywhere else. But I'm sure not happy here anymore.*

I had, of course, been searching for answers to the big mysteries my grandma posed back in 2002, but as I read Roy's words, I realized that what kept me going was a desire to answer the questions I often asked myself. Will I ever be fully happy outside of Louisiana? Would Roy have been happier somewhere else? He never made the leap that I did. As far

as I could tell, he never got his driver's license. He never drove to visit
Jo or anyone else, so he never tested his own hypotheses. If he'd left,
maybe he would have found happiness, but maybe it would have been
the kind of incomplete happiness I experienced, a rootless good marked
by the kind of yearning that can never be quelled as long as home is a
place you've fled. Somehow, even without traveling, Roy seemed to already know what I'd learned in the world beyond—for misfits, no place
is ever right.

I closed his journal with a big sigh. Years ago, maybe the first time
I went down with Aubree and Aaron to film, my grandma told me that
she'd been surprised by how interested I became in Roy's story. "It was
like it burnt a hole in you," she told me. It was still burning a hole in me,
even as I held the thing I'd so desperately wanted. I read, but I didn't
feel sated. I told myself I'd search later for Mrs. Alred or Carolyn Perry.
I wondered if Ann Russell knew anything more than Roy's journals
revealed. I was grateful for the big thing Mark and Cheryl had done for
me. They'd braved the curse, and they'd packed up Roy's journals and
brought them to me. But I knew I'd never feel satisfied with only one
reading. I set 1987 down, and I told myself that I had to find a way to
come back and read it again.

Roy had written far more than I had anticipated about his clothes
and his appearance, but I didn't find nearly as many entries as I'd hoped
to about Jewel. I suppose it made sense. I only wrote about my mother
when things were really bad between us, and even then, I jotted just a
few lines. Roy's journals only offered the vaguest hints about the woman
who raised him. Once, in February 1978, he noted that it was the anniversary of her death, and in 1979, after he'd attended one of the McVays'
funerals, he wrote that the ceremony reminded him of his mother's.

*They buried Mr. McVay today. I went to the funeral. There
really was that many people there. I rode onto the graveyard with
Ann's brother. He went by his self, or he would have been, but
he let me ride with him. I guess I'll go to church tonight. I don't
really feel like going. All the funeral and things took me back so
long ago when mama died. The memory come back to me so clear.
We didn't have a lots of kin folks like the McVays did. There was*

*only my step-father and his brother and family and mama's four
nephews. They all left right after the funeral, and my step-father's
brother took him home with them for a week, and for the first
time in my life, I was left completely alone at night. I was 32 years
old, but I really was like about a 12 year old child. I had to grow
up all at once. I don't know how I made it.*

How many times had I thought about Jewel dying? I'd pictured the
scene in my head dozens of times, but I'd never imagined what Roy felt
like. I'd always assumed he was an adult when she died, so I'd believed
he hadn't suffered that much. Maybe I couldn't have pictured it before
my own mom died, but now I read his words, and I thought about the
night I flew back to Columbia after my mother died. I had crawled into
my sofa bed and played every recorded voicemail my mother had ever
left me. None of them were particularly interesting. Mostly she just
asked why I never called her back. She sang "My Special Angel" into my
voicemail a few times, and once, the year I turned thirty-three, she sang
"Happy Birthday."

I was thirty-four when my mother died, two years older than Roy
had been when he lost Jewel. I suppose I was an adult, but my age hadn't
mitigated anything. My mother's death obliterated me. It knocked me
off my axis, and even now, more than three years later, I cry at least once
a week, missing her. Of course Roy suffered, I know now. How had I
ever assumed he hadn't?

I READ THE ENTRY a second time, and something dawned on me.
Roy didn't mention my great-grandmother Rita Mae. He didn't describe
a bathtub full of alcohol or the storm Rita Mae had supposedly braved
when she darted across the street to hear Jewel's last confession. Rita
Mae wasn't even listed among the funeral attendees.

I'd spent my career trying to hew as close as possible to the truth of
things, but that night in the cabin, I began to accept that there were some
answers I'd never have. Maybe the story my grandma passed down wasn't
the right one, but it had been the one I needed to hear. I'd felt so relieved,
sitting at her wobbly kitchen table that Fourth of July. I'd been so sure
that the rest of my life would be lonely, but then my grandma had spun

this *tale,* and I began to imagine the tiniest shimmer of light stretched out before me. I'd chased that feeling. I'd chased it for so many years that, over time, what I was looking for began to change. Did it matter why or how Roy wound up in Delhi? In the end, what I really wanted to know is how he felt once he got there. The diaries offered ample evidence.

I closed the 1979 journal. None of us spoke for a minute or two. Outside, the wind was whipping the lake into makeshift waves, and I listened to the water slosh against the deck as I searched for another good entry.

"Wait a minute now," Mark said. "Roy wrote in print there. Boy, that's really good print, look at that."

He handed me the journal he'd been reading. I didn't understand what Mark's fascination with cursive and print writing was, but I prepared myself to seem shocked by Roy's sudden shift to print as I crawled toward Mark. Once I inched close enough, I saw that the page Mark had been reading was brown and half-covered by another piece of paper Roy had affixed with about twenty pieces of tape. I creeped closer. At the top of the page, I saw, Roy had written a title: "The Town Misfit."

"I think it's a poem," I said.

Mark stood. I was still on my hands and knees, hovering to the side of the notebook, but I read the poem out loud.

The Town Misfit

I'm the town misfit, and I live here all alone
I've got no friends or family, nothing to call my own
I'm always broke and hungry, and lonely as can be
I'm the town misfit, nobody cares for me

I've went to different churches, and I tried to fit in
I've searched this whole town over, trying to find a friend
I've tried all their parties, but I couldn't fit in you see
I'm the town misfit, nobody cares for me

I've worked in the cotton fields, and I drove a big old truck
I tried for country music, but I didn't have much luck
I scrubbed floors for rich folks, cut grass till I couldn't see
I'm the town misfit, nobody cares for me

I've eat at rich folk's table, and also with the poor
I've walked the streets of Delhi till I couldn't walk no more
There's not much in this town that I haven't tried you see
I'm the town misfit, nobody cares for me

When my life on earth is over, and it's time for me to die,
No one here will miss me. There will be no one to cry.
If I make it up to heaven, will I then find a friend?
Or will I still be a misfit, with no place to fit in?

I finished reading, but I waited a beat before looking up. Everything people had told me was here. The preachers, the cotton fields, the country music career that never took off.

I turned back to the journal. All the tape had gone yellow, and black mold crept up the center of the page. I read the last stanza again. *"No one here will miss me."* I touched the blue ink, believing somehow that doing so would bring me closer to Roy, then I jerked my head up.

"Roy was wrong," I said.

People missed him. My grandma had missed Roy her whole life. Archie Lee Harrell missed him, and so did Lou Henry and the McVays, and I knew Mark and Cheryl must have, too. Otherwise, why would they have held on to Roy's things? He'd been dead nearly thirteen years, and here the four of us were, still remembering him, missing him in our own ways.

"You know," Mark said, "one thing about Royce, the way she was treated by some people and the way her life went, society was robbed of potential. How many potentials does our society rob by bullying and treating people like Royce was treated? Royce could have been a nurse. She could have been, for all I know, a journalist because of the way she loved to write. That's sad, isn't it?"

Mark pointed at me when he said "journalist," and I suspected he understood why I'd been knocking on his door for so many years. He seemed to be saying that if things had broken a different way, Roy might have had the life I had. I nodded in affirmation. I don't know how, but everyone suddenly seemed to understand that the night was nearing its end. Cheryl stood. She grabbed the trash bags and reached for the journals. I asked if she wanted help putting them away, but she shook her head no. Mark stood, so I stood, then he turned to me.

"Well," he said, "if I move, I plan on burying these in that yard. But I'm not going to tell whoever buys the place where they are. I'm going to put them in a good, strong, plastic box and bury them kind of deep."

Even then, after two hours of reading, I felt that familiar ache claw through me. Maybe I could wait until the Kings moved. Maybe I could buy their land or just sneak over and dig until I found the journals again. I knew how ridiculous this desire was, but nothing seemed to quell it. I thought of my grandmother again. *It was like it burnt a hole in you.*

I watched Mark and Cheryl slip each journal into a bag, then we all stood and lingered. Aubree stepped around the room, angling the camera to catch one last look at all of us. In the footage, we almost look like distant family members at the end of a holiday dinner, close somehow, but awkward. When Cheryl slid the last journal into a bag, I stepped toward the Kings, and my voice broke as I tried to say goodbye.

"I don't even have the words to tell you what I feel. Thank you."

"Well," Mark said, laughing, "if Royce didn't want us to see them, we may not live much longer."

I didn't believe in the curse, but still, I asked Mark if he would call me when he made it home. He laughed again, then he transferred the trash bags to his other hand.

"I kinda decided that since you've been so persistent on this, maybe Roy did want you to see 'em."

I walked Mark and Cheryl to the cabin door. They disappeared down the boardwalk, and Roy's diaries were gone. I cried for a while on the cabin floor. I so badly wished I could tell my mom and my grandma about the journals. I closed my eyes and imagined bringing pictures of Roy's pages to the carport. I could almost hear my grandma say, "Those were Roy's thoughts, honey."

My grandma always believed that Roy was an earthly angel, and suddenly I hoped that she was right about the afterlife. Maybe Roy was in the heavenly band, playing songs for my grandmother again. Maybe my mom was there, too. Was she right? Were they all strangers in Heaven? I pushed the thought away. In my Promised Land they were all together, living side by side in mansions on a street more beautiful than Hell.

I opened my eyes. I texted my brother, and I called Frankie, but I didn't feel as relieved as I'd thought I would. Eventually, I reached over and turned the camera off.

I know Aubree and I left town the next morning, but for the first time in years, I didn't tape anything, so I don't remember the details. That day, like most of the others the year my mom died, is lost to the black hole of grief. Maybe I drove through Delhi sure I'd move back to Louisiana. Maybe I felt at peace or maybe I didn't. Whatever I felt leaving my mother's hometown, it was just a blip, as gnawing and uncertain as all the other competing things I felt that year and the years after.

I had hoped reading Roy's diaries would settle something inside me. If I could solve his mysteries, I thought, I would decipher my own. I would know where I belonged. But I understand now that most of what haunted me before might haunt me forever. I drove away from Louisiana, but I returned. I am still returning, even now.

Acknowledgments

I wish I could give every journalist a partner like Aubree Bernier-Clarke. They spent eleven years asking me questions and pushing me to make one more phone call. They sat in every awkward living room, and they slept on the world's least comfortable bunk bed—all on their own dime—because they believed in this project long before anyone else did. Most of the time, I was pouty. I didn't want to answer questions. I didn't want to make hard phone calls. Aubree persisted. Thank you, buddy, for your relentless positivity and wild ideas. Thank you for collard greens, big salads, and chocolate-almond cold brew. You're my family, by biscuits, if not blood.

Christopher, you make every moment bigger, better, and more fun. I'm so grateful for the easy way you talk to strangers. I'm thankful for your jokes, your songs, and sweet curiosity. Thank you for remembering with me.

Aunt Cindy, thank you for loving me unconditionally, and thank you for keeping everyone alive with the stories and pictures you've saved. I couldn't have written this without your memories. When I think about what I've gained in doing this project, you're always the first person I think of. Thank you for being as nosy and nostalgic as I am.

Dad, you've always made me feel like I could and should be a writer. Thank you for selling those comic books. Thank you for answering even the hardest questions. *Michael, I love youuuuuuu.*

TNC, from the moment I picked you out, life has been better. No one loves like you do. Thank you for sharing forts, clothes, Barbie dolls, IHOP pancakes, rap songs, country songs, and so much else. I'm certain you're the reason I survived most years.

ACKNOWLEDGMENTS

Alicia Fletcher, whole chapters of this book would be missing pieces without your memories. Thank you for talking about Mrs. Allen and demon exorcisms and S.P. and the year the men left base. Thank you for being such a great friend to my mom.

Anna Stein, thank you for saying yes even though I didn't have the goods. Thank you for making me go back one more time. You are the fastest emailer and coolest agent. I knew, as soon as I talked to you about Dolly Parton, that no one else would do. I'm even more sure now.

Lexy Bloom, thank you for your incisive questions and gentle prodding. I love having a straight editor who adores the Indigo Girls and isn't afraid to talk about the hard stuff. Thank you for pushing me to dig deeper and write clearer.

Thank you, Kathleen Fridella, for shepherding this book through production and catching every small thing. Thank you, Louise Collazo, for improving my sentences with your deft copyedits and checks.

Sam Freedman, thank you for the beat-downs and beatitudes. Thank you for teaching me that I need a comma before "then," and thank you for saying, "Don't act like you don't have skin in the game." I'm so proud to be a part of your pantheon of ancestors.

Andrea Elliot, thank you for calling this book a book. Thank you for pushing me to apply for Sam's class, and thank you for sending me songs and books after my mother died.

Aubree and I mostly paid for the trips to Delhi ourselves, but 207 people gave to a Kickstarter campaign when we were near broke. The Regional Arts and Culture Council also gave us a grant. The Anne McCormick Foundation gave me a scholarship to Columbia, and the Lynton Foundation endowed the Columbia book-writing grant that enabled me to take a month off to write the first chapter. Thank you all, and thank you also to the folks at the J. Anthony Lukas Prize, whose Work-in-Progress Award provided a crucial boost as I finished this book.

Aaron Wong and Erin O'Connor are wonderful filmmakers who agreed to work for free in the early days of this project. Thank y'all for tagging along to a town in the middle of nowhere, and thank you for making such beauty of the place that feels most like home.

Thank you, B. Frayn Masters and Back Fence PDX, for giving me an early stage to work out my feelings about this story.

Marlena Ray, thank you for keeping my arms in working order, and thank you for asking enthusiastic questions for twelve years. You made me feel like this book was worth doing.

Martha Kenney, interim, thank you for helping me write the last few chapters. Thank you for getting me through. The time you gave me is one of the great gifts of my life, and if my grandma were still here, I'm sure she'd say you must be an earthly angel.

I wrote most of this book during the pandemic, which would have been horribly lonely if I hadn't had Claudia Meza, Ben Herold, and Bethany Barnes texting me nonstop. Thank you, Meza, for all the long, brainy texts no acknowledgments could sum up. Thank you, Ben, for the bookbag full of honey buns and one-dollar bills. Thank you for texting about the NBA's best jerseys, worst haircuts, and sexiest players. Thank you, Bethany, for your book recommendations, always-right songs, and endless poring over the dramas we lived through.

Thank you to Brian Goldstone, Amanda Darrach, Meg Kissinger, Justin Lynch, and Sage Van Wing, all of whom read early versions of the earliest chapters.

Thank you, Kate B., for believing in me even when I was mumbling scared at Powell's, 2012. Thank you for saying I'd get the journals. I don't think I would have persisted if you hadn't written to ask how it was going. You taught me to be brave and unrelenting, empathetic but not soft. I never do a story without thinking of your words. Stupid Casey. *The mess is the story.*

Thank you Mitxu, Mike, Nikki, Nick, Patrick, Megan, and all of the kiddos for making me believe in family again. Y'all are healing and hilarious, loving, witty, special. You made me feel like I belonged, and I am so grateful to have spent time in your glow.

Nicole Gilson, ISP, thank you for turning the world to color again.

Hayes Young, B, thank you for teaching me boundaries and vulnerability. Thank you for growing with and toward me, and thank you for always being the family I need.

Lizz Gardner was there for all of the good parts and most of the bad. Penny, you and I are bound for life. Thank you for hashing out the early parts of this book with me. Thank you for New Spaghetti and KYTech and Brad and pomes and The Now Sounds. Thank you for going to Cups with me, February 2002, and thank you for being the keeper of all my giddy secrets. I'm forever your babie, and, babie, you're mine.

Tali Woodward, thank you for our rambling conversations and lost circles. Thank you for knowing exactly what to send, April 2018. Thank you for talking to me about American cheese and so much else that horrid night. Somehow I knew, that first day in your office, that you were my person, and you've shown me over and over again how right I was. Thank you for teaching me to write better sentences. Thank you for hoarding Andes mints and editing this book (eventually!!). You have made so much happen for me. How could one paragraph sum it up?

Bird, wild-brain wanderer, the moment I first saw you was one of the most important events of my life. Maybe I'm dramatic, but the rest of the world dimmed, and there you were, tiny, radiant, a vision of what my life could be. Thank you for daring across my dorm bed. Thank you for Mary Oliver and "The Predatory Wasp." Thank you, like-minded companion, for fielding my shadow book the lockdown year we spent digging for an Edge. You already know how many of these chapters started as emails to you. Thank you for your (long) beautiful (daily) replies. Thank you for your perfect mixes. *I dreamed you were a poem*. I love you like Celie loves Shug, like Shane Koyczan says, like the magnets in that Tegan and Sara song. *Whatever the mess,* I'm so grateful for our space in the stitch. (I'm sorry about the crickets.)

Anna Griffin, how did I luck into a best friend in possession of the world's best and fastest brain? You read this book first and often, and you answered every editing question, even the dumb ones about single words or errant commas. You know me better than anyone, so you called bullshit when it was right, and you let me pout and protest until I reluctantly agreed that, yes, I hadn't felt this way or that at just the right narrative moment. You taught me how to slow down and pick scenes, and you've improved everything I've written since I was twenty-four. You always tell me "you get what you pay for," but I know you've given me an immeasurable amount more than that. Goat videos, Nong's soup, BAM. *Antelope,* you do it all. I love you till diapers, till the next life or wherever your heathen gods let you and Big Sexy land.

CFWMDW, our person, P above everything, you were the light at the end of a tunnel I thought would always be dark. You showed me what good can mean. Thank you for being the fan who never doubted me. Thank you for cooking one million good meals. Thank you for moving to "Manhattan" and working at a chest of drawers so I could write this book in silence. You made me laugh. You taught me how to hope. You did the Gilly dance almost every time I asked. *La da dee dee, oh . . .* I'm so grateful I got to experience your meticulous edits and wide-open heart. Life with you was so much fun. Somewhere in the great beyond, I'm sure my mother is voting me out for letting you slip away, but I hope that someday, over corn dogs, we can get together on an island in the stream and tell her it all ended OK anyway. You're my family for life and whatever is after that. *Perpetua, P. Esto perpetua.*